A CULTURAL HISTORY
OF GARDENS

VOLUME 4

A Cultural History of Gardens

General Editors: Michael Leslie and John Dixon Hunt

Volume 1
A Cultural History of Gardens in Antiquity
Edited by Kathryn Gleason

Volume 2
A Cultural History of Gardens in the Medieval Age
Edited by Michael Leslie

Volume 3
A Cultural History of Gardens in the Renaissance
Edited by Elizabeth Hyde

Volume 4
A Cultural History of Gardens in the Age of Enlightenment
Edited by Stephen Bending

Volume 5
A Cultural History of Gardens in the Age of Empire
Edited by Sonja Dümpelmann

Volume 6
A Cultural History of Gardens in the Modern Age
Edited by John Dixon Hunt

A CULTURAL HISTORY
OF GARDENS

IN THE AGE
OF
ENLIGHTENMENT

Edited by Stephen Bending

Bloomsbury Academic
An imprint of Bloomsbury Publishing Plc

B L O O M S B U R Y
LONDON · OXFORD · NEW YORK · NEW DELHI · SYDNEY

Bloomsbury Academic
An imprint of Bloomsbury Publishing Plc

50 Bedford Square
London
WC1B 3DP
UK

1385 Broadway
New York
NY 10018
USA

www.bloomsbury.com

BLOOMSBURY and the Diana logo are trademarks of Bloomsbury
Publishing Plc

Hardback edition first published in 2013 by Bloomsbury Academic
Paperback edition first published in 2016 by Bloomsbury Academic

© Stephen Bending 2013, 2016

Stephen Bending has asserted his right under the Copyright, Designs and
Patents Act, 1988, to be identified as Editor of this work.

British Library Cataloguing-in-Publication Data
A catalogue record for this book is available from the British Library.

ISBN: 978-0-8578-5032-4 (HB)
978-1-8478-8265-3 (HB set)
978-1-3500-0992-9 (PB)
978-1-3500-0995-0 (PB set)

Library of Congress Cataloging-in-Publication Data
A catalog record for this book is available from the Library of Congress.

Series: The Cultural Histories Series

Typeset by Apex CoVantage, LLC, Madison, WI, USA
Printed and bound in Great Britain

CONTENTS

ILLUSTRATIONS

INTRODUCTION

CHAPTER 1

CHAPTER 2

CHAPTER 3

CHAPTER 4

CHAPTER 5

CHAPTER 6

CHAPTER 7

CHAPTER 8

GENERAL EDITORS' PREFACE

The volumes of this series explore the cultural world of the garden from antiquity to the present day in six particular periods. Each volume addresses the same eight topics, determined by the general editors for their relevance to garden history across different times and cultures. Thus a reader interested more, say, in planting or in types of gardens could read through the chapters devoted to those issues in successive volumes. Contrariwise, either of those interests might be contextualized by a volume's discussion of other aspects of the garden in a given period. There is therefore both a horizontal and a vertical way of using these volumes. Further, each volume includes both its editor's introduction, which rather than abstracting or summarizing the other contributions, surveys the period from a fresh vantage point, and a bibliography, which encompasses references from all the eight chapters augmented with that editor's additional readings.

HISTORY

These volumes are a historical enquiry and not an encyclopedia. They do not pretend to be comprehensive, either geographically or chronologically. The authors of the individual chapters have been encouraged to foreground what seem to be the most significant episodes and examples of their particular topic, leaving it to the reader to envisage how other sites that he or she knows better might further illustrate, challenge, or qualify the given analyses. But in every instance, we intend there to be some narrative of one particular theme as it

exists, unfolds, or develops during a particular historical period. The definitions of these historical eras must be taken with some caution and elasticity,
since a chronology of garden making does not always fit the divisions of time
devised for and endorsed by other histories: André Le Notre did his work after
1650 but is arguably more usefully considered in a volume focused on the Renaissance than on the Enlightenment; similarly, Gertrude Jekyll and William
Robinson were designing before 1920, but we understand their work better
within the cultural content of the modern age.

CULTURAL HISTORY

There are of course many modes of history that have developed over the centuries. A relatively new one addresses the cultural context of human activity.
"Culture" derives from the Latin *colere,* which has as some of its meanings
"to inhabit," "to respect," "to pay attention to"; it emerges also in our words
"colony" and "cultivation." Gardens, then, must be considered as driven by
and evidence of a whole congeries of human concerns; they are not, above all,
to be examined in terms of their merely visual appearance, materials, or stylistic histories. The diversity and density of human involvements with those sites
we call gardens mean that the discipline of garden history draws upon adjacent
disciplines such as anthropology, sociology, economic, and political history,
along with histories of the arts with which the garden has been involved. So
three large questions are posed: why were gardens created? How were they
used or visited (there being no handy term for the "consumption" of gardens)?
And how does their representation in different arts express the position and
value of the garden within its culture in diverse periods? Regretfully, we were
unable to extend the range of these volumes to include the garden making of
China and Japan among other Eastern cultures, although inevitably the rich
examples of such gardens have been invoked on occasion.

GARDENS

The range of places that can be envisaged within this category is enormous
and various, and it changes from place to place, and from time to time. Yet
this diversity does not wholly inhibit us from knowing what it is we what to
discuss when we speak of the garden. Yet the garden is typically a place of
paradox, being the work of men and women, yet created from the elements of
nature; just as it is often acknowledged to be a "total environment," a place

may be physically separated from other zones but answering and displaying connections with larger environments and concerns. Gardens, too, are often created, and subsequently experienced, as commentary and response: a focus of speculations, propositions, and negotiations concerning what it is to live in the world. Both the physical gardens and the ideas that drive them are cultural constructions, and their history is the topic of these six volumes.

John Dixon Hunt, University of Pennsylvania

Michael Leslie, Rhodes College

Introduction

STEPHEN BENDING

The last thirty years have seen an enormous, and enormously fruitful, expansion of approaches to European gardens and to garden history of the period 1650–1800. All periodizations are of course arbitrary, and these dates are not intended as markers of absolute or abrupt change; indeed the idea of periods, of homogeneous movements, of the geographical and chronological uniformity of fashions in garden design have all come under scrutiny in recent years.[1] In one sense, both the title and the shared structure of each volume of this Cultural History of Gardens seek to address these problems. The chapter themes in particular (design, meaning, use, representation, and so on) point to the multiple ways in which gardens can be understood, but it's also important to recognize the contributions from individuals as interventions in an ongoing debate and as explorations of aspects or pathways, rather than as magisterial surveys. The latter approach, indeed, has arguably been one of the problems of garden history in our period: the language of the survey tends to occlude its own ideological agenda and normalize its own point of view—a point, of course, only too well understood by the seventeenth-century writers of prospect poems. Conversely, suspicion of the larger view has brought its own problems, and a resistance to grand narratives can lead to the proliferation of the local and particular that loses sight of a bigger picture. The reader of this volume will therefore find a combination of approaches offered: crucially, while contributors may focus on a particular aspect, or on a "national" style (for example, as the supposedly "new" form, the English landscape garden, often appears in popular garden history as the great invention of the period, many take this as their theme), each chapter is intended primarily as an exemplar of a methodology that might be applied to different case studies.

The contributors to this volume are more than capable of speaking for themselves, and so in this introduction—rather than rehearsing their arguments—I want to map out some of the larger issues for garden history in our period and to make some suggestions about possible ways forward. In the following pages, therefore, I address the nature of our sources and the continuing influence of Enlightenment thinking on the practice of history and on popular narratives of progress in garden design; I suggest that we can further expand our interests from garden design to garden *use*, not only by owners but by visitors, not only by individuals but as it appears in the wider cultural imagination; and I draw on the curious absence of women from mainstream garden history to suggest some of the ways in which the field of garden history may be further developed.

SOURCES AND THEIR HISTORIANS

It perhaps only slightly overstates the case to characterize much of early garden history—from the eighteenth century onward—as predominantly an exercise on paper, involving literature and fine art. Major published works on the theory of gardening and garden visiting to which historians have traditionally turned include André Mollet's *Le Jardin de Plaisir*, the various guides to Versailles (some published under the auspices of Louis XIV[2]) along with Madame de Scudéry's *La Promenade de Versailles*, Evelyn's *Sylva* and his fascinating *Elysium Britannicum* (though it was not to appear in print in our period), Dezallier d'Argenville's *La Théorie et la Pratique du Jardinage*, Stephen Switzer's *Ichnographia Rustica*, Jean-Denis Attiret's *Letters* (describing the Chinese imperial gardens of Yuan Ming Yuan), Horace Walpole's *Essay on Modern Gardening*, Thomas Whately's *Observations*, Jean-Marie Morel's *Théorie des Jardin*, René-Louis de Girardin's *De la Composition des paysages*, C.C.L. Hirschfeld's *Theorie der Gartenkunst*, and Humphry Repton's *Observations on the Theory and Practice of Landscape Gardening*. These in turn are frequently read in conjunction with works of imaginative literature ranging from Jean Jacques Rousseau to Ann Radcliffe and from Milton to Erasmus Darwin and the Abbé Delille. Many more could be added to such lists, of course, and these works certainly open up to us contemporary understandings of garden design. However, one of the major changes in garden history over the last thirty years has been the recognition that such high-status works are only one element of a much larger archive of materials on which the garden historian can draw, and this in turn has changed the ways we might now attempt to construct the cultural meaning of gardens.

Contemporary history and theory of the eighteenth-century garden, then, tell a particular tale, but so too do the highly conventional and often long-standing practices of visual representation (see Richardson in this volume), and there is often a mismatch between different kinds of sources. Crucial here are both the limits of sources and an understanding of their conventions—inevitably a challenge for the garden historian who seeks to be multidisciplinary but is likely grounded in one particular discipline. The literary historian attuned to the complex codes of poetry and the generic conventions of the novel may not be best placed to decipher the equally highly coded visual conventions of maps and estate plans, high art and low caricature, topographical views and conversation pieces, but all are inevitably freighted with a set of expectations, the primary concern of which need not be accurate description. Even within what we might loosely term the literary, poetry, philosophy, and history are in frequent discord, while the still underused world of contemporary diaries and letters often suggests a further mismatch among the claims of designers or the writers of histories, the lived experiences of those who inhabit spaces, and the language in which each might choose to represent themselves to others. Garden archaeologists and cultural geographers, in particular, have done much to complicate this picture by insisting on physical evidence and on the use of less apparently glamorous sources such as estate maps and local records.[3] Notably, in *Polite Landscapes* (1995), Tom Williamson demonstrated the inadequacies of relying on printed sources at the expense of material and archaeological evidence and insisted on the need to cross-reference multiple forms of source material. It has become increasingly apparent that the big theoretical statements—Walpole's *Essay* perhaps the most obvious[4]—can only ever be partial narratives. It should be conspicuous, for example, that women largely remain absent from what tend to be termed the major movements in garden design; town gardens have only recently been given serious attention;[5] kitchen gardens have largely been sidestepped by the scholarly world;[6] and the country gardens of the middling sort remain largely unexplored.

As much work over the last decade has shown,[7] new stories can be told, and those stories frequently emerge from the insistence that gardens can only be understood in relation to the wider world of which they are a part—however much the physical rhetoric of a garden may appear to claim its separation. Indeed, while the proliferation of sources for the garden historian in our period may appear overwhelming, perhaps even disabling, approaches that range from—and at times elide—the economic and the symbolic, the personal record and the public agenda, consumption and conduct, marketing and professionalism have combined to demonstrate what a dense cultural site the garden is as a space, a commodity, a representation, and an arena for self-fashioning.[8] As a result, perhaps the most profound question asked in garden history at the moment is what the garden is. In a sense, that question needs to be asked precisely because so many gardens from our period have apparently "survived" and because that survival proffers the all-too-seductive sense that the physical space is its own answer to the question. The changing interpretations of a garden like Stowe should put paid to that, of course, as new evidence has come to light and as old evidence has been reinterpreted. For example, Ronald Paulson's alignment of the Grecian Valley with Thomas Whately's expressive landscapes[9] has been superseded by readings that recognize the iconographic importance of the (variously named) Temple of Concord and Victory and that draw on evidence—unavailable to Paulson—of statuary at key points around the valley.[10] Beyond such specifics, however, is a larger disciplinary issue: cultural geographers and archaeologists have done much to challenge histories of gardens based solely on verbal accounts,[11] but recent work has also argued that the physical layout is itself only a part of what or how the garden "means."[12] It is not just that the survival of gardens, in combination with a variety of scholarly approaches, destabilizes the interpretation of individual sites; there is also a larger conceptual uncertainty in terms of disciplinary objects and epistemes that to some extent reiterates the period's own ambiguities concerning the status of garden and landscape and the loosening of terminology around the act of gardening. Here the insights of an object-based material culture may prove particularly valuable with their insistence on placing objects (including gardens) in the context of social relations, cultural practices, and symbolic meanings.[13] That is to say, when we ask what is the garden, our answer must inevitably include not only physical landscape but eighteenth-century history and theory and the recognition of the garden as an imagined space both in the lives of individuals and in the cultures they inhabit.

At the heart of the matter is the nature and value of textual, archaeological, and visual sources for the study not only of individual gardens but for the understanding of the wider cultural landscape at any given historical moment. As I have already suggested, like eighteenth-century garden visitors, modern garden historians tend to see from particular points of view and it is as well to recognize the limitations in a field that may wish to be interdisciplinary but that tends to be at best multidisciplinary and more often a conglomeration of subject-specific insights. A less upbeat answer to the question what is the garden, therefore, might be that in modern scholarship "the garden" tends to devolve into the disparate sources and biases of the discipline-based historian. A more upbeat answer would be that works such as this Cultural History of Gardens[14] at once recognize such disciplinary and indeed national separations while inviting synthesis.

HISTORY AND PROGRESS

As a cultural history, this volume inevitably makes much of *change* across the period, but one of the most interesting developments in recent garden history— brought about once again by the literally groundbreaking work of garden ar- chaeologists—has been work that is beginning to demonstrate continuities and long-term traditions, which, though they may be dismissed by the avant garde of the eighteenth century as old-fashioned, nevertheless formed a major part of the European garden landscape.[15] Much historical writing on gardens requires and is indeed predicated upon fashion: forms that broadly continue across centuries, that are not so prone to changes in fashion, or crucially (however er- roneously), that do not seem to lend themselves so obviously to intellectual or emotional complexity—again, kitchen gardens come to mind—have attracted limited scholarly attention. Perhaps that is bound to be so, but it is worth recognizing the limitations of any cultural history—including this one—and recognizing also, therefore, that the culture of which we speak is as much our own as it is that of a past age.

The emphasis on change in itself accounts for one of the most tenacious of narratives in garden history that traces "progress" across nations, and that in our period would run thus: Italian Renaissance, French formal, Dutch, En- glish landscape, and then perhaps picturesque or gardenesque. Certainly, by the mid-eighteenth century, the landscape gardens created by English landown- ers both great and small were often claimed as a new and peculiarly English invention. And indeed one of the myths of the English landscape garden in the eighteenth century was of its almost miraculous "discovery" as a wholly native art in the early years of the Hanoverian succession. According to this narra- tive, the older style of "formal" and geometrical garden, heavily influenced by French and Dutch models, was swept away by a new delight in nature and an attempt to imitate its forms. In Walpole's famous phrase, painter and early landscape gardener William Kent "leaped the fence, and saw that all nature was a garden."[16] If this was a championing of "nature," however, it was also a championing of nation. Walpole, like many of his contemporaries, claimed the English landscape garden as Britain's great contribution to the arts, and he did so in the context of a widespread recognition that in other areas—whether painting, sculpture, or music—the English could not compete with their continental neighbors. In this sense, the rejection of geometrical form in favor of the "English" aesthetic of variety was claimed not just as a change in taste, but as a demonstration of England's inherent (though only recently established) liberty and its rejection of foreign tyranny.

In recent years, however, garden historians have challenged this politicized history of gardens and shown it to be the ideological construct it always was, with its nationalist agenda and its insistence on property, progress, and the power of great men. John Dixon Hunt (1986) has demonstrated the powerful influence of Italian designs on English gardens of the late seventeenth and early eighteenth century and suggested that it is here we should look for the origins of the "English" style. Tom Williamson (1995), by exploring the histories of individual gardens (rather than the histories produced by contemporary writers), has challenged the claims for a gradual transition from the "unnatural" to the "natural," from the "formal" to the "informal," and has demonstrated how patchy such changes could be. Douglas Chambers (1993) has taken another approach and shifted the chronology of the landscape garden's genesis back toward the middle of the seventeenth century by looking to Virgil's *Georgics* as a sustaining myth for the garden. And in this volume, Rachel Crawford argues for an "English" style of gardening widely recognized across Europe long before the appearance of the landscape garden. This last point should alert us to another issue, which is that while we might now question the rhetoric of national difference, that rhetoric was nevertheless fundamental to a period characterized as giving birth to nationalism in its modern form.[17] European travelers were keen to diagnose gardens precisely in terms of prevailing but often contradictory accounts of national character—which tended to revolve around such interrelated issues as masculinity and effeminacy, pragmatism, philosophy, economics, liberty, and empire—all used in turn to make claims about the relative cultural status of nations and the progress of civilization.[18]

The emerging science of comparative history was itself linked to another major feature of our period, the development of a truly global commerce, and this should alert us to another problem concerning periodization and the ways in which we might characterize an "age." For, just as we might refer to our period as the "Age of Empire" or the "Age of Enlightenment" (a subject to which I return in a moment), so might we follow the lead of McKendrick, Brewer, and Plumb (1982) in Britain and of Roche (2000) in France and characterize it as an age of "Consumption"; this in turn confronts us with the far from even patterns of consumption and the radically different influences of the Enlightenment across Europe. Only relatively recently has a case been made for a British Enlightenment, for example,[19] while its influence across Europe could be heavily dependent upon the power of the monarchy and the development of public institutions.[20] Similarly, patterns of consumption inevitably varied widely across Europe, not least in relation to global empires, the size of cities, the wealth of middle-class populations, and the influence of the aristocratic elites. Thus, for example, the socioeconomic conditions that sustained country estates in England and France can be framed in quite different ways—Girardin's Ermenonville appears to fit quite neatly in some respects into a narrative of French radical thinking; if one changes country and with it from a physical to an imagined garden, Sarah Scott's idealized landscape garden in *Millenium Hall* (1762) may have a similarly sympathetic purpose for its less fortunate inhabitants (and indeed it shares some of the characteristic design features that we might term "English" or "modern" or "natural"), but that sympathy is framed in terms not of the radical but of the return to an older culture of moral economy of rights and duties. And we can complicate this still further once we recognize—as David Hays (2006) has argued—that for all its apparent radicalism, its embrace of the local population, and its adherence to "nature," Girardin's garden—like that owned by Scott's fictional women—was wholly reliant, and indeed predicated upon, individual wealth, the sanctity of property, and the continuation of an established social hierarchy.

The moral usefulness claimed by both Girardin and Scott highlights another important issue for us, which is the ongoing and endlessly problematic relationship between profit and pleasure. Profit of course could signal many things, ranging from the economic to the spiritual, or indeed a combination of the two;[21] and for garden visitors across our period the balance of those different meanings was likely a touchstone for their moral evaluation both of the garden and of its owner. By the late eighteenth century, English travelers frequently reported their disappointment that continental pleasure gardens were also a source of income for their owners, but any landowning Englishman would know only too well that the apparent nonproductivity of the landscape garden was more rhetorical than actual and that while landscape gardens may suggest a world apart from commercial capitalism, they were fully implicated in a culture of commodities and strikingly concerned with spending money and with conspicuous display.[22] Conversely, of course, those same English travelers would frequently lambast the great French gardens for their ostentation, lack of productivity, and waste of resources. Thus, for example, we find agriculturalist Arthur Young at Chambord, in the Loire Valley, writing:

[W]e saw the environs, of which the park or forest forms three-fourths; it contains within a wall of about 20000 arpents, and abounds with all sorts of game to a degree of profusion. Great tracts of this park are waste or under heath, &c. or at least a very imperfect cultivation: I could not help thinking, that if the king of France ever formed the idea of establishing one complete and perfect farm under the turnip culture of England, here is the place for it.[23]

Standing on the battlements of this French royal palace, Young looks out over a landscape created for hunting and leisure but imagines instead a landscape transformed by "the turnip culture of England"—shorthand for the methods associated with Norfolk husbandry, with the agrarian capitalism of enclosure, with the benefits of new technology, crop rotation, large-scale farming, and low rents. Away from home and freed from the constraints of his own society, he challenges the value of an archetypal, aristocratic, designed landscape, and the limited productivity of the park can be replaced by Young's vision of the socioeconomic utility of the farm.[24] We should also recognize, however, that the championing of the profitability of "improvement" was far from new. It would be quite wrong to align Young's stance neatly with the concerns of, for example, John Evelyn and his circle at the beginning of our period—not least because Evelyn was so clearly inspired by the French and Italian gardens he had seen on his travels, because a religious imperative is absent from Young's writings until very late in his life, because Young's tenuous grip on gentry status made his position quite unlike that of the royalist gentleman Evelyn, and because Britain's economic state, in particular its agricultural productivity, had changed fundamentally between 1650 and 1800—but they nevertheless shared a concern for the national importance of horticultural improvement and the need to proselytize on its behalf, and they shared also a belief that profit—however defined—was a central part of man's relationship with the natural world.[25]

The relationship between gardens, productivity, a culture of commodities, and a language of improvement (replete with an easy or uneasy merging of profit and piety) was, then, fraught with contradictions, and different frames of reference inevitably tell us quite different stories. Gardens by definition mark out their own difference from the productive agricultural land around them, but the significance of that difference can be read in numerous ways. Thus, for example, while large-scale French-style gardens continue to be caricatured in Anglo-Saxon garden histories as a wasteful aristocratic or monarchical domination of nature, it has been suggested that the landscape parks of the second half of the eighteenth century became so widespread because they seemed to offer a shared aesthetic space and to assert a class identity common to both the propertied middling sort and an aristocratic elite.[26] Seductive as they may appear, neither of these accounts in itself allows for the multiplicity of meanings of the garden or adequately encapsulates the range of ways in which they might signify and engage with the world around them. As Thierry Mariage (1999) has convincingly argued, for example, the purpose of Versailles was not simply "aesthetic"; rather, its technological innovations, its complex economic organization, and its successful demonstration of global marketing was part of a large-scale attempt to reorganize and revitalize the French economy. Similarly, a good case can certainly be made for later eighteenth-century landscape gardens distinguishing themselves from economic profit while cementing the ties of polite society through a shared aesthetic, but Brownian gardens in particular remain notoriously disputed and the complexities of relating style and fashion to specific or self-consciously framed class identities would bear far greater exploration. What claims of an apparent progress toward a broadly middle-class capitalist aesthetic should alert us to, surely, is the problematic nature of progressivist narratives and the ease with which historical accounts of gardens slip into a Whig teleology underpinned by modern assumptions about the nature of the natural (on which more later).

FIGURE 0.1: Versailles, main axis. photograph by Stephen Bending.

In garden history, the willingness to follow a certain "progress" of the arts across nations—and with it the inexorable rise of the "natural"—also leads to misunderstandings of particular moments of gardening activity. Thus, for example, perhaps because the French style associated with Louis XIV is so strongly linked with the late seventeenth century, only fairly recently has attention turned to English gardening in the same period and an attempt been made to understand English garden writing of that time not as a prophetic precursor to the mid-eighteenth century but as the articulation of wholly contemporary gardening theory and practice. As John Dixon Hunt has argued, for example, Stephen Switzer's work makes far more sense in the context of later seventeenth-century understandings of the garden's intimate and intertwined relations with the agricultural and horticultural world of which it was a part rather than as anomalous prophecy.[27] Indeed, that powerful narrative of an increasing "naturalness" in design is itself in part responsible for the willingness of many garden historians to take eighteenth-century (English) rhetoric at face value and thus to insist on an absolute differentiation between "French" and "English" gardens that fails to recognize the close ties between the work of Le Notre and the likes of Alexander Pope and Robert Morris.[28] Gardens, that is, are always about nature (and therefore also about culture), but what a particular culture understands, and indeed sees, as natural remains historically specific in ways sometimes obscured by the teleological histories of progress that remain so powerful in modern garden history.

The problem of progress is not simply a matter of debate for twenty-first century historians, however; it is central to intellectual debate in our period and at the heart of what has become known as the Enlightenment. That term, *Enlightenment*, whether used broadly to denote a period, or more specifically to focus on a particular intellectual and ideological stance, has become a subject of much discussion in recent years, raising fundamental questions not only about ideas of progress, but about historical method, civilization, nature, nation, imperial expansion, and the relations between Europe and the wider world.[29] This is not the place to rehearse the history of the Enlightenment, but some of its central concerns are of particular interest to us.

One of the less controversial accounts of the Enlightenment traces the development of scientific knowledge in Europe from the mid-seventeenth century onward, and such knowledge was certainly crucial to the construction of some of the major gardens of the period, ranging from the complex mechanics of hydraulic engineering at Vaux and Versailles in the seventeenth century, and the less obvious but nevertheless complex work of "Capability" Brown's water systems at Croome or Wotton; to the navigational advances that massively expanded the reach of European shipping and brought back from around the globe both the knowledge of other cultures—including their garden design (see Charlesworth and Mowl in this volume)—and the "exotic" plants which were to shape the gardens of King Louis XIV at Versailles and the one-time republican poet William Mason at Nuneham (see Symes in this volume).

ENLIGHTENMENT GARDENING

It is not just the expansion of technological and scientific knowledge, however, that links gardens to the so-called Age of Enlightenment; as I have already suggested, central to the Enlightenment too is the idea of progress and the place of the arts as the marker of civilization.[30] Once again, Walpole's claim in his *Essay on Modern Gardening* is only perhaps the most striking example of the confidence in modern design, but whereas Walpole's narrative is effectively a hatchet job on all gardens before the English landscape garden, more usually the idea of progress runs alongside an equally strong but diametrically opposed account of classical greatness and modern corruption. We can see a version of this played out at Stowe, of course, with the ruinous Temple of Modern Virtue set alongside the perfections of the Temple of Ancient Virtue, and both set opposite the Whig narrative of progress found in the Temple of British Worthies. Across the channel, at Girardin's Ermenonville, modern philosophy appears as a temple in the process of construction even as the presence of an "ancient" dolman points to the pleasures and virtues of a simpler past. Indeed, if the Enlightenment sets much store by the language of the simple and the natural, it also of course relies upon a concept of the primitive, which is played out in the construction of primitive huts, of hermitages, and of "ancient" ruins. Here the "primitive" is required in order to demonstrate a sense of progress and modernity, but it also operates as a source of nostalgic pleasure, as a signifier of ancient virtues, and, more cynically, as a means of sidestepping the commercial present of which the garden is inevitably a part. That is, part of the attraction of eighteenth-century gardens—then as now, surely—is that they offer a complex arena for the expression of conflicting but ultimately interconnected cultural frameworks where use of the classical may signal modern decline or a formula for improvement; where the yearning for primitive virtues, or a pastoral nostalgia for a simpler past (whether that be William Shenstone's *ferme ornée*, Marie-Antoinette's *hameau* at the Petit Trianon, or Condé's at Chantilly), can be expressed through conspicuous display.

FIGURE 0.2: Stowe, the Temple of Ancient Virtue. Photograph by Stephen Bending.

FIGURE 0.3: Ermenonville, the partially built Temple of Modern Philosophy, with Rousseau's Tomb on the island in the lake. Photograph by Stephen Bending.

FIGURE 0.4: Versailles, Le Hameau. Photograph by Stephen Bending.

Another issue emerges here too, and this is once again related to the problems of progress. As Michel Baridon has ably demonstrated, a strong case can
be made for linking the rise of the English garden style in the eighteenth century to the increasing dominance of an empirical scientific model, its assumptions about the natural world and about how that world might be known.[31]
This may well be the case, but it is also the case that by concentrating on that
model one runs the risk of tipping over once again into a Whig history of progress, which, in tracing the onward march of rationalism, leads us to underplay
other aspects of the garden experience. Were we to shift our frame of reference
from design to, for example, religious belief, our sense of both change and
periodization might well be entirely different: Milton regularly makes an appearance in later English writing as a prophet of the "English" style, but one of
our period's most striking features is undoubtedly the sheer volume of religious
writing that emerged not only from the press but from an increasingly literate
population: central to that writing is the use of the garden as a metaphor for
the personal immediacy of religious belief, and if we return to our question
of what is the garden, one further answer would be that it is a space enabling

the articulation of interior spiritual life (see Crawford in this volume).[32] John Prest's excellent study of the Garden of Eden as a trope in European gardening has of course already alerted us to the importance of religion,[33] and the fascinating work on Evelyn and the circle around Samuel Hartlib places religious belief center stage,[34] but for the latter part of our period, piety and the garden remains a strangely underexplored area.[35] We need not rely on the likes of the Methodist Countess of Huntingdon's claim to convert servants through garden walls: eighteenth-century letters and diaries are full of references to the garden as a place of pious meditation and worldly temptations, and yet modern scholarship's interest in eighteenth-century religion has been curiously limited. That is, "progress" can hide from us the equally strong pull not of the modern but of the traditional, not of the rational but of the religious; and indeed when we ask ourselves how eighteenth-century individuals inhabited the garden, many of the models to which those individuals turned were fundamentally classical and biblical.[36]

What complicates this further is that while such an account suggests a historical frame of reference for the garden as a site of nostalgia for a simpler past and as a demonstration of modernity and civilization, that understanding was likely merged with a further geographical agenda that set the country against the city, and indeed that understood the garden from the perspective of the civic, commercial, and complex present.[37] The tension between the ancient and the modern, between the purity of the past and the progress achieved in the present, between the rational and the religious, between the country and the city inevitably raises a larger question about just what it is one *should* do in or with a garden. As we have seen, any number of theoreticians are willing to tell readers how to behave, and, as we have also seen, modern scholarship still places strong emphasis on the intentions of owners and their apparent designs upon visitors. It is here also, however, that the Enlightenment interest in perception becomes of particular importance not least because of its intimate relation to matters of taste and the inevitable embroilment of taste in the fluid and contested world of social relations and status. As nature itself became one of the central subjects of Enlightenment investigation, so too did the means of perceiving that natural world; indeed accounts of the apparently objective and empirical exploration of nature nevertheless assumed the central importance of the perceiving individual, and perception—as Hume among others noted— could and probably would be inflected by emotion even as claims were made for objectivity and detachment.[38] In our time, a version of this appeared in what (following Thomas Whately) became known as "expressive" gardens— essentially the landscape gardens of the later eighteenth century in which the individual is apparently left to his or her own emotional devices—but more recently garden historians have begun to rethink this account and to turn instead to the wider frames of reference and alternative agenda that a perceiving individual might bring to a garden or articulate in the reimagining of a garden that inevitably takes place in any verbal composition. It is to the perceiving individual and to the sense of an audience, therefore, that we should now turn.

RECEPTION AND THE USE OF GARDENS

John Dixon Hunt has argued persuasively for the end of our period as a watershed in the understanding of garden design, suggesting that until the late eighteenth century there was a common recognition that the garden necessarily used artifice in order to interpret nature; that with the rise of "natural" gardening in Europe, at least, the well-understood distinction between objects and representation all too easily collapses into an apparently undifferentiated "nature"; and that accounts of the garden that lose sight of representation's role in design have predominated over the last two centuries.[39] Central here is Hunt's recent emphasis on the garden as a third nature to be understood in the context of, and always in relation to, a first, which is wilderness, and a second, which is cultivation. Hunt rightly stresses the function of the garden as a form of representation, and crucially the relations between the garden and what is beyond it. This use of "third nature" is itself a particular take on a longer-standing recognition of the garden's relation to the world beyond and reiterates in the world of garden history what has already been argued in art history and cultural geography.[40] Most usefully, however, the term highlights and seeks to provide a means of separating out the merging and conflicting accounts of nature with which gardens inevitably operate. As a culturally specific historical construct, "nature" always carries different kinds of ideological freight: "third nature" invites us to recognize and attempt to articulate what that freight might be in a particular context.

We can complicate the model, however, by turning to another term popularized by Hunt: *afterlife*. It has of course long been recognized that there can be a fundamental mismatch between the intentions of designers and owners and the experiences of individual visitors—not least because there are frequently very different stakes at play and because individuals bring with them their own accounts of the world.[41] As Hunt's third nature suggests, accounts of nature must necessarily be accounts of the cultural frames of reference and the modes of understanding necessary to articulate an individual's place in the world: if gardens are a knowing account of their relation with the world beyond, accounts of gardens are at least as much an image of that larger world, but crucially, they need not take as their basis the assumptions of garden owners or garden designers.

In some ways, of course, the model of afterlife may still suggest the primary importance of design and the intentions of designers because use by others is what comes after, but it points usefully to the need to take account of the variety of ways in which individuals might respond to a designed object. Such variety of response is not of course unique to gardens—though the range of responses may be—nor does it need to come long *after* the designer's work (Repton's constant negotiations not only with his clients but with their families and friends is a case in point[42]); but what marks gardens as different from other kinds of aesthetic objects is that they change from season to season, year to year, and decade to decade, and thus unlike, say, a painting, viewers look at literally different objects (thus, for example, William Kent's extensive drawings of garden designs offer a carefully arranged and theatrical vision of such sites as Rousham or Chatsworth,[43] but a modern viewer can't help but be struck by the sheer change of scale affected by the growth of trees around the architectural structures and thus by the very different experience apparently on offer). As numerous accounts of garden making suggest, conflicting responses to gardens, even as they are being made—which, with gardens, is almost continually the case—is inevitable and also inevitably an account of culture. Hunt has suggested that a new history of reception might need to focus on individual gardens, as George Clarke's valuable *Descriptions of Lord Cobham's Gardens at Stowe 1700–1750* (1990) has done, but any such history would need to be careful not to conflate individual with necessarily "major." By definition, the majority of gardens cannot be major, but the use of less celebrated sites can still tell us much about gardens and about the cultures that produced them. Not least—as I suggest later—the mass of evidence available to us from diaries and journals, published and unpublished tours, sketching, annotation, and the like can open up to us alternative perspectives that in turn help us to place the garden within the larger cultural tussles by which a society understands itself.

This turn to reception has itself been one of the most interesting moves in recent garden history. Unlike any other art forms, the construction of the garden placed man, or woman, within a physical statement of how he or she understood his or her place in the world, geographically, temporally, morally, and spiritually. It is also the case of course that the eighteenth-century garden visitor—or owner—might be cheerily oblivious to most of these claims, inhabiting instead, for example, a world of fashion, class interests, and social competition. Other inhabitants of the garden—those who labored, for example, but whose experiences are now almost entirely lost to us—would surely have experienced gardens in quite different ways again. The gardener at Rousham may have had a peculiarly acute understanding of General Dormer's garden in the mid-eighteenth century;[44] for many further down the social scale we are largely left to speculate as to whether working in the garden "felt" very different from other forms of agricultural labor (though the likes of Shoemaker poet James Woodhouse at least give us a partial sense of what might be at stake for a literate working man[45]).

This range of responses to the garden is now being recognized in critical and historical writing,[46] and has moved garden history away—in part at least—from earlier obsessions with design, designers, and the recovery of design intention. This suggests, of course, that just as gardens articulate themselves in relation to the world around them, so garden history is shaped by changing accounts of the eighteenth century, whether that be history from below, the influential work of E. P. Thompson and Lawrence Stone, the emergence in the 1980s of the "New Eighteenth Century," or the recent object-based focus of consumption studies. Each in its way has made more difficult the cheery isolationism of a popular garden history based more in fantasies of pastoral pleasures than the rather less comfortable—but more exciting—world of ideologically engaged interdisciplinary scholarship.

Two connected points are worth making here. One is that if we look only to those theoretical statements on garden design that tend by their nature to align themselves with landowning interests, we inevitably gain a very partial view of the cultural meanings of the garden; the other is that when we turn to that wider range of sources we can begin to see more clearly why gardens were of such particular importance not only to their owners but to their visitors. Certainly gardens could articulate and seek to justify the interests of owners, but beyond the concerns of the patrician elite, we should also be aware of a whole range of discourses for which the classically freighted aesthetic theory on which their apologists drew has only the most limited relevance—hence, for example, the importance of guidebooks as both a symptom of and a source for the understanding of consumption; and hence also the need to read such public accounts both with and against the more private world of letters and journals.

One of the strengths of recent garden history in our period is the range of approaches now taken in an attempt to understand what and how gardens mean. Thus, while we have sophisticated analysis of the nuanced and often highly politicized meanings of gardens generated by owners and their close circles of friends (in this volume, see, for example, Eyres on the political iconography of landscape gardens), we benefit also from an increasing interest in the possible resistance to this—something to which David Lambert points in his account of the modern use of some of those same landscapes. Resistance, or re-use, is not, however, a new phenomenon, and as the back story to Lambert's chapter it may be helpful here to provide some brief examples of how eighteenth-century visitors (rather than owners) attempted to make other people's gardens their own.

Lambert uses the Leasowes as one of his examples of modern departures from the official agenda, but as he notes, the story begins much earlier. If one were to read only William Shenstone's published theoretical statements on gardening (most notably his influential "Unconnected Thoughts"[47]), one might reasonably conclude that gardens are about aesthetic, emotional, and intellectual experience. They certainly are; but gardens, including Shenstone's, are inevitably also *about* property, and one of the ways in which their owners' stance can be resisted is by challenging those property rights. At the Leasowes, Shenstone frequently complained of the local villagers breaking down his boundary hedges, picking his flowers, and ignoring the aesthetic signposts of his carefully crafted poetic landscape in favor of their own less educated but rather longer-established practices. One of his responses was to alter the garden accordingly, with new poetic "keep off the grass" inscriptions joining the more erudite Latin mottos around the estate. Other landowners reacted in a rather less subtle fashion, and the man traps and spring guns found on many estates were only a more brutal sign that the nonlandowning poor refused to see gardens as the aesthetic objects their owners claimed; they are also of course a reminder that owners saw their gardens in quite different ways as well. But even where one might assume some kind of shared aesthetic response to designed landscape because of class and education, individual interests and agenda could make the experience of the garden quite different, and the sophisticated meanings ascribed by owners might have only the most limited purchase.

Central to debates about aesthetics in the Enlightenment is the ongoing wrangling over subjective and objective accounts of taste—something of which eighteenth-century garden visitors are at times acutely aware (not least because claims for the universality of aesthetic theory—notably those of Shaftesbury and Addison—often rested upon landscape examples). We can see some of the ways in which this works if we consider a group of visitors' accounts of the same gardens, and here Piercefield in south Wales is a good place to begin. Close to Tintern Abbey and looking down on the river Wye, Piercefield was laid out by Valentine Morris in the middle of the century. Morris's father had made a vast fortune from slavery and cattle on his estates in Antigua, and if we would now characterize this money as new commercial wealth, Morris himself attempted to transform it by recreating the mythic life of medieval hospitality, opening his cellars to all and sundry, feeding every passerby, and lavishly entertaining guests of all ranks. Many of the "major" garden writers of the eighteenth century visited Piercefield, from George Mason and Thomas Whately to the famous picturesque traveler William Gilpin. Unlike Mason or Whately, Gilpin was not a substantial landowner, but in his tour of Piercefield, as elsewhere, he offers confident judgments of its picturesque and sublime scenes, and is happy to judge its defects and offer advice to its owner. At the same time, it is important to recognize that the judgments in Gilpin's tours were substantially toned down between the manuscripts first circulated and the accounts finally published: acts of self-censorship articulate Gilpin's recognition of the kinds of social and aesthetic compromise that becomes necessary in the shift from private experience to polite public representation. Given Gilpin's characteristically critical response to "made scenery," Piercefield got off very lightly. By contrast, at the Leasowes, one can trace through the series of revisions in his manuscript notebooks the way in which the personal reproach of Gilpin's note that he "laughed at his inscrip[tion] inviting the naiids to bath" has to be massaged in the published text into a more carefully worded discussion of why the inscription, by a muddy pool, might be less than appropriate.[48] As Richardson argues in this volume, landscape gardens are notably absent from most visual satire, perhaps because of the common values they were perceived to embody, but if criticism does not tend to appear in visual publications, manuscript sources can give us an insight into how criticism might be molded into appropriate public statements.

Gardens invite, perhaps even expect, a response from their visitors precisely because they offer themselves as a designed space, as a space designed to speak, and therefore as a space in which to engage in dialogue (one need think only of the insistent gesturing of Rigaud's staffage in the widely circulated engravings of Chiswick and Stowe). But if we read travelers' accounts of gardens as some untroubled account of a physical reality rather than considering how seeing is itself mediated; and if we read only in order to enumerate *what* was seen by a visitor, rather than exploring how garden representation might articulate a sense of audience, we lose an essential element of what and how the garden might mean.

A further crucial question for the garden historian, then, is not simply to ask what visitors might do in and with a garden, but what the visitors' object of attention might be—the physical landscape or the sense of self. The answer, of course, must be both, and we can see something of this if we return to Piercefield. In Robert Dodsley's 1761 account of the garden, he writes of "bold and numerous" rocks, of surprising heights, of the romantic windings of the river Wye at the foot of the cliffs, of the "Pride and Grandeur" of the scenes and of their extensive prospects; he also adds "a more particular Description of the Scenes and Views I have attempted to describe," essentially a list of all the different objects and viewpoints found around the estate.[49] For Dodsley, that listing of objects produces a "better understanding," demonstrates his socio-aesthetic status, and becomes a means of laying claim to a garden he does not own. However, for other travelers, that insistence on particularity is itself a demonstration of aesthetic incompetence. Thus, for example, in the *Tour through Derbyshire to the Lakes*, by a "Gentleman of the University of Oxford," Dodsley is abruptly taken to task by the author, who claims, "Particular descriptions, the more minute they become, are the farther from giving the reader a distinct idea of the place, whose beauties they enumerate; witness Mr. Dodsley's tedious detail . . . I shall dwell only, therefore, on such beauties as may be relished, without passing through the medium of sight."[50] More radically still, when Methodist leader John Wesley visited Piercefield in 1769, after offering a wholly conventional account of the garden's beauties, he concluded, "And must all these be burned up? What will become of us then, if we set our hearts upon them?"[51] Such attacks on the triviality, indeed immorality, of physical gardens are inevitably an attack on those who own them: in questioning the aesthetic value of such design, a spiritual engagement with the garden here implicitly challenges landed culture's self-representation and justification. More than this, we need then to understand the garden as a site in which conflicting responses can cohabit in the mind of the visitor, and indeed as spaces that can elicit and make apparent the contradictions that inevitably emerge when public and private identities confront one another.

As garden historians, we need to recognize the significance of such shifting responses within an individual and the cultural pressures that might produce them; we also need to recognize that if these responses may be tempered by class, by wealth, by property owning, they also can be predicated on the forms of gender identity that remain so oddly absent from the majority of garden history. For women, that is, things could be quite different, and that difference lay not least in the way Enlightenment thinking normalized gender inequalities as part of the natural order. As Dorinda Outram has argued, in its Enlightenment guise, "natural" could mean any number of things: "it could mean 'not socially defined'; not 'artificial'; 'based on the external physical world.' " But as she also notes, "overwhelmingly, [it] was used, often in a mixture of all of these meanings, to legitimate and control arrangements which we in the twenty-first century would see as socially created."[52] Nowhere is this more the case than in the ubiquitous alignment of male with culture but female with both nature and artifice, a version of which is at the heart of one of the most influential—but fictional—gardens of the period, Rousseau's *La Nouvelle Héloise* (1761). At Clarens, Julie's garden is described as natural, but it is kept this way by the combination of Julie *and* the practical estate management of her husband. If Clarens functions as the site in which Saint-Preux can leave behind the solitude of the Alps and the heightened emotion they engender in favor of calm reflection, it also functions, of course, to reduce women to their apparently biological limitations while claiming to celebrate their sensitivity to nature and their role as the markers and upholders of civilization. It was not least for this reason that Rousseau proved such a difficult figure for many eighteenth-century women, but especially for those who gardened.[53]

WOMEN IN THE GARDEN

It was not just Rousseau, of course, who sought to limit women by aligning them with an account of the natural, for, alongside the domestic's concomitant, which is the limiting of education, ran that widespread eroticization of women in landscapes that saw them as figures of seduction in gardens, of punishment in gardens, and of disgrace in gardens. The combination of casual male erotics, limited female learning, double standards of propriety, and gendering of power relations is, I would suggest, central to women's experience of the garden in the eighteenth century.[54] This is not to argue that women who found themselves in gardens necessarily defined themselves wholly in such terms; it is, however, to argue that we should recognize the pervasiveness of such language and its influence on women's self-representation, whether that self-representation drew on the language of piety or botany, philosophy or fashion.

Women were of course amongst the many visitors to gardens in our period. However, another of the popular myths of the garden is that large-scale gardens were the creation and the domain of men. If one lists the famous names of eighteenth-century landscape design in Britain, for example—London and Wise, Bridgeman, Kent, Brown, Repton—they are all (in this case professional) men; in France, one might look to the Mollets, Le Notre, and Le Blond at the beginning of our period and to Girardin and Morel at the end; even in Russia, with the example of Catherine the Great, much of the attention of garden historians turns to the world of male designers. Indeed, with its fascination for design and for narratives of formal change, garden history has until recently had little place for women. With few exceptions, to read garden history is to read a story of men.[55] When women appear, they do so within the confines of the flower garden, of recognizably domestic spaces, or as quirky exceptions in a male-dominated world of large-scale landscape design. But we should surely question the curious absence of women and of women gardeners in the majority of histories, whether written in the eighteenth century or in our own day.

It is not that women are said to have no place in gardens, but that their place is characterized as domestic, small scale, private rather than public, devotional rather than political, and so on. Women are routinely mentioned in contemporary sources—Stephen Switzer, for one, named the Duchess of Beaufort and the Countess of Lindsey amongst his important gardeners of the early eighteenth century. For all that this may suggest a world of gardening free from gender distinctions, however, women in fact confronted quite different problems from men when they took to gardening on a large scale—Switzer is in no way unusual, for example, in associating the women he names either with exotics and piety (Beaufort) or with a practical participation (Lindsey) that "has something in it that looks supernatural."[56] In this area, then, garden history still has a lot of work to do.

What academic garden history has been good at doing over the last two decades is insisting on an understanding of the garden as a cultural rather than just a physical place, on recognizing the garden as an ideological as well as a geographical location. With its fascination for great men and great designs, however, it has spent less time asking if women can be neatly subsumed within such accounts of class, taste, and politics. Part of the problem with traditional garden history of course is the listing of "greats" and the assumptions on which that operates. For the significance of the garden lies not only in its major innovators and master practitioners but in the depths to which it penetrated eighteenth-century culture, the importance it was given as a national art, and the emotional significance with which individuals invested it. We take nothing away from "great" men by arguing that gardens offer us rather more to think about; and if the insistence on great works and great designers effectively relegates women to little more than footnotes, we must look elsewhere for their presence in the garden.

It is undoubtedly the case that flower gardens grew increasingly associated with women as an extension of indoor domestic spaces.[57] At the beginning of our period, Amalia von Solms, wife to the prince of Orange, was a dedicated collector of flowers for her gardens at the Noordeinde Palace; in the mid-eighteenth century, Lady Walpole was celebrated for the flower gardens she created in Italy; and when one turns to the remaining evidence of Henry and Caroline Holland's gardening work at their seaside estate of Kingsgate, Kent, in the 1760s and 1770s, it is Henry Holland who designed large-scale garden structures with an angry political agenda while Caroline created a small flower garden. At their main estate, Holland Park, the Hollands—like many married couples—in fact present us with a far less simple gender divide, but whether in English conduct books or in Rousseau's novels, that divide was frequently asserted.

There are exceptions to this, of course—for example, Queen Caroline at Kew or Catherine the Great at Tsarskoe Selo—but on the whole what is championed in public writing that links women with gardens is a form of domestic moral worth. Perhaps the most influential English version of this is found in Addison's account of Aurelia in her garden in *The Spectator*,[58] but women writers followed his lead throughout the eighteenth century, and the link between women and flowers is particularly insistent. Notably the garden becomes a site for the exercise of female virtue, a place in which to demonstrate one's understanding of appropriate female conduct in the polite world, but also, conversely, as a private female sphere set apart from that public world.

Some women, however, gardened on an altogether different scale, creating their own landscaped estates either by buying in a designer like Brown or—more often than most histories suggest—designing for themselves or with their partners and taking an active and sometimes physical role in the creation of their landscapes. Moreover, when we turn to the accounts of gardening left to us by eighteenth-century women, passive acceptance of gender roles and the cultural narratives that support them is far from universal. Rather, gardens are recognized as the opportunity for a self-fashioning engagement with cultural norms and narratives, a space in which the disparate agenda of eighteenth-century culture would inevitably have to be confronted.

One of the most powerful aspects of the garden in the eighteenth century is that it allowed men and women, the elite and the lowly, those who owned and those who merely visited, to claim its rich cultural resources as their own. In this they were aided by a great wealth of religious, literary, and practical writing that made the garden as much a metaphorical as a physical space. In many cases, encomia on country life could, in principle at least, be claimed by both men and women, and the garden could offer a shared space for labors at once physical and intellectual, moral and emotional. In important ways, this is just what the idea of the garden did offer both to men and to women; but it also allowed for a breaking down of those apparently shared interests along gender as well as class lines, and it was aided in this by the great mass of writing that claimed the garden as its subject while addressing issues spreading well beyond the cultivation of trees and flowers—the world of letters and of cultural imagination was not just some literary exercise for women who gardened, rather it was a crucial part of the way in which they engaged with a world beyond their apparent rural seclusion.

Tom Williamson (1995) has argued that a stress on the literary has misled us into a false account of eighteenth-century garden design by emphasizing what was written over what actually happened on the ground. That is undoubtedly right, but we might also turn it around; for, while we can describe with relative certainty the physical layout of a garden and its changing appearance, that is only one part of its existence: its significance lies at least as much in what is brought to it by an individual as in what is physically present, and if we want to put women back into garden history, we should be less concerned with those narratives of innovation in design that have always championed the work of men, and turn instead to the sources in which women actually appear and to the cultures on which they drew. We should turn, that is to the letters, journals, and diaries, to the fiction and to the poetry in which women's gardens continue to have their existence. My point here is not to argue that when women created or inhabited gardens their actions and experiences were wholly different from those of men; it is, however, to argue that those experiences could be crucially different because of the cultures of gender with which men and women lived. We should also resist the notion that eighteenth-century women gardeners simply fit into our existing models of garden history but in a less interesting way because they do not appear at the forefront of innovation.

A BRIEF CASE STUDY AND SOME SUGGESTIONS

Having made that appeal, I want to conclude this introduction with an example of what I have in mind and to suggest how this may offer us further ways forward as we explore the place of the garden—whether owned by men or women—in a cultural field that must necessarily range way beyond the aesthetics of design.[59] Elizabeth Montagu, the "Queen of the Bluestockings" and one of the most famous female intellectuals of the mid-eighteenth century, is, of course, mostly associated with the sociability and literary culture of London rather than with a life in the country. But like many fashionable eighteenth-century women, she in fact spent up to half of each year not in London, but at her country estate, in this case Sandleford in Berkshire.[60] At the center of cultural life in London, it should perhaps be no surprise that Montagu described country life as at times, "Sedentary, solitary, lazy and dull," but this needs to be set against an altogether different account of the country that centers on repeated accounts of sitting alone on a garden bench:

If I sit on some contemplative bench on a summers day, I know that I soon throw myself, and all the circumstances that belong to me, into the vast Ocean of Animal life . . . and in so large a company all that is personal is lost . . . humbled without being mortified I acquiesce in the general laws, and determine to enjoy my short day of Being like the Animals about me.[61]

So here Montagu appears to represent the experience of the garden in terms of philosophical contemplation, Christian resignation, and personal insignificance. Writing from Sandleford, she offers us a classic rehearsal of garden meditation that aligns her with a tradition we can recognize from aristocratic women poets of the seventeenth century; from physico-theologists like John Ray and Bishop Burnett; from nearer contemporaries like James Thomson; from the writings of Rousseau (whose *Solitary Walker* the passage closely prefigures); from the pages of *The Spectator*, and so on. Ostensibly, then, Montagu claims that her garden signals both its own and Montagu's limited significance in the greater scheme of things—the garden bench on which she rests leads her to a loss of "all that is personal" and allows her to forget the social world that has given her importance. And as she moves from the local and the specific to the general and the universal, her particular location seems to lose its significance in favor of the absent and the elsewhere. Read in this way, the figure of a woman sitting in a garden appears to be shorthand for piety and otherworldliness—and the importance of the garden is that it can remove the individual from the social world and from sociability.

But this self-image might also be framed in other ways. If this philosophical piety seems to dismiss the garden as unnecessary to an understanding of the creation—one can as well meditate on a leaf or a flower—Montagu's apparent rejection of the garden is surely complicated by the bench on which she sits: because if the bench is an opportunity for a reverie that moves her beyond the social world and its false values, it nevertheless signifies the private property, the wealth, and the leisure on which her own meditative opportunities rest. Thus if one can argue that sitting on her bench, Montagu demonstrates Christian piety and a rejection of worldly concerns, one can also argue that when sitting on her bench, Montagu demonstrates the importance of property, landowning, and leisure in order to have the luxury of meditation. And indeed it is no contradiction to argue for both of those positions at the same time.

One can complicate this account still further, however, because while Montagu chooses to represent herself as a lone figure in a garden thinking of God, the choice of the bench also does something else—it suggests the possibility of company while quietly marking its absence. Here, then, the garden appears as a place of social failings, haunted by the sense of an absent social world—in many letters by women gardeners, that is, it holds an awkward cultural position as an object of sociability (the subject described and shared in a letter to another) while also being a marker of social absence—a point to which I return in a moment.

As Stephen Daniels (2002) has argued, Montagu's insistence on the "sober" and retired character of her landscape should also be read in the context of gardens celebrating not learned ladies, fine ladies, or women in retirement, but rather women as sexual objects in the fantasies of men. Daniels has in mind the gardens created at West Wycombe for Sir Francis Dashwood, and as Wendy Frith (2002) has shown, it was here that Dashwood notoriously celebrated an aggressive masculine sexuality in a landscape that not only included a temple of Venus and numerous titillating inscriptions, but was said to be laid out in the form of a reclining female nude. The formal structure of the garden need not be as extreme as Dashwood's, however, for women to be implicated in the erotic language of the garden: as Montagu was to find out in the letters of her friends, that same battle could be waged as easily in the imagined spaces of a quiet pastoral landscape as in the more overtly libertine structures of Dashwood's West Wycombe.

As I have argued elsewhere,[62] Montagu was acutely aware of the gendered fantasies of her close male friends, and her self-representation as a contemplative woman on a bench was also a response to the ubiquitous sexualization of women in gardens. Thus, for example, in a letter of 1764, Lyttelton imagines Montagu in her garden and offers what is effectively a mini-compendium of classical rapes and seductions as he busies himself with thoughts that are quite as much about her body as they are about her bodily well-being:

> Don't you read too long under the shade of your Garden? Does not the Warmth of the Sun make you sometimes too forgetfull of the Coldness of the Wind? Pray, Madam, remember, it is recorded in the History of the Thracians, that a rape was committed by Boreas on a Lady of that Country. Don't imagine that he carried her off in a Whirlwind. No—he slily insinuated himself into her bosom under the favour of a warm Sun, which made her neglectfull to guard it against him with the necessary caution. Do you therefore be more carefull: but, if the mild and benignant Zephyrus should come and court you in your garden, open your breast to him boldy, and let him sport there as he does among the Lillies and Roses: he will do you no more harm than he does them . . .[63]

Montagu's self-representation as a contemplative woman on a bench is surely also a response to the almost casual sexualization of women in gardens of which Lyttelton's letter is only a mild example, and this adds a further set of possibilities to just what Montagu's sense of herself in her garden might be. One might extend such suggestions much further, of course, setting the letter, for example, in the context of popular fiction, which not only made gardens places of seduction but of punishment after seduction; or elaborating on that difficult relationship women inevitably had with the gendered Rousseauvian pleasures of nature; or exploring Montagu's further self-representation as an icon of charitable behavior who orchestrated happy pastoral feasts for her rural workers; and so on. But the example of Montagu and her garden should highlight the further questions we must surely ask of the garden and of the individual's relation to the garden: what kind of cultural space is constructed both by and around the individual in the garden and to what kinds of sources must we turn in order to understand that space? How does the creation and inhabitation of a garden place both owners and visitors in dialogue with the world beyond its boundaries? If individuals draw on their cultures' discourses in order to frame themselves in particular ways, how might they nevertheless be framed and interpreted by others? What do we learn by exploring non-canonical sources, and how might "thick description" alter our sense of the garden's significance in relation to the interlocking but often clashing cultural discourses and agenda with which it inevitably engages? Such questions do not of course preclude the important work of garden reconstruction and the establishing of just what was happening on the ground, but I hope even these brief examples suggest some of the ways in which we might reimagine garden history not only as a series of design issues, or as an account of garden experience based on theoretical texts from the period, but also as a form of lived experience that might be quite different from these concerns.

Garden history in our period remains excitingly open to new possibilities. The proliferation of sources of all kinds—so central to and characteristic of these years—invites us to see many kinds of gardens and many forms of relations between gardens; it also invites us to think further about how the garden—physical or imagined—might engage with or be the arena for other kinds of cultural agenda. The recognition of a gendered garden history will undoubtedly reshape our larger narratives of garden design—as both garden archaeology and the detailed cultural analysis of individual sights have been doing for many years—but so too will the new interest in reception and the emerging study of emotion. As the following chapters suggest, we may no longer attach ourselves to the narratives and agendas generated by the needs of eighteenth-century society, but the questions they raise—of nature and artifice, of progress and modernity, of emotion, gender, class, and religious belief—remain with us.

CHAPTER ONE

Design

TIMOTHY MOWL

In the 1650s, many Western European gardens were following or preparing to follow the Italian-Franco-Dutch style of design of long central axes, flanking parterres, and side screens of controlled woodland. At the same time, other countries, notably but not exclusively England and Russia, made a stand in favor of extending centralized gardens to engage more with the land for virtuous profit (agricultural and horticultural productivity) rather than in the service of aristocratic pomp. In each country, there was also a parallel, but contrary, movement toward gardens designed to respond to nature or the imagination. So Europe faced three alternative garden directions: geometric, productive, and introspective.

Tsar Aleksei Mikhailovich (1645–76), the father of Peter the Great, was devoted to garden improvements and the acclimatization of plants like melons, vines, and mulberries, though he also had a fondness, like Tsar Boris Godunov (1598–1605) before him, for palace pavilions set on islands in artificial lakes. But neither his Vineyard Garden nor the Apothecary's Garden[1] on his estate at Izmailovo outside Moscow were directly related to a parent palace: both, by their design and scale, required laying out across virgin forest land. The forty-acre Vineyard Garden grew crops—rye, wheat, barley—and poppies, white currants, flowers, and herbs in a series of diminishing squares. Circular gardens at each corner of the outer square were dedicated to four orchards, one for pears, one for plums, and one each for white and red cherries. In design terms, the Apothecary's Garden was a fifteen-acre circle of three inner concentric bands

divided by ten paths radiating from the core.² On the surviving survey plan,³
the multiple areas are marked for medicinal herbs, vegetables, gooseberries,
and groves of birch, sweet briar, mulberry, apple, and rowan trees.

Tsar Aleksei's Prosyansky Garden was a design of diminishing squares, but
centered more aesthetically upon a pavilion with four winged dragon fountains
and a flower bed. A plan also survives for a pleasure palace with a garden,
designed for Izmailovo, strictly geometrical again,⁴ with a central maze planted
with black currants and cherries. Outside it lie sixteen square parterres of tu-
lips, narcissi, and scented herbs. The remainder of the square area was to be
planted with fruit trees. In a harsh climate like that of Russia, a garden's first
duty had always been to produce food. These two gardens had readily appre-
hensible designs based on simple geometric shapes, yet they were also focused
on maximizing the products of nature through an assiduous and scientifically
minded horticulture.

However, at the same period, Patriarch Nikon, who ruled from 1652
until his deposition and confinement in a monastery garden in 1668, founded
the New Jerusalem Monastery at Istra in 1656. It had a surrounding garden
designed to recall the topography of the real Jerusalem,⁵ including a Sea of
Galilee, Mount Carmel, and Mount Taber; two rivers to represent the Jor-
dan and the Euphrates; and even a house of King David from which he spied
Bathsheba bathing in the garden of Uriah the Hittite. The garden was much
admired, and a nineteenth-century visitor reported being guided along an avenue through a wood to "a little white building embosomed amid drooping
arches,"⁶ where Patriarch Nikon lived for twenty years. Carved out of a forest,
with wandering waters, isolated mounts, architectural features of a biblically
eclectic nature, and a little arched pavilion, it would have been similar to some
of the north Italian *monte sacre*, and in its historical, evocative design, to the
later English Arcadian garden of the mid-eighteenth century. In Holy Russia,
the Bible was the controlling literary factor that brought historic eclectic references in to turn otherwise geometric and utilitarian gardens into places of
surprise and enchantment. In Augustan England, where a newly empowered
parliament saw itself as a modern version of the Roman Senate, the poetry
of Virgil and Horace was the controlling literary force and it required classical temples and grottoes. But in both countries, the eclectic references would
have created adventurous, rather than regular, ornamental gardens. Russia had
made this garden move some decades before England.

In contemporary England of the 1650s, there had been by parliamentary,
not royal patronage, a similar dual move: not only one toward geometrical
estate designs aimed at improving productivity, but another, not to a garden
of overt biblical symbolism, but to a garden that appreciated God as nature's

gardener, designing far more impressively than men. Interestingly, and perhaps not coincidentally, the sponsor behind both these approaches—the utilitarian and the nature centered—was an East European, Samuel Hartlib (ca. 1600–62). Born in Elbing to an English mother and a Lithuanian merchant father, Hartlib (or Hartlieb) was an "Intelligencer," communicating through copious letters with and among agricultural experts (and many others he thought had profitable ideas). He may have been aware of the gardens at Izmailovo and their simple productive geometry.[7]

Hartlib was excited by the hopeful pansophist doctrines of another East European, Moravian Jan Amos Komenski (1592–1670), best known by the Latin form of his name, Comenius. Pansophism was a Christian rationalism; Eden had been God's garden design and so, according to pansophism, the way to banish hunger and want, to make human happiness general, was by educating farmers and gardeners.

Hartlib settled in England in 1628; Comenius himself sought refuge from the Thirty Years' War in England in 1641 (before fleeing when the Civil War erupted in what he had hoped would be an oasis of peace). Hartlib's "Office of Address" spread information on newly developed crops like sainfoin and on superior systems of crop rotation, contributing to the large-scale increase in agricultural efficiency that enabled England to change from a net importer to a net exporter of grain in the later seventeenth century.

Among Hartlib's many publications was his 1653 *Discoverie for a Division*, written jointly with Cressy Dymock. This featured dramatic plans, one square and one circular,[8] to show how an ideal estate and garden combined should be set out. Immediately around the house, Hartlib's circular design set four gardens—B, C, D, E—each with a distinct purpose: "choice fruits or flowers," "Physical plants," "Kitchin Garden," and "Orchyard." Instead of the usual twin pavilions devoted solely to pleasure rather than utility present in earlier Jacobean layouts, there were "Bake House," "Brewhouse," "Dare" (Dairy), and "Landry" (Laundry). As the circles widened concentrically, just as at Izmailovo, there were fenced areas for animals, corn, and, last, for pasture. As a clear proof of Hartlib's influence and success, the grounds of Thorpe Hall, Peterborough,[9] home to Oliver St. John, who became Oliver Cromwell's deputy and lord chief justice, copied precisely the utilitarian divisions; while an old royalist soldier from the antiparliamentarian camp, Colonel John Milward of Snitterton Hall in Derbyshire, did just the same.[10] Milward adapted Hartlib's design to a steep valley slope with the "Privy Garden" above the "Kitchin Garden." A scientifically designed fish pond sat below the kitchen garden and the orchards, with fish breeding and netting areas.

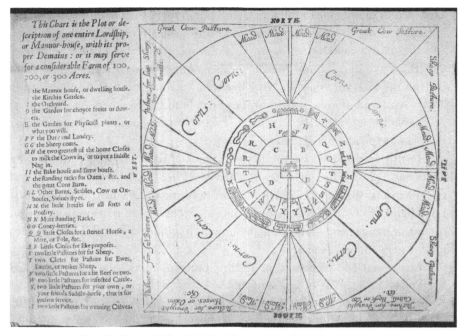

FIGURE 1.1: Hartlib Plan. © The British Library Board. 234.e.32 (1) pg A3r.

Hartlib's conception of God as the perfect gardener, an improving deity with agricultural projects, meant he saw no difficulty in combining practical designs with theological enthusiasm. Urged on by Hartlib, Herefordshire clergyman John Beale published *Herefordshire Orchards a Pattern for all England* in 1657, that decade so fertile in new garden designs. As well as encouraging all farmers to plant fruit trees as generously as Herefordshire farmers already did, Beale launched boldly into religiously inflected design with a brilliantly appreciative description of his local Backbury Hill.[11] This he saw as the ideal God-given natural garden of peace, recreation, and beauty. Beale's innovative perception, which historically anticipates garden designs of the next century and of Romanticism generally, was his claim that "there is a kind of beauty, and a sure refreshment in a wilderness; at least it is a good sight if appendant to a pleasant garden."[12] One has to be careful of anachronism and the assumption that such terms meant the same in the mid-seventeenth century as they did later; nonetheless, it is exciting to think that here one encounters part of the prehistory of Horace Walpole's idea that for William Kent all nature was a garden. Beale's enthusiasm seems to have been unrelated to the Roman classical poets.

Hartlib and Beale were members of the scientific groups that founded the Royal Society after the restoration of the monarchy in 1660. A later president of the Royal Society, Isaac Newton, proposed a vision of creation as God's supreme handiwork, structured by forces capable of rational explanation. The resulting sense of the universe as a marvelous, orderly machine susceptible to an enlightened, scientifically educated human understanding surely contributed to the confidence of members of the senatorial English aristocracy, celebrating themselves and their rise to imperial power with classical and historical references in gardens and landscapes characterized by self-assured but respectful collaboration with nature's genius: "Paints as you plant, and, as you work, designs."[13]

In the early eighteenth century, English garden design began to move away from the geometrical order most characteristic of the designed landscapes of the French monarchy and toward gardens that imitated nature, but also drew on new trends in French theories by A.-J. Dézallier d'Argenville[14] and Jacques-Francois Blondel (1737): Blondel took notice of French criticism of English gardens, D'Argenville himself urged more grassy plots and more views over landscape beyond the immediate garden. Also influential were ideal natural landscapes in visual art and in literary descriptions. Yet only later in 1734 was the design for the gardens of Carlton House described as being laid out "after Mr Kent's notion of gardening, viz., to lay them out without either level or line."

The reasons for this gradual revision have been much debated: a reaction to the monarchical absolutism of Louis XIV; a new appreciation of the landscapes in paintings by such artists as Claude Lorrain, Nicolas Poussin, and a host of Dutch and Flemish painters, which depicted idealized classical as well as rural scenes. There is also some evidence, however, of the influence of Chinese gardens, news of which, together with increasing visual material (as simple as a willow pattern plate), was reaching Europe in increasing quantities as a by-product of trade with the Indies. Sir William Temple, an English diplomat who, perhaps significantly, had served as ambassador to the Netherlands (England's greatest rival in Far Eastern trade), wrote in *The Gardens of Epicurus* (1685; printed 1696) a tantalizing account of the "scorrn" of the Chinese for European "proportions, symmetries, or uniformities," saying that a child with a ruler could achieve as much:

[T]heir greatest reach of Imagination is employed in contriving Figures, where the Beauty shall be great, and strike the Eye, but without any order or disposition of parts, that shall be commonly or easily observ'd. And though we have hardly any Notion of this sort of Beauty, yet they have a particular word to express it; and where they find it hit their Eye at first sight, they say the *Sharawadgi* is fine or is admirable, or any such expression of Esteem. And whoever observes the Work upon the best India Gowns, or the painting upon their best Skreens or Purcellans, will find their Beauty is all of this kind, (that is) without order. (131–132)

Temple had experimented in the 1690s with the charm of the asymmetrical in a small wooded area at the far end of his Moor Park estate in Surrey. Significantly, Temple gives us a sense of growing access to such novel design ideas: "Something of this I have seen in some places, but heard more of it from others, who have lived among the *Chineses*" (131). His remarks were taken up by Joseph Addison in *Spectator* no. 414 and by Samuel Molyneux, both praising "the beautiful Scaravagie," Temple's own invention for Chinese design, "without any Order or Disposition of Parts." No Chinese gardeners are known to have traveled to England, and only a few men, like Sir William Chambers (1723–96) in England and French Jesuits, had any experience of Chinese models; but knowledge of Chinese aesthetics was gradually increasing.[15]

Since the sixteenth century, Chinese garden makers had elaborated an extensive repertoire of garden designs. What seized the European imagination were irregular garden layouts, decorative buildings, and the Chinese delight in what were called on borrowed views (in Chinese *jiezing*), prospects outward to choice landscapes beyond the garden walls. These developments were largely seen in the mid-eighteenth century, but early hints suggest their importance: Addison specifically singled out Italian and French estates with their extensive landscapes, and Stephen Switzer argued for the same spread of "Frequent plantations" in *Ichnographia Rustica* of 1718, where he also explained and illustrated the larger landscape of Paston Manor. Switzer, like Addison before him, also praised John Milton's poetic evocation of Eden in *Paradise Lost* and its landscapes. When Pope in 1734 called for designers to "call in the country" into their gardens, he was articulating the same interest in wider views.

Furthermore, by contrast with the ordered, geometric, and even dull landscapes of Bourbon autocracy, which certainly had their followers elsewhere among the European nations, the gardens of the newer English style evoked liberty and emulation of an idealized classical world. Not only the triumphant British aristocracy could deploy such an aesthetic, however; enlightened despots like Catherine the Great of Russia and Frederic the Great of Prussia could express their improving modernity by surrounding an oppressively grand palace with a delightful clutter of eclectic garden buildings like that of Hanoverian Kew.

Key elements of the new garden style were fresh understandings of the term *variety*, along with elements of concealment and intrigue. Axes and flanking *bosquets*, answering *parterres de broderie* and *parterres de gazon*, and the large structures of Grand and Petit Trianon at Versailles seemed lacking in variety, though some of Vaux Le Vicomte's enclosures down the sides of the main garden as well as the hide and seek elements of Versailles bosquets (constantly changing) allowed an element of privacy and intrigue and the opportunity for human scale and fun. Yet the grand style associated with Louis XIV was at least as oppressive as impressive, as affirmed vehemently by Louis de Rouvroy, duc de Saint-Simon:

> Truly, the magnificence of the gardens is amazing, but to make the smallest use of them is disagreeable, and they are in equally bad taste. To reach any shade one is forced to cross a vast, scorching expanse and, after all, there is nothing to do in any direction but go up and down a little hill, after which the gardens end. The broken stones on the paths burn one's feet, yet without them one would sink into sand or the blackest mud.
>
> Who could help being repelled and disgusted at the violences done to Nature? Numberless springs have been forced to flow into the gardens from every side making them lush, overgrown and boggy; they are perpetually damp and unhealthy and their smell is even more so. The fountains and other effects are indeed incomparably fine, although they require a great deal of attention, but the net result is that one admires and flies.[16]

Jan Kip and Leonard Knyff's bird's-eye views of English geometric gardens[17] may seem to yield the same impression, and although more variety can be discerned in many of them, Alexander Pope's witty weariness at Timon's Villa:

> And when up ten steep slopes you've dragg'd your thighs,
> Just at his study door he'll bless your eyes.[18]

confirms Saint-Simon's resentment and disdain at the "lavish cost, and little skill." The English garden took Europe by storm in the eighteenth century not least because it was more surprising, more various, and more entertaining, as well as economical in upkeep.

King Charles II (1630–85) may not have been a master gardener, but he did propel André Mollet (died 1665) in 1661 into a masterstroke of European town planning in St. James's Park in West London.[19] Mollet had one favorite design plan, which he deployed here and also in Holland, Sweden, and often in France. From a double half circle of trees, Mollet liked to launch out a goose foot, or *patte d'oie*, of double avenues, each avenue usually planted with fashionable limes for their fragrance. Strictly speaking, though this is a bold design strategy, it does not produce a satisfying garden unless some of the areas between the avenues are planted as woodland or confused expensively with parterres. A royal park, St. James's was nonetheless an amenity for the capital's residents (ideally, the fashionable), an impressive public space of parade for wealthy and consequently influential Londoners. Close to the royal necropolis and parliament at Westminster and to St. James's Palace, the park enabled access to a monarchy that deployed the common touch—John Evelyn (1620–1706) observed Charles II flirting openly with Nell Gwyn over her park garden wall;[20] and the king was content to be seen feeding the ducks.

But it was not Mollet's actual design that made St. James's Park a triumph; it was the siting of the design and the relationship of the park to the city and the nation. The palace gardens of the Chinese empire had functioned for centuries as symbols of the unity in diversity of the state and as magnets to attract spiritual power and to offer moral refreshment.[21] Though vast in area, they were intended, like bonsai trees, to be miniatures of the whole empire, containing typical temples of the four major regions, representative animals, cultural symbols, and even the palaces of conquered rulers transported bodily to imperial gardens.

Politics, spirituality, and a keen aesthetic awareness of natural beauty were thus gathered together, but not in any geometric axial design. In 1644, the Ch'ing dynasty had taken over from the Ming, who had ruled from 1368 to 1644. It would rule until the republic of 1911 and prove as eager as any of the preceding dynasties to create impressive and consolidating gardens. Two great Ch'ing emperors, K'ang-hsi (1654–1723) and Ch'ien-Lung (1735–96), were obsessive garden builders in an eighteenth century that saw Europe become increasingly conscious of Chinese trade and intrigued by glimpses of Chinese culture.[22] Visitors to China were rare. Trade between the Netherlands and especially Sweden was, however, active, and, under those auspices, Sir William Chambers, working for the Swedish East India Company, visited Canton in 1744 and 1748. He subsequently made much of these contacts both in work for Kew Gardens, also published in his book of 1763, and in his publications, first *Designs of Chinese Buildings, Furniture, Dresses, Machines and Utensils* (1757), which was later absorbed into a major French publication on garden design, and *A Dissertation on Oriental Gardening* (1772).

But long before Chambers made his extravagant claims for Chinese design in England, French Jesuits had been exploring and writing about Chinese gardens. Matteo Ripa engraved the summer palace and gardens at Jehol in the 1710s, a copy of which Richard Boyle, third Earl of Burlington, purchased in 1724. Ripa's work was soon followed by Johann Bernhard Fischer von Erlach's *Entwurff einer historischen Archikektur* (1721), which also illustrated Eastern examples. Jean Denis Attiret (1702–68) was a Jesuit and artist who went to China in 1737, and his account of the Yuan Ming Yuan (*A Particular Account of the Emperor of China's Gardens near Pekin*) was published in 1752, somewhat abridged, in a translation by Joseph Spence (writing under the pseudonym of "Sir Harry Beaumont"): Attiret was particularly struck by Chinese "variety" and the gardens' "natural" qualities.

The vogue for Chinese temples and summer houses spread rapidly in England, with structures like the Chinese House at Shugborough in 1747 modeled on notes from a visitor to the Far East, with others at Wroxton and Studley Royal, or the delicate frivolities of Woodside, Berkshire, created for Hugh Hamersely and depicted lovingly by Thomas Robins. Publications by William and John Halfpenny promoted *Rural Architecture in the Chinese Taste*, and many other pattern books used Chinese examples. But the French were even more absorbed in this Chinoiserie than the English, partly because they saw in Chinese gardens a means of challenging the preeminence of the "English" garden. Thus it was that the "jardin anglo-chinois" was promoted as a counter foil to "real" "English" landscaping, most forcibly by Georges-Louis Le Rouge. His *cahiers*, serially published between 1776 and 1787, were entitled *Détails des nouveaux jardins à la mode* or sometimes as *Jardins anglo-chinois*. They republished materials from a wide range of English gardens, showing plans of Chiswick, Esher, and Kew among others, and borrowing from other English pattern books, including the whole of Chambers's 1757 *Designs*. But they also devoted cahiers XIV to XVII to the gardens of Yuan Ming Yuan, and illustrated Chinese work in Europe that included the Chinese House at Desert de Retz, Chinese bridges at Schwetzingen, a Chinese kiosk for the Hermitage and another at Rambouillet, the pagoda at Chateloup, and a Chinese barge at Steinfort. In short, Le Rouge represents probably the best repertoire of European gardens as they were seen by the second half of the eighteenth century.

In the fifty-odd years between the restoration of the Stuarts to the throne in 1660 and the well-staged arrival of George I (1660–1727) from Germany in 1714, the formal gardens Kip and Knyff illustrate, many designed and laid out by London and Wise, appear to have played themselves out of favor, not just by their expense and their tedium, but by the sheer unpredictability of their design. There is no agreed upon national design in the pages of *Britannia Illustrata* (1707), though Switzer offered his own agenda in the *Ichnographia*, just as D'Argenville and Blondel sought to do in France. The political changes of the forty years after the Restoration had left the English aristocracy uncertain as to which way to turn to please an almost rotating monarchy.

When George I arrived, by aristocratic invitation, he came from the Herrenhausen Palace of his Welf dynasty in Hannover, and Herrenhausen boasted a predictably conventional axial layout almost a mile long, climaxing in a giant fountain.[23] Yet almost as soon as King George was enthroned, one strand of English garden design abandoned rigid axiality and geometry, increasingly adopting a more relaxed and playful landscaping that would evolve into an English garden style that would take Europe by storm in the later years of the eighteenth century (or so England liked to think; the French had other ideas, and eventually so did most of Europe and the United States.[24] George I liked simple Palladian architecture and enjoyed private performances of Shakespeare; pomp and circumstance bored him. His tastes may have contributed to British architecture and garden design becoming more simple and relaxed. Like the gardens of the Chinese Ch'ing emperors, Yuan Ming Yuan Garden (the Garden of Happy Harmony), these new "English Gardens" would embrace and enhance their topography of lake, woods, and hills; borrowed views would be commonplace, contrived circuits would carry delighted visitors from one temple to another, to grottoes of contorted rocks, and to pleasure pavilions where tea might possibly be taken.

It is worth drawing attention to the apparent paradox here; but it is only apparent. The garden style most closely associated with England in the eighteenth century is closely connected with an English ideology of landscape and nature identifiable in the century of the Stuart monarchy and the Interregnum, even when that period's actual landscapes look so unlike those created later. The roots are not found in the elements of visual design itself; rather, they are found in a more dispersed but more powerful congeries of cultural attitudes, scientific and philosophical developments, the experiences of trade and travel, and the challenges and triumphs of religion and politics. French models may have prevailed from 1661 under Charles II; Dutch models with an emphasis on canals and "greens" after 1688 under William III of Orange (1650–1702) and Queen Anne (1665–1714). But, in the long term, more influential were the urgent concerns of John Evelyn's *Sylva* (1664) and John Rea's *Flora* (1665). These ideas and cultural movements, though yielding no distinctly visual proposals, constituted the bedrock for new design principles.

Kip and Kynff's *Britannia Illustrata* records shaggy, French-style hunting forests at Westwood, Uppark, Ashdown, New Park, and Cassiobury; straight avenues criss-cross everywhere so that they seem to have become an aristocratic obsession: the higher the rank, the more the avenues. Ducal Badminton in Gloucestershire has twenty-four focused on a random point in its park and twenty more upon the Duke of Beaufort's actual house.[25] But the standard design, exemplified at Eaton Hall, Cheshire and at Swillington in the West Riding, is of two double avenues in front and behind the main house, theoretically slicing directly through the middle of it in one long axis of authority, with parterres a mere incident on its course.

The characteristic Dutch garden design of the period was Mollet-inspired, from his "Plan for an Ideal Garden" in the 1651 *Le Jardin de Plaisir*.[26] This is distinctly un-English as it sites the house centrally in a huge rectangle with wide gardens at its side as well as the usual gardens fore and aft. It also has three rows of double avenues at the sides, leading up to an exedral ending with three more avenues leading to the house, not out of it as in his St James's layout. The Dutch seem to have reveled in the inclusiveness of this design; Zeist, Huis ten Bosch, Zorgvliet, and Heemstede all followed it, with the usual intense Dutch infilling of flowery parterres.[27] But in late seventeenth-century England, only Ragley Hall, the Conways' seat in Warwickshire, follows this format of a central axis with flanking sectors.[28] The straight canals of Staunton Harold and Melton Constable, from the same period, may have been polite compliments to Dutch "King Billy."[29]

One English design feature rarely remarked upon is the preponderance, alongside the patterned parterres, of homely but extensive vegetable gardens, often with a clear commercial purpose. Houses in large towns were naturally most profit inclined. The Pierrepoint house in Nottingham and Lord Burlington's Chiswick Villa are examples of aristocrats' commercial gardens. Althorp in Northamptonshire, Ragley Hall, Eaton Hall in Cheshire, Bryanston in Dorset, and Orchard Portman in Somerset all have quite disproportionate areas given over to vegetables. The last of these has vegetables, avenues, and only the most minimal parterre. These vegetable plots were obviously integral features of the designs; whether they reflect Dutch influence is arguable. Even Windsor Castle had its fair share.

One surprising feature of this formal garden period is the unimaginative layout of the flower and fruit enclosures. Like the avenues, a multitude of enclosures seems to mark the houses of the higher-ranking aristocrats.

Lowther in Westmorland, the Lonsdales' seat, Chatsworth in Derbyshire, and Longleat in Wiltshire are the most overburdened.[30] They are not easy to count, but Lowther has about thirty of these squares crammed together—higgledy-piggledy parterres, vegetable plots, orchards, tree nurseries—slung away to one side of the house, which has only very small formal pleasure areas. London and Wise's Longleat again has some thirty unrelated rectangular garden areas climbing a hillside, where they abruptly evolve into the nine rides of "The Grove," a forest garden. The ducal pair, Chatsworth and Badminton, are the most ambitious and, from some points of view, the worst designed. Badminton has an excuse because it lies on a dull plateau of poor soil. The Chinese would never have sited a palace so unrewardingly when attractive valleys lie quite close by. But Chatsworth ignores the steep rise of land to the north; its great cascade and its canal are both later improvements more responsive to its topography. One seventeenth-century straight canal, now filled in, seems to have been dug to distract from the existence of the real river parallel to it, as if natural riverbanks were something of which to be ashamed. However, we also have hints here of an inherited French scheme by which natural, meandering rivers were canalized: André Le Nôtre did this at

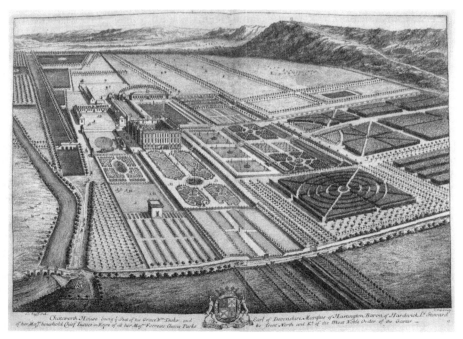

FIGURE 1.2: Chatsworth, from *Britannia Illustrata*. Courtesy of University of Bristol, Special Collections.

Vaux, and Temple did it at Moor Park, Surrey, where a canal paralleled the adjacent river.

All this ostentation was about to evolve into the enchanting Arcadian gardens of the eighteenth century, and it is possible to identify in the confusion of formal improvisation the elements that would soon cohere to create gardens of informal design. It was left to the English to aim at Arcadia reborn in a natural pagan simplicity of temples in leafy woodland; for this they invoked memories of Roman classicism and the strong tradition of masques and pastoral operas that dominated first royal performances and then public theaters in England. The first move toward this evocation of Arcadia in architectural terms is rarely noted as it has been demolished, but it was a classically domed viewing pavilion that Sir Thomas Tresham, a Northamptonshire recusant, built in 1596 at Rushton Hall, whilst directing operations from his prison cell in Ely.[31] He had experimented with Christian symbolism on an earlier garden building, the triangular Warrener's Lodge, but then made a deliberate move to pagan forms in the ambitious Hawkfield Lodge with its viewing gallery and Ionic porches set at a distance from the main house on the perimeter of the park.

An American-born Englishman made the next Arcadian steps. Captain George Evelyn, John Evelyn's cousin, built a Doric fronted grotto-temple to Venus, cut into the steep, sandy hillside facing Wotton House in Surrey in the 1650s. It survives, with its original fresco of Venus seated on a dolphin.[32] John Evelyn was away in Paris when Captain George, who had spent some time in Rome, no doubt admiring the gardens of villas like the Borghese, designed and presumably paid for this numinous but dark building. Evelyn complained ungenerously that the captain "was mistaken in the Architecture of the Portico, which tho' making a magnificent show, has greate faults in the *Colonnade*, both as to the Order, which should have been *Corinthian* & the Ornaments, the rest is very tolerable."[33]

John Evelyn missed his chance to build upon the achievement of his cousin with a predictably chaotic layout at his own house at Sayes Court, near Deptford,[34] and it was left to Thomas Archer (ca. 1668–1743), designing for the first and only Duke of Shrewsbury, to contrive between 1707 and 1710 an Arcadian cluster of classical buildings in the woods of Heythrop House in Oxfordshire.[35] Equally instrumental was Stephen Switzer (1683–1745) who, working for London and Wise's Brompton Park firm, spotted the group— Cold Bath, Nymphaeum, and Octagonal Pool—and praised the achievement in his 1718 *Ichnographia*, a widely read, impressively erudite publication that picked up Hartlib's view of the garden and the park designed as one integrated whole.[36] This was a design step of prime importance, and Switzer offered in

Ichnographia several plans to show how farmland, lakes, woods, drives, and garden buildings could be fused together not by straight avenues but by curving waters and sinuous walks. Geometry was outdated, and Switzer had the wit to see that a casual group of classical buildings was aesthetically superior to magnificence and pomp. "There is," he wrote with reference to such gardens, "Pleasure in these Natural, Twinings, and private Walks, to a quiet, thoughtful, studious, Mind."[37]

This expresses a basic shift in the national sensibility: a new English sensitivity to the complex conversations between the human, nature, culture, history, and art that Augustan contemporaries may have been waking to during the Enlightenment. Switzer is explicit and, significant in an age that saw both a triumphant aristocracy and a growing segment of society with cultural ambitions, he asserted that the creation of such a resourceful landscape was within the grasp of many. The Earl of Carlisle's contemporary Wray Wood at Castle Howard in Yorkshire, which he had praised for its relaxed charm of winding paths, was an expressive construct, but with a much later Temple of Venus and statues imported from abroad. Switzer realized that primroses and violets in a wild wood with a few simple classical garden buildings and cold baths for private nudity next to a walk "set round with little Nitches, Seats, and Benches" was something "any Gardener can contrive."[38] Heythrop, not Castle Howard, was "the first attempt of this kind, I ever saw, and which has in a great measure prompted on these rural thoughts."[39] It was "truly delightful, rural, easy and pleasant,"[40] and spelled the end of expensive garden formalism. Switzer had framed an idea, and an idea calls for a change of design, but in this case a change to a deliberate absence of any prescribed design.

That humble building cluster at Heythrop pays no attention to its wider topography. That was its weakness. It lies in random order on the sloping ground of an ill-drained wood; it commands no views and is hidden from sight; it was a place for the Duke of Shrewsbury's private, naked frolics. The next vital design step forward was to site such buildings strategically in a more flattering topography.

Once again *Britannia Illustrata* offers clues as to the way design was heading. The characteristics of the gardens of the previous century, with their straight axes and evident geometry, forced designers to invent surprises and atmospheric relief. In the heart of the dense woodland behind Sir George Fletcher's Cumberland seat, Hutton-in-the-Forest, was an enchanted Arcadian glade, circular and geometric it is true, but enhanced by four fountains, two small classical pavilions, a circular streamlet, and a central statue.[41] A straight ride leads from the glade to a grotto. The design of the garden has the relish of the Arcadian, but it fails to escape from the constraints of geometry or to relate to the surrounding topography. Guisborough Priory in Yorkshire makes a different eclectic point.[42] Towering over its bowling green, geometric duck island, and vegetable beds is the dramatic Gothic wreck of the Augustinian priory, entirely dysfunctional in practical horticultural terms, yet preserved consciously as a numinous reminder of the historic past.

Charles Bridgeman (died 1738) acted as a kind of intermediary between these two cultures of garden and landscape design. A man trained to garden geometry, from which he never quite departed, yet with a keen eye for the implications of topographical substructures, he could sense where an avenue shape was implicit in a hillside, where a circle could be imposed, where linking rides were required.[43] Amesbury Abbey in Wiltshire exemplifies his skilled rigidity of response.[44] There he had to cope with a steep wooded hill, the end of which he cut into his favorite form, an amphitheater. One wooded slope he sliced into a great diamond, centered precisely on a grotto dramatized by six statues. The hilltop drive moved first through a circular glade, then through a square one; he shaped a millpond into an exact circle; all connecting drives were straight; and yet it worked as an environment in which the visitor experienced an intimacy, a pleasure, and an invitation to thoughtfulness and the apprehension of beauty entirely remote from Saint-Simon's experience of Versailles. Appropriately, much later in the 1760s, an exquisite Chinese tea house was set on a bridge over a stream.

Bridgeman shrewdly perceived natural geometries at Rousham in Oxfordshire; to turn this remarkably small pleasure ground into his pastoral and Arcadian masterpiece, William Kent (1685–1748) intervened delicately but decisively: naturalizing a river bank, moving the medieval bridge to create a compelling vista from and to an existing small temple, curving a rill, drawing the eye out over the agricultural landscape through eye catchers, opening alleys to invite the visitor to move between and link in the imagination different scenes and experiences.[45]

Rousham was not alone in this golden age of English garden design. When a lively topography of water and hills came together, as it did at Stourhead in Wiltshire and at Studley Royal in Yorkshire, with a rich, sensitive patron, Arcadias were achieved physically by such elements as lakes and pools resulting from dammed streams, and in the imagination by statues and temples invoking literature and the visual arts, myth and philosophy. The cult or practice of nude bathing (not entirely surprising, given the amenities of interior

FIGURE 1.3: Rousham Rill. Photograph by Tim Mowl.

bathrooms) should not be forgotten: in his exquisite Grotto of the Nymph at
Stourhead, Henry Hoare sometimes bathed naked with companions who had
been put up at the local inn, all to the music of French horns.[46] Arcadias could
release the human spirit, and the design of the grotto offered both privacy and
a perfectly composed *shakhei* view through a rockwork arch, provided with a
curtain for privacy, across the lake to the valley church and the Gothic Bristol
High Cross. England, more than any other European state, was impelled by
its quest to revive the Augustan Rome of Horace and Virgil. England had no
precise design formula, though landscape paintings and hints and memories of
Italian garden visits could offer guidance: composition from Claude Lorrain,
details from Gaspard Dughet (1615–75), and mythography from Nicolas Poussin.[47] In creating Augustan Arcadias to gratify pseudo-senatorial aspirations,
the English aristocracy had stumbled upon an entirely fresh garden styling that
fired the imagination and sensibilities of continental rivals: France, Germany,
Sweden, Russia, even the Italian states.[48] The influence of the gardens of French

autocracy never quite recovered from the defeat of France in the War of Spanish Succession (1701–14) and the consequent shift in the balance of European power; by contrast, a new and newly assertive Great Britain become a potent ally with a confident and vibrant culture to be copied, and, of course, rivaled and excelled.

France and Germany played the garden game with formidable results, perhaps attributable to superior craftsmen and a more cerebral, analytical approach. In France, one may identify a dual approach. One was basically encyclopedist and philosophical, a spin-off from Denis Diderot and Jean d'Alembert's *Encyclopédie or Dictionnaire raisonné des sciences, des arts et des metiers* (1751–65) with an aim "to reunite in one garden all times and places" (as Carmontelle wrote of the Jardin de Monceau), or the implicit gathering of older civilizations at the Desert de Retz.[49] The second was political and inspired by Jean-Jacques Rousseau: a quest for natural simplicity and self-exploration, a sentimental awareness, and civic reponsibility.[50] This last was exemplified by the Marquis de Girardin's Ermenonville, where Rousseau (1712–78) himself lived, died, and was buried in thoughtful simplicity. Ermenonville had three lakes, cataracts, grottoes, winding woodland walks, a classical philosopher's temple, and a keen attention to pre-Revolutionary ideals. The French, with their lively rococo culture, always stressed rusticity more than the English, like Claude-Henri Watelet's Moulin-Joli, based on islands in the Seine, with its exquisite delicacy of trees, frail bridges, and fragile cottages.[51] The famous Hameau in the Petit Trianon of Versailles was only one of many settings; Chantilly, Betz, Beloeil, and Rambouillet were all constructed for aristocratic peasant role-playing. Temples of friendship were almost standard.

Nothing in Germany, or indeed Europe, quite matched Prince Leopold of Anhalt Dessau's Worlitz for its fresh and intelligent concept of parkland and society. Apart from its notorious, occasionally erupting volcano,[52] designed with Germanic earnestness to study volcanology, it copied English ironwork (a miniature Shropshire Ironbridge), but also practiced an enlightened agrarian culture and gave tenants religious freedom and their own lending libraries in its parks. It had classical temples, a Gothic house, busts of famous men, Roman baths, an amphitheater, and paths for the sentimental and the imaginative. Throughout Europe, the so-called English garden was subjected to considerable local and philosophical adjustments, with design schemes and individual features colored by a mix of the exotic and the philosophical. At first glance, many of these gardens were merely eclectic—Mauperthuis's Doric Grotto and Egyptian Pyramid of 1761, which led into an English Garden,[53] the exquisite design detail of Potsdam's Chinese Tea House (1754–7), the Turkish tent

FIGURE 1.4: Vaux, main axis. Photograph by Stephen Bending.

at Schwetzingen's 1785 mosque.[54] But they also often reveal a detailed and scrupulous agenda, sometimes Masonic (Olausson) in the Jardin Monceau and maybe Desert de Retz, and with a keen attention to the ideas of *perfectabilité*, the sense that all past cultures, suitably understood in the new Enlightenment, had found new landscapes, literal and philosophical, that distinguished them firmly from English models.[55]

This golden age of serendipity need never have ended, but the Industrial Revolution concluded it before its time by providing light, efficient guns to shoot pheasants and fast, well-sprung carriages for comfortable transport.[56] In essence, the post-1748 gardens of Lancelot "Capability" Brown (1716–83) and his many imitators are design simplifications of the eclectic Arcadias that preceded them: there were still garden buildings, but fewer; pleasing dispositions of woods; lakes; and smooth, grassy slopes.[57] But Brown did have a standard design formula, which could be adapted to all except the wildest or most level terrains. He would plant a circumferential belt of trees, usually followed closely by a carefully graded, well-surfaced drive mounting any knolls that could offer wide park views. In the middle distance, he would create a natural-looking lake, its furthest banks snaking away around a wooded corner, as if to suggest a major river. The foreground would be dotted with tree clumps, planted for diversity of foliage.

The assertion of "a standard design formula" marks a major topic implicit in this chapter. For much of the period up to the mid-eighteenth century, in

Britain, continental Europe, Russia, China, and Japan, there had been ambiguity concerning the "designer." Throughout this chapter so far, the patron or proprietor has been assumed to be the creative mind shaping the design. To be sure, contemporary accounts that attribute artistic genius to the owner may well have been flattery; but it is clear that, just as the concept of the architect as artist, rather than merely a builder, had to fight for recognition somewhat earlier, the attribution of the design of a garden to a "landscape architect" rather than its owner occurred only gradually in the eighteenth century. Bridgeman may again be seen as a transitional figure in England; by the time Horace Walpole elevated William Kent to the artistic pantheon, the identification of his particular landscaped parks with Brown was well under way. The client's genius lay in selecting the artist, not in the design. Acceptance of the term *landscape architect* came later, but the primacy of the designer was becoming established. In France, it was probably Jean-Marie Morel who invented the term *landscape architecture*, and his careful study of natural processes set out in Geroges LeClerc, comte de Buffon's forty-four-volume *Histoire naturelle* underpinned his own distinctive work.[58]

Underpinning his dominance was Brown's technical command of earth engineering, comparable to Morel's thorough understanding of landforms and topography. He had several teams of trained men controlled by reliable foremen who would, for a price and strictly to Brown's own carefully drawn up contracts, turn an unkempt marshy valley, like that around Croome Court in Worcestershire, into smooth slopes of welcoming green turf where the land had been drained, enriched, and reseeded.[59] Brown's particular mastery was in creating earth dams of well-tempered clay pounded down into a layer of stone. The whole was then planted with trees and threaded with a walk affording, from tree alcoves, pretty glimpses of the new lake, usually with a leafy island, that the earth dam had created. No one walking Brown's massive dam below the lake at Hewell Grange, Worcestershire would ever suspect they were on an artificial feature. Brown's skill lay in his tactful trimming and manicuring of nature. If the resultant landscapes are sometimes a trifle bland, that was what landowners enjoyed. There was an economic motive to this simplification: Arcadias of temples like Stourhead came expensive. When required, Brown could always offer a Gothic dairy, as at Sherborne Castle in Dorset, or a stern Greek Doric lodge, as at Wynnstay Hall in north Wales, but his ideal landscapes were perfect backgrounds for grazing deer or prize cattle. Any enclosing cattle fences were discreetly concealed.

That was the broad, Brownian picture, but he did not attract in his lifetime over 150 commissions, literally changing some of the face of England, by aesthetics alone. The attraction of his designs was that they opened the wider landscape of a park to ladies and to "sportsmen" of the shooting fraternity. Arcadias had essentially been gardens to walk around. Brown's parks were created to be driven around fast and in safety in those new well-sprung carriages. That explains a certain tedium to a Brown design; it is not meant to be lingered over, but to be enjoyed at a spanking pace: the perfect treat for idle visiting ladies. A landowner could show off his estate with no hard horse riding and circumnavigate it in a half hour's drive with no interruption to polite chat. Drives, as opposed to rides, were the first attraction. Then Brown would plant alongside these drives, or at a short distance from them, the long narrow tree groves that were proving ideal for rearing pheasants.

Brown's defining stroke was Blenheim. There he had John Vanbrugh's imperial Grand Bridge straddling a deep theatrical valley, but only over a miserable canalized stream, the Glyme.[60] He saw his chance and took it with bold genius. Not only did he dam the Glyme to create a shimmering lake, but he also drove it over a resounding cascade reinforced with stones to resist the pounding of water. The lake was Brown's masterpiece, nationally acknowledged as such. *Ben Hur* could be filmed on it successfully, driving chariots two abreast across Vanbrugh's imperial viaduct that now bridged Brown's broad waterway, splendidly overlooked by the towers of Vanbrugh's castle-palace. Brown had flooded most of the thirty-three rooms of the bridge and put out of action the pumping machine that brought water up to the palace, but for a truly great landscape design, possibly the greatest in the country, it was worth it. He also had an eye for design detail, which led him to save one length of the old causeway across that once marshy valley and turn it, planted with red alders, into Elizabeth Island, which composes perfectly. Brown died a prosperous landowner, admired by his king, at ease with the dukes who eagerly employed him, and generally hailed as a national treasure. This was not the view, however, of the generation that succeeded him; garden design thrives upon reversals.

Richard Payne Knight (1751–1824) and Uvedale Price (1747–1829), two like-minded, environmentalist landowners of the Welsh border, detested Brown's bland softening and tidying up of landscapes. Brown had swept his lawns up to the very doors of his houses, hiding gardens away behind distant brick walls, as at Longleat. Knight and Price wrote convincingly for a return to terraced gardens around the skirts of a house to visually enliven the division between house and park. They called for nature in the rough, for visible gnarled roots of trees, for fallen tree trunks, rushy verges, and broken sandy banks: the Savage Picturesque[61] as depicted in

FIGURE 1.5: Blenheim Lake. Photograph by Tim Mowl.

paintings by Jacob van Ruisdael (1628/9–82) and Salvator Rosa (1615–73). When Brown was safely in his grave and the oleaginous Humphry Repton (1752–1818) set out to be the master's natural successor in garden design, he ran into a blizzard of critical anger from Payne Knight for offering a manicured treatment for Ferney Hall, next to Knight's Downton Castle, on the Shropshire-Hereford border.

Poor Repton never quite recovered. For the rest of his career, his designs, presented in the Moroccan leather Red Books of "before" and "after" watercolors of the proposals,[62] hovered between smooth, predictable Brownian solutions—lakesides naturalized, trees planted tactically to expose beauties and cover blemishes, drives concealed or sited to capture better views—and attempts at the roughness advocated by Payne Knight and Price. He claimed, following the perceptions of René-Louis Girardin's *De la Composition des Paysages* (1777), to enjoy humanity's homely impact on landscapes: gates, hedges, children playing, workers digging, cattle grazing, carriages passing; what he termed "inhabitation." Being Repton he searched for compromises as assiduously as he sought commissions, though many of his schemes remained unexecuted. However, Brown never laid out a more visually enriched or more exciting approach drive to a patron's house than the one Repton unrolled for John Scandrett Harford, a rich Quaker banker, at the Blaise Castle estate just outside Bristol. The carriage drive still sweeps under a Gothic lodge, plunges down and out of a deep gorge with backward glances to an earlier mock Gothic castle, all to reach a house sited mere yards from a public road. On the way the drive passes a rustic cottage and a mill and gives onto a vertiginous precipice walk where visitors can relish with an artist's eye the trail of smoke from the cottage chimney slanting across the ravine.

At heart Repton was a suburban garden designer. He anticipated the flood of mass-produced artifacts that poured from the Great Exhibition of 1851: bird baths, pigeon cotes, trellises to create little garden privacies, sentimental statues of half-naked nymphs, wall fountains, pergolas, ready-made balustrading, greenhouse equipment, and, most of all, conservatories full of exotics to blur and confuse the links between a house and its garden. Through these and the precious watercolors of ladies' gardens with their intricate flowerbeds dotted with vases, urns, and seats, he ushered in the gardenesque style, long before the term was coined in 1832 by John Claudius Loudon (1783–1843). Repton's favorite clients were industrialists, though he groveled happily to lords, offering even the Duke of Bedford at Woburn a lobby to prevent damp, a glass-roofed orangery, a flower passage, an aviary, a vinery, and a forcing house for grapes and peaches. Repton was the garden herald of the Industrial Revolution, and his Red Books, which made his name with garden historians by their cunning charm, were essentially advertising confidence tricks: "employ me and pull back the flap of my watercolour illustration to see what you could get!" His design had its greatest impact, after his death in 1818, on the nineteenth century, which was not so much an age of garden design as of maximum consumption; our modern garden centers are temples to Repton.

Repton's confrontation with the picturesque and his agile reassessment of the role of landscape architect, a term Loudon would eventually confer upon him, is by no means the end of the story. In the complicated multinationalism of the long eighteenth century, there is also the newly emerging world of the United States, where revolution played as vital a role as it did in France. It is often thought that Thomas Jefferson was, at least as a gardenist, a dedicated Englishman; yet his residence in and admiration for France plays out at both Monticello and above all in the geometry of Poplar Forest (Brown). And in both sites, natural scenery, social customs, and political exigencies all worked to shape a thoroughly American landscape culture. If the "English" picturesque played out so richly and variously among European nations, it is also apt to recognize that by the end of the eighteenth century, country seats throughout America were beginning to realize their own designs and relish their own national ideology.

CHAPTER TWO

Types of Gardens

MICHAEL CHARLESWORTH

If we leave out gardens made for production of vegetables and fruit, two broad types of garden were made during the period. Each contains several ramifications, however, by which a wider variety of forms of garden can be identified.

LARGE-SCALE GEOMETRICALLY DESIGNED GARDENS

These gardens are especially associated with France during the period of absolutist monarchy (1614–1789) since the most spectacular are two designed by André Le Nôtre (1613–1700): Vaux-le-Vicomte (1656–61), for Nicolas Fouquet, and Versailles (1661–1715), for Louis XIV. However, large gardens of this type could be found throughout continental Europe and the British Isles. The form was particularly associated with royal palaces but was not exclusive to them.[1]

A palatial house usually stands in the center of one side of the garden. Immediately adjacent to it, the ground is leveled and occupied by parterres, rectangular areas crossed by gravel paths. The areas between the paths are planted with hedging material such as box in patterns that can be figurative (the owner's coat of arms in some late seventeenth-century parterres in Scotland, for example) but often abstract in the form of arabesque patterns. Color can be provided by bedding plants, but is sometimes supplied instead by yellow sand, red brick dust, and (black) coal. Parterres need to be kept immaculate (including watering to control dust), and their upkeep is labor-intensive and

FIGURE 2.1: Caserta main axis. Photograph by Stephen Bending.

expensive. Urns and statues, balustrades, and (less often) low stone walls and pools can be found in and around parterres.

Further from the house, divisions of the garden are formed by high hedges, still held in a rectangular framework of broad paths. In most cases, these en-closures (bosquets) cannot be looked into from the outside. Some contained labyrinths or spaces designed in the shape of circles and stars. Within those of the king's gardens at Versailles were water features, mostly fountains designed so that the water shooting from the fountain took on a perceptible form in the air (a water obelisk, for example, and fountains whose jets arc in the form of the royal French badge, the *fleur-de-lys*). At Vaux, one fountain's jets formed a gate: opposite this stood a real wrought-iron gate, so that the garden design playfully coaxed visitors to think about form and differing materials; the repli-cation of a familiar, conventional form in unlikely transient unstable material.[2] Where water was lacking, the bosquets could harbor statues and statue groups.

Beyond the bosquets, continuing to depart from the house, opened a more extensive, and more ambiguous, distant space. At Vaux, the principal avenues of alignment projected into the surrounding woodland (used for hunting), embracing it too as an extension of the garden. The main garden at Vaux, grouped except for some prepared surprises within one main view from the house, and spread across, rather than along, a valley, gives a sense of enclosure despite its size. It terminates in a giant statue of Hercules resting after his labors and facing back to the house. The feeling of enclosure contrasts with Versailles (also designed by Le Nôtre). There, the palace and the terrace of parterres occupy the highest part; the rest of the garden extends outward and away over a broad apron of slopes and the flatter spaces below. Large lakes—the Grand Canal and the Pièce des Suisses—provide distant, emphatically man-made rectilinear features, and the resolution, as it were, of the design in the areas further away to either side remains ambiguous, tempting exploration. At Sceaux, designed by Le Nôtre for Colbert, Fouquet's replacement as Louis XIV's chief minister, topography provided the designer with the opportunity for considerable elements of surprise. The initial view of the garden, stretching across a shallow basin-like valley, conceals steep drops in height with, at their bottom, broad canals and pools. One of the sloping drops features a long cascade; visitors can descend, delightfully following its course. Topography determined much about design in the large-scale geometric garden: at Herrenhausen, in

FIGURE 2.2: Cascade at Sceaux. Photograph by Michael Charlesworth.

Hanover, designed by Martin Charbonnier and Sophia, Electress of Hanover, the flat site supports the rectangular plot of the palace and its gardens on a level space. The garden is filled with bosquets and parterres, here terminated and enclosed by canals in the Dutch manner. Exploration demands all the enclosures be exhausted.

The framework of gravel paths that penetrates, contains, and articulates the spaces of these gardens thus extends over a varied topography and needs to provide access to a variety of types of space. Such a framework necessitates joints; far from being awkward, these provide skillful designers with opportunities. Versailles's Latona fountain is situated just below the terrace of parterres in a space giving on to bosquets. It marks a change in levels and slope as well as a change in conceptual handling of the design; it also articulates continuity across the garden, in a scheme based on the myths of Apollo. This fountain represents an episode from Ovid's *Metamorphoses*: Apollo's mother invoking divine help to transform obstreperous peasants into frogs. Down the *tapis vert*, the green carpet of lawn, in a pool at the nearer end of the Grand Canal, a statue group shows Apollo, the sun god, urging his chariot horses up out of the water to begin a new day, but also, in this conjunction, seeming to answer his mother's cry for help.[3]

The Latona fountain provides a triumphant feature at a transitional place that left blank would have suggested uneasiness. The development of such places of transition was a strong feature of this type of garden. Slopes accommodated ponderous stone terraces penetrated by grottoes housing statues, often taking the form of reclining river gods. Streams and rivers crossing the site provided the opportunity to develop rectilinear canals, sometimes as surprise features only visible from nearby. The edges of parterres demanded topiary—usually abstract spheres and cones—as well as low hedges: terraces necessitated balustrades with urns, basins, and statues raised on heavy plinths. The size, weight, and emphatic character of these features contribute one of the pleasures of the geometric garden.

Such features, including bosquets and geometrical form, reveal the derivation of these and many other European gardens that emulated them, from earlier, large-scale Italian gardens such as those of the Villa Aldobrandini, at Frascati (1598–1603), and the Boboli Gardens in Florence (1549–1637). Even though some elements of the Italian examples were developed far beyond their original scale, and others, such as the water jokes, were not adopted by the French, the essential connection should be noted: the Italian celebration of the beauties of geometry and proportion, conceived at the time as the foundation of beauty, underlies the design of geometrically based gardens of the period 1650–1800.

Designs of this type and on this scale were clearly perceived as expressing power. Cardinal Richelieu is credited with inaugurating this type, at Richelieu (1631 onward) and Rueil (1633 onward), both since destroyed, before Fouquet's Vaux and the king's Versailles were developed. However, Le Nôtre showed he could apply similar design principles on a much smaller scale, as his garden for the Château de Castries, not far from Montpellier, exemplifies. At Castries, he had just enough room for a grand terrace and grotto, with staircase, before at the bottom having to turn the main axis crossways for best use of the available space. Beneath a canopy of plane trees, small channels (*rigoles*) distribute the water from a huge, mossy fountain into a large circular pool. The place is delightful.

Encouragement to meditate on relations between form and materials was not confined to fountains. From a distance, geometric topiary made vegetation look smooth, immaculate, even hard. Close up, the same features become soft and penetrable. As Bernard Lassus has put it, such topiary retards the contrast between two orders of things.[4] Between stone house and natural shapes of the surrounding woodland's trees, the parterres and hedged bosquets (with their intermittent architectural features) provokingly display combinations from throughout the intervening spectrum of art and nature.

EXTENDED FOREST GARDENS

Extensive-, *Forest-* and *Rural-Gardening* are phrases associated with English designer and seed merchant Stephen Switzer (1682–1745). Switzer is not usually remembered as an exceptionally important designer. In England in his lifetime, Charles Bridgman, together with two people for whom Switzer worked, George London and Henry Wise, were clearly more famous figures. Yet Switzer's three-volume book *Ichnographia Rustica* (1718) describes a type of aristocratic garden derived from the continental models discussed previously. Whether he invented this classification of garden or codified what was already well discussed and practiced in the circles in which he moved is debatable, although I incline to the latter view.

Switzer argues that a landowner's whole estate can be brought into a design and that this can be achieved through one or two big defining avenues linking house and parterre to agricultural land in the distance. At Wentworth Castle, an avenue extends southward over the brow of the hill to end at the edge of a field, and a smaller avenue runs parallel to join a star-shaped pattern of avenues cut through a wood. A second large avenue reaches eastward from the house toward a narrow wooded valley at the bottom of the image. Both avenues cross enclosures for deer, cattle, and horses. Switzer advises that diagonal avenues should be kept to a minimum.[5] He had views about parterres: "parterres are, generally speaking, too large, by which Means the Expence of Gardening is not a little rais'd, and that which is the most valuable of any Part of the Garden, I mean Wood, and, consequently, Shade, very much diminish'd."[6] Wentworth Castle had a fountain court in front of the house, one double parterre south of the house, a fruit garden in the southeast corner between the two, and then bosquets uphill behind the house: two laid out with Union Jack patterns and one enclosing a bowling green. Switzer might have approved this pattern, with only one double parterre.[7] In addition to diminishing the size of parterres, Switzer advised that "Grass, Gravel, and Sand, or Cockle-shells interwoven with another" provide the "neatest and cheapest Way of making Parterres."[8]

In developing woodland into ornamental features, Switzer also suggests moderation in cutting existing trees: "how common it is for Layers out of Gardens to resolve upon some regular Scheme in the Closet, and from it to cut out their whole Design; so that down go all the Oaks, Beeches &c. that have been some Ages coming to Perfection."[9] He advises avoiding the "Error of Regularity" and accommodating design to preexisting natural landforms as well as trees.[10]

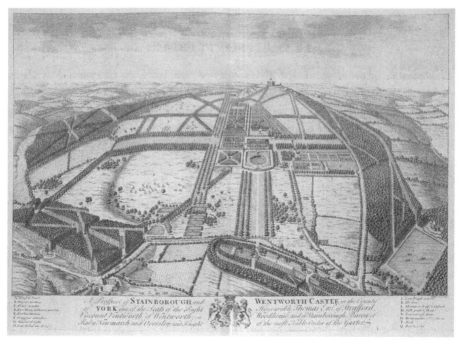

FIGURE 2.3: *A Prospect of Stainborough and Wentworth Castle in the County of York*, Thomas Badeslade, 1739. © The British Library Board. All Rights Reserved. 191.g.15–16.

The symmetry of the big continental geometric gardens had always been more apparent than real, even at Vaux, the most symmetrical of them, and Switzer advises against large-scale symmetry, arguing that when each side resembles the other you end up with no more than "half a garden."[11]

The gardens Switzer describes—with small parterres, nonsymmetrical layouts of large avenues relating the house to the wider landscape, and woods cut through with patterns of avenues—can be recognized all over Britain in the first four decades of the eighteenth century, at least, in the engraved views produced by Kip and Knyff and by Badeslade. They represent the adaption of grander-scale, regal continental models, which reflected the economic and political centralization of European courts, to a British context of power, wealth, and innovation in garden design dispersed among the landowning class after the 1688 settlement.

Switzer also draws our attention to "designing and laying down some little Spots of Gardening, in the Manner that the Ichnography or Plan of a Building is; and by the Means of Eugh [yew] and other tonsile Greens, to imitate the Elevation thereof, in Columns, Pilaster, Niches, &c."[12] He mentions Winchendon and the "beautiful Hollow" at Kensington as examples of gardens planted to imitate architecture; and we may add the south parterre at Stowe, the garden of Carlton House, London, Alexander Pope's garden at Twickenham, the lime walk at Sherborne Castle, the "temple of Pan or Silvanus" at Hall Barn, Lord Petre's Thorndon Hall and his design for Worksop Manor, and Switzer's own design for Nostell Priory.[13] None of these have survived, but twentieth-century examples of Switzer's "ichnography" exist: the gardens of Sissinghurst Castle in Kent and the parterre at Chatsworth laid out to replicate the ground plan of Chiswick House. The architectural treatment of plants (clipping to suggest arcades, colonnades, niches, and even string courses) could of course be found in bosquets at Versailles and in other continental gardens.

DUTCH GARDENS

The specific character of the topography of the Netherlands helped the development there of a particular type of geometric garden. The character and size of gardens during the period were limited by the predominant terrain and, in the province of Holland at least, the large number of canals. Smaller in scale than the geometries of France and Britain, symmetrical, rectilinear, enclosed by canals, walls, fences, and hedges, Dutch gardens tended to feature parterres and orchards rather than bosquets. They also devoted quite large areas to flowers: Dutch horticulture was in some respects spectacularly advanced.

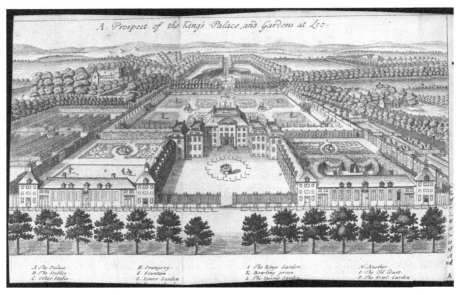

FIGURE 2.4: *A Prospect of the King's Palace and Gardens at Loo,* from Walter Harris, *A Description of the King's Royal Palace and Gardens at Loo* (1699). Courtesy of the Wellcome Library, London.

By the end of the seventeenth century, some places in the ownership of the royal family, such as William and Mary's Het Loo and the Count of Nassau-Odijk's Zeist, were taking on the grander scale of French or British geometrical gardens, featuring bosquets and sculptures and extending the avenues of the garden into adjacent wooded or farm lands. Empire in the East Indies and South America stimulated interest in and culture of exotic plants. Tropical shells no doubt helped inspire shell grottoes. The first half of the eighteenth century saw an acceptance of meandering paths in bosquets, the retreat (in size) of parterres and expansion of tree cover, and other tendencies related to what was happening in Britain. Duin-en-Berg (ca. 1730), for example, displayed asymmetrical geometry very similar to some of the designs disseminated by Switzer or Batty Langley.[14]

LANDSCAPE GARDENS

From the early 1730s, in England, a new type of garden—landscape gardens—emerged. Landscape gardens strive to efface the traces of their own artistic making, at least in comparison with the previously dominant geometric layouts, and thus banished topiary, parterres, fountains, hedged bosquets, and straight avenues. Instead, bushes and trees displaying more of their natural habits of growth, lawns, pools, streams and waterfalls, open groves, and meandering or serpentine paths (or eventually no paths at all) were preferred. In 1734, Sir Thomas Robinson wrote to the Earl of Carlisle (the owner of Castle Howard) announcing that "There is a new taste in gardening just arisen" and that "a general alteration of some of the most considerable gardens in the kingdom is begun," based on the gardening ideas of William Kent (1685–1748), "to lay [gardens] out, and work without level and line."[15] Robinson means without a spirit level (used for leveling lines and surfaces) and without a plumb line (for straightening). The contours of the new gardens would follow the natural topography of their sites, assisted only by approximate optical judgments by the designer. A second implication is that divisions, compartments, clearings in the new gardens will no longer be rectilinear.

Landscape gardens aim to look like the products of nature, rather than human artifice, and of time and history as opposed to the stasis, always brand new, of geometrical gardens: "this method of gardening is more agreeable as when finished it has the appearance of beautiful nature, and without being told, one would imagine art had no part in the finishing. . . The celebrated gardens of Claremont, Chiswick, and Stowe are now full of labourers, to modernize the expensive works finished in them, even since everyone's memory."[16]

Robinson asserts that another principal benefit is diversity, or variety: "By this means the 12 acres of [the Prince of Wales's garden at Carlton House in London] . . . is more diversified than anything of that compass I ever saw."[17] However, we know from contemporary maps and views that Carlton House featured an array of flowerbeds symmetrical around an elongated central space adorned with plant-covered arbors in the architectural form of arcades. This is what Robinson (or his informants) considered as "the appearance of beautiful nature"; so at the beginning of the landscape garden the departure from the topiary and regularity of parterres was of a relative character. It became more absolute in later decades. Rousham in Oxfordshire, Esher Place in Surrey, and the landscape extension embracing bridge, lake, and mausoleum at Carlisle's own Castle Howard would soon be added.

One of the places Kent first worked (before those mentioned previously) was Queen Caroline's Richmond Gardens, where in 1732 he designed a hermitage and a grotto, "Merlin's Cave." The hermitage was made by Caroline as a place to enshrine portrait busts of thinkers (some scientists, some clergymen) whose works had advanced natural religion, or deism.[18] This way of thinking, to give it a brutal summary here, considered that the natural world furnished evidence not only for the existence of but also about the character of the beneficent creating deity,[19] rendering the Bible potentially obsolete, although Church of England clergymen worked hard to reconcile deism with orthodoxy.[20] Caroline's chaplain, Samuel Clarke, wrote a classic deist treatise[21]; her old tutor, Gottfried von Leibniz, had displayed considerable interest. Insofar as Richmond Gardens can be identified with Kent, the beginnings of the landscape garden involve celebration of the comprehension and spiritual understanding of the natural world deriving from the new science. Some decades later, the first edition of the *Encyclopedia Britannica* emphasized this connection with gardens. The entry for "Garden" is rather pedestrian and anti-French in tone, suggesting that gardens should imitate nature and abominating Versailles. The writer singles out one of Versailles's bosquets that imitates the appearance of a grove of trees "by a group of jets d'eau" of a fountain as appearing ridiculous. The entry emphasizes the deist aspect, praising Kent's "admirable" method for "embellishing a field" (meaning a field of vision) and sums up:

> Rough uncultivated ground, dismal to the eye, inspires peevishness and discontent. . . A field richly ornamented, containing beautiful objects of various kinds, displays, in full lustre, the goodness of the Deity, and the ample provision he has made for our happiness; which must fill every spectator with gratitude to his Maker, and with benevolence to his fellow-creatures. Other fine arts may be perverted to excite irregular, and even vicious, emotions; but gardening, which inspires the purest and most refined pleasures, cannot but promote every good affection. The gaity and harmony of mind it produceth, inclining the spectator to communicate his satisfaction to others, and to make them happy as he himself is, tend naturally to establish in him a habit of humanity and benevolence.[22]

This, the peroration of the article, is deist in its essence: the signs of the Deity and his goodness are present in nature, resulting in sociable optimism and contentedness. In this view, gardens are as much about the interchange of emotion as about visual beauty (feelings of "grandeur" and "gaiety" are cited earlier).

In practical terms, the ha-ha wall, or sunk fence, enabled the new form of garden. Located at the edge of the garden proper, between the garden and the land outside (most often this was parkland), the ha-ha concealed the division that prevented livestock from entering the garden and permitted an unimpeded view to the landscape beyond. Some yards beyond the boundary, the level of the land was gradually lowered, sloping to a depth of five or six feet against the garden; the exposed edge of the garden was then supported by a wall. The full consequences of this invention, the origins of which are obscure, can be understood when we have considered the question of how views in and out of the new gardens were composed.

Poet William Shenstone (1714–63) coined the term *landscape gardening* in his essay *Unconnected Thoughts on Gardening* (1764): "Gardening may be divided into three species—kitchen-gardening—parterre-gardening—and landskip, or picturesque-gardening: which . . . consists in pleasing the imagination by scenes of grandeur, beauty, or variety."[23] The word *landscape* (*landskip*) first came into the language in the seventeenth century to designate a type of painting, and even in our day it has not lost its associated ideas of pleasure and aesthetics.[24] In Shenstone's time, the original usage was still strong: "I have used the word landskip-gardiners; because, in pursuance of our present taste in gardening, every good painter of landskip appears to me the most proper designer."[25] Shenstone believes that the new garden design is and should be closely related to pictorial artistic practice and that gardens should be designed in a "picturesque" way so as to form pleasing three-dimensional pictures akin to contemporary landscape painting to be first apprehended as views and then, unlike paintings, entered and explored. However, Shenstone's "picturesque-gardening" or "landskip-gardening" is not solely and exclusively visual. In his first Unconnected Thought, he argues that it "consists in pleasing the

FIGURE 2.5: The ha-ha at Rousham House, Oxfordshire. Photograph by Michael Charlesworth.

imagination," and in his fourth Thought, he reiterates that "Objects should indeed be less calculated to strike the immediate eye, than the judgement or well-formed imagination; as in painting." It might strike us as paradoxical that elements in paintings are not there to "strike the immediate eye," but the apparent paradox has been explained in the third Thought:

> There seems . . . to be some objects, which afford a pleasure not reducible to either of the foregoing heads ["the great, the various and the beautiful"]. A ruin, for instance, may be neither new to us, nor majestick, nor beautiful, yet afford that pleasing melancholy which proceeds from a reflexion on decayed magnificence. For this reason, an able gardiner should avail himself of objects, perhaps, not very striking; if they serve to connect ideas, that convey reflexions of the pleasing kind.

Good landscape gardening, therefore, consists of the composition of elements that are felt and sensed as much as seen. The "able gardiner" aims at the stimulation of feelings, the association of ideas and trains of thought. The picturesque way of seeing is too often interpreted as purely visual, whereas it was a way of associating ideas and stirring emotions and sentiments.

Shenstone was not a landscape painter, and he does not give a very coherent idea of how a landscape painter could be of practical help in the design. Specific recommendations are made by another landowner who visited and greatly admired The Leasowes, Shenstone's *ferme ornée*, in the 1760s: the Marquis de Girardin, creator of his own landscape garden at Ermenonville (Oise), France, from the 1760s.[26] At Ermenonville, Girardin actually employed a landscape painter, Georg-Frederic Mayer (died 1778: described on his gravestone in the grounds as "a landscape painter and an honest man"). Girardin describes the usefulness of a landscape painter in the treatise he wrote on composing landscapes, *De la Composition des paysages, ou, des moyens d'embellir la nature autour des habitations, en y joignant l'agréable à l'utile* (1777):

> Keep the Painter in your company. If you find that the view from the salon is interrupted by obstacles, climb up to the top of the house. From there, single out within the countryside the backgrounds and distant prospects which afford most interest, and take care to retain whatever there is in the way of constructions or established plantations that can be utilised in the composition of your picture. Then let the Painter make a sketch in which he composes the foreground in relation to the background that the countryside offers you.[27]

This passage anticipates the practice of Humphry Repton, who was his own artist and who presented his proposals to clients in a series of "Red Books" that illuminated the designer's ideas in the form of before and after views of the same terrain.[28] Girardin's passage also shows the design being created from the outward to the inward, or from background (which because of its size and distance would be vastly expensive or impossible for the landowner to change) to foreground (which could be changed). This takes us back to the ha-ha.

At the time when the ha-ha emerged, conventional alternative forms of garden enclosure included fences, walls, and hedges—all barriers that deny continuity (and often can't be seen through). Supplementing these in Britain in the period 1700–40 was a form of terrace that has been termed a "bastion wall" whereby the wall that supports the garden's terraces very slightly resembles a fortification in the massiveness of the barrier it presents to the surrounding

FIGURE 2.6: Sledmere House, east Yorkshire: The view from the house across the line of the ha-ha to the eye-catcher, "Sledmere Castle." Photograph by Michael Charlesworth.

terrain. Such walls and bastions are usually raised well up above the surrounding areas. Examples still survive at Castle Howard, Stowe, Bramham Park, Duncombe Park, and Grimsthorpe Hall. The "bastion wall" is sometimes taken to be a transitional barrier, but unlike the ha-ha there is no real or implied continuity between the garden spaces and the land outside. Outward views often begin with an exhilarating plunge into empty space.

With these other barrier forms, therefore, there is no necessity for a continuum of planting types or land use, as the discontinuity between inside and outside is plainly acknowledged. This is not the case with a ha-ha, which is designed to present a seamless visual continuity. This affects the design of the whole. To have a parterre within the ha-ha and cattle or deer grazing outside would announce a discontinuity as plainly as if there was a fence or hedge. One fundamental aspect determining the appearance of landscape gardens, therefore, was that whatever was outside the garden proper, whether woodland, parkland, or farmland, exercised a determining influence on what could be designed within. In practice, this meant that parterres and topiary were not generally part of the classic form of landscape garden, where in some cases grass extended right up to the walls of the house. Even flower gardens represented particular problems for designers.

FLOWERS IN LANDSCAPE GARDENS

As Mark Laird has comprehensively shown, there were plenty of flowers in landscape gardens, both in the pleasure grounds within the ha-ha (what I termed the "garden proper") and in specialized flower gardens.[29] In the pleasure grounds, flowering shrubs of all kinds were used, as were rambling and climbing plants. Sections of the garden dedicated to flowerbeds were also established and maintained. At Sledmere House, east Yorkshire, this was a walled garden at some distance from the house, with low trees and bushes planted outside the brick walls to conceal it from view. At other places, flower gardens were concealed by trees on four or at least three sides so that their bright colors would not intrude on the views from the outlying park and disrupt the naturalistic prospects.[30] A third solution was adopted at places such as Cannon Hall, Cawthorne (and, on a much more modest scale, Mystole House, Kent): Laird describes the flower garden at Cannon Hall within a pleasure ground that "spread out beyond the side axis like the wings of a bird or butterfly."[31] In other words, the landowner sacrificed some of the lateral spread of the main prospect from the front of the house in the interests of accommodating pleasure grounds that included flower gardens. Richard Woods, Cannon Hall's designer, laid out circular planting beds and serpentine flower borders for "Roses and all sorts of common and sweet flowers."[32]

The most famous of eighteenth-century flower gardens is that at Nuneham Courtenay, made by William Mason for the Earl of Harcourt, beginning in 1775. Its form is something of an epitome or miniature version of the design of landscape gardens and parks then spreading across the whole country. (The landscape garden at Nuneham Park itself, by Lancelot "Capability" Brown, involved the destruction of the old village, the conversion of the church to classical architecture, and the planting of the usual clumps and belts of woodland.) The flower garden was triangular with pushed-in sides. The edges were planted up with trees and bushes, rather like the encircling belts around the edges of a park. A meandering serpentine path guided visitors close to the periphery rather than across the middle, as the carriage drives and path-ways through parks tended to do. It also brought visitors to the architectural features (the Temple of Flora modeled on classical Roman temples, a grotto and a covered seat, the "bower") and to the sculpture, consisting of busts of classical deities and a handful of modern figures. The major part of the garden was put down to lawn in which were clumps of shrubs (as clumps of trees would figure in the grassland of parks). One or two mature standard trees stood around (a large elm, a spruce), and the main element that has no equivalent in landscape parks outside is the flowerbeds that spread at intervals over the lawn. The fame of Nuneham's flower garden rests not only on its beauty and relative rarity but also on its associations with French philosopher Jean-Jacques Rousseau, who is commemorated with one of the busts and by an inscription of deist persuasion from his writings: "Si l'Auteur de la nature est grand dans les grandes choses il est très grand dans les petites" ("If the author of nature is great in great things, he is very great in the little things").[33] Rousseau had also been enshrined at the Marquis de Girardin's Ermenonville, where he died in 1778.[34]

LANDSCAPE PARKS

In eighteenth-century Britain, landowners extended the definition of gardens to embrace large areas of land that supported grassland and trees outside the pleasure grounds. These areas, known as parks, had a long history. In their eighteenth century manifestation, they were economically productive areas varying in size from about fifty acres to hundreds, or even more than a thousand acres.[35] Trees were planted in landscape parks in belts, especially near the furthest boundary of the park, to enclose it optically from the world beyond; in clumps, as elements in the visual design; and sometimes as individual specimens. These woods represented a capital investment by the landowner that, when desired or necessary, could be felled and sold.

The grassland that stretched between the clumps and belts of trees also represented a financial return for the owner because it supported livestock. Convention dictated that certain animals were acceptable in parks: deer (associated with aristocratic hunting and valuable as meat for the owner and as an exclusive gift to others, since buying and selling venison was prohibited); and sheep (associated with the idealized and innocent world of Arcadia and with the pastoral in verbal and visual art). Thomas Gainsborough added two sheep to the background of his portrait of Mrs. Richard Brinsley Sheridan to enhance the pastoral feeling. William Beckford took a small flock of sheep to his house in Portugal to give it a more English, aesthetic, and pastoral atmosphere.[36] Cows and cattle were also acceptable for something of the same reason. So integral were they to the design of parks that the "browsing line" they created at the bottom edge of the branches and foliage of trees by eating the leaves and shoots (up to the level beyond which they could not reach) was anticipated by designers such as Repton as part of the planned finished whole.[37]

The people who came into the park to look after these animals—shepherds and milkmaids—feature in poetry and landscape art of the day,[38] but other types of agriculture—and their human attendants—were excluded. Pigs were not normally encountered nor were ploughed fields, since the harder physical work of arable farming dispelled the feeling of leisure the park was designed to foster. Rare exceptions to this, neither typical nor representative, were the estates made by famous agricultural improvers.[39] Also, ploughland and stubble fields disrupted the color scheme of parkland.[40]

Parks therefore combined beauty with utility, the aesthetic with the economic. With their smooth, even curves and gentle transitions, the landscape parks corresponded with the definition of the "beautiful" articulated by William Hogarth and Edmund Burke. Burke influentially differentiated between the beautiful and the sublime, the latter characterized by its "ruling principle" of terror; for that, a far wilder landscape would have to be found or made. Hawkstone in Shropshire qualifies, as does the man-made volcano at Wörlitz, near Dessau in Germany. Sublime parks can be found, but they are far rarer.

Like the pleasure grounds, parks would be ornamented with buildings. Usually, as with the beautifully positioned temple in the grounds of Godmersham Park, Kent (belonging to Jane Austen's brother), they were classical in idiom, but Gothic buildings like the castle at Sledmere were popular, and more exotic Chinese, Turkish, and, occasionally, Indian buildings could be encountered. Generally, only a sprinkling of such structures was necessary, as opposed to the scores of features found in landscape gardens where livestock was not present, such as Stourhead, Stowe, and Ermenonville.[41] There are only half a dozen structures in Petworth Park, four or five at Sledmere. Some of these structures have practical as well as aesthetic functions: Sledmere's deershed; boathouses on ornamental lakes; even the house, which itself becomes an eye catcher when viewed from a distance.

The precise boundaries of the park were concealed from visitors so that a subtle blending with the countryside outside was effected. Viewed from a plane approaching Gatwick Airport, Petworth's park appears as a very large rectangle; but no visitor exploring its spaces will be aware of that shape. The primary psychological effect of large landscape parks, with the land's surface showing under the soft undulations of turf, and trees standing around in carefully placed natural-seeming groups, is one of tranquility. Hazardous natural features have been removed, unauthorized visitors (such as poachers) deterred by traps, and in some places (such as Sledmere and Nuneham) the rural community relocated or dispersed, leaving only the village church incorporated as a visual element in the landscape. The calm and peace of the landscape garden was there only for the privileged owning family and its visitors. However, exceptions to this were Girardin's Ermenonville and Shenstone's The Leasowes, where the owners encouraged villagers to use the landscape gardens. Ermenonville offered amusements such as archery butts and two dance floors.

THE FERME ORNÉE

Parkland was not the only way to resolve relations between gardens and the wider country. *Fermes ornées* (ornamented farms) were a relatively rare type of garden during the period, but some, such as Philip Southcote's Woburn Farm in Surrey, enjoyed exceptional fame. The most famous was Shenstone's The Leasowes.[42] Here, the landscape garden embraced a whole farm without it ceasing to be productive, supplementing usefulness with areas dedicated to beauty, leisure, and pleasure. Shenstone relied on the farm's productivity for his income, and was keenly concerned with the balance of purposes; poetically and conceptually, he integrated his farm with its surroundings by means of inscriptions at the highest points and a hilltop seat offering wide views as far as the Welsh mountains. On the seat was inscribed:

DIVINI GLORIA RURIS!
(The Divine Glory of the Countryside).[43]

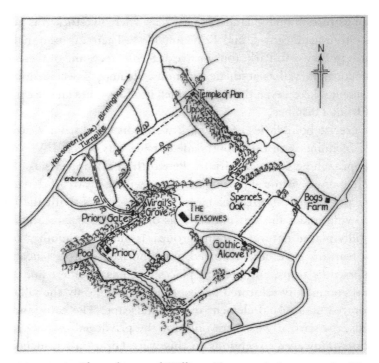

FIGURE 2.7: *Plan of part of William Shenstone's ferme ornée, The Leasowes.* Drawn by Robert Williams.

Visitors are thus encouraged to celebrate the view, acknowledge the deist suggestion, perceive The Leasowes and the surrounding countryside as an integrated whole, venerate the poet Virgil from whom this line comes, and perhaps reflect on continuities between Roman civilization and eighteenth-century Britain.

At another part of The Leasowes, a contemporary guidebook tells us, "the path winds up the back part of a circular green hill, discovering little of the country till you enter a clump of stately firs upon the summit. Over-arched by these firs is an octagonal seat, the back of which is so contrived as to form a table or pedestal for a bowl or goblet thus inscribed—To all friends round the Wrekin!"

The Wrekin, the hill thirty miles away, mentioned in what is described as "an old Shropshire" drinking toast, was visible.[44] We notice Shenstone's art immediately: the route leads visitors for maximum surprise at the top; the hilltop is planted with a distinguishing grove; the idea of a circle of friendship is subtly prepared by the seat that faces the whole panorama, as well as in the inscription. The landscape garden's two hilltop features are complementary: the vernacular inscription here opposes the other's august Latin; there is an implied contrast between near (the English fields) and far (the Roman fields); between present and past; between human society and enjoyment of nature; and ultimately between friendship and conviviality, on one hand, and suggestions of the ineffable (of "glory" and "divinity") on the other. All point to an enjoyment of the immediate, the daily, and the human, after basking in the exalted, the grand, and the poetic, the conjunctions unified and stabilized by the similar terrain of the views.

Hilltops thus become crucial features at this ferme ornée; hedges lead and disguise paths; in particular, the small streams and valleys that crossed The Leasowes could be treated artistically to endow them with meaning: Virgil's Grove, dedicated to the celebration of poetry; and a ruin of a priory (doubling as a tenant's dwelling) next to an artificial pond.

There was a farm, with cultivated fields, at Marie-Antoinette's le Hameau (1783–8) (in the Petit Trianon area at Versailles). This farm is not a ferme ornée. At Versailles, the entire farm was a garden ornament included with an entire imitation village within the garden as conceptual features.

ANGLO-CHINESE GARDENS

Whether the landscape garden was influenced by the design of Chinese gardens was discussed in the eighteenth century. With few exceptions, British writers since the 1750s have tended to disparage the idea.[45] This was not necessarily the case, however, at the very beginning of the landscape garden.

Sir Thomas Robinson's letter to the Earl of Carlisle, quoted earlier, included this suggestion:

> [T]his method of gardening has the appearance of beautiful nature . . . without being told, one would imagine art had no part in the finishing, and is, according to what one hears of the Chinese, entirely after their models for works of this nature, where they never plant straight lines or make regular designs.

China was certainly commemorated in landscape gardens, usually in the form of isolated Chinese buildings (such as the Chinese Teahouse (1754–7) at Sanssouci, Potsdam, Germany, which, however, stood in a geometric layout). At Studley Royal, near Ripon in Yorkshire, the hillside around the Chinese pavilion appears to have been altered to provide an appropriately "Chinese" setting. As early as 1744, a visitor found that the landowner planned to erect a pagoda ("a Chinese house of a pyramidical form, with a gallery encircling every story") to occupy "the point of a ridge which encloses on each hand a valley finely wooded and washed by a rivulet. One side is formed into a number of small terraces interspersed with rocks, which makes a Chinese landscape."[46] Humphry Repton's Chinese Dairy (1804) for Woburn Abbey, with two Chinese buildings facing across a pond, and plantings of *hydrangea macrophylla* (then thought to be originally from China) and Mandarin ducks, also clearly attempted to create an entire setting. Other examples include Chinese buildings (since disappeared) at the Désert de Retz near Paris, by François de Monville in the period 1774–89;[47] the House of Confucius at Kew gardens, built in the 1740s and so one of the early Chinese buildings in English gardens.

There was serious interest in Chinese culture during the eighteenth century. The philosopher Leibniz was deeply interested in Chinese philosophy, perhaps because he thought it lent support to his notions of a natural religion, emphasizing the contemporary value of Confucianism in his Preface to *Novissima Sinica* (1699) and asserting that China surpasses Europe in the "principles of civil life," that is, ethics and politics. If corruptions become even worse in Europe, Leibniz writes, he could see the need for "Chinese missionaries [to be] sent to us to teach us the use and practice of natural religion, just as we send missionaries to them to teach them revealed religion."[48] English deists concurred: "Navarette, a Chinese missionary, agrees with Leibniz and says that 'It is the special providence of God that the Chinese did not know what was done in Christendom; for if they did, there would be never a man among them but would spit in our faces.' "[49] Such ideas of Chinese civilization and

FIGURE 2.8: Chinese Teahouse (1754–7) at Sanssouci, Potsdam. Photograph by Stephen Bending.

good government surely constitute the primary context for Chinese buildings in landscape gardens. In England, Henry St John, Lord Bolingbroke, and his friend Alexander Pope both wrote admiringly of Confucius; in France the Abbé Raynal praised Chinese government in his strongly antislavery *Philosophical and Political History of the Establishments and the Commerce of the Europeans in the Two Indies* (1774–80).

Such interest in Chinese civilization among Europeans does not necessarily prove the influence of Chinese garden design on the character of the European landscape garden. But the possibility cannot be simply dismissed.

POETIC GARDENS

Some landscape gardens make extensive use of poetic inscriptions carved into seats, buildings, or other features to suggest to the visitor/reader associated ideas, a mood, or an elevated way of thinking. Others use no inscriptions. Ultimately, gardens become poetic by virtue of the feeling of the whole, apprehended by the visitor's judgment. It is as much a question of how the garden makes us feel as of what the garden features are and what they refer to. We call "poetic" things that embody or give rise to elevated or profound ideas and sensations, and things that transcend conventional material concerns. A poetic garden feature leads to the "virtual" or "noumenal" level referred to by John Dixon Hunt,[50] what I termed the "mythic" space just the other side of the garden's real space.[51]

CHAPTER THREE

Plantings

MICHAEL SYMES

In the late seventeenth century, and throughout the eighteenth, plantings not only in Britain but across Europe were dominated by introductions from abroad, especially from North America. Colonization was the enabler, or facilitator, and the results were to have a radical and permanent effect on the appearance of gardens. Introductions can be seen partly in terms of empire but also in trade and the opening up of new avenues, such as John Tradescant the Elder visiting and bringing back plants from Russia.

Methods for planting were also taken more seriously. Practical handbooks had been available for a century, but post-Restoration authors added further dimensions. John Rea's *Flora* (1665) gave instructions for laying out a garden, while John Evelyn's *Sylva* (1664), prompted by the impulse to plant trees on a massive scale to replenish the stocks depleted by ship building, concentrated on forestry and became the standard work on trees.

All planting and gardening had to be done by hand. Basic implements remained largely the same, but introductions meant that more sophisticated ways had to be found to nurture tender plants from abroad. There was thus a great increase in the number of greenhouses and orangeries, the latter giving architectural scope for buildings of considerable invention and elegance: they often served a social purpose as well. Awareness of climate and soil conditions spread, as did scientific and botanical interest in what was grown. On the agricultural front, new revolutionary methods of maximizing use of the soil

and the fields (e.g., crop rotation), with some new technology, complemented
the growth of interest in ornamental plantings.

The regions that fed European nurseries and gardens included North America (largely the British and French colonies) and the Middle East. Later in
the eighteenth century, expeditions opened up sources in China, Australia, the
Indies, South Africa, and South America. The East India Company was responsible for sending several hundred species home, including grewia, hibiscus,
and several sorts of fig. Joseph Pitton de Tournefort (1656–1708), creator of
one of the systems of plant classification, held a post at the Jardin des Plantes
in Paris and was commissioned by Louis XIV to visit Greece and Turkey in
1700–2. The latter was a remarkable region, especially for flowers. Hans
Sloane set off with the Duke of Albemarle to Jamaica in 1687 and collected
many exotic plants in the West Indies, publishing an account of his travels in
1707.

At the instance of Bishop Henry Compton, John Banister (ca. 1650–92)
went to the West Indies in 1674 as an Anglican minister, and subsequently to
Virginia. He combined his missionary work with plant collecting, and sent
specimens back to Compton, to the Chelsea Physic Garden, and to the Oxford
Botanic Garden. Among the more striking plants he dispatched were the
swamp bay (*Magnolia virginiana*), the first magnolia seen in Europe; the sweet
gum (*Liquidambar styraciflua*); the scarlet oak (*Quercus coccinea*); red oak
(*Q. rubra*); balsam fir (*Abies balsamea*); and the honey tree (*Gleditsia triac-
anthos*). These caused a sensation and proved lastingly popular in their new
homes. Part of the excitement was that these novelties would flourish in the
British climate, which was found to be not too dissimilar to that of the eastern
seaboard of New England.

Mark Catesby (1682–1749) also went to Virginia, in 1712, traveling later
to Jamaica. In 1722, a syndicate sponsored him for a four-year plant collecting expedition to the Carolinas and Bahamas. He took European plants out
with him, but sent back, and returned with, even more wonders than Banister
had found. Surviving such adventures as unwittingly sharing his bed with a
rattlesnake, he introduced the Carolina spice bush (*Calycanthus floridus*), the
catalpa or Indian bean (*Catalpa bignonioides*), wisteria (*Wisteria frutescens*),
and the great magnolia (*Magnolia grandiflora*).

What gave the greatest impetus to the transatlantic plant trade was the
contact between John Bartram (1699–1777) in Pennsylvania and Peter Collinson (1694–1768) in London. This partnership, which lasted for nearly forty
years, was responsible for introducing up to 200 new American species into
Britain and for countless thousands of seeds or plants (mostly seeds) being

distributed by Collinson as agent to many landowners all over the country. From 1735, when Collinson provided seeds for Lord Petre, a regular business evolved, with owners ordering, via Collinson, five-guinea boxes that normally contained the seeds of about 100 different species, generally trees or shrubs. Bartram initially concentrated on locations close to his home a short way from Philadelphia, but later expeditions to adjoining states and further south to the Carolinas, Georgia, and Florida were reflected in new material added to the standard nucleus in the contents of the boxes.

Sometimes there were special consignments to order, while dried specimens were sent for identification to the Oxford Botanic Garden. Apart from Collinson, Bartram dealt directly with leading botanists and collectors such as Mark Catesby, Philip Miller at the Chelsea Physic Garden, and Johann Jakob Dillenius at Oxford. After Collinson's death, Bartram tended to use Dr. John Fothergill of Upton, West Ham (1712–80) as his main contact. He also dealt with others in Europe, such as J. F. Gronovius of Leiden, Queen Ulrica of Sweden, and Pehr Kalm, also from Sweden and a pupil of Linnaeus. *Kalmia latifolia*, common in Pennsylvania, was named after him.

The trade was not all one way. Bartram obtained many seeds and plants from Europe, since the American colonists' tastes were often for European rather than native species. Cedar, cypress, and pinaster arrived from England, but did not always flourish. Collinson sent Bartram some Russian rhubarb together with a recipe for rhubarb pie. Collinson, indeed, had many correspondents and did not depend exclusively on Bartram for material: he obtained the Tree of Heaven (*Ailanthus altissima*) from Père d'Incarville, a missionary in China, and plants from Persia, Russia, Gibraltar, Nuremberg, and Siberia.

French collectors and explorers were also active in America. André Michaux (1746–1803) followed up expeditions to western Asia and Persia in the 1770s by traveling to the French colony of Louisiana. Once established there, he spread his interests and connections through the former British colonies (post-War of Independence), instigating gardens in New Jersey and South Carolina. His extensive expeditions resulted in the shipment of sixty thousand plants back to Paris. He wrote *Flora Boreali Americana*, the most complete work on American flora of its time.

A sample of the especially notable introductions that have made a lasting impression shows the wide range of origins during the eighteenth century. The weeping willow (*Salix babylonica*) officially arrived from China in 1730, but may well have been known earlier; the camellia (*Camellia japonica*) came from Japan in 1739; the ginkgo (*Ginkgo biloba*) from China in 1750; the Lombardy poplar (*Populus nigra* var. *italica*) from Italy in 1758; the common rhododendron (*Rhododendron ponticum*) from Turkey and other countries in 1763; the buddleia (*Buddleja globosa*) from South America in 1774; the tree fern (*Dicksonia antarctica*) from Australia in 1786; and the monkey puzzle (*Araucaria araucana*) from Chile in 1796.

COLLECTORS AND COLLECTIONS

The acquisitive urge has always existed. In the case of collecting plants, the impulse was usually twofold: one impulse was indeed to amass as large and varied a holding as possible, but this was often accompanied by genuine botanical interest. Furthermore, many owners saw the opportunity to extend their range of plants (trees in particular) as a means of enhancing the appearance of their gardens. So it comes as no surprise to find a good many collectors in the age of new introductions, and to see a rise in the number and importance of gardens owned by collectors.

The seventeenth century witnessed the start of an expanding process of collecting, mainly through the Tradescants and particularly from the new North American colonies. The first major collector in our period was Henry Compton (1632–1713), who became the bishop of London in 1675 and created a garden of exotic trees and shrubs at Fulham Palace. He was said to have had over a thousand species of exotics, and was dubbed "the Maecenas of botany." Much of his collection came via John Banister, the missionary and plant collector sent over to Virginia by Bishop Compton, and Compton is credited with more than forty introductions. After his death, his stock was dispersed and found its way into various commercial nurseries such as Gray's.

The precocious Lord Petre (1713–42) established gardens, nurseries, and an almost unrivaled range of stoves (hothouses) at his home of Thorndon Hall, Essex. By the age of seventeen, he had built up a large library of works on botany and gardening, and by the following year he had proved his practical interest by growing some remarkable exotics in the hothouses. In 1736, still only twenty-three, he commissioned Philip Miller to draw up a catalogue of his vast collection of plants. In 1740, nearly five thousand trees were planted in the park, all grown from seed in Petre's nurseries, and in the next two years about forty thousand more followed, mostly North American species. The imported plants were listed in a sixteen-volume *Hortus Siccus* (herbarium of dried plants), one of the ways in which a collector could record his or her collection. After Petre's tragically early death at twenty-nine, the estimated 219,225 plants in the nurseries were offered for sale.

At Thorndon, Petre designed a layout from 1732, which, understandably for the time, was largely formal—avenues, drives, canals, ponds, and nursery areas. However, the plantations (some of which were of mature trees that had been moved) in themselves determined a new direction—clumps and groves, with shrubberies for the smaller plants. Initial botanical interest led to a gradual awareness of the aesthetics of planting, with attention paid to perspective, grouping, shape, and color—"painting with Living pencils," as Petre's work was described.[1]

The other major collector at this period was Archibald Campbell (1682–1761), Lord Islay and, from 1743, the third Duke of Argyll. After a political career in Scotland, where he first took an interest in gardening, he went south and in 1722 purchased sixteen acres that formed a modest basis for his garden and nursery at Whitton, Middlesex, which by 1750 had expanded to fifty-five acres. The treemonger (as Horace Walpole called him) was not only a collector with a wide range of plantings, but actually the first to grow several species in England. These included the Siberian stone pine (*Pinus cembra*), the Lombardy poplar (*Populus nigra* var. *Italica*), the paper birch (*Betula papyrifera*), and the Carolina holly (*Ilex opaca*). Seventeen species are said to have been introduced by him.

FIGURE 3.1: *View of the canal and Gothic tower at Whitton*, engraved by William Woollett, 1760. Author's collection.

Argyll's nursery covered nine acres, but the plantations filled the rest of the grounds quite densely. The layout was, again, formal, centered on a canal leading to a triangular Gothic tower. His trees came from many sources, since he was active long before the Bartram-Collinson trade, which he joined in 1748. American sources included Mark Catesby and the Houston collections from Georgia, and possibly other botanists and collectors such as John Clayton, Alexander Garden, John Mitchell, and Cadwallader Colden. But he also obtained much material from Spain, Hungary, and as far afield as Russia.

Another collector of note was Charles Lennox, the second Duke of Richmond (1701–50), as was his son, the third Duke of Richmond. By 1741, he was in the Bartram-Collinson scheme, and he was an eager buyer of much of the Thorndon riches after Lord Petre's death. Collinson said that Richmond had the best collection of hardy exotics in England at his estate of Goodwood, Sussex. Richard Pococke reported that he had seen "thirty different kinds of oaks and 400 different American trees and shrubs which compose a wilderness and a fine wood cut into ridings."[2]

The next generation brought forth a collector who also created one of the greatest gardens of the eighteenth century, the Hon. Charles Hamilton of Painshill, Surrey (1704–86). Hamilton created a naturalistic pictorial garden, unlike the predominately formal gardens of the owners mentioned earlier, with a subtle spread of views and perspectives, a varied array of architecture, skillfully designed water, and plantations that ranged from floriferous shrubberies to a dense dark evergreen wood. Much of what Hamilton planted was of North American origin, though he acquired only two boxes from Peter Collinson and had other channels for obtaining such material, principally nurseryman Alexander Eddie. A direct contact abroad was the Abbé Nolin, garden adviser to Louis XV and Louis XVI and inspector of the royal French nurseries. He corresponded with Hamilton in the years 1755–9, during most of which time England and France were at war, which meant that plants and seeds sometimes had to be exchanged via third parties. The exchanges opened up new territory for Hamilton: the French possessed a large part of North America, both in Canada and to the west and south of the English eastern seaboard colonies, and also had colonies, for example, in Africa (Nolin offered Hamilton seeds from Senegal).

The correspondence reveals Hamilton's enthusiasm as a collector, avid for the latest and newest. But he was also a practical grower and very interested in how trees and shrubs would flourish. He had the eye of an artist and arranged his plantings to give a varied effect, and his unique combination of arboriculturist and designer was widely recognized.

England also boasted many other fine collections. At Syon House, the Duke of Northumberland employed "Capability" Brown, and the grounds were "planted with all the foreign hardy trees and shrubs that could be procured, at that time, in the London nurseries; and the place now [1838] contains many very fine old specimens of cedars, pines, planes, gleditschias, robinias, catalpas, and more especially of deciduous cypress."[3] At Croome Court, Worcestershire, another Brown commission displayed "some of the finest specimens of foreign trees and shrubs in the country."[4]

Some collectors were happy to share their knowledge: thus, Charles Dubois of Mitcham, Surrey circulated information about how to grow exotics.[5] Such information was by no means widespread, and John Loudon bemoans the dearth of specimen trees, readily available in nurseries and found in botanic gardens, in many pleasure grounds. He attributes this lack to insufficient knowledge as to how to grow them.[6]

A collection of trees would now commonly be called an arboretum, but the word was unknown in the eighteenth century—Loudon first used the term in 1806.[7] The basis for Loudon's concept seems to be (a) a comprehensive collection and (b) an arrangement conducive to scientific study, though in practice collections called arboreta would normally be selective rather than complete. In the eighteenth century, there were certainly collections that, if they existed today, would appropriately be called an arboretum, such as Bishop Compton's or the Duke of Argyll's at Whitton. Painshill, Goodwood, Syon, Croome, Wilton, and Bowood would also be candidates. Hamilton's emphasis on conifers at Painshill might also merit the specialist term *pinetum*. Loudon's own assessment was that Kew possessed one of the first equivalents of an arboretum, east of the orangery, covering five acres with hardy trees and shrubs.[8]

NURSERIES AND BOTANIC GARDENS

Nurseries had been known in Britain since the Middle Ages, but quality control arrived in 1605 with the granting of a charter to the Company of Gardeners. From that time, plantsmen and seedsmen established nurseries of a recognizably modern kind, initially in and around London where the company could exercise its authority. During the seventeenth century, the trade in flowers and other ornamental plants expanded to equal the provision of fruit trees and vegetables that had been the staple of a previous, more utilitarian age.

The first great nursery was that at Brompton Park in south Kensington, partly where the Victoria and Albert Museum now stands. It was founded by George London and three others in 1681, London later running the business with Henry

Wise. This was the major nursery in England, and not only was it a provider, but London and Wise were also the leading garden designers of the time and indeed became the royal gardeners. Their large-scale baroque designs, as seen extensively in the engravings of Kip and Knyff, required copious quantities of trees for lining the long avenues, so it was of great commercial advantage that they were also the suppliers of the trees. At this time, they used mainly native species.

In the wake of the success of Brompton Park, many other commercial nurseries started up in the metropolis. Thomas Fairchild at Hoxton, who experimented with hybridization, Robert Furber at Kensington Gore, and Christopher Gray in King's Road, Fulham were early in the race to challenge the supremacy of Brompton Park (and indeed overtook it after the departure of London and Wise). James Gordon, after working for Lord Petre at Thorndon, set up his own nursery at Mile End in 1743, and James Lee, who had worked at Syon for the Duke of Northumberland and at Whitton for the Duke of Argyll, founded the Vineyard Nursery, Hammersmith with Lewis Kennedy two years later. It was a common path for a skilled and experienced gardener to establish a nursery business in his own right: George London had started out as a gardener to Bishop Compton at Fulham Palace.

Nurseries had their ups and downs largely according to the people who ran them. Thus, the Hackney nursery established by John Busch in 1756 achieved its greatest eminence under the subsequent owners, the Loddiges family. London as the center gradually lost its monopoly as provincial nurseries, such as those run by the Telford and Perfect families in Yorkshire, or the Dicksons in Edinburgh, began to cater to the local regions.

Botanic gardens, which developed from medieval physic gardens, fulfilled some of the functions of nurseries in propagating and nurturing plants, though without the commercial imperative. The earliest in England was Oxford (1621), followed by Edinburgh (1670) and the Chelsea Physic Garden (1673). The latter achieved its greatest prominence in the eighteenth century under Sir Hans Sloane (from 1722) and the gardener in charge, Philip Miller, who ran it for nearly fifty years and turned it into the best-stocked botanic garden in the world. The purpose of the garden was to provide plant material for study, teaching, and research, and it served as Miller's base although he traveled around and advised many owners and cultivators and was an all-around authority on gardening.

The Royal Botanic Gardens at Kew evolved from the two adjoining ornamental grounds of Richmond Gardens and the gardens of Kew House. Princess Augusta, the widow of Frederick, Prince of Wales (died 1751), worked with Lord Bute and architect William Chambers to enhance the Kew House grounds, and in 1759 a small area of 3.6 hectares was established as a botanic garden under the supervision of William Aiton the Elder, who had trained at the Chelsea Physic Garden. From this modest beginning, the botanical importance of the site steadily grew. On Princess Augusta's death in 1771, Joseph Banks (later Sir Joseph) was appointed as horticultural and botanical adviser, a position he held until his own death in 1820. He was enormously influential in the botanical world and raised the profile of Kew by, in particular, sponsoring (and sometimes joining) plant hunters to gather specimens from all over the globe, starting with Francis Masson's expedition to South Africa in 1772.

Other botanic gardens included those of William Curtis, founder of the *Botanical Magazine*, at Lambeth Marsh from 1771; James Sherard at Eltham; and William Swainson at Twickenham, said to have contained every available tree and shrub.[9] John Stuart, the third Earl of Bute (1713–92), who had advised at Kew, had botanic gardens at his own properties of Kenwood, Luton Hoo, Bedfordshire, and Highcliffe in Hampshire. Despite his resistance to the new Linnaean nomenclature, Bute was commemorated by Linnaeus who named a genus after him, though perhaps Linnaeus took some mild revenge by misspelling his name in "Stewartia," which by botanical rules cannot be corrected.

SHRUBBERIES

The idea that the eighteenth-century garden was devoid of color, flowers, and intimate planting, which held sway for so long, was banished once and for all by Mark Laird in his groundbreaking and transformational book *The Flowering of the Landscape Garden* (1999). Through a mixture of archival research, field archaeology, and visitors' descriptions, it has been possible to reconstruct (if imperfectly because incompletely) an idea of how those most ephemeral of garden features, shrubberies and flower gardens, might have looked at the time. As a result of such investigations, not only has our knowledge of these features increased substantially, but there has been in recent years a number of restorations in historic gardens of shrubberies planted according to eighteenth-century patterns and principles. Among many examples may be cited Painshill, Stowe, Croome Park, and Osterley. While it cannot be claimed that the results are entirely historically accurate, because minute details of plantings will never be known, the appearance of such shrubberies is at least of the period and has added enormous appeal and interest to the effect of some very well-known landscape gardens.

A shrub is basically a woody plant, smaller than a tree though sometimes it can attain the height of one. A shrubbery should, accordingly, consist of a collection of such plants and appear as a group of bushes. However, the eighteenth-century shrubbery might contain slim trees as well as shrubs, and herbaceous (non-woody) material might also be introduced, thus blurring the definition. The shrubs would often be of a flowering kind, which made the presence of flowers per se entirely compatible. The word *shrubbery* appears for the first time in 1748, according to the OED, when Lady Luxborough wrote to William Shenstone about her garden at Barrels, Warwickshire. She does not use the word self-consciously as a coinage: indeed her use of it is matter of fact, as if the word were commonplace, and by 1749 both correspondents were employing it freely.

Shrubberies, as they developed, particularly after 1750, fell into two categories. Either they formed a self-contained assemblage or acted as a more diffuse bordering of a straight or meandering path. Philip Southcote at his *ferme ornée* at Woburn Farm, Surrey had had a circuit walk that from time to time wove through a border on each side consisting of flowers at the front, shrubs in the middle, and trees at the back. A similar walk was created by "Dickie" Bateman at Grove House, Old Windsor at an equally early date (the 1730s). Even if *shrubbery* was not the appropriate word for these early essays, the idea of the ornamental circuit path led to later developments that can be recognized as shrubberies.

The idea of the gradated or graduated shrubbery, structured in tiers from small at the front to large at the back, was termed *theatrical shrubbery*. Mark Laird's book gives many examples of both theatrical and nontheatrical shrubberies, and there are several surprises. Principal among these is Lancelot "Capability" Brown's interest in shrubberies—at estates such as Croome Court, Worcestershire; Syon House, Middlesex; Petworth, Sussex; and Belhus, Essex, he spent considerable time and trouble working on them. An estate did not necessarily have to be large—actor David Garrick's small riverside lawn at Hampton, Middlesex sported a range of plantings including two (suitably) theatrical shrubberies.

Slightly larger and just down the river from Hampton was Horace Walpole's Gothic confection of Strawberry Hill, where a circuit walk wandered through woods and where shrubs aplenty were found, whether in groups or forming a graduated shrubbery next to the house. The plants provided a great deal of color, justifying Walpole's description of his garden as "*riant*": syringas, honeysuckles, lilac, and several attractive trees such as the robinia, Chinese arbor vitae and (of course) a strawberry tree.

A shrubbery walk was often part of the longer circuit walk, and might well take the form of lines of laurel. At Croome, for example, a recreation of Brown's shrubbery furnishes planting on both sides of the path down the hill toward Robert Adam's glorious orangery. At Stowe, the path along the upper side of the Grecian Valley leads through a replanted shrubbery, giving flavor to the entry into the pleasure grounds. At Painshill, several shrubberies served different purposes. One was near the house, providing exotics of particular botanical interest inside and outside an orangery; another clothed the zigzag paths down from the Gothic temple and on the level toward the Chinese bridge; and island beds and shrubberies decorated the "Elysian plain," the plateau in the vicinity of the Temple of Bacchus.

Shrubberies could adorn both formal and informal layouts. In the garden of Carlton House, where William Kent was supposed to have initiated the idea of laying out grounds "without level or line," the design, though still in fact quite geometrical, incorporated flowers and shrubbery planting. William Woollett's engraving of 1760 was twenty-five years after Kent's work, so may represent some later thinking, especially with regard to the lower-growing species, but there is evidence that shrubs, climbers, bulbs, and flowers were supplied in profusion,[10] and the overall effect was immensely colorful. Figure 3.2 shows

FIGURE 3.2: *View of the garden at Carlton House*, engraved by William Woollett, 1760. Author's collection.

the engraving, in which we can see arcaded hedges, flower beds, and a good deal of shrubby underplanting around the trees.

FLOWER GARDENS

Flower gardens were often, though by no means always, the province of the woman of the house, and designs were accordingly made to suit her. Thus, among the most well-known gardens of the time were those designed for the Duchess of Beaufort at Badminton and Netheravon, Wiltshire; for Lady Burlington at Chiswick; for Princess Augusta at Kew; for the Duchess of Portland at Bulstrode; the "Ladies Garden" at Redlynch, Somerset; and for Lady Elizabeth Lee at Hartwell, Buckinghamshire. The gardens presented one main annual display—the practice of "bedding out" and changing the display two or three times a year did not come in until Victorian times—and the garden would be a discrete area with a recognizable identity. Beds, and their design, could vary immensely from a simple circle or ellipse to a series of irregular or mathematically worked out shapes.

Flower gardens usually consisted of small areas of lawn with beds of various sizes and shapes, focused on a garden pavilion, and were found in large gardens from the 1730s. William Kent designed Lady Burlington's at Chiswick, while "Dickie" Bateman devised two at Grove House as part of a circuit walk around a large meadow. These were the pioneers, but they were followed by a large number not only of flower gardens but flowerbeds which might not in themselves constitute a full garden. Thomas Wright, mathematician and garden designer, proposed flower gardens for Badminton and Netheravon (the first not executed), and used his geometrical skills to draw up intricate patterns for a "rosary" flower garden for Beckett Park, Berkshire, consisting of intersecting circles imposed on flower beds, or beds inserted between the lines.

About 1762, William Chambers laid out a flower garden at Kew in front of the aviary. A small central basin in the quatrefoil shape beloved of "Gothick" architects was echoed by four beds around it with the same curves. Beyond a circling path around these beds lay a radial pattern of small individual beds divided by paths that connected with the outermost encircling path. At about the same time, the "Ladies Garden" at Redlynch, the seat of Stephen Fox, the first Earl of Ilchester, was created as a series of small irregular beds centered on a pavilion and accessed by a serpentine walk through clumps of shrubs.

"Capability" Brown, not known for his love of flowers, nonetheless included several floral features in his designs for landscape parks. At Petworth, Sussex, his shrubbery clumps would have had flowers at the front, and nearly twenty years later (1771) he was still proposing a circular flower garden and serpentine path for Lowther Castle, Westmorland, and the following year a flower garden in the shape of a flower for Brocklesby, Lincolnshire, and for "Miss Constable's garden" at Burton Constable, Yorkshire.

The most famous of all flower gardens was the one known as Mason's Garden, after poet-gardener William Mason, at Nuneham Courtenay, Oxfordshire. The heir to the property, Lord Nuneham, created a flower garden that became overgrown and disorderly, much to the displeasure of his father, the first Earl Harcourt, returning home after duty away. The first Earl preferred a more formal approach, along the lines of Chambers's flower garden at Kew, but the plan was referred to Mason, who suggested a compromise. The result, implemented from 1773, saw a range of kidney-shaped beds edged with box and arranged irregularly on a lawn. In 1777, Paul Sandby composed two watercolors of the garden, engraved by William Watts. Figure 3.3 shows the beds, with the conservatory wall to the left, in a view looking toward the focal Temple of Flora. Planting is of the tiered, graduated fashion. There was a serious,

P. Sandby pinx.²   W. Watts sculp

View of the Flower Garden at Nuneham, from the Statue of Hebe, to the Temple of Flora

Published according to the Act by G. Kearsly, at N.º 46 in Fleet Street Aug.¹ 1777

FIGURE 3.3: *View of the flower garden at Nuneham Courtenay*, engraved by William Watts after Paul Sandby, 1777. Author's collection.

moral side to this garden, which had a circuit walk, inscriptions, urns, and busts. Lord Nuneham wrote a description that laid emphasis on the inscriptions and the sentiments consequently evoked. The flowers were intended to uplift as well as please, and cultivated and wild flowers were mingled in the beds to express freedom. In later years, the garden became more "romantic" with festooned bowers and the beds treated as shrubberies drifting on to a forest lawn.

A few years later, Placido Columbani (following an earlier proposal from Richard Woods) designed the Elysian Garden for Sir John Griffin at Audley End, Essex. Reached by a tunnel arch, this garden opened up into a secluded spot bounded by evergreens. A blue and white circular tent, rockwork, a cascade, and Robert Adam's Teahouse Bridge complemented the plantings of azaleas, geraniums, roses, magnolias, kalmias, and rhododendrons. Undulating paths wove round the garden, which lay on both sides of a stretch of water.

Although flower gardens were often designed for women, it is unusual to find one created by a woman, as is the case at Hartwell, where Lady Elizabeth Lee designed a number of circular, elliptical, and kidney-shaped beds for a plot well away from the house in 1799. Detailed plantings are indicated in sixteen sketches for these beds, enabling the main circular bed to be re-created as the centerpiece in the walled garden at Painshill, where there is an exhibition of eighteenth-century plantings and introductions. Lady Elizabeth was the sister of the second Earl Harcourt, and thus had a family connection with Mason's Garden at Nuneham Courtenay, which was clearly an influence.

In 1797, a plan was drawn up for a flower garden at Kenwood, north London. What is interesting is that the shape of the beds (mostly thin crescent moons) echoes the sort of design that would have been cut out in turf in an embroidered parterre of a century earlier. Humphry Repton worked at Kenwood in the 1790s, but the plan is not in his hand. However, he was keen on introducing flower gardens in a varied series of small gardens near the house in some of his commissions after 1800 (Ashridge, Hertfordshire, and Endsleigh, Devon are the best examples). He had, in fact, shown a taste for them early in his career, at Courteenhall, Northamptonshire in 1791. His proposal for Lady Wake's flower garden shows a radiating petal-like pattern, together with a separate "corbeille" (a circular bed edged generally with basketwork).

LINNAEUS AND THE BINOMIAL SYSTEM

The world of botany and plant identification was transformed by the work of Swede Carl Linnaeus (1707–78). During a stay in the Netherlands, he published a number of works including *Systema Naturae* (1735) and *Genera*

Plantarum (1737), in which he developed the system of classification known as his "sexual system," based on the number of stamens and stigmas of plants. This led to the publication of his *Species Plantarum* (1753), which represents the foundation of modern botanical nomenclature. Up to that time there had been a number of systems for naming plants, such as John Ray's or Tournefort's classifications, which usually involved a long, cumbersome description in Latin. The binomial system devised by Linnaeus was a brilliant simplification and also an effective and convincing means of classification. Although it has subsequently been subject to change and challenge, it has remained the basis of modern taxonomy. In essence, the two-word name of a plant, for example, *Quercus suber* (cork oak), gives the genus first and the species within the genus second. Varieties or special forms can be indicated by a third name, so that the common yew is *Taxus baccata* and the upright Irish yew *Taxus baccata* var. *fastigiata*.

The binomial system spread with varying degrees of rapidity across Europe and the botanical world. In Britain, it was taken up quickly in some quarters, but Philip Miller, the doyen of botanists and the author of the *Gardener's Dictionary* (1731 and subsequently), remained obstinate for a while, being a loyal follower of Ray and Tournefort. Not until the seventh edition of the dictionary (1759) did he acknowledge the Linnaean system, while full adoption of the binomial nomenclature had to wait until the eighth and last edition (1768).

Linnaeus's classification had enormous impact on the whole business of collecting and growing plants and trees. It meant, for example, that plants traveling from one part of the world to another could be identified and recognized, and it also provided a universal language of identification. Prior to Linnaeus, confusion in terminology could result in an owner or collector ordering a specimen he later found he already had. It was also a much more scientific way of understanding botany and thus in tune with Enlightenment ways of thinking.

CONTINENTAL PLANTINGS

In mainland Europe, we find considerable evidence of plantings that varied and expanded according to the era and the availability of new species. In France, Louis XIV had imported mature trees (few of which survived) mostly from the royal forests in the north to sustain the groves, avenues, and bosquets of Versailles, but at the Grand Trianon and at Marly he indulged in floriculture on a vast and intensive scale. At the Trianon, the displays were stupendous, with ninety-six thousand flowers and two million plants sunk in pots. There was a "Cabinet des Parfums" for the rarest scented flowers, and others could be found in borders, plate-bandes, pots, vases, and parterres. At Marly, eighteen million bulbs were planted in four years, and flowers vied with shrubs and trees for magnificent effect.[11] All this was, however, for the king's greater glory, and is very different from later eighteenth-century plantings, which reflected an approach much more in tune with the Enlightenment. In 1759, Louis XV started what was to become one of the most important botanical gardens in Europe at the Trianon, with the advice of botanist Bernard de Jussieu (who adopted the Linnaean system) and the father-and-son chief gardeners, Claude and Antoine Richard. In turn, Marie-Antoinette transferred the botanical collection to the Jardin des Plantes in Paris, while establishing an early Alpine garden with appropriate planting at the Petit Trianon. Other impulses came from John-Jacques Rousseau, whose pursuit of the natural led to the cultivation of wild flowers, and the Abbé Nolin, who collected widely from the French colonies.

There was also the suiting of planting to mood along with a growing romantic sensibility: thus the Valley of the Tombs at Betz was planted with melancholy species—Italian poplars, cypress, and thujas. This can also be observed in some German romantic gardens of the time such as Seifersdorfertal.

The Netherlands supported a large number of nurseries, not only providing bulbs for use at home but supplying many other countries. In Italy, the impetus for planting had perhaps died down from its peak in the great Renaissance botanic gardens, but it should be remembered that Venice remained a gateway to the East, furnishing imports from the Near and Far East of all kinds including plants, some from China. Bulbs from the Netherlands appeared in Italian parterres, followed by a renewal of interest in fruit and flowers from far away, this time in a more natural setting.[12]

THE EFFECT OF PLANTINGS

The introduction of exotics changed the face of the landscape garden. In the early eighteenth century, when formality reigned in the garden, the range of species was small and generally predictable. Native species were used for lining avenues—lime, elm, beech, horse chestnut—and were planted more for geometrical than botanical reasons. Occasionally there would be a variation in the type of tree grown, such as the "abele walk" at Stowe composed of white poplars, but by and large avenues and walks were intended to impress rather than to provide novelty.

Even when William Kent and others began to challenge geometry in the 1730s and to suggest more naturalistic ways of planting, the palette was for a time still restricted. Kent, from his decade in Italy, drew Italianate impressions of scenes in gardens he was working on, with such characteristic Mediterranean trees as the cypress and stone pine depicted, but both species were well established in Britain by that time anyway. In fact, a number of trees had come into Britain in the seventeenth century that, by the time of the landscape garden, could be said to have become naturalized—the larch (1620), robinia, cedar of Lebanon, and swamp cypress (all 1640s), tulip tree (1650), black walnut (1656), the liquidambar (1690), and scarlet oak (1691). All could in theory have been found in gardens of the early eighteenth century, but in practice few were until the advent of the landscape garden and the influx of other introductions.

Kent did, however, struggle to introduce some realism into planting, even if sometimes he strained too far: Horace Walpole tells us he placed dead trees for naturalistic effect in Kensington Gardens but was laughed out of such excess.[13]

Walpole gave credit to the Duke of Argyll for providing the motivation and momentum for introducing exotics into the landscape, thereby transforming its appearance:

> The introduction of foreign trees and plants, which we owe principally to Archibald duke of Argyle, contributed essentially to the richness of colouring so peculiar to our modern landscape. The mixture of various greens, the contrast of forms between our forest-trees and the northern and West-Indian' [=American] firs and pines, are improvements more recent than Kent, or but little known to him. The weeping-willow and every florid shrub, each tree of delicate or bold leaf, are new tints in the composition of our gardens.[14]

The effects were noticeable and remarked on by visitors: German architect F. W. von Erdmannsdorff, visiting Painshill in September 1763, commented that most of the garden looked like a wood or forest, and that since it had a large number of different foreign trees it displayed a landscape with a wonderful variety of colors.[15]

While many owners took full advantage of the introduction of exotics to add visual appeal to their gardens, the landscapes laid out by "Capability" Brown were, in general, confined to a limited range of natives, beech predominating. At Bowood, indeed, his contract specifically barred him from dealing with exotics.[16] The reason is twofold: Brown's designs were often simplified and minimalist in terms of decoration, and he was aiming at an essentially idealized English scene, so traditional timber was required.

The volume of introductions also meant an increase in shrubberies away from the house and the use of underplanting; in other words, shrubs or flowers planted around trees or in woods. Such underplanting was used in the woods at Rousham, Oxfordshire and in the groves designed by Joseph Spence, who, for instance, planned the planting of larch, almond, acacia, and cherry with an understory of honeysuckle, jasmine, and laurustinus.[17] The result of such mixed plantings can be seen in William Woollett's 1760 print of the lake and grotto island at Painshill. Mark Laird has identified the plantings, which illustrate Hamilton's varied approach.[18] To the left of the bridge is a shrubbery acting as a screen, with a tall larch in front and what is probably an elm. Slightly behind is a clump of elm or oak. On the right of the bridge, on the grotto island, are three trees in the foreground: a spruce, a pine, and a robinia. The latter is underplanted with laurel, and the young cedars further back appear also to be underplanted. The screen on the left is, as Thomas Whately described it, "composed of the most elegant trees, full of the lightest greens, and bordered with shrubs and with flowers."[19] Although the experience of going round Painshill was multilayered in any case, the plantings contributed immeasurably to the sense of variety and contrast.

FIGURE 3.4: *View of the lake and the west side of grotto island at Painshill*, engraving by William Woollett, 1760. Author's collection.

BRITISH GARDENERS ABROAD

Plants and knowledge about how to grow them were often disseminated by gardeners who had trained at nurseries or worked in gardens in Britain and then found employment on the continent. As the landscape garden spread in popularity in Europe, the demand for those experienced in cultivating it in Britain increased. Continental owners and rulers often asked specifically for a British gardener to come over and create such a garden for them, which would involve laying down turf and lawns and the planting of trees and shrubs as well as park design. Knowledge of growing tender exotics in hothouses was also sought, so there was botanical as well as landscape input.

Sometimes continental gardeners would come to Britain to learn techniques and acquire planting knowledge. Thus, German gardeners came to learn at John Busch's nursery in Hackney (he was himself of German origin). Owners might come over to England themselves to study either gardening or agricultural improvement, such as Prince Franz of Anhalt-Dessau, who visited Bowood specifically for the latter purpose.

Thomas Blaikie, a Scottish gardener, spent most of his working life in France, though he never troubled to master French. As well as creating landscape gardens he traveled around France and recorded his visits with some contempt for French ideas of the English garden. He encouraged gardeners from England and Scotland to go to France, and while on occasional visits back to Britain collected plants for his French employers.

Johann Graefer, German by birth, trained in England under John Busch at Hackney and also under Philip Miller. After working for Lord Coventry at Croome Court and James Vere at Kensington Gore, he joined the nursery firm of Thomson and Gordon in Mile End, east London, around 1776. In 1786, at the instigation of the queen of Naples and Sicily, Graefer went over to Naples to create a fifty-acre English-style garden to one side of the fabulous baroque layout at Caserta. This included a vegetable and a botanic garden as well as many ornamental features. Gravel was imported from Kensington and exotics obtained from Hammersmith nursery. The year 1789 saw the publication (in England) of his *Descriptive Catalogue* of over eleven hundred plants, an important work that covered name, size, suitability of soil, time of flowering, color, and native country. Intended mainly for a British readership, the catalogue nonetheless contained a good many plants from Italy.

The Haverfield dynasty that dominated both Kew and Richmond Gardens as gardeners from 1758 (Kew) to 1795 (Richmond) produced a scion who, after working at Kew, moved to Schloss Friedenstein, Gotha, Germany, where an English-style park was created from 1769. Haverfield (first name uncertain) took with him a number of exotics from Kew.

Russia, principally as a consequence of the Anglomania of Catherine the Great, embraced the landscape garden eagerly and sought British architects and gardeners. Charles Cameron, Catherine's favorite architect, not only designed part of the palace and some garden buildings at Tsarskoye Selo, but at Pavlovsk was responsible for palace, garden buildings, and design of the park. Of the gardeners, John Busch and his son Joseph were perhaps the best known, working mainly at Tsarskoye Selo. Originating from Hanover, John Busch set up his Hackney nursery in 1756, and when he moved to Russia in 1771 at Catherine's invitation, he brought with him a knowledge of plants that enabled him, particularly by means of hothouses, to grow fruits and plants previously unknown there or that would have been expected to fail.

Other British gardeners in Russia included the Sparrow brothers, who worked mostly at Gatchina, another of the royal gardens; James Hackett, who continued at Gatchina after the Sparrows; William Gould, who landscaped the Taurida Palace gardens in St. Petersburg; James Meader, who laid out the English park (now destroyed) adjacent to the grand formal gardens at Peterhof; and several others, Scottish gardeners in particular.

The exodus of gardeners to Russia had benefits back in England. John Busch, shortly after his arrival in Russia, sent Lord Coventry a box of Russian plants including ferns, birch, aloe, lilies, and rhododendrons. In addition, the popularity of the English garden in Russia prompted the exchange of several specimens from Siberia, such as the bergenia, an aconite, and the sedum (*Sedum populifolium*) now so familiar in British gardens.

An Irish gardener, Denis McClair, went to Poland in 1790 at the request of Princess Izabela Czartoryska, who was already employing an English gardener and designer, James Savage, at her well-known park at Puławy. McClair (rendered in Polish as "Mikler Dionisy") worked briefly both there and at Arkadia, another famous landscape park, before establishing an extensive practice creating gardens in the landscape style, particularly in eastern Poland, in the early nineteenth century. He sent *Rhododendron luteum*, among other specimens, back to Britain.

The planting scene in the eighteenth century was, accordingly, a vibrant one in which plants increasingly crossed continents, generating excitement in collectors and creating new possibilities in the appearance and design of gardens. The range of form, color, size, and shape available was infinitely expanded during the century, giving impetus to the freedom expressed in the landscape garden and to a new floriferous approach to gardens.

CHAPTER FOUR

Use and Reception

DAVID LAMBERT

This chapter starts with the premise that the meaning of historic gardens is culturally determined and resides in the ways we represent them today. As Stuart Hall has observed, things or places in themselves "rarely if ever have any one, single, fixed and unchanging meaning. . . It is by our use of things, and what we say, think and feel about them—how we represent them—that we *give them a meaning*."[1]

The eighteenth-century garden is, as much as any other thing or place, subject to this filtering and evolution in contemporary culture. Thus, for example, Lyme Park in Cheshire is now, for all its colorful history as the seat of the Leg family for nearly 600 years, inextricably linked for millions with Jane Austen: as the National Trust's online guide announces, like a showground barker, "Famous scene in *Pride & Prejudice* (1995) where Darcy emerges from a lake was filmed here."[2]

My second basic premise is about the products of elite culture in general. As Walter Benjamin advised:

[C]ultural treasures have an origin which [we] cannot contemplate without horror. They owe their existence not only to the efforts of the great minds and talents who have created them, but also to the anonymous toil of their contemporaries. There is no document of civilization which is not at the same time a document of barbarism.[3]

Unearthing more of that origin and that anonymous toil is critical to establishing a wider sense of elite culture's value as national heritage.

MORE THAN ONE POINT OF VIEW

There is more than one point of view in looking at a historic garden today. History is about power and conflict: as Michel Foucault observed, the past is not "an acquisition, a possession that grows and solidifies; rather it is an unstable assemblage of faults, fissures and heterogeneous layers that threaten the fragile inheritor from within or from underneath."[4] In practice, interpretation and presentation of history often construct a spurious coherence from a selective use of historical data.

While partial points of view have dominated the presentation of country houses and their designed landscapes, recent years have seen a dawning awareness of this shortcoming. In 1997, English Heritage published a modest leaflet entitled *Sustaining the Historic Environment*. This document was significant in heralding a shift in thinking on the historic environment, suggesting that "it owes its present value and significance to people's perceptions and opinions, or in other words to their personal beliefs and values." Hence, the expert evaluation of significance needs to be counterbalanced by a recognition of the "value of local perception and . . . of other people's non-expert values." This paved the way, theoretically at least, for a heritage discourse that acknowledges the pluralist nature of history and of significance.

HERITAGE AND INHERENT VALUE

Just as meaning is produced, so, in modern conservation terminology, is value or significance. Hall's insistence that meaning is culturally constructed is evident in modern thinking on heritage:

> While places, sites, objects and localities may exist as identifiable sites of heritage . . . these sites are not *inherently* valuable, nor do they carry a freight of inherent meaning. . . What makes these things valuable and meaningful . . . are the present-day cultural processes and activities that are undertaken at and around them, and of which they become a part.[5]

In other words, what is conserved is what those in power want to conserve, its wider value being established retrospectively.

In the United Kingdom, this can be seen in the rise of the country house as national heritage. The country house and its park were not always viewed as icons of a shared heritage. This significance was constructed in the twentieth century, for example, in the pages of *Country Life* in the 1930s; in the postwar acquisitions of the National Trust; in the work of SAVE Britain's Heritage in the '70s and '80s; or in the Victoria and Albert Museum exhibition, "The Destruction of the Country House, 1875–1975." Prior to this, there was little sense that the nation at large had a stake in the country house.[6]

In establishing its Country House Scheme in 1936, the National Trust embarked on saving these places well in advance of public support for "such a symbol of conspicuous 'taste' and social inequality," because of the political power of those who wished to save them.[7] Subsequently, the heritage agencies have, with more or less success, sought to legitimize this policy by developing ways of presenting them more inclusively. This is what interpretation does.

Elsewhere, debate over meaning/s and significance/s likewise challenges heritage management. The significance of the World Heritage Site at Riversleigh, in northern Queensland, for example—designated in 1994 for its fossil fields—is the subject of an ongoing contest between the Aboriginal community, mining companies, tourism companies, and local government.[8]

INTERPRETATION AND COMPLEXITY

Hall defines "representation" of things, or in this case, places, as "the words we use about them, the stories we tell about them, the images of them we produce, the emotions we associate with them, the way we classify and conceptualise them, the values we place on them." Interpretation is, then, not the innocent matter of *translating* between a past language and the present; rather, in *re-presenting* these places, using certain words and images, certain concepts, often unexamined, we are in effect, making them anew. Meaning is a "dialogue" between the past and the present, "always only partially understood, always an unequal exchange . . . [it] is produced rather than simply found."[9]

Heritage interpretation needs to recognize the complexity of history, its "profusion of entangled events."[10] Referring to the archaeological interpretation of the Paca garden in Anapolis, Maryland, Dan Hicks has written in favor of an "awareness of contingency and complexity . . . to replace the emphasis upon meaning with more nuanced approaches" and a new approach "constructing moments at which multiple levels exist at once—provisional stabilities that resist epistemological closure."[11]

Current practice on interpretation tends to eschew complexity in favor of simplification. An authoritative British guide to interpretation advises that "a reading age of 9–12 is a good level at which to write your text." It adds, "there is nothing more off-putting than too many words on a panel or leaflet. . . Keep it short and simple!" The preferred textual style addresses the reader in the first person, using metaphors and analogies ("Jays are a bit like us. When we're hungry we pop to the fridge for some food. . .") and direct questions ("Can you imagine living here during the [Highland] Clearances. . .?"). It concludes, "Always keep your audience in mind and talk to them using simple and clear conversational language . . . let your writing tell a story." While no one should underestimate the difficulty of explaining to a modern audience cultural meanings that may be hundreds of years old, it is hard to avoid the inference that such simplification is a reductive process.[12]

Interpretation also needs to understand the multiple contemporary perspectives on historic sites. The origins of a site, and its anonymous toil, represent stories that potentially can appeal widely, but in practice most interpretation is not so "nuanced"; it is restricted not only by the editorial choices of professionals but also by the available data, and data on anonymous toil is in short supply. In practice, there is simply not room for the hooks that might engage every possible visitor. As a result, while it is true that efforts are being made to interpret sites with a wider potential audience in mind, at present it remains the case that most country house presentation is characterized by a "lack of social commentary and the exclusion of working areas of houses on visitors' tour routes."[13]

INTERPRETATION AND MARKETING

Interpretation's shadow is marketing: they are frequently addressed in a single strategy document for a heritage site. And the marketing of a site—its advertisements, events, and retail activities—also implies a version of history, an interpretation. This discourse is more pervasive and far-reaching than the guidebook, and almost invariably unexamined.

Marketing is big business and increasingly critical to the funding of a historic property. The fact that the target audience of many properties is the middle-class homeowner, for example, is reflected in the expansion of modern guidebooks beyond a technical catalogue or itinerary to include a section along the lines of "Living at Knightshayes" or "Saltram and its Owners" or "The Leghs and Lyme"; that is, the country house as a home; Castle Howard's advertising strap line is "There's no place like this home."[14] On the contrary, very few guidebooks describe the experience of working in a country house or garden.[15]

As Laurajane Smith notes, "above all else, these houses are about power; their architectural design is not about ensuring a sense of 'home,' but is an explicit statement about the status and power of the family within."[16] Marketing involves minimizing that power and emphasizing the domestic. Increasingly, most noticeably in the shops, but also in the marketing of National Trust paints and wallpaper and in the sale of garden furniture and tools, the emphasis is on the relationship of the country house to the home of the visitor affluent enough to visit the site and then to buy into the commodities on sale; that is, the historic house and garden as lifestyle.

Thus at Chatsworth, one of the most successful private brands, it is claimed that the "spectacular shop" "reflects aspects of country house living—from the still room to the drawing room." It specializes not in objects designed as mementos of the visit—that is, objects that embody one's inferior status as a visitor—but instead, reproductions of china, tinware, and sculpture in the house itself, by which visitors can vicariously buy into the role of owner. The garden shop offers a similar faux authenticity in the sale of plants grown on the estate.[17]

The "visitor experience" is increasingly stand alone, or parallel to direct experience of the place and its strangeness; not only mediated by but replaced by the experience of the visitor center, the shop, and the restaurant. The guide to interpretation cited earlier states, "the real product is the interpretation not the building."[18] It can sometimes seem almost impossible to directly confront the place itself: Colonial Williamsburg has become the symbol of a "theme park" approach to heritage, with actors, reconstructions, and stage sets, all simplifying and sanitizing the past.[19]

The confusion is perhaps irresolvable. Cultural critic Michael Bywater has made the interesting observation in relation to "heritage" branding, for example the use of Victorian lettering and archaic language, that a genuinely old-fashioned item had "become its own avatar": "by insisting, semiotically, on its own authenticity, it had mythologised itself at the cost of the authenticity upon which it was insisting."[20] We can see the phenomenon everywhere; any drive along a country lane will sooner or later reveal a pub decorated not only with its name board but with an additional sign announcing "Country Pub" or "Traditional Village Pub." And perhaps too we see it in the sign or guidebook that announces a "historic garden."

THE AGE OF CONSERVATION

For better or worse, we live in an era of conservation. Modernist architect Frederick Gibberd thought it for the worse: "Preservation is a symbol of a culture in decline," he wrote in 1982.[21] Since the eighties, the failings of "the heritage industry" have been analyzed and derided as a symptom of such a culture.[22] But now, with membership of heritage organizations outstripping that of political parties, the evidence of popular participation in heritage requires a more measured response than mere dismissal.[23]

Smith has pointed out that "heritage tourism may have more deeply layered or nuanced cultural and social meaning and consequence than its characterization as a leisure activity and economic industry often allows."[24] Cultural historians such as Marxist Raphael Samuel have argued against such dismissiveness, asserting that heritage is a far richer and more socially diverse phenomenon than liberal critics allow.[25]

But if this is an era of conservation, it has recently also become an era of doubt among conservationists. Over the last ten years, conservation agencies have engaged in a prolonged bout of soul searching over the issue of broadening intellectual and physical access. This is partly a result of the professionalization of heritage management, which has necessitated a more rigorous approach to decision making; it is also a result of the need to justify conservation expenditure in an era of competitive bidding for funds from public sources.

In the United Kingdom over the last decade, English Heritage published *Power of Place* (2000) based on the first major survey of public attitudes toward the historic environment; the Heritage Lottery Fund published *Broadening the Horizons of Heritage* (2002), as well as advice on Audience Development Plans and Access Plans; in 2006, Heritage Link launched *Embracing Difference*, a program to encourage the participation of minorities in heritage; and in 2007, the National Trust launched a major consultation on what its future priorities should be, *Join In*. These bodies are all reexamining their contribution not to conservation but to social justice.

HISTORIC GARDENS IN AN AGE OF CONSERVATION

The conservation of historic gardens is a latecomer to the heritage sector. In the United Kingdom, ancient monuments have been protected and conserved since the Ancient Monuments Act of 1882 and the founding of the Royal Commission for Historic Monuments in 1908; buildings since the 1947 Town and Country Planning Act; natural habitats since the setting up of the Nature Conservancy and establishing of national Nature Reserves and Sites of Special Scientific Interest in 1949; townscapes have been protected since the creation of Conservation Areas in the 1967 Civic Amenities Act. In contrast, parks and gardens have only been technically historic since the establishment of the

English Heritage Register of parks and gardens in 1983, and unlike these other interests, still have no statutory protection in the planning system.

As a result, conservation of historic parks and gardens has borrowed many of its practices and thus legitimacy from the older, more well-established disciplines. Axioms such as "conserve as found" borrowed from the conservation of ancient monuments, or the principles laid down in various international charters, are applied to parks and gardens as a way of including them in the family of conservation interests. Unfortunately, many of these principles fit more or less uneasily with the specific nature of parks and gardens.

For example, the authoritative UNESCO Burra Charter (1979, rewritten 1999) prioritizes fabric, when for gardens, fabric is necessarily evanescent. It distinguishes between restoration—subtracting from fabric—and reconstruction—adding to fabric—when replacement of fabric is essential to landscape management. At the heart of conserving historic gardens lie the twin processes of cutting back and planting—removing fabric and adding new. To try to legitimize garden conservation in terms derived from monuments is a hopeless task: preservation cannot be applied to living, dying things. As Stewart Harding has commented: "Fabric in gardens is in the end not the object of conservation. It is the meanings and the sensual, spiritual and visual aspects of parks and gardens which are of the greatest importance. Conserving fabric can seriously and negatively impact on the conservation of these less tangible aspects."[26]

Related to this preoccupation with material fabric, "authenticity" is a touchstone in conservation management. It has dominated Western thinking about historic buildings since the days of William Morris and the founding of the SPAB, and has been referred to as "the near-sacred calling of heritage professionals towards authentic fabric."[27] Again, it has been imported from buildings and monuments practice into garden conservation, but it is highly problematic in a heritage asset the fabric of which is growing and short-lived. Not only is the material itself in a process of constant change, but its landscape effects, the spaces and vistas it frames, are also inherently changeable and vulnerable to that change. It could indeed be argued that material authenticity is at odds with design authenticity if the material now blocks a vista or dwarfs a building.

RECEPTION OF HISTORIC GARDENS—THREE EXAMPLES

If the dominant professional discourse on conservation still fails to accommodate the requirements of historic landscapes, so the dominant discourse on interpretation fails to reflect the potential audience. This is especially ironic given that parks and gardens potentially offer an experience that by its nature is more accessible than most types of heritage. John Dixon Hunt has referred to the sensuous, "haptic" qualities of the experience of landscape[28]; Neil Higson, for many years the lead landscape architect for the Milton Keynes Development Corporation, has spoken of "the labyrinth of freedom that is landscape architecture."[29] By their very nature, gardens are literally living heritage, not requiring any resuscitation to bring them to life. The breadth of public interest in gardening, embracing all aspects from vegetable growing to TV shows on garden makeovers, and the surprisingly long tradition of permitted public access to private parks, should make connecting historic parks and gardens to contemporary life a relatively straightforward proposition. In practice, results are mixed.

At Studley Royal, the National Trust's new (award-winning) visitor center is located close to Fountains Abbey, which stands at one end of the historic garden. In a triumph for architectural antiquarianism, however, the trust's route takes the visitor into the garden via the abbey. This is like entering a theater via backstage, for the abbey, acquired after much effort by William Aislabie in 1768, was designed as the culminating focal point of walks that approached it from the other end of the canal, so that it was seen at a distance in a landscape frame. The trust's arrangement destroys the garden's great dramatic effect at a stroke. Very few visitors approach from the Ripon end, where the descent through parkland to the lake offers the great landscape experience of the garden unfolding to its climactic vista. Instead, the visitor walks from the abbey to the Ripon gate, then must turn and walk back to Aislabie's "Surprise View" of the ruin. The "Surprise View" is signposted by the trust without a trace of irony, likewise the quotation from Arthur Young in the guidebook: "Ruins generally appear best at a distance."[30]

Studley Royal offers a paradigm for the modern experience of the eighteenth-century garden. The audience has expanded exponentially, and the democratization of a formerly elite landscape is welcome, with ice creams for sale beside the lake and rugby balls taken on to the lawns of the water garden.[31] But at the same time as visitors obviously enjoy the landscape, the loss of an eighteenth-century way of seeing Studley Royal, the turning inside out of its greatest aesthetic effect, cannot be ignored. Democratization has failed to transfer a key element of the place's significance.

Elsewhere, we can see how elements of the significance of an eighteenth-century landscape can be eclipsed by other interests. At Hackfall, in north Yorkshire, Aislabie's sublime wooded walks hanging high over the valley of the river Ure have been managed by the Woodland Trust since 1989, with a

FIGURE 4.1: Visitor processing—the entrance to the visitor center at Studley Royal, October 2007. Photograph by David Lambert.

consequent emphasis on native woodland flora and fauna, which allowed the ornamental buildings to crumble and the designed vistas to disappear amidst a welter of new, self-sown trees. Fortunately, the establishment of a new Hackfall Trust, a grant from the Heritage Lottery Fund, and the restoration of the unique banqueting hall at Mowbray Point by the Landmark Trust should see this imbalance addressed.

Similarly, at Moccas Court in Herefordshire, the site's management is divided between a nature reserve in the old deer park run by the government agency, Natural England, and a country house hotel in the immediate park and garden. For Natural England, the park is primarily an ecosystem: as the foreword to its book on Moccas states, it took over the site when "parkland nature conservation strategies and the Veteran Trees Initiative were inconceivable . . . we were still up against ecologists who simply did not regard parkland as a form of woodland."[32] While the efforts of Natural England in conserving Moccas are admirable, to see a park on which both Brown and Repton worked as no more than "a form of woodland" represents a very different angle of approach from that of garden or cultural historians.[33]

However, it is a fact that designation for its nature conservation importance, as a Site of Special Scientific Interest in 1963, predates by over twenty
years any formal recognition of the importance of Moccas as a designed
landscape.[34]

REPRESENTATION: THE CONTEMPORARY PICTURESQUE

The apparently broad terms of Gilpin's original definition of the picturesque—
picturesque objects are those "capable of being illustrated in painting"—meant
in practice a rigorous, and now faintly comical, practice of selection, modifica-
tion, and exclusion.[35] The picturesque was a rigid aesthetic, dedicated to a very
particular way of seeing, concentrating with exquisite refinement on the surface of things, which can be characterized as a kind of relentless superficiality.

Gilpin of course dedicated many thousands of words to defining what he
meant. In contrast, the dominant contemporary aesthetic for representations
of historic gardens, as illustrated, for example, in the National Trust's sumptuous new book on its gardens, is accompanied by no such exegesis.[36] The
aesthetic is entirely unexamined, and yet, judging from the common features
shared by the photographs produced by different photographers, it is quite as
rigid as Gilpin's.

One review of the new book remarked that it was "a very attractive coffee
table book, full of high quality images"; another that "this is a book to dip
in and out of before and after visiting National Trust properties."[37] That is,
the images seduce and allure in their own right, preparing the way for a visit
to the place itself, as well as acting as a memento. Given the proliferation of
photographic and other modern media images, experience of the garden itself
is often preceded now by experience of representations of the garden. Photographs and other media images create a set of reference points, a visual and an
intellectual framework, for reception.

These images are powerful representations and complex signifiers. The
most obvious characteristic is that the gardens are empty of people. It has been
argued that the sight of a visitor dressed in today's fashion would instantly
place the image in a particular time, which would soon date, not something
that inhibited depictions in the eighteenth or nineteenth century, which invariably include figures. Gardeners too are absent, with garden labor represented
merely symbolically, for example by an artful composition of tools arranged in
the vegetable garden. These impressions of timelessness and effortlessness are
seductive, but both are political.

Second, it is notable that the aesthetic behind these representations pitches
itself at the purely visual, for example:

Stowe is the most complex of English gardens and for the full account of its conception, development and meaning, you should turn to John Martin Robinson's book, *Temples of Delight*. But no deep understanding is needed in order to appreciate its beauty—the open meadows, the lofty plantations of beech, lime, oak and chestnut with their yew, holly, cherry laurel and box understorey, the waterside fringes of alder and ash, and the golden architecture.[38]

While a picture can speak more effectively than words, at the same time it can also serve to forestall debate about meanings, whether historical or contemporary.

The third characteristic is the large number of close-ups, on a plant or a feature, excluding the physical context just as the text excludes, because it is too complex for the common reader, the intellectual or historical context. Thus the images of Stourhead, for example, are dominated by maples in the foreground, with the structures and the designed landscape obscured and relegated to the background.

Fourth, we note that anything considered "intrusive"—the telecommunications mast on the hilltop, the contrails of airplanes, the glitter of the roofs of parked cars—is carefully excluded, again editing out the contemporary physical context.

Thus it could be concluded that these representations prepare the visitor for an experience dominated by close-up inspection of plants and buildings, removed from their physical, intellectual, or design context. They also create a profound ambiguity in the visitor experience, namely the place of visitors in scenes consistently represented as devoid of human movement or activity, places produced with no labor, and in which there is no place for the visitor. Indeed, these representations subtly cast the visitor in the role of an intruder, out of place, disturbing the scene by his or her very presence. Their unspoken message is that when we enter these gardens, we do so, at some deep, even unconscious level, as trespassers. As we shall see, there are other ways of representing gardens and garden experience.

WAYS OF NOT SEEING: THREE EXAMPLES OF THE DEMEANING OF THE HISTORIC GARDEN

Interpretation acts as a cultural filter, omitting and editing on the basis of a largely unacknowledged set of presumptions. It also tends to create a powerful counterimage: thus, to refer to West Wycombe or Wentworth Woodhouse as "temple-strewn gardens," for example, is not just to fail to acknowledge the design intention behind those buildings, but also to erect an idea of frivolous extravagance that has proved a highly appealing simplification of what was going on in such gardens.[39]

This tendency culminated notoriously in the National Trust guide to "follies," lambasted by the New Arcadian Journal, *Blast Folly*.[40] This was a caustic attack on an approach that decontextualized garden architecture, that willfully ignored the serious intent behind many garden buildings and insisted on seeing them as mere architectural sports created out of whimsy or eccentricity. The New Arcadians demanded close reading of these buildings in their historical context, recognizing their role in the garden as a whole and their production in the context of eighteenth-century cultural politics.

Another way in which gardens are decontextualized is in their separation, both physically and in interpretation, from their original, much wider estate setting. Designed landscapes like Stowe were experienced through a network of ridings and drives around the estate as a whole, in which the garden was a core or climactic element. This way of viewing not only the garden but the park and the whole estate often also incorporated the home farm as a feature, and the enjoyment of enlightened agriculture and the patriotism it embodied was a key feature in sites such as Holkham, Shugborough, Woburn, or Wimpole.[41]

Hunt observes that, "how visitors experienced the extensive gardens relied on what is rarely acknowledged in modern commentary, the considerably larger territory belonging to an estate of which gardens were but a part."[42] But the problem is not just one of modern commentary but of landownership. The twentieth century saw the great estates broken up into ever smaller units, and most historic gardens are now mere fragments of larger wholes.

A third example of the reduction of meaning is the way in which the sexual element of much eighteenth-century garden design is removed in genteel interpretation. Gardens such as Castle Howard, Hackfall, Rousham, West Wycombe, Stowe, The Leasowes, and Stourhead have strong elements of sexual allusion built into their iconography and design.[43] And the molded forms and lush planting of the landscape garden are still more than capable of inspiring a libidinous response in viewers today. However, contemporary interpretation almost invariably edits out such cultural references, sacrificing a rich vein of entertainment and understanding for modern audiences.[44]

WAYS OF SEEING: FIVE ALTERNATIVE STRATEGIES

Preconditioned by selective visual imagery and marketing, mediated by interpretation and signage accessed via assorted visitor processing practices, ticketing, retail, and refreshment amenities, the contemporary experience of historic parks and gardens is a complicated matter. Once within the site, the visitor is still not at liberty, but guided and influenced by a range of hints, some overt, some covert; some consciously designed by managers, others inadvertent and unconscious. However, there are ways of accommodating a wider degree of freedom within a historic garden.

Stourhead Revisited

In the summer of 2002, under the aegis of head gardener Richard Higgs, the National Trust inserted into the landscape at Stourhead a number of modern reconstructions of vanished eighteenth-century features. Painted silhouettes of the statue of Apollo and the temple were erected on the terrace; the Chinese bridge was recreated in painted polythene on a suspended frame of wires; the Turkish tent was recreated by the local yurt company while the simple umbrello seat was rebuilt in contemporary materials. In addition, skiffs allowed visitors to see the grounds from the lake. The justification was to give visitors a deeper understanding of the eighteenth-century design. Interpretation boards accompanied each of the insertions, with tours led by guides in period costume. The installations saw a thirty-five percent increase in visitors, responding to this innovative approach to interpretation.

FIGURE 4.2: The painted polythene bridge at Stourhead, 2002. Photograph by David Lambert.

Aesthetically, it was a knowing nod to the often paper-thin theatricality of the eighteenth-century experience: no one aware of the extensive use of wood and plasterboard in the eighteenth century could object to the spirit of these installations. The structures challenged notions of authenticity too—while self-evidently pastiche in themselves, they were arguably authentic insertions in terms of the landscape as a whole, successfully restoring an authentic experience when viewed from a distance as part of an overall landscape composition. They also wittily encouraged a contemplative visitor to ask questions of our attitude to history and the line between history and heritage: a *tromp l'oeil* silhouette of a statue, found on examination to be only an inch or two thick, might suggest reflections on the nature of what we see when we look back at the distant past through the lens held up by the heritage industry.

In a commentary on the exercise, Higgs wrote: "Interpretation boards cluttering the landscape, actors destroying the peace and tranquillity, and visitors messing about in boats, can only be justified if this is done to interpret the significance of the garden, and in the spirit of the place. Whilst gardens often succeed best when they are totally naked of any interpretative material, *Stourhead Revisited* explored new ways of bringing the history of a place to life in an innovative and exciting way."[45] The ambivalence expressed here ran throughout the exhibition itself: its humorous irony and self-awareness lifted it far above most "interpretation."

Stowe and Rousham

Two great eighteenth-century landscapes, only a few miles apart, illustrate fascinating issues in the management of historic landscapes. The gardens at Stowe are now managed by the National Trust; Rousham is still owned by the descendants of General Dormer who laid it out in the 1730s and '40s. Stowe has been undergoing an extensive program of landscape restoration since the National Trust acquired the grounds in 1989; at Rousham nothing seems to have changed for centuries.

The experience of visiting Stowe is dominated by delight at the recently restored vistas and the immaculate maintenance. As at Studley Royal, the newly accessible landscape brings its own modern delights—a family playing with a frisbee in the Grecian Valley below the Temple of Concord and Victory, for example, or a child in combat trousers running after her parents through the Elysian Fields. But inevitably, the way-marked route reduces the measure of delight in discovery, discouraging visitors from the choice and variety that appear to have been an essential part of the garden experience—it was Stowe, after all, where interpretation continues to present a garden with a strict intellectual and geographical program, where Pope described how after breakfast, "Everyone takes a different way and wanders about till we meet at noon."[46] It is possible that such an approach was a privilege reserved to guests of the house; Stowe very quickly introduced a specified route via the guidebooks of Benton Seeley and others from 1750 onward. However, this approach, of freedom and discovery within a designed landscape, is not encouraged now at Stowe, where the NT shares the grounds with the school and with a private golf course formed in 1974. And while the NT route offers sumptuous landscape pictures, the visitor is led through them by the discreet insistence of the way marking.

In contrast, the forks and junctions in the paths at Rousham—gravel, grass, or faintly beaten earth almost entirely free of signage—leave visitors to make a route for themselves, to appropriate the terrain through those choices. As Chuang Tzu, the fifth-century Chinese sage, observed: "a path is made by walking on it."[47] In a sense, the visitor is allowed to appropriate the garden's geography through the engagement required by these bifurcations: Rousham has become famous among historians for the gardener's letter that describes "the way to view Rousham," but while this allows for a rising crescendo of designed effects, it is clearly not the only way to perambulate the site. Ironically, while Rousham fails almost every modern test for access, the very absence of interpretation and guidance accommodates the visitor in a way institutional ownership could never do.

Rousham is close to the heart of the conundrum of the adaptation of a place which was elite to a place which is appealing to, or for, an audience. Its minimal interpretation, minimal visitor processing, minimal marketing is both admirable and deplorable. On one hand, Rousham, with its honesty box and absence of any kind of checks, has been described as open "under the most civilised and reasonable system of entrance anywhere in the country."[48] On the other, the lack of signs and directions is sublimely indifferent to the public: there are no brown signs reassuring you as you progress further away from the main road, no welcome signs telling you that you have arrived at a place where, for a fee, you can feel you have a right to be. The sense of trespass could be overpowering. What redeems the experience is the demonstrable trust in the visitor; the casual, take-it-or-leave it encouragement to linger and to confront the unknowability of the past on its own terms.

Heligan

Voted Garden of the Year 1995 by *Country Life*, Garden of the Year by the *Good Guide to Britain* in 2000, and The Nation's Favourite Garden by *Gardeners' World* in 2003, Heligan, or as the project has brilliantly named itself, "The Lost Gardens of Heligan," has clearly tapped into a powerful vein of popular imagination. In the last decade of the twentieth century, the idea of history as loss, as fragments of a vanished coherence, was hugely powerful.

The restoration project at Heligan combined "traditional" conservation practice, as required under grant aid from the government's Countryside Commission, with a sharp eye for marketing. Under the inspired guidance of Tim Smit, the restoration project was branded with a showman's eye for publicity in a series of books, articles, and TV programs. The ten-part documentary series of the same name won the Garden Documentary of the Year award in 1998. Arguably, no other garden project has received more publicity, resulting in the project being dubbed "the garden restoration of the century" in *The Times*.[49]

The project ran from 1990 to 1996, the last years of the Conservative government that had dissolved the postwar consensus under the banner that "there is no such thing as society," and the timing does not seem coincidental, for it was not simply the marketing that broke the mold. The interpretation of the site, the stories selected for retelling, were pioneering. It focused on the image of a prelapsarian world of social cohesion, which vanished with the First World War: "We were fired by a magnificent obsession to bring these once glorious gardens back to life in every sense and to tell, for the first time, not tales of lords and ladies but of those 'ordinary' people who had made these gardens great, before departing for the Great War."[50] The foregrounding of the labor of gardeners, especially in the kitchen garden, caught the national imagination. The painstaking restoration of every aspect of the working kitchen gardens allowed an audience of practical gardeners to be engaged as no other historic property had done before.[51]

If restoration of the kitchen gardens was about resurrecting the site in its nineteenth-century heyday, elsewhere the project played up the romantic nature of the gardens in their more recent history of dereliction. The paradox inherent in restoring the "lost gardens" was accommodated by different management priorities in geographically distinct areas. Elsewhere, in "The Jungle" and "The Lost Valley," the management regime sought, unconventionally in terms of conservation philosophy, to maintain an element of that romantic ruination. Vegetation was cleared and cut back selectively, with wildly overgrown plants allowed to remain because they preserved something of the late twentieth-century atmosphere that first captivated Smit and played to the contemporary fascination with that myth. It identified the garden's ruined state as key to a contemporary reception of the site and to unlocking mass public appeal.

The Leasowes

In some ways it is hard to classify The Leasowes as a success or a failure in terms of contemporary conservation practice. It has succeeded, if it is a success, by default, irrespective of the aim of the HLF conservation project to restore the garden of William Shenstone. As a project, it ran into significant difficulties and had to reframe its priorities and indeed its overall object.[52] The objective of restoring Shenstone's landscape was always a compromise: although much of the garden survives spatially, Shenstone's creation was physically so fragile, and intellectually so reliant on a particular way of seeing, that "restoration" was a hopeless task.[53] And yet, compromised and hemmed in by suburbia though it is, post-Shenstone the place has established its own character as a locally cherished landscape.

Its special qualities disappeared within years of Shenstone's death, and no other garden's afterlife has been quite so minutely and gloomily enjoyed: Goldsmith, Johnson, Gilpin, Isaac Disraeli, and others all reveled in the contrast between the poetics of the garden and the decaying reality. For Hugh Miller, visiting The Leasowes in the 1840s, the contrast between the famous description by Robert Dodsley in Shenstone's *Poetical Works* and the material reality of the ruined garden framed the experience. His lengthy account of his visit is full of gloom, at the waters of the spring falling "dead and dull into a quagmire," the "faintest traces" of paths, and a "black, lazy swamp with thickets of bramble all around;" Miller depicts himself picking his way through the ruins of rotten oak posts and collapsed heaps of bricks, stalking "along the once trimly-kept walk, through a stratum of decayed leaves, half-leg deep."[54]

And yet, Miller, unlike the others, redeems The Leasowes in his account. "An eye accustomed to contemplate nature merely in the gross," he writes, "might not find much to admire." "But one not less accustomed to study the forms than to feel the magnitudes—who can see spirit and genius in . . . the convexity of a mossy bank, in the glitter of a half-hidden stream, or the blue gleam of a solitary lochan . . . will still find much to engage him amid the mingled woods and waters, sloping acclivities, and hollow valleys, of the Leasowes."[55]

This remains the case. Shenstone's garden may have almost entirely disappeared, but The Leasowes is now an urban arcadia of its own. Grandparents and children walk their dogs, families picnic, youths fish, couples wander hand in hand, and golfers pull their trolleys through Virgil's Grove. The HLF restoration project may have failed to restore Shenstone's landscape, but it has reinvigorated a place that after a century of public access has developed, parallel to the authorized version of its history and heritage, an unauthorized and

FIGURE 4.3: A modern urban arcadia, The Leasowes on a Sunday morning, October 2007. Photograph by David Lambert.

undocumented history and heritage of local use by successive generations, and this continues to thrive.

Perhaps the subtlest response was Ian Hamilton Finlay's, whose inscribed stone bench in Virgil's Grove placed above a sad trickle of water quotes Dodsley and refers to a bubbling rill in a knowing gesture to the spirit of the place:

> Here the path begins gradually to ascend beneath a
> depth of shade, by the side of which is a small
> bubbling rill, either forming little peninsulas, rolling
> over pebbles, or falling down small cascades
> all under cover, and taught to murmur very agreeably.

In his *Proposal* for *the Leasowes*, 1992, Finlay made the point that the inscription described the scene not as it is now but "as it was in Shenstone's time." He recognized that the stream no longer flows "in the lively form described" but suggested that it is instead " 'restored' by means of the text."[56] Thus, just as Shenstone insisted in his use of texts around the garden, Finlay encouraged us to visualize in the fancy or mind's eye a scene that does not actually exist in front of us. In Shenstone's case, the imaginary scene was a classical fantasy; in Finlay's, an eighteenth-century fantasy. Both take the "real" landscape as raw material for a "fairy" landscape that exists somewhere between what is before the eye and what can be conjured in the mind's eye by the visitor's willing imagination. In the same way, Patrick Eyres takes the graffiti on another bench as the starting point for a whimsical flight of fancy on the original poetics.[57] For Finlay and Eyres, the garden continues, as it did for Shenstone, to comprise a prompt for the imagination, rather than just its material reality.

The Gateway Gardens Trust

One of the most innovative historic garden projects of the last ten years is not a site at all, but an educational initiative. Because it concerns itself with the culturally excluded, it casts a fascinating light on reception of heritage. The Gateway Gardens Trust has a simple enough mission: it arranges visits to historic gardens for groups who would otherwise never get the chance to visit such sites: inner-city school children, ethnic minorities, disabled, women's groups, rehabilitated offenders, single mothers, the homeless, the mentally ill.

Mark Humphries, education officer for the Trust, has commented that the common sense among minorities of being "out of place" in a historic garden is in fact a two-way process. That is, they are excluded not only by their own sense of self ("I don't belong here"), but also by the attitudes and actions, often unconscious or very subtle, of staff and visitors. As education officer, Humphries's role is not only to advise and reassure the visiting groups but also to advise and reassure the staff who will present the garden to them.

One of the most innovative of the Gateway's projects has involved digital cameras. Hard-to-reach groups were given cameras for their visit and invited to take pictures of whatever they wished, with the results collected and sent back to the group for an exhibition; a nationwide exhibition at Dinefwr House was held in August 2007. A camera offers a new way of looking—many of the participants had never used one before. And a new way of looking represents a new way of thinking and relating to a place, especially one that is potentially intimidating or confusing.

Susan Sontag has rather cruelly described the photography of travel as "assuag[ing] general feelings of disorientation that are likely to be exacerbated by travel. Most tourists feel compelled to put the camera between themselves and whatever is remarkable that they encounter. Unsure of other responses, they take a picture. This gives shape to experience."[58] She is right in a way;

but her analysis is a kind of negative image. The positive is that photography is a weapon by which the dispossessed can take possession—we speak, after all, of being "armed" with a camera—a means of handling (almost literally) an experience that could otherwise be overwhelming, the reverse in fact of what she describes as a way of "refusing" experience.

First off, and simplest in the Gateway project, the loan of a camera and the freedom to use it represented an important gesture of trust; it also imposed at the same time a new level of responsibility. And because there were often not enough cameras to go around, the gesture also involved sharing within the group. All these things deflected the intimidation of the site itself.

But still more interesting, the framing and taking of photographs offers the viewer a way of relating to the site, one that offers a new level of control of the environment through the selection and framing of shots and a level of active participation and negotiation with the place. Wandering with a camera— "taking" photographs—offers a way of appropriating the place, of creating a personal geography, of discovering and negotiating unfamiliar space. A camera, in a word, offers power; it restores the balance between the historic site and the unfamiliar visitor.

In just the same way as, for a timid visitor to a sublime scene in the Lakes, a Claude glass reduced chaotic nature to order in the palm of the hand, so a digital camera, with its instant result, frames and orders a potentially overwhelming space. However, it is also fascinating to recognize that the images framed are in many ways the opposite of the Claudean picturesque, or indeed the modern picturesque of the exquisite but solemn "historic garden view" epitomized in the National Trust book. Rather, in a kind of anti-picturesque, these views are of people, and people having fun, or of the gardening staff at work, or of odd corners normally overlooked. In place of the careful composition of the professional shot, these snaps are instantaneous, multiple, and whimsical; they eschew the monumental in favor of the fleeting and everyday, but are nonetheless equally engaged with the historic garden. The Dinefwr exhibition represented, indeed celebrated, an alternative way of looking at and experiencing gardens.

The guided tour, however inadvertently, can easily reinforce the sense of being "out of place" through the cultural references that stud the discourse. The ultimate way to enjoy a garden is the free walk, but for many people this is a daunting undertaking, so it needs to be carefully prepared. Gateway visits are set up after an initial meeting with the group to understand its background and any particular needs. The introduction on site can then set the garden in terms of familiar contemporary cultural references rather than just historical

FIGURE 4.4: Photograph taken on a Gateway Gardens Trust visit to Dyffryn Gardens with Cyrenians Cymru, May 2007. Courtesy of the Gateway Gardens Trust.

ones, for example, by highlighting to a West Indian group plants imported from particular Caribbean islands. A group can be given particularly relevant items to search out as a way of offering structure, so that each discovery is a kind of token of ownership. Or participants, once welcomed, can wander singly or in groups, with or without a guide: *Solvitur ambulando*—it is solved by walking.[59] Every step gets the measure of a place; alienation and attraction working themselves out in the walker's mind step by step.[60]

CONCLUSION

Whether the wonders of a historic garden have an autonomous power to delight everyone, or whether people need to have those wonders pointed out by interpretation is too deep a question for this chapter. Ultimately, that is to ask whether the human response to beauty is innate or culturally determined. The historic garden is a complex experience and, in contemporary culture, a problematic one. Historical meanings that might engage a much wider audience have often been edited out, and we engage with them via a highly charged process of mediation, a process framed in terms that all too often remain unexamined and freighted with a host of cultural assumptions. But at the same time, gardens continue, nonhistorically, to exist as gorgeous, sensuous experiences to which everyone is capable of responding, provided presentation does not obtrude. For this, it is not interpretation that is required, but a welcome, and a welcome can take the form not of effusiveness but of trust.

Class, the tyranny of the eye, shortage of time, commodification, and consumption, all play a part in the way we now relate to eighteenth-century gardens. Perhaps what we need to restore, as much as any "heritage fabric," is a way of seeing: slower, more meditative, associative, poetic; the garden not as fabric but as a series of prompts to the imagination, which may be historical or may be contemporary, a free space the viewer is allowed physically and mentally to explore and make sense of. For this, we need to leave the place to cast its spell—"trust the tale" as D.H. Lawrence said—rather than preface it at every turn with interpretation, which should be available on demand but otherwise kept out of the picture. Such an approach would allow for a wider appreciation both of historical meanings and an enriched, if unpredictable, experience of remarkable landscapes.

CHAPTER FIVE

Meaning

PATRICK EYRES

As the most extensive of contemporary artworks, the garden offered such a major opportunity for cultural display that it was an essential commodity within the flourishing consumer culture inhabited by the European elite. Although commodification of gardening was well under way by 1700, the century's progress was significant precisely because the audience of consumers broadened from that of the elite to include the bourgeoisie. The same tendency was also evident in the increasingly fashionable leisure pursuit of country house and garden tourism. It is no surprise, then, that the most conspicuous gardens throughout Europe were those of royalty and the aristocracy; nor that the swelling ranks of upwardly mobile gentry and bourgeoisie also required up-to-date gardens, usually through acquisition of country estates. Cultivated as landscapes long before the term *landscape garden* was coined, this type of garden was the dominant subject of gardening discourse—and these gardens were created as landscapes of ideas wherein meaning was embedded intentionally. Indeed the relationship between landownership and power ensured that meaning was consistently, though in the broadest sense, political. The garden was a conspicuous signifier of status, wealth, identity, and patriotism. The garden also signified the landowner's aesthetic and horticultural connoisseurship, which would be evident in the sylvan and botanical compositions and, simultaneously, in the poetic, philosophical, and painterly associations invoked by the landscape, architecture, sculpture, and inscriptions. In short, the ability of gardening to embody and communicate complex messages created the opportunity to synthesize personal aggrandize-ment, political ideology, and aesthetic vision with horticultural fashion. By dis-cussing particular themes first within a number of English case studies, and then in a wider European and North American context, this chapter will illuminate the diversity of meanings found in the gardens of the eighteenth century.

The case studies have been selected from different regions to exemplify the cultural politics that articulated the interests of the English landowning elite. They have also been chosen to qualify the common perception of the landscape garden as aristocratic, rural, and privately owned. Consequently, this selection encompasses the gardens of royalty, gentry, and the bourgeoisie, as well as the aristocracy. The examples demonstrate that these privately owned retreats increasingly welcomed, indeed encouraged, a public audience, and that, although predominantly located in the countryside, they addressed not only a regional but also a metropolitan audience focused on the city, Parliament, and the court. Indeed they exemplify the landscape garden as an aestheticized site of active ideological engagement through which owners could intervene in political debate, often in innovative and provocative ways. Whereas the range of meanings addressed here emphasizes the interrelationship of commerce, empire, and the landscape garden, all the case studies underline the landscape garden as an artistic project on a grand scale.

As these gardens were experienced both in situ and through published accounts, these case studies have also been chosen to acknowledge the role of print media within the lively, argumentative, and often contradictory discourse of gardening that flourished throughout the century. The variety of meanings is evident in the extensive array of publications that ranged far beyond the specialist press: treatises on garden design and estate management, texts on visual symbolism, garden guidebooks, poetry and plays, topographical and political prints, newspaper reports and magazine articles, and books on ag-riculture, travel, and regional history. All these gardens were promoted and discussed in ways that were not only approving and celebratory, but also critical and satiric, even polemical—and the amateur, landowning patron was among the participants as well as the bourgeois professional, for example: the de-signer, poet, journalist, artist, and publisher.

In brief, the diversities of meaning within these case studies remain legible to the informed eye within the fabric of each garden—whether this is extant, vestigial, or restored. Hence this discussion is illustrated with a selection of the bird's-eye overviews drawn by Chris Broughton for the *New Arcadian Journal* between 1991 and 2005. As their purpose is to visualize the extant features of each garden, topographical accuracy has been set aside and artistic license has been applied to the perspective of the terrain and the scale of the features. Some drawings even reconstruct gardens that have either substantially changed or vanished altogether. Nonetheless, in all of them, the relation of the architecture, sculpture, and water to the landform and planting is clearly delineated to further appreciation of the ways in which meaning was (and remains) communicated.

~ § ~

At the beginning of the eighteenth century, certain factors conjoined to swell the ranks of aristocratic landowners eager to invest in gardening and to create new patrons amongst the gentry and the upwardly mobile bourgeoisie. The creation of a Protestant constitutional monarchy following the Glorious Revolution of 1688 and the development of a maritime empire through warfare with the Catholic powers, France and Spain, helped forge a radical new sense of national identity. Lords Shaftesbury and Burlington were among those urging the creation of a distinctively British style in the arts that would befit an ascendant power, and gardening began to acquire the cachet of a patriotic statement.

Studley Royal and Wentworth Castle were created early in the century by upwardly mobile Tory politicians, while Wentworth Woodhouse was the product of an ambitious Whig dynasty. Each family hailed from county gentry and this was the social milieu that the Aislabies of Studley Royal inhabited throughout the century. Both Studley and Wentworth Castle reveal the garden as a representation first of social elevation through career success, and subsequently of a rehabilitated status following political downfall. Their extant features—landform, plantation, water, architecture, sculpture—demonstrate that the early English landscape garden emerged as a pragmatic synthesis of French, Italian, and Dutch princely models. French political and cultural hegemony ensured that, by the late seventeenth century, the vocabulary of Louis XIV's epic garden landscape at Versailles had forged a model for the grand baroque garden that became fashionable across the continent. Promoted by an extensive literature, the French style was modified to suit the requirements of garden cultures in other countries, as exemplified by the Anglo-Dutch manner.[1] Thus the gardens of the English elite emulated the ways in which their European counterparts drew upon Roman precedents to articulate personal, dynastic, regional, and national identities—and sculpture played an important didactic and metaphorical role in this process.

Imported from Flanders during the late seventeenth century, the new technology of lead casting transformed the English market for sculpture and provided a ready supply of affordable statuary suited to the outdoors. By the

1720s, the fashion for embellishing gardens with replica antique figures had become widespread—and the siting of classical sculpture was recommended to catch the eye, to enable contemplative navigation, to adorn particular spots, and to invoke parallels between the ancient and modern worlds that would invest the landowner with the civic virtues of imperial Rome. The elysian water garden at Studley was intended to display the status of John Aislabie, a Hanoverian Tory who became a minister in the Whig government. However, by the time the statues were chosen during the 1720s, Aislabie was in retirement, a disgraced politician, and his investment in gardening had become a cultural bid for social rehabilitation.[2]

The statues of combat situated on one side of the canalized river—Hercules slaying Antaeus, Roman wrestlers, and the (now absent) dying gladiator—were suggestive of Aislabie's struggle and mortal wounding within the parliamentary arena whilst, on the other side, the presence of Bacchus (god of fertility), Endymion (romantic love), and the erstwhile Galen (medical pioneer) suggested solace and personal regeneration. As god of the sea, Neptune would be appreciated as the appropriate statue to preside over the moon pools in front of the Temple of Hercules (later renamed Piety). However, the temple's original dedication would have prompted the traditional associations of this heroic and deified mortal. On one hand, Hercules personified heroic virtue, as exemplified by the twelve virtuous labors that combined physical and intellectual prowess; on the other, he embodied the familiar Choice of Hercules between virtue and vice. Within the temple, this choice would have been symbolized by the busts of two Roman emperors: Vespasian for good government and Nero for bad. Similarly, comparison with the pleasurable distractions symbolized by the statue of the naked Venus de Medici inside the (former) Temple of Venus would have emphasized the dominant theme of Herculean civic virtue.[3]

The form and value of sculpture was rarely taken for granted. It was defined, criticized, promoted, and challenged within gardening discourse, and its relationship to the landscape in which it was placed would shift, quite literally, in response to changing fashions in design. By mid-century, progressive opinion regarded sculpture as passé. At Studley, William Aislabie reengineered the watercourse downstream from his father's water garden to create the picturesque serpentine river that flowed through sculpture-free terrain embellished by seven rustic bridges and a pair of hilltop features.[4]

The neighboring landscapes of the Wentworths were created by upwardly mobile branches of the same family. The conspicuousness of competitive mansion building and gardening between 1710 and 1750 publicly articulated the dynastic one-upmanship of a rivalry that simultaneously aspired to power in the national realm of party politics and government. Wentworth Woodhouse (Whig) is in the foreground and Wentworth Castle (Tory) is in the distance. In 1717, Wentworth Castle was described by its creator, the first Earl of Strafford (second creation), as his monument. As such, it was perceived as a physical totality of mansion and landscape, buildings and sculpture, plantations and waterworks, whose collective meaning commemorated Strafford's career in the service of the Stuart monarchy. Although the gardening intentionally signified Strafford's achievements and aspirations, his loyalty to the Stuarts would necessitate a treasonous subtext encoded within patriotic commemoration. Strafford had served the last Stuart, Queen Anne, as a minister in her final, Tory cabinet. His subsequent exile from the center of power after the accession of Hanoverian George I (1714) by the king's Whig government proved so alienating he transferred his allegiance to the exiled Stuart (Jacobite) cause. The extant Stuart commemorations created between 1713 and 1734 are signified within the first Earl of Strafford's baroque house; by his wilderness in the pattern of the union flag, created through the union of England and Scotland in 1707; by Stainborough Castle, the replica of a medieval castle built on the highest point of the estate as a monumental garden building; and by the Queen Anne Obelisk.[5] After the irrevocable defeat of the Jacobite cause at Culloden (1746), the

FIGURE 5.1: *Overview of The Wentworths, South Yorkshire* (Wentworth Woodhouse in the foreground, with distant Wentworth Castle). Courtesy of Chris Broughton.

Hanoverian monarchy was for the first time secure on the British throne. This triumph was proclaimed at Wentworth Woodhouse through construction of two belvederes: the Hoober Stand and the Doric Temple. By 1747, successive elevations in the peerage enabled the Whig first Marquis of Rockingham to outrank and out-swank the Tory, Stuart-favoring rival at Wentworth Castle.[6]

The overview of the Wentworths illustrates the blurring of landscape architecture and sculpture through the deployment of inscribed obelisks and the statue-topped column. However, only one of the lead statues has survived. This is the Blackamoor, a representation of a kneeling African supporting a sundial on his head. This proved the most popular of the lead figures produced for gardens, and it demonstrates the commercial pragmatism of contemporary sculptors. The statue originated in the personification of Africa that derived from the emblematic treatise, *Iconologia*, by Cesare Ripa (1593), which had informed the sculptural program at Versailles.[7] Needless to say, the popularity of the Blackamoor and its presence at Wentworth Castle illuminates the inter-relationship of commerce, empire, and the landscape garden. Strafford's great achievement was as Britain's chief negotiator at the Peace of Utrecht (1713). The lucrative bounty of the treaty included the "Asiento," the "contract" that secured British control of the slave trade between Africa and the Spanish Empire in the Americas and the Caribbean. Consequently, the popularity of the Blackamoor invites particular questions. One is, as a representation of Africa, must the statue implicitly symbolize the human produce "offered" by the continent? Another is whether any of these landscapes were *not* created from investments in the slave economy. These investments were not only in the slave trade, but also in shipping, in services to the colonial plantations and their owners, and in their produce (for example, sugar, cotton, rum).[8]

~ § ~

The financial resources that initially funded West Wycombe and Stowe were inherited from wealth accumulated through overseas trade. Like the Went-worths, the regional competitiveness of these gardens was also enacted in the arena of national politics. The art of political gardening was famously prac-ticed at Stowe to articulate the opposition Whig critique of government virtue and policy—first by Lord Cobham and then by his successor, Earl Temple. Thus Stowe confirms that a garden, although familiarly a place of retirement, could equally become a symbolic counterattack against the dominant political culture. By way of contrast, the theatrical flamboyance created by Sir Fran-cis Dashwood at West Wycombe was partly an irreverent satire on the more illustrious *gravitas* of Stowe.[9]

The political gardening at Stowe is renowned for criticizing the pacific foreign policy of successive governments while simultaneously promoting the benefits of commercial empire. Indeed the preoccupation with North America provides a useful example, throughout this chapter, of shifts in meaning prompted by the interrelationship of commerce, empire, and the landscape garden. During the 1730s and 1740s, Cobham's critique centered on the landscape to the east (or left) of the mansion through the conjunction of sculpture and garden buildings: the Temple of Ancient Virtue and the Temple of British Worthies and also by the Temple of Friendship, the Palladian Bridge, and the Gothic Temple of Liberty. Consider the interior of the Palladian Bridge, which originally contained the sculptural relief by Peter Scheemakers entitled *The Four Corners of the World bringing their Produce to Britannia*. Through personifications of Africa, America, Asia, and Europe it portrays each continent as a bountiful resource.[10] However, North America was clearly located as the jewel in the imperial crown through the flanking mural portraits by Francesco Sleter of colonial founders Sir Walter Raleigh (Virginia) and Sir William Penn (Pennsylvania).

Although empire in North America was acknowledged at West Wycombe by the statue of Penn that formerly topped the sawmill, Dashwood's commemorations were largely through the fun of exuberant showmanship. West Wycombe was not only commodified by the sale of prints, but the replica

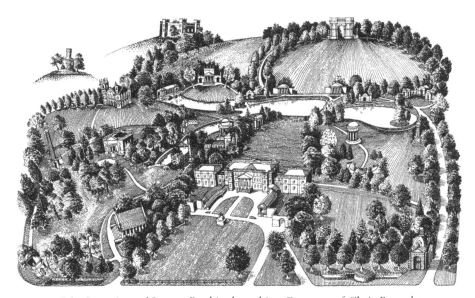

FIGURE 5.2: *Overview of Stowe, Buckinghamshire.* Courtesy of Chris Broughton.

warships illustrated in some of these announced that Naumachias were among
the entertainments of this garden during the 1750s. The Naumachia was a
mock naval battle "fought" in patriotic celebration of the Royal Navy as the
bulwark of the nation's defense and agent of imperial expansion. Forts, docks,
and batteries were constructed as garden features, and the Naumachia became
a phenomenon of aquatic theater throughout Britain during the eighteenth
century.[11]

Naumachias and prints exemplify the way the private landscape garden
became increasingly public in the course of the century. As garden tourism
became a popular leisure pursuit, many landowners intentionally played to the
expanding audience. The owners of Stowe, for example, began an active program of self-promotion during the 1740s by encouraging publication of guide
books, topographical prints, poetic eulogies, and "puffs" in the London press,
as well as offering visitor accommodation in a public house built just outside
the garden.[12]

The way in which West Wycombe and Dashwood's neighboring Medmenham Abbey became infamously publicized demonstrates that the printed word
could create new meanings about gardens. The crisis over the peace treaty of
1763 mobilized an alliance of aristocratic and bourgeois Whigs that escalated
into a movement to reform the parliamentary system. When the Stowe Whigs
resigned from government as a matter of principle, Dashwood remained.
Consequently, Whig activist John Wilkes penned a ribald critique to discredit
him—in prose whose waggish salaciousness matched the (allegedly) libidinous
indulgencies of the Hell Fire Club, of which both Dashwood and Wilkes were
members, and whose now notorious carry ons occurred at Medmenham Abbey.
Thus the tantalizing elision of heady description and impish fiction leaves the
reader sighing with the hope that the explicit statuary at Medmenham really
did exist.

The rakish humor of Wilkes's unsubstantiated allegations prompted a later
generation of Dashwoods to demolish the Temple of Venus at West Wycombe.
Nonetheless, once reconstructed in the late twentieth century, the venerean
mount and temple continue to symbolize the pleasures through which the satirist
impugned Dashwood's sexual virility. The temple (1748) was apparently topped
by a sculpture of Leda and the Swan, as if to suggest the ravishings presided
over by the statue of the Venus de Medici within the open rotunda. Nevertheless, the figure of Mercury survives and, as the one who leads the souls of men
to paradise, is critically positioned above the entrance to Venus' Parlour—the
grottoesque apex of the wall that, like open thighs, curves away on either flank.
Wilkes left no doubt that this symbolic vagina represented the shrine at which

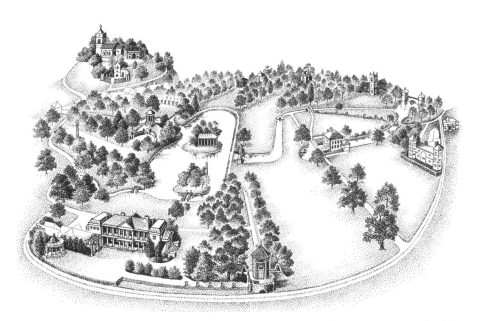

FIGURE 5.3: *Overview of West Wycombe, Buckinghamshire.* Courtesy of Chris Broughton.

Dashwood had formerly worshipped with alacrity, and also that the elderly and debauched politician was no longer able to sustain these devotions.[13]

The notoriety of this incident confirms not only the effectiveness of print media in shaping the consumption of meaning, but also that the same sculpture could signify differently from one garden to another despite, or according to, the agenda of each landowner—and the Venus de Medici provides a splendid example. Of all the sculptural representations of the goddess of love, the Venus de Medici was privileged as the epitome of beauty and emphasized as such by William Hogarth, who placed her as the centerpiece of the key illustration in his book *The Analysis of Beauty* (1753). However, the posture of the naked Venus de Medici would also attract opposing interpretations: one hand is positioned across the breasts, the other in front of the loins. Thus, to some, the statue was modestly poised to conceal the goddess's nudity; to others, the figure emphasized female sexuality by highlighting erogenous anatomy.

Through his satire on West Wycombe and Medmenham Abbey, Wilkes appropriated the garden as a site for the media's customary use of sexual satire for political purposes. However, his success relied on the perception of the garden as a sensual domain rife with sexual allusion where, at least in the imagination, active physical gratification could be enjoyed. Renowned in Italian and

French gardens, the libidinous associations of the Venus de Medici were also invoked in England. Endowed with sexual connotations, the presence of the statue signified that a garden was not just "A Lovely Place" (*locus amoenus*), but also "A Place for Loving" (*locus amorem*).[14] For example, the promenade of the 1720s garden at Stowe circumnavigated the open Venus Rotunda, which displayed a gilded version of the statue and tantalized with a series of buildings that, conveniently furnished with "luxurious couches," were dedicated to the pleasures of the flesh.[15] Whereas the couches in the erstwhile Temple of Sleep were to assist recovery after the raptures of the garden, those in the Temple of Venus were intended for "pleasuring."[16]

It is hardly surprising that the morality associated with this statue was contested. Some would excoriate the figure as an emblem of licentiousness; others would lambaste it (and classical statuary in general) as irreligious, pagan idolotry; elsewhere the sexual associations would be mediated to encompass the virtuous as well as the carnal.[17] An example of the latter can be found in the much acclaimed topographical poem, *Castle Howard* (1732), through which Lady Irwin extolled the dynastic meaning of her father's landscape (the third Earl of Carlisle). In so doing, she described how the presence of temples to Venus and to Diana were integral to the relationship of mansion and garden to the epic mausoleum. As expected, a statue of the Venus de Medici inhabited the (former) Temple of Venus, and the Temple of the Four Winds was originally dedicated to Diana. Notwithstanding, the poem reconciled the carnality of Venus with the chastity of Diana to celebrate the garden as a paean to marriage as the social contract that ensured the dynastic continuity sanctified by the lineage interred in the mausoleum.[18]

Like the Venus de Medici, statues of Hercules could be found across Europe, from Medici gardens in Tuscany to the Versailles of Louis XIV. Whereas the figure's personification of heroic virtue would be enlisted on behalf of princes and landowners, the well known Choice of Hercules would invoke the worthy moral decision, such as the preference of civic virtue over carnal vice, of industry over idleness. Examples may also be found at Stowe and Stourhead, the latter created by a Whig banking dynasty. The randy masculinity of Stowe's garden of Venus had prevailed before Cobham quit government in 1733 to join the opposition Whigs. By way of contrast, the Eastern gardens created during the 1730s and 1740s applauded the civic virtues associated with temples dedicated to British Worthies, Friendship, Liberty, and Ancient Virtue. Hence the gardens cultivated on either side of the mansion invested Cobham's political gardening with the virtuous choice.

As in Lady Irwin's *Castle Howard*, a marital sexuality fecund with dynastic heirs was enacted at Stourhead through a sculptural representation of the Choice of Hercules. The garden tour comprised an anticlockwise perambulation around the lake. Within the Pantheon, originally intended to be dedicated as the Temple of Hercules, the eponymous hero stands between Flora and Ceres. Posture and gaze favor Ceres, goddess of harvests and fecundity, rather than Flora—symbolic of the fleeting and frivolous blossomings of spring. Moreover, Stourhead offered another encounter with the moral choice. Shortly after leaving the Pantheon, a grottoesque ruin recreated the topography that visualized the moment of decision in paintings (one of which hung in the mansion). Will the visitor ascend the hillside in search of virtue or enjoy the ease of vice on the lakeside path? Crowned with the Temple of Apollo, the summit of the garden continues to reward the virtuous with the panorama of this sylvan and watery Arcadia.[19]

Although Louis XIV had adopted the cachet of heroic virtue and the virtuous choice at Versailles, the appropriation of this aura by William III from his political adversary demonstrates the way Herculean iconography was deployed within distinctive European cultural geographies. Throughout the palace and gardens at Hampton Court, the English king personified himself as heroic virtue laboring on behalf of the Protestant nation. Consequently, until defeat of the Stuart claim to the British throne, the virtuous hero took on an additional resonance for Whig supporters—as the symbolic champion of British Protestant nationalism, as exemplified by the Hercules within the Ionic temple on the terrace at Wentworth Woodhouse. Similarly, the moral choice could signify loyalty to the Protestant succession—and those marginalized by this anglicized heroic virtue would be the familiar "unnatural" and "unruly" vices, representative of the un-British and un-Protestant French, Spanish, and Stuart Jacobites.[20]

~ § ~

The later landscaping at Stowe, by Earl Temple, was contemporary with the creation of Kew Gardens by Augusta, Dowager Princess of Wales. The political gardening at both places proclaimed a triumphalist celebration of imperial expansion. However, it is important to differentiate between the motives behind these gardens because they articulated the rival agendas of royal government and Whig opposition. Thus Kew was designed as a representation of the Hanoverian monarchy, which was now thoroughly "naturalized" and at the helm of an imperial nation. By comparison, Stowe promoted the critique of the Whig aristocracy that regarded itself as the bastion of the Protestant constitutional monarchy now perceived as threatened by royal ambition.

The victorious strategy of William Pitt the Elder during the Seven Years' War (1756–63) inspired his brother-in-law, Earl Temple, to develop Stowe as an imperial landscape marked by the Temple of Concord and Victory at the head of the Grecian Valley and the Triumphal Arch that crowns the southern horizon. This process exemplifies the way sculpture became peripatetic as gardens evolved. Earlier, Lord Cobham had pragmatically relocated statuary to create new meanings. In the 1760s, his "naturalizing" successor, Earl Temple, similarly recycled to signify afresh; such as the sculptures of mortal combat that were repositioned in the Grecian Valley to complement the temple's victorious theme. Redesigned in the early 1760s, the temple too was adorned with sculpture—notably Scheemakers's relief, which was ingeniously relocated to the pediment from the Palladian Bridge. This portrayal of the four continents as a British mercantile resource was substantiated by the new, interior medallions. Although representative of victories in all four continents, the majority commemorated expansion of empire in North America and Canada.

Nevertheless, a problem with monuments is that the time they take to design and build weakens the immediacy of either commemoration or critique. This conundrum was often resolved by pragmatically naming structures in progress to communicate the point. At Kew, wartime success was immediately promoted through naming two of the new temples Victory and Bellona, the latter after the Roman goddess of war. Although Stowe's temple was renamed Concord and Victory to commemorate Pitt's war strategy rather than the royal peace terms, the medallions were installed after the treaty was signed. Thus, in order to project his gardenist critique into the public domain, Earl Temple mobilized the London newspapers, Whig periodicals, and the Stowe guidebook—and these publications were used over the next thirty years to reinforce the critical dissent from royal policy encoded within the temple.[21]

Whereas the naturalism of Stowe's Grecian Valley represents the ascendancy of the English landscape garden, the emblematic design of Kew demonstrates that other garden styles coexisted with the dominant fashion. Moreover, while Earl Temple's gardening remains legible through careful restoration by the National Trust, the vestigial presence of Augusta's Kew is intimated only by the few buildings that survive within the fabric of the present Royal Botanic Gardens. Thus the overview is a reconstruction of the royal garden designed for the princess by her long-standing friend and confidant, the third Earl of Bute, and adorned with a prolific quantity of buildings by the architect, Sir William Chambers.

The circuit path commenced at the palace and followed the garden's wooded margins. The succession of architectural encounters that punctuated

FIGURE 5.4: *Overview of Kew Gardens, London*. Courtesy of Chris Broughton.

the journey of horticultural and geographical discovery symbolized the prosperity of Britain under the Hanoverian monarchy. Initially, the tour disclosed the botanical enterprise which, nurtured by horticultural science, was represented by the utilitarian orangery, Great Stove, and the water pump that supplied botany and lake alike. The classical temples within these gardens were dedicated to natural forces essential to plants: the Sun, Arethusa, Pan, and Aeolus—the latter situated on a mount between the Chinese Aviary (an islanded Pavilion) and the House of Confucius set astride the lake's edge. The score of other buildings had, beside those functions intimated by their dedications, another significant and imperial message.

Bute and Chambers were able to commemorate the global conflict that was exactly contemporary with the garden's development. Although the opening of the Seven Years' War had been ominous for Britain in all continents, on August 1, 1759, the victory won at Minden by British and German forces under the command of Augusta's kinsman, Prince Ferdinand of Brunswick, introduced the *Annus Mirabilis*, the year of victories worldwide. Yet it was the German victories with their Hanoverian associations that the royal designers chose to celebrate, and it was from the world of classical antiquity that Chambers selected the architectural models for the circular Temple of Victory and the porticoed Temple of Bellona.

The Temple of Victory was set high on an artificial hill as a belvedere from which the garden could be surveyed. The royal narrative clearly located victory as the key to the benefits of commercial empire. The ruined triumphal arch stood adjacent to symbolize imperial Rome (and also to provide daily access for the flock of sheep that grazed the central meadows). Just across the sheep pasture, the arch was complemented by the twin-towered Gothic cathedral. Together, they signified that British victory would create a new trading empire more extensive than that of Rome and the Middle Ages. Even the grazing sheep played a signifying role, for they suggested the importance of farming and the wool trade in Britain's export economy. The arch and cathedral also framed the three garden buildings furthest from the palace: the alhambra, the pagoda, and the Turkish mosque. These represented ancient cultures that were still powers in the world. On either side of the pagoda, the alhambra and mosque pointed beyond Europe, past Moorish and Ottoman cultures to one still more exotic, China—thus suggesting an imperial trade and influence that victory had rendered more accessible. By signifying the far-flung scale of the commercial empire presided over by the Hanoverian monarchy, Bute and Chambers appropriated Pitt's victorious wartime strategy on behalf of the court and royal government.

Today there is no hint that Augusta's Kew endured a quarter century of political and stylistic controversy. Indeed the ferocity was fueled by the attempt of her son, King George III, to reassert royal command of government. Thus Kew became the discursive site of an ideological collision between royal and Whig agendas: praised by loyal Tory partisans and condemned by opposition Whig polemicists. Just as in the case of Wilkes's satire of Dashwood's gardens, the Whig critique was intended to discredit royal government. Once again the garden was positioned as the site of alleged couplings through the saucy caricatures that sexualized the relationship between Augusta and Bute. The inference to be drawn was that the Tory courtier (Bute) was the power behind the throne and held in his thrall the royal mother (Augusta) and her son (King George).[22] So insistent was the satiric assault that one is left wondering whether the princess and the earl acquired an unwarranted notoriety or actually did frolic in carnal pleasure. Nonetheless there is no doubt that the garden's concluding temple fell victim to the discord over the peace terms negotiated by Bute's government. In the landscape designed to celebrate the benefits of victory and demonstrate the interrelationship of agriculture, botany, commerce, and empire, the concluding Temple of Peace should have reinforced the benevolence of Hanoverian reign. Instead the political furor persuaded the royal designers to leave this building discreetly unbuilt.

~ § ~

By way of contrast to these elite landscapes, the Dorset Pantheon, The Leasowes, and Goldney exemplify bourgeois modes of gardening distinct from those of the aristocracy. Nonetheless, they shared the cultural imperative whereby the landscape garden served as a representation of modernity through the synthesis of aesthetic pleasure and commercial profit. Early in the century, Whig commentator Joseph Addison noted in *The Spectator* that this practice was more prevalent abroad, especially in France and Italy. In those countries, gardening and forestry artfully and usefully intermingled within the wider land-scape of the country estate. Addison's celebrated proposition was that English estates should be gardenized in a similar manner, with fields and woods inter-laced with paths and aesthetically embellished to conjoin profit and pleasure.[23] Clearly, Addison was proposing developments already under way at the time of writing. Nevertheless his proposal envisioned the aristocratic landscapes of improvement as well as the humbler scale of the *ferme ornée* cultivated by the gentry and bourgeoisie.

Thomas Hollis and William Shenstone were cultural innovators whose inscribed landscapes were integral to the farmland of their country estates. Whereas Shenstone had inherited The Leasowes and his income through his family's background in farming and the minor gentry, Hollis had inherited manufacturing wealth and invested in farmland. Both chose to inhabit preexist-ing farmhouses rather than to emulate the fashion for country house building. Thomas Hollis in particular eschewed aristocratic modes of gardening in favor of practices appropriate to bourgeois contexts. On his estate, he conjoined

FIGURE 5.5: *Overview of the Dorset Pantheon* (Corscombe and Halstock). Courtesy of Chris Broughton.

FIGURE 5.6: *Overview of Goldney, Bristol.* Courtesy of Chris Broughton.

the patriotic concerns of improvement with his unique program of "planting" Whig ideology into the very soil of his land. Throughout 1772–3, he renamed his farms, fields, and woods in the parishes of Corscombe and Halstock to create the Dorset Pantheon.

Hollis was active in the Whig associations that allied the aristocracy and bourgeoisie in the campaign to curb the power of the crown and protect the civil liberties of subjects at home and in the American colonies. From his home at Urles Farm, high on Corscombe Down, Hollis took solace in the panorama that encompassed his thirteen farms. The libertarian virtues codified by the names given to 207 of his fields and woods were triggered by the title of each farm. Ten were renamed to memorialize canonical authors from the Whig pantheon of heroes: Buchanan, Harrington, Locke, Ludlow, Marvel, Milton, Neville, Russell, and Sydney, with Harvard, over five miles away on the horizon, renamed after the founder of the eponymous university. For Hollis, Harvard Farm symbolized the regeneration of liberty in the North American colonies, and he renamed the adjacent farm after liberty itself. Hollis's political gardening embraced the past and the present to envision an American future based on the Whig foundations of public liberty. His support for the American cause was so renowned that his premature death in 1774—fourteen months before the war of words escalated into armed conflict—was lamented equally in Britain and the colonies.

Although renowned as a conceptual "temple" of liberty, the pantheon of
Thomas Hollis is now invisible. Nevertheless, surviving names scattered across
the Ordnance Survey map sustain a vestigial presence. Some of these are identified on the overview. "Comprehension Coppice" at Locke Farm celebrates
one of the texts through which political philosopher John Locke promoted
the revolutionary Whig heritage of contractual monarchy. This aspiration was
realized through the Revolution Settlement of King William III. "Settlement
Copse" at Harvard Farm commemorated this achievement whereby the Whig
legislation passed between 1689 and 1701 not only established Britain's constitutional monarchy and parliamentary democracy, but also became regarded
as the cornerstone of British liberty. Apprehensive of the king's ambition, the
Whigs considered its defense a patriotic duty.[24]

By the time of his premature death in 1763, poet-gardener William Shenstone
had acquired such a reputation that his *ferme ornée* at The Leasowes became
an obligatory destination on the tour of the English Midlands. Indeed his
poetic embellishment of the ferme ornée was so distinct from aristocratic gardening that he created a model for proprietors of equally modest estates and
incomes. Published posthumously in 1764, Shenstone's *Unconnected Thoughts
on Gardening* comprise the lyric design principles in which he also coined
the term *landscape gardening*. Melancholic, amorous, and commemorative of
friendship, Shenstone's pastoral was created by the variety of pools, cascades,
seats, urns, sculpture, and inscriptions that punctuate the hilly terrain of The
Leasowes.[25] These features drew attention to views and atmospheres within the
garden as well as to prospects of the wider landscape beyond, and the poetic
experience was complemented by the sound of cattle lowing and enlivened by
the cascading water of the two streams that tumbled down wooded dells to
fill the Priory Pool. The overview records that The Leasowes is substantially
extant. The sylvan dells and pool are maintained as a municipal urban public
park, while the greenswards and house are leased as a private golf course—and
the route of the "Circuit Walk" outlined by Robert Dodsley in his *Description
of The Leasowes* (1764) can still be traced. Commencing at the Priory, named
after the purpose-built Gothic ruin, it winds its way uphill in an anticlockwise
direction to the highest point and then descends to the climactic Virgil's Grove.

The poet's reflections on sculpture are illuminating at a time when it was
being removed from the rolling greenswards of the aristocratic landscape garden. Contrary to the opinions of many critics, Shenstone championed lead statuary in his *Unconnected Thoughts* and appreciated its aesthetic and economic
qualities. He also recommended the use of other sculptural objects such as urns
and obelisks, along with such suitable appendages as trophies, garlands, and

mottos.[26] The Leasowes also became the site of critical satire, and this example confirms that for certain audiences the meanings associated with gardens were irreligious, even blasphemous. Mr. Wildgoose, *The Spiritual Quixote* of the title (1773), devoted his travels to denouncing the distractions of luxury consumption. Appalled by the profane gardening at The Leasowes, he secretly pulled down a lead statue to punish Shenstone for his idolatry. Although this example appears extreme, the critique of garden sculpture as an un-Christian phenomenon was widespread. Indeed the cultural value of lead statues was denigrated throughout the century, especially in the satires that mocked the aspirations of the upwardly mobile urban nouveau riche.[27] Nevertheless, although the ferme ornée had been borrowed to satirize the religious zealotry that condemned garden statues as pagan idols, this episode was equally a "puff" that acknowledged the renown of The Leasowes by Shenstone's old friend, novelist Richard Graves—which is probably why the Piping Faun was chosen as the target of Wildgoose's assault rather than the more problematic Venus de Medici in Virgil's Grove.

By way of contrast, Goldney exemplifies the many sites of bourgeois suburban gardening which, of practical necessity, were on a far smaller scale. The port city of Bristol and its coterie of Quakers and Merchant Venturers profited hugely from the combination of commerce, empire, and warfare. The city's trade in slaves, sugar, and munitions created much of the new wealth that funded the ring of mansions and landscape gardens laid out on the heights around the city. Established by Thomas Goldney I, a grocer and merchant, the wealth of this trading dynasty was consolidated and amplified by his son and grandson through their investment in new technologies, iron and brass works, as well as in licensed privateering during the wars of Spanish and Austrian Succession (1702–13, 1739–48). While Thomas Goldney II acquired the property, Thomas Goldney III enlarged the estate and created the garden, designed to celebrate the benefits of trade.

Situated on the Clifton hilltop, Goldney commanded extensive views of the river Avon, the city, and the surrounding countryside. The overview encompasses the salient features. The martial prospect terrace (1754) dominates the foreground. Beyond lies the house and garden with, to the right (ca. 1760), the orangery and canal. By 1768, the statue of Hercules was stationed on the terrace between the two crenellated prospect towers: the engine tower (1764), and the belvedere (ca. 1739). Further to the left, the equally martial bastion (ca. 1748) projects as a fortified spur. The prospect terrace also provided an ingenious means of entombing the subterranean grotto (1739–64). While the entrance is on the garden side of the terrace, the exit may be seen below and to the right of the belvedere. The grotto extended from this point to the engine tower, which camouflaged the beam engine that pumped water to the grotto's cascade as well as to the canal.

All these garden features emphasized the source of the owner's wealth. Whereas the bastion commanded views of the river and distant sea, bristling with the sails of merchant ships, the terrace overlooked the port where busyness amidst the forest of masts also signified burgeoning commerce. Similarly the grotto symbolized the fruits of these commercial voyages. Almost all the corals and shells used to decorate the interior came from the Caribbean and West African seas; that is, from the triangular route of the slave trade. Similar associations were generated by the garden's sculpture: by the river god in the grotto, the Neptune beside the canal, and the combative Hercules atop the prospect terrace. This Hercules is the dynamic hero of the labors rather than the contemplative philosopher—redolent of the heroic virtue of this Whig merchant and of the assertive pursuit of commercial profit. In siting his Hercules so conspicuously on the great prospect terrace with its vistas of the river and its freight, Goldney was perhaps conscious of the hero's popularity as a patron of trade among the merchants of imperial Rome. This kind of iconographical value is implied by the contemporary eulogy that hailed Goldney as a "minor Stowe." Thus, in his poem *Clifton*, Henry Jones (1767) infused Goldney with the *gravitas* of the renowned aristocratic landscape.[28] Certainly, the imperative of commerce and empire, embedded in the political landscape at Stowe, was equally shared by the mercantile Goldneys and Thomas Hollis. For his part, Hollis had animated Stowe's imperial iconography,[29] while Shenstone was to influence the Temple-Grenville Whig landscape at Hagley[30] and eulogize Lord Lyttelton.[31]

~ § ~

Thomas Whately, in his influential *Observations on Modern Gardening* (1770), defined the way Addison's aspirations had been realized and confirmed that a shift had taken place in the meaning and use of the term *garden*. The expanded perception encompassed the wider landscape, the farm and the forest, while the functions of gardens could include a range of activities that have little or nothing to do with gardening, such as walks, agriculture, riding, forestry, and hunting.[32] Translated into French, Whately's book was among those that disseminated the characteristics of the English landscape garden, a style familiar through the designs of Lancelot "Capability" Brown and subsequently associated with his self-appointed successor, Humphry Repton. The style was also disseminated by the reports of European visitors such as Count Kielmansegge, who observed that the "Nature" of both garden and countryside had become so improved it was difficult to distinguish between them.[33] Indeed the familiar signifiers of canals, fountains, temples, and statues had given way to allow the parkland to lap around the house itself and to open vistas of greenswards grazed by flocks, bounded by woodland, and punctuated by clumps of trees, sinuous water, and distant monuments. It was precisely this kind of landscape that was enjoyed from the Whig Palladian palace at Wentworth Woodhouse.

It is telling that, also in 1770, agricultural writer Arthur Young set the tone for the subsequent paeans to the patrician landscape of Wentworth Woodhouse. Young considered that the house, park, woods, and temples, along with the surrounding agricultural countryside, comprised a bounteous Arcadia.[34] As an epitome of the culture of improvement, Wentworth Woodhouse demonstrates the way in which the landscape garden had become integral to the productivity of estate agriculture and even industry. Indeed agricultural improvement was matched by the parkland where flocks, timber, and distant monuments were complemented by open cast coal mining and the fishing lakes whose water powered a mill and supplied a transport canal. Indeed Young's account exemplified the way in which agricultural journalism promoted the patriotic association between landownership, gardening, and farming. In addition, it created specific meanings that acknowledged the second Marquis of Rockingham as the imperial peacemaker. When prime minister in 1766, Rockingham had repealed the infamous Stamp Act, equally hated at home and in the American colonies. Young thus conjoined farming and statesmanship as fitting signifiers of Rockingham's patriotism and heaped compliments on the husbandry and gardening of an aristocrat who, as leader of the Whig opposition, was an irritant to King George III.

The success of the royal assault on the Whigs had rallied a number of parliamentarians to the traditional idea that defense of the Revolution Settlement was the constitutional duty of a Whig patriot. As the head of one of the wealthiest Whig dynasties, Rockingham acknowledged it was his responsibility as an aristocrat to undertake such a course of action. Under his leadership, the Rockingham Whigs became the grouping that offered the only coherent parliamentary opposition to the governments of George III. As a result, Wentworth Woodhouse displays slippage from the Whig orthodoxy of the first Marquis (already noted) to the oppositional Rockingham Whig critique of the second Marquis and his successor, the fourth Earl Fitzwilliam. After the crisis over the American colonies escalated into armed conflict in 1775, Rockingham's dissent from King George's war was signified by Keppel's Column (1778) and posthumously by the Rockingham Monument (1789).

An unexpected political victory spurred Rockingham to complete the eye catcher already under way on the southern horizon of the park and to dedicate it as Keppel's Column. The court-martial of the Rockinghamite Admiral Keppel after an indecisive naval battle against the French had been intended by the government to discredit opposition to the war. Nevertheless, the trial backfired: Keppel was acquitted, the government ridiculed, and the critical patriotism of the Rockingham Whigs vindicated. Although Keppel's Column stood as a critique of the government's unpopular war, Rockingham's dedication to the admiral saluted naval integrity and thus applauded Britain's armed forces.[35]

Having initiated peace negotiations with the American republic, Rockingham's premature death in 1782 curtailed his second premiership. The Rockingham Monument crowned the concluding phase of landscape gardening at Wentworth Woodhouse. Designed by John Carr for Earl Fitzwilliam as an eye catcher just over a mile to the east of the mansion, the setting was enhanced by advice from Humphry Repton. It is worth comparing the overviews of Stowe and West Wycombe with that of Wentworth Woodhouse to appreciate that the compact terrain of the earlier landscape gardens is a cornucopia of temples, statuary, and pavilions. By way of contrast, and characteristic of the later English landscape garden, the monuments at Wentworth Woodhouse are dispersed throughout this extensive and bounteous Arcadia, whether within the agricultural estate or at different extremities of the parkland. Indeed an earlier lakeside temple was even removed in order to improve the spacious aura of naturalness.

The elegant neoclassicism of the monument's three tiers is topped by a circular tempietto, while the arched central story displays a sculptural sarcophagus to symbolize the dead hero, and the interior of the ground floor enshrines the principal Rockingham Whigs. As such, the monument exemplifies the tendency to remove sculpture from the landscape altogether in favor of installation within distant and eye-catching buildings that would be visited in the course of the parkland tour. Thus the combination of architecture and sculpture creates a cenotaph dedicated to remembrance that subsumes the functions both of a temple of political friendship and of a pantheon of contemporary British worthies.

Inside the monument, Edmund Burke's eulogy to Rockingham is emphatic that "This monument [. . .] was not built to entertain the eye, but to instruct the mind." Its purpose was to enshrine the civic virtue of Rockingham's program and his political coterie, to distance them from the king's disastrous war, and to emphasize his patriotic role as peacemaker. Around the central and life-sized statue of Rockingham by Joseph Nollekens, each of the four wall niches supports a pair of portrait busts—of Charles James Fox, John Lee, Frederick Montagu, and Sir George Savile by Nollekens; the Duke of Portland and Lord John Cavendish by John Bacon the Elder; Admiral Keppel by Joseph Carrachi; and Edmund Burke by John Hickey. Burke's *Eulogy* is inscribed into the statue's pedestal and presents Rockingham as the ideal Whig statesman, an imperial hero, and the peacemaker who restored: "Increase to its [Britain's] commerce; independence to its publick [*sic*] councils, and concord to its empire." These points are emphasized by Montagu's poem that concludes the inscription:

> No Fields of Blood, by Laurels ill repaid,
> No plunder'd Provinces disturb his shade:
> But white-robed Peace compos'd his closing Eyes,
> And join'd with soft Humanity her sighs.

The subsequent accounts of the landscape of park, gardens, and estate, published well into the following century, were permeated with the tone of Arthur Young and reproduced the inscribed eulogies of Burke and Montagu.[36]

Amidst the masculine landscapes addressed by this chapter, the two Marchionesses of Rockingham, both active Whigs, created gardens that exemplified a feminine modernity. Within the military-style bastions of the parkland's Rockingham Wood, the first Marchioness created a garden of exotic and picturesque diversions which, further enhanced by her successor and daughter-in-law, won accolades in print from visitors between 1750 and 1783. During the 1760s, the second Marchioness also created a small landscape garden in neighboring Tankersley Park that encompassed the ruin of the old manor house, small lakes, plantations, a Gothic bridge, and the Tuscan belvedere known as the Lady's Temple.[37] During the 1770s, she created a flower garden in the pleasure grounds of the mansion in the fashionable style devised by William Mason for Lord Harcourt at Nuneham Courtenay. Indeed her political connections and the Rockinghamite sentiments of Mason allow the speculation that the two might have collaborated at Wentworth Woodhouse.[38]

~ § ~

These English case studies confirm that landscape gardens articulated ideas integral to the political, commercial, and aesthetic interests of landowners, whether aristocrats, gentry, bourgeoisie, or royalty. The concluding examples clarify that similar concerns are evident in Enlightenment gardens across continental Europe and the American republic. In his *Diary of a Journey to England* (1761–2), Count Kielmansegge is typical of the many continental visitors whose summary of the formal repertoire of English landscape gardening encapsulates the popularity of Stowe and Kew: irregular walks through trees, shrubs, and flowers (native and foreign), a winding lake, waterfalls, bridges, summer houses, seats and benches, heathen temples, ruins, colonnades, hermitages, and mosques.[39] Appreciated as the fashionable style of modernity, this genre of landscape design and its associations with the liberties of the landowning classes found a favorable reception with elite audiences across the European mainland from France to Russia. It especially appealed to monarchs and aristocrats who considered themselves to be, variously, up-to-date modernizers, politically reforming liberals, benevolent autocrats, or connoiseurial aesthetes. However, in other cases, meaning lay in a cultural distinctiveness that eschewed the fashionable elements of landscape gardening.

Certain extant gardens are renowned for the ways in which the Arcadian repertory outlined by Count Kielmansegge was deployed, as well as for the meanings embedded within the terrain. For example, at Worlitz, Ermenonville, and Arkadia (respectively in Germany, France, and Poland), the agenda of each landowner is inscribed within the garden as a reflection upon the wider politico-cultural environment. At the *gartenreich* of Worlitz, developed by Prinz von Anhalt-Dessau from 1764 to signify his enlightened modernity, the addition of such dramatic and theatrical features as the iron bridge and the volcano connoted his engagement with industrial innovation and the natural sciences. The landscape of Ermenonville was created between 1766 and 1776 by the Marquis de Girardin and developed to position him in relation to the ancien régime of the French monarchy. Furthermore, to identify the Marquis as a man of liberty, the garden commemorated the literal presence and then the memory of the contemporary critical thinker, Jean-Jacques Rousseau. At Arkadia, which dates from around 1780, the Garden of Allusions is rife with the meditative reflections of Masonic symbolism. Moreover, the significance of her iconography was so important to Princess Helena Radiziwell that she wrote the guidebook to the park.

Elsewhere, diversities of meaning were articulated in ways intended to differentiate between the Arcadian repertory characterized by Kielmansegge's description and gardens specific to the cultural and political geography of a place. One such is the memorial grove in the park of the Jægerspris Palace outside Copenhagen. The contemporary Danish advocate of the landscape

garden, C.C.L. Hirschfeld, argued that the potent nationalist agenda differentiated this grove from other dominant models, such as the French statue-rich
gardens of the Louis XIV era and the memorializing temples of the English
landscape garden.[40]

The fifty-four memorials commemorating heroes of politics, science, religion, warfare, and the arts were sculpted and installed by Johannes Wiedewelt
between 1777 and 1789. Collectively, these comprise a litany of national worthies composed on behalf of the monarch by Ove Høegh-Guldberg as part
of a wider politico-cultural program to promote Danish-ness. Consequently,
Wiedewelt chose not to design the Jægerspris grove as a landscape garden but
as a network of intimate glades within an expanse of dense woodland scrub
noted for its gnarled oaks, tall beeches, and dark fir trees. Thus, through successive encounters with each solitary memorial within this sublime landscape,
the visitor would experience a cumulative meditation on the heroism of modern Danish history and culture.

The memorial to the Colbiørnsen family (1779) comprises the ruined section of a house destroyed by fire in order to evoke the selfless gesture through
which the family frustrated the Swedish siege of Frederickshald in 1718. In a
similar vein the memorial to Ivar Huitfelds (1784) is composed of a fragment
of a shattered warship to signify the heroic decision to fight his blazing vessel
to the end and perish in the act of enabling the Danish fleet's escape from the
Swedish surprise attack of 1710. The monument is reminiscent of the ros-
tral column at Stowe (1747). According to George Clarke, this was originally
topped with a statue of Neptune bearing the wooden warship fragment that
killed the gallant Captain Grenville during a battle with the French.[41] However the distinctiveness of the Jægerspris grove is emphasized by the innovative
form of Wiedewelt's memorial to Huitfelds compared with the resolutely classical monument at Stowe.

The citizens of the United States of America were also keen to differentiate
the gardens of the new republic from English models, especially those that were
royal and aristocratic. By pragmatically adapting classical republican precedents, American gardeners deployed formality to delineate an ordered space in
opposition to the wilderness beyond. The ideological imperatives of republican
rigor and equality among citizens that defined civil society and national culture
were further signified by a moral insistence to counterbalance ornamentation
with the usefulness of husbandry.[42] At the same time, the gardens of prominent
citizens were hailed as places that both naturalized and heroized the republican virtues of American worthies and imbued their domains with the aura
of liberty. The Mount Vernon of Washington and the Monticello of Jefferson

are well-documented examples. John Searson's poem, *Mount Vernon* (1799), is redolent of the Virgilian tradition of pastoral poetry and exhorts the reader to "see Great Washington retir'd" in his peaceful Arcadia, a blissful harmony of rural nature and the human mind. Nonetheless, published in the immediate wake of Washington's death, the poet's account of vistas that yoke nature and retreat with liberty and commerce strikes a chord with the gardens of those mercantile, bourgeois, and Whig Englishmen, such as Thomas Hollis and Thomas Goldney III, who had supported the American cause. Searson urges the reader to "See . . . on th' beauteous Potowmack [*sic*] . . . ships and vessels . . . where thousand fishes glide."

Thomas Hollis had approved of the critical writings of John Adams, and honored him by naming a field "Adams" at Harvard Farm on the horizon of his Dorset estate. Through the ideological program of his agricultural pantheon, Hollis had envisioned the handing on of public liberty from English Whigs to Americans. Even though he never lived to see it, the creation of the new republic realized this vision. After the war of independence, Adams became ambassador to London, then vice president and finally president of the United States of America (1797–1801). During 1788, Adams's correspondence speculated on the dual task of gardenizing his estate at Braintree outside Boston, which he described as the farm of a patriot, and commemorating the Englishman he regarded as the great literary benefactor of his native state, Massachusetts. In a manner that invoked the Dorset pantheon, Adams pondered whether a meadow, a hilltop, and a brook were worthy of the names Hollis-Mead, Hollis-Hill, Hollis-Brook. In so doing, Adams identified an agenda of meaning whether or not this was realized on the ground. In both these American examples, ideological affinities with England were sustained despite the wider cultural quest for differentiation.

CHAPTER SIX

Verbal Representations

RACHEL CRAWFORD

SETTING THE STAGE: THE THEATER OF HORTICULTURE

"[F]or *perfect deceit* equals *reality*," writes George Mason in *An Essay on Design in Gardening*.[1] Defoe's *Robinson Crusoe* (1719) could be the paradigm that proves Mason's aphoristic comment: at an initial glance so perfect in its mimesis of the transformation of space into place that its first readers thought it a genuine travel account; an empirical narrative in which a castaway cultivates what he perceives as a savage state into an Englishman's estate; and an estate in which all depends on the island's capability to provide a habitation while appearing a perfect replica of nature. Deceit thus operates in what Crusoe considers his island estate at two levels: at the level of narrative, which promotes the efficacy of empiricism—its measurements, observations, rational judgment, experiment, and experience—to designate truth in a fictive mode; and at the level of symbolic form, in which the reader perceives art as nature and deceit as truth.

Similarly, in Goethe's *Elective Affinities*, the first crisis to effect the eventual separation of Charlotte from her husband, Edmund, is the disfiguration of her garden—a natural garden that respects the terrain of rocky protrusions and rough paths of which it is a part, thus paying tribute to Germanic sublimities of mountain, rock, and ravine believed to have formed the backbone of that hardy yet spiritual Teutonic race.[2] Her husband's best friend, the Captain (Otto), introduces instead *his* plans for the garden, produced through surveys, measurements, and schematics, translating it from Charlotte's not entirely comfortable paths and seats to a mathematically exact English garden, the fashion of Europe at the time. In words any reader familiar with Isaiah, or Handel's *Messiah*, would recognize—"Every valley shall be exalted, and every mountain and hill shall be made low: and the crooked shall be made straight, and the rough places plain"[3]—the Captain explains, "She had only to break away a corner of the rock, which is now but an unsightly object, made up as it is of little pieces, and she would at once have a sweep for her walk and stone in abundance for the rough masonry work, to widen it in the bad places, and make it smooth."[4] The inevitable product, the intent of which, despite its mathematical formulas, is to feign the natural, replaces Charlotte's Germanic garden with a little piece of England created amidst the rougher, soul-uplifting terrain of her native place.

Goethe's antipathy for the church and the pleasure he found in an ironic, Faustian nature would not have excluded him, having been raised in a power-fully Lutheran nation, from familiarity with Jesus's popular injunction, "Enter ye in at the strait gate: for wide is the gate, and broad is the way, that leadeth to destruction. . . Beware of false prophets, which come to you in sheep's clothing, but inwardly they are ravening wolves."[5] While Goethe himself may have felt more empathy for the Captain than for Charlotte, he nevertheless tells the story through the virtual lips of a sentimental narrator. A portion of this story involves the advice of the old friend Mittler, who, like the seer Tiresias (and conveniently apposite to his own name), mediates the roles of the actors around which the novel revolves; as such, he assumes the function of Schlegel's prophet, "the his-torian looking backward"[6]; and in the role of this functionary discerns from the beginning the culmination of so small an act as the equivocations involved in the translation of a garden from one idiom to another, the false outworking that results from displacing a fabricated England into *natural* German terrain, and the grander, *performative* outcome of a garden grown in the theater of the nation-state.

So the deceits of art operate in multiple ways. The singular irony in Defoe's and Goethe's legerdemain is that for many Protestants representation created considerable theological debate—for Martin Luther who did not object to it and for John Calvin, an avowed iconoclast. The fundamental problem inhered in the relationship between things and idolatry. Augustine's observation that words constitute a special category that embraces both signs and things com-plicated the problem. Augustine observes:

There are other signs whose whole use is in signifying, like words. For no one uses words except for the purpose of signifying something. From this may be understood what we call "signs"; they are things used to signify something. Thus every sign is also a thing, for that which is not a thing is nothing at all; but not every thing is also a sign.[7]

Gardens parallel Augustine's description: as a symbolic system, they occupy the domains of the natural and the symbolic. While the natural may precede the conventional in this case, it nevertheless, like the conventional, provides a rift through which idolatry may find a way, but also provides a potential hermeneutic, as John Bunyan illustrates in *Pilgrim's Progress*: in the *tableaux vivants* in the House of Interpreter, allegory converts things into signs.[8]

A graphic example of this hermeneutic process may be found at Het Loo in the Netherlands at the turn of the eighteenth century. Het Loo, the summer retreat of the House of Orange-Nassau, memorializes a symbolic system that represents itself as that of a Dutch *Stadthouder* and the road that it fronts as that of an ordinary town thoroughfare. The royal gardens themselves were characterized above all else by their riot of water and the conveyance through canals from reservoirs. In addition to the great canals and others of middling size, one of its many Lilliputian canals deviates into an intricate formulation of the initials of the king and queen, R.W.M.R.; a crown above the initials, moreover, formalizes the meaning inherent in the letters. As in Bunyan's allegory, God's Book of Nature represents the transformation of material things into the Word, the natural into a symbolic system that suggests the hermeneutical nature of the gardens as a whole, a code that can be analyzed, systematized, and ultimately made legible. Everything may not, as Augustine points out, be a sign, but in this case we are directed to interpret the signifying system of the garden as a whole.

By virtue of this hermeneutic, the garden provided a rich source of meanings for Protestants, though not for Protestants only. Drawn from some of the most salient moments in the biblical narrative, from the originating anecdote in the Garden of Eden, to the testing ground of the Son's incarnation and betrayal on the Mount of Olives, to fruition in the New Jerusalem, the garden is a focal point, and garden images contribute essential plot elements in the sequence of events necessary to salvation. The garden brings into focus forms through which nature explicates a soteriological narrative; yet, even as Christian critics judge art's inherent deceit, its fascinations lure them to revisit its themes, whether through the linguistic emphasis of evangelical Protestantism or the iconic one of the High Church, including Catholicism.

Considered mimetically, gardens present a conundrum: if they imitate nature, they provide organized images of God's Book, the revelatory natural volume that places salvation within the purview of all peoples. Though mimesis constitutes only one aspect of representation, that aspect is nevertheless essential to understanding gardens during the decades between 1650 and 1800: instructional manuals and guidebooks, especially, present gardens with a linguistic precision that often exceeds that of visual images, as Joseph Addison concurs: "Words, when well chosen, have so great a Force in them, that a Description often gives us more lively Ideas than the Sight of Things themselves."[9] Before (and to a degree, even after) Stephen Switzer's *Nobleman, Gentleman, and Gardener's Recreation* (1715) verbal precision, in both England and France, was devoted primarily to useful gardens: fruit, herb, vegetable, and flower gardens.[10] We think, for example, of manuals and treatises produced by Philip Miller (1724–68) and Jean de la Quintinye (1693), whose enthusiastic affection for the cultivation of vegetables, herbs, and flowers, the boundaries between which were porous, spilled over into lyrical renditions of their beauty.[11]

Throughout Europe, ecclesiasts developed sophisticated theories of garden representation derived from their comprehension of what constituted idolatry. Catholic countries, however, more or less escaped this dilemma. At Versailles especially, André la Nôtre's use of representation was constrained less by religion than by a narrative of the personage of the king and royal power.[12] Considered as a representation of things metaphorical or things metonymical, such as the power of the throne, representation by its very nature had to admit the evidence of things unseen; furthermore, when drawn into the signification system of language, as Augustine contends, words do not abandon their status as empirical objects; they may assume the properties of idols even in the absence of graven images. Words thus participate in the fictive economy of art, which in mimetic representation produces a parallel reality. Thomas Whately, in *Observations on Modern Gardening* (1770), and Henry Home, Lord Kames, in *Elements of Criticism* (1762), produce a genuine change in garden writing when they detach this reality from a moral system and reattach it to a pugnacious aesthetics in which art allies itself with pragmatism and deceit inhabits an extra-moral category.

In England, the conventional history of gardens, as John Dixon Hunt pointed out decades ago, is based on assumptions drawn from an erroneous interpretation of statements made in the eighteenth century and earlier. I would add to his more political correction that this convention was also seen as beginning with a fall late in the seventeenth century into an imitation of continental, especially French, formality, and a rebirth in the eighteenth century into the genuinely English landscape park characterized by extent, imitation of nature, and titled estates. In this narrative, the park reaches its apogee between 1730 and 1790 when an expressive methodology replaces the emblematic.[13] Switzer continues to articulate this interpretation in the first chapter of *The Nobleman, Gentleman, and Gardener's Recreation*, and its prevalence in twentieth-first century coffee table productions and even scholarly work intimates that this history will become a mythology of the English garden.[14] In such a mythology, the seventeenth century becomes precursor to *le jardin anglais* in the later eighteenth century throughout Europe, a view that makes sense only in hindsight, and could not have been the supposition of gardenists in the seventeenth century.[15] I focus instead on the linguistic trajectory provided by written representations of gardens in instructional manuals, fiction, and poetry. This trajectory reveals a different story in which aesthetics replaces typology and the emblematic remains, although its efficient cause shifts from the spiritual to the political. The idiom that accompanies this trajectory emphasizes a relationship between horticulture and the unfallen world that includes the garden's salvific potential, responsible proprietorship, frugality, utility, and simplicity—what Switzer cast under the rubric *simplex munditiis* and carried over effortlessly into the extensive style of gardening. In his words, just as *simplex munditiis* reflects "an unaffected Simplicity and Neatness in the Words, Actions, and Dress of a Man or Woman, so in Gard'ning and all the whole Cycle of Arts, it signifies a noble Elegance and Decency, a due Proportion and clear Majestick Mein in the several corresponding Parts thereof, and without straining it too hard."[16] Although this approach articulates a primarily Protestant idiom, it is not limited to Protestantism as the ensuing fashion for *le jardin anglais* suggests; moreover, Protestantism itself has no import apart from the Catholic matrix in which it was engendered and gestated: *simplex munditiis* is meaningless without the miraculous intricacies that provide signification in rich ornamentation and ritualistic splendor toward which even Protestant artists aspire: the plain style itself has intricacies that lie beyond the hermeneutic power of the Logos.

MIMESIS AND DIMINUTION

Of the Netherlands, Walter Harris (William III's court physician) remarks on the simplicity of the countryside, which he sees as lacking in variety, since it has "in one place the same Aspect and Resemblance to that in another, as an Egg is like to an Egg . . ."[17] In addition, the "*Apparel* of the [non-Noble] *Dutch* is grave, and free from levity"; they eat simple food—primarily fish—and their

"Church is without dispute the chiefest *Honour* and *Glory* of the *Reformation*, and the brightest Example of True Moderation, between the gay Decorations and Paintings of *Superstition* on the one side, and the mean and homely Addresses to Divine Majesty on the other."[18] Thus the Dutch exemplify the marriage of Calvinism with the famed toleration necessary to their economic success in the seventeenth century.

Harris closes his introduction to *A Description of the King's Royal Palace and Gardens at Loo* with a reflection on the austerity of his own rhetoric:

> I . . . leave it to the Reader to make a true judgment . . . from the *Description* it self, which is at least natural and plain, and as perspicuous as the nature of such Descriptions (sometimes necessarily intricate through the great variety of matter) will admit, though indeed very destitute of the ornaments and flourishes that are usually made in the describing *Great Things*, to make them appear *Greater* than they *really* are.[19]

Harris therefore inadvertently calls upon the aesthetic of *simplex munditiis* and the rhetoric of the *sermo humilis*. At Het Loo, although "gay decoration" offsets gravity, Harris's "natural and plain" language nevertheless reveals the intricacies by which gardens, even in the mode of *simplex munditiis*, may exceed language, so that any garden, theoretically, may fall into that aesthetic if the language used to describe it maintains an austerity and perspicuity that, in a linguistic fallacy, makes things appear "as they *really* are."

Despite the systemic allure of Het Loo, I confine myself here to the ingenious and even whimsical uses of water, the symbolic core of the garden and material foundation of most of the Dutch provinces in the seventeenth and eighteenth centuries. Het Loo's canals do more than demarcate elements of the garden, proliferating into various sizes, from the Great Canal to some a mere seven inches wide, from fountains not more than *jets d'eau* to fantastic elements of the simulacrum through which the gardens cohere; thus, in a conscious mimesis of the Low Countries, the broad Lower Garden nearest the palace is sunk beneath the main water level and surrounded by a "dike" of sloping turf, providing the sense of a little world that supplements the outer world it adds to *and* replaces, intensifying it in the same way a group of small Tritons may supplement a large Triton and together form a fountain that amplifies symbolic references to the sea. The fountain sculptures, especially, demonstrate how a garden's "fabric" may communicate the symbolic system of a country; Het Loo foregrounds its debt to the sea rather than, as in Spain, for example, drawing upon a Moorish code that formulates gardens as *mappae mundi*, thus symbolizing the almost universal idea in the West that the garden constitutes a little world.

Hydraulics constitute the most important techne of Het Loo; relying on a "remarkable" system of "natural conveyance of water that does constantly run, and is not forc'd up with Engines into great Cisterns" and thereby supplies marvelous and diverse configurations of water from six reservoirs, the vivers.[20] Harris comments on the practice of continuously renewing the vivers with fresh water to preserve the sweet scent of the waterworks with distinct anti-Catholic bias:

[T]he very famous *Water-works* of *Versailles*, have in this regard a very great disadvantage and inconvenience, because they soon contract corruption and after they are forc'd to play, are found to cause an *ill stench* in the *Gardens*. Whereas at *Loo* the water is always sweet, and there is no need of Commands, or Preparations for a day or two before, in order to make it run.[21]

Like Versailles, however, the variety of waterworks has an extraordinary quality that even in print infuses those gardens with liquidity: at Het Loo, the Great Canal and its increasingly diminutive simulations; brooks and viaducts; reservoir-fishponds and pools; fountains, jets d'eau which escape from the tines of Neptune's trident, mouths of miniature dragons, nostrils of dolphins and tongues of sea horses, and spouts from the gilded horn of a Triton and four lesser Tritons; cascades, sheets and double sheets of water, down-turned bells both large and small, falls and multiple falls into shell-like basins that spill into shell-like basins, and showers of small rains. Like the river that runs under Paradise in *Paradise Lost*[22] that provides a natural hydraulic mechanism, Het Loo's canals lose themselves under walkways, terrain, or even other canals to reemerge into the open air.

The hydraulic effects of Het Loo tend toward more and more water moved through lesser and lesser gradations, which produce correspondingly greater visual effects. Some might see in this tendency toward smallness, rather than toward the greatness of the sculptures of sphinxes or presiding deities, the *style précieux*—shells and pebbles take the place of marble, a preference established by Italian practice, while *parterres à l'Anglaise* resemble textiles of cut velvet woven on gauze. More like the "Dainty China Country" in *The Wonderful Wizard of Oz*,[23] the diminutive impression the gardens yield evokes Baum's porcelain landscape whose delicate inhabitants speak, move, and break—and so suggest the frangible, ephemeral, and artifactual side of nature in its domesticated state. The water system taken as a whole contributes to the sense that Het Loo is its own little world, one that generates a mimesis of the Netherlands—its debt to, and fear of, the sea. Rendering the sea in both its real and mythical estate, the symbolic system signifies perfect management of the sea's encroaching waters and, in the antisense, fills the grounds with the liquid song of moving waters that bear the trace of a threat only tenuously controlled.

The following description of a fountain at Het Loo, pruned almost to excess, exemplifies the Dutch inclination during this period toward contraction and repetition. Such descriptions underscore the Dutch tendency against feigning extension—the fantasy that would dominate the mid- to late eighteenth-century English landscape—and through a scattering of images explodes the rhetorical space of the text with each increasingly smaller feature. Repetition in ever-smaller forms accentuates the diminution for which the Dutch style has been both famed and scorned. I begin well into the description, initiated by Harris's comment that "The Park is a *great space of Ground* containing many Long Green Walks, Groves, Nurseries, Fountains Canals, Cascades, the Viver, and divers Corn-fields, within the Pales":[24]

> In the middle of this *Cascade* . . . there are four little *Boys* a *fishing*, and drawing a *Nett* full of Fish; the four little *Boys* are of Stone, with leaden Network coloured like Stone, in their Arms; and through a great deal of this Net-work placed between the *Boys*, the water falls into a large wrought *Basin*, and from this *Basin* the water falls again in five several places between other Net-work. Two of these falls of water from the said Basin are made into a Stone *Canal* below, that runs along the side of the Wall, under the Stone Bridges into the *Canals* on the North and South sides of the *Cascade*.
>
> [*He describes three other falls and a further conveyance of the water through statues and canals that form sheets of water that eventually fall into a single basin.*]
>
> In the middle of the common Basin there is a large inverted *Bell* of water, near two yards high, and the *diameter* of its *basis* on the top seems to be much about two yards likewise. About this *Bell* there do arise twelve Spouts which throw up the water about eight foot. On the North and South sides of the Basin, . . . there are other *lesser Bells* of water inverted, on each side one. . . [*He describes the spatial context of the common basin.*] Moreover . . . there are made to rise, when

'tis thought fit . . . about fourscore the most minute Spouts that can
be conceived. They are like a shower of small rain, artificially made in
a certain order. . . Every one of these little *Spouts* . . . is covered with
a small Copper Cover, that has five little holes through which the
water does rise in five small branches, like to a very small shower of
Rain.[25]

The diminutive elements in the design of Het Loo's gardens draw attention
to human dimension and the manipulation of human scale. Human beings
step over or wander beside *miniature* canals, in the two senses that they
diminish and replicate the Great Canal, thus bringing attention to illusions
of scale that Jonathan Swift manipulates in *Gulliver's Travels* (1726). The
garden highlights human form and eschews the manipulation of perspec-
tival distance prominent in Italian gardens and in the grand canal at Versailles, where, as one walks toward the end farthest from the palace, the
canal gradually widens, revealing the stratagem that provides the appearance
of unaltered width from the palace. Instead, at Het Loo the Lower Garden
is surrounded by dike-like slopes of turf into which stairs must be cut for access, down the corners of which may fall water into a succession of shell-like
basins, while the walks above made of broad strips of lawn, gravel, and dirt
parallel canals of varying widths.

Its human dimensions, its exposed divisions, and repetition of topiaries
and canals would seem characteristic of a style that declares itself as taking
an unorganized set of images and making them legible through art; yet the
artifactual quality of Het Loo, set against its wilderness, as well as its many
architectural elements, including topiaries of vernacular cottages at the corners
of the queen's arbors, windows cut through the hedges that surround her private garden, seats of turf within her garden, and curving arbors which, from
above, simulate a monarchical crown, suggest something quite other: it fore-
shadows the dual process that would become a staple of estates a half-century
later—that art feigns nature and nature feigns the impress of symbolic form.
Like those gardens, it enacts the structural opposition that reifies the wall that
separates the artful garden from the artless wilderness, the Hedge of Grace that
figures in Puritan literature as a boundary between the Elect and the Philistines.
The topologies of nature become by convention nature and not-nature; and
despite its Lilliputian quality and consciousness of excess, Het Loo nevertheless fulfills our expectation of landscape that has been ordered into a form
quintessentially Dutch.

The Het Loo of the seventeenth century and early eighteenth century provides a subtle truth; its overt manipulation of nature discloses the plasticity of natural form: gardens are not just mediated and manipulated, but metaphoric. In a direct sense, they map the domain of nature onto the domain of images, symbolically linking the illegible forms of nature with everyday objects; canals, dirt paths, cottages, idealized seats of turf, window openings into hedges underscore the human proportion. Symbolic representations of these objects survive the translation into literature, whether fictive or descriptive, as artifactual forms. Like all visual art, they synthesize disparate cognitive spheres, the pure noumenal realm of nature with the symbolic, aesthetic world of images.

ERROR: VIEWS AND MAZES

Le jardin anglais emulated, in at least one fundamental way, Versailles, which well before the middle of the eighteenth century became the cynosure of gardens that emphasized aesthetics over spiritual uses and placed a nationalistic and state symbolic at the core of garden design. Thus, despite its natural contours, the English garden, while bringing something uncustomary to the European garden, also brought with it something already deeply familiar—the garden that served the state, a symbolic core arising from the developing concept of the nation. Politicians themselves referred to the English garden's variety as simulating mixed government, its serpentine paths as representing English forms of freedom, and so forth. Milton's *Paradise Lost*, also, brought with it the interpretive possibilities of its uses in the interest of the state.

Instruction manuals contemporary with *Paradise Lost* were likewise dedicated to public environmental concerns for recreating vanished fruit gardens and felled forests following the ravages of the countryside before and during the Interregnum. Political ramifications can be found in treatises as persuasive as John Evelyn's *Sylva*, with its appended collection of essays on making cider, metaphorically, a method of rendering the vinous spirits of English race from the English fruit.[26] Milton, with his close ties to Evelyn and other members of the nascent Royal Society, wrote an epic that demonstrated his own knowledge of horticultural practice and its native uses. Paradise in the larger contours of its mountain seat, combines a well-designed timber forest with a fruit garden that, together, like Evelyn's *Sylva*, manage the arboreal needs of a nation that, in recovery, had a specifically ecological agenda in timber and fruit. (In addition, the convex, stadial design of timber trees that surround the walls of Paradise owes a debt to the Italian incorporation of theater design into gardens.[27]) The environment was not, of course, central to Milton's high argument. The inclusion of figures of speech into the tributaries of the poem suggests that the "flowers of language" comprise a linguistic horticulture of more use to Adam than God's Book; knowledge of the latter of which was restricted in a figurative version of eating the fruit of the Tree of Knowledge. The warmth with which Raphael receives Adam's curiosity about the cosmos contrasts sharply with his response to Adam's curiosity about the world around him. Contrary to instructional manuals that advise gardeners to learn God's doctrines from their gardens, Raphael restricts God's Book to the heavens:

> To ask or search I blame thee not, for Heav'n
> Is as the Book of God before thee set,
> Wherein to read his wond'rous Works, and learn
> His Seasons, Hours, or Days, or months, or Years:
> This to attain, whether Heav'n move or Earth,
> Import not, if thou reck'n right; the rest
> From Man or Angel the great Architect
> Did wisely to conceal, and not divulge
> His secrets to be scann'd by them who ought
> Rather admire.[28]

The Ptolemaic universe provides a provocative if outmoded trope for Milton's narrative: its errant inner circle of wandering stars, which earth inhabits, and its inaccessible outer Empyrean offer a figure for the narrative itself. Raphael's words thus artfully address the work of feigning in the production of the poem.

Moreover, the seventeenth-century critical tradition that posits Paradise as a precursor to the English garden indicates that nature does not give itself to us freely but requires the hermeneutic task of untangling art from lies. Milton's description of Paradise falls soundly into a system that interrogates the relationship between art and deception and art and nature in an historical time when art existed on an etymological borderline that lay simultaneously between the representation of beauty and mechanical skill and between art and nature. Milton explicates his concerns about the representation of Paradise and its relationship to art and truth in the fourth book when he disrupts a topographical

account of the river flowing beneath Paradise, that like the disappearing and
reappearing canals of Het Loo, emerges at the boundary of Eden, with a divert-
ing moral purpose

>   to tell, how, if Art could tell,
> How from that Sapphire Fount the crisped Brooks, . . .
> Ran Nectar, visiting each plant, and fed
> Flow'rs worthy of Paradise which not nice Art
> In Beds and curious Knots, but Nature boon
> Pour'd forth profuse on Hill and Dale and Plain.[29]

An instrumental question concerning topography pervades this passage:
does Milton refer to Eden entire, since Adam and Eve survey the prospect the
slope affords, or restrict the scene to that part of Eden called Paradise—to the
garden, or its view over lands neighboring the Paradisal mount? As a secondary matter, this question denotes the fact that Paradise, placed on the sloping
side of the mountain rather than a flat summit, has an enhanced view over
Eden, outside its domain, and a topography that aids its hydraulic system. Its
slope emulates Italian gardens such as those of the Principe Doria or portions
of the Villa Lante and the gardens of Frascati, something similar to those
Milton had seen when he visited Italy from May 1638 until June 1639.[30]
More important, the entire sentence also queries truth in reference to that
proffered by the mythological golden fruit that "Hung amiable, Hesperian
Fables true,/ If true, here only, and of delicious taste."[31] Both these excerpts
fall within the ambit of representation and telling. Milton's use of the phrase,
"if Art could tell" recalls the diction of Spenser's Bower of Bliss in *The Faerie
Queene*, particularly concerning the area that *neighbors* the bower where
"The art, which all that wrought, appeared in no place."[32] This translitera-
tion of Utopia creates a metonymic displacement in which the area fast by the
Bower of Bliss shares in its beauty and provides a precursor for the slippage
in Milton's text between Paradise and Eden in which Eden partakes of the
garden's ideal estate. The lands of Eden that surround the Paradisal mountain and drink of the same waters that run beneath Paradise, but through
Eden, *were* Paradise's prospect, its view *and* the place to which Adam and
Eve were consigned after the Fall. It foretells God's fortuitous grace to his
creation in which the rain falls on the just and the unjust alike[33] and produces
flowers *worthy of Paradise*, but remains outside the symbolic system that
makes nature intelligible, outside the formal English designs Adam and Eve

maintain in their Paradisal home, for, closely explicated, their garden does indeed reveal its formality.

The Hesperian fable speaks rhetorically to the role of truth in Milton's polysemous narrative of a fruit garden with parallel yet conflicting lines of interpretation. Both Spenser and Milton describe scenes that replicate nature almost perfectly, but insufficiently to prevent the cognitive disturbance that results from a slippage between art and nature. The core of the matter rests in the truth of the fable, "true,/If true, here only": true only within the rhetorical space of the poem. The concept of representation shifts to a different level, in which, to pilfer a trenchant discrimination made by Coleridge, rhetorical representation has priority over the object of representation in logic rather than in time.

A logical rather than temporal relationship helps to account for the fact that in *Paradise Lost* Raphael dislocates the interpretation of God's Book from the hermeneutic frame of the garden to the inaccessible Ptolemaic cosmos. In Ralph Austen's garden manuals, by contrast, fruit gardens epitomize God's Book;[34] moreover, Austen threatens to jeopardize his system of profit and pleasure by celebrating words themselves as material sources of worship, a pleasure in language that characterizes instructional manuals. In the tradition of Paradise, gardenists characteristically recommend carefully implanted forms of error, such as the maze. French broderie, unlike the grassy English plat, evokes the form of the maze, complete with entanglements, intersecting vectors, and twisted lines of herbage. Even the most pragmatic manuals incorporate visual plans for parterres or knots that elude linguistic description. In Stephen Blake's *The Compleat Gardeners Practice* (1664), as in other garden manuals, plans for knots include one for the labyrinth.[35] Language fails at the level of complexity that error requires and such images reinforce the Protestant suspicion of idols and their amplification of the second commandment, which bans the worship of images.[36]

Mazes indicate the magnetic quality images of error created in the garden, in part because of their visual intricacy, in part because of the mythos of error that accompanies gardens historically, and in part because of the etymological link between error and wandering, the latter of which infiltrates gardens from Jane Austen's shrubberies to the oneiric wildernesses of Flaubert; yet, mazes also speak to the biblical promise that, when tempted, the elect will find a way of escape. In the biblical scheme, error not only signifies wandering, but also as Flaubert comprehends, temptation and escape, failure and recompense. *The Legend of Saint Julian the Hospitaller* tells the tale of a man who

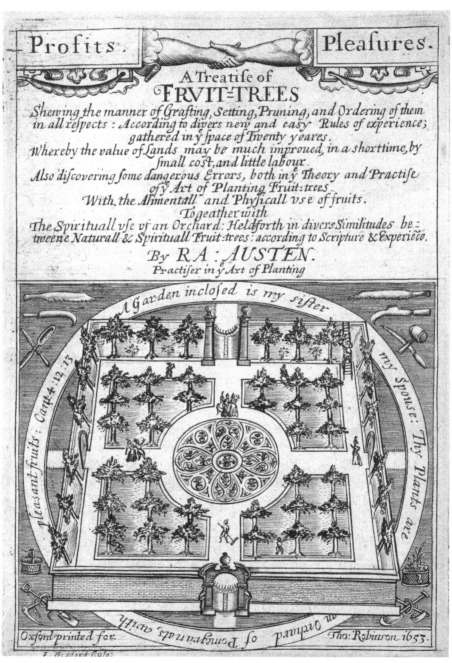

FIGURE 6.1: *A Garden inclosed is my sister my Spouse*, Ralph Austen, Title Page, *A Treatise of Fruit-Trees* (1653), RB 64523. This item is reproduced by permission of The Huntington Library, San Marino, California. Austen's title page exemplifies the necessity of learning to read and interpret God's Book of Nature. On the literal plane,

lives without grace, who wanders wildernesses spiritual and physical, but who also, after a catastrophic fall, gives up his possessions, survives in the sparest of shelters, and finds a life of humility, penance, and finally rest.[37] The maze of error gives way to the center of grace. Just as the garden promises a place of contemplation, so the maze within the garden provides a contemplative core, which found, provides rest. Rubrics of mazes, such as Dezallier's, often represent at their centers such a place—whether the rudiments of a garden, an image of two people evocative of Paradise, or a single tree as though, in Emily Dickinson's representation of a prairie, "the reverie alone will do if bees are few."[38] The maze in John Smith's imaginary estate resonates with the biblical language used to describe the New Jerusalem. *Paradise Lost* provides a darker image: the closer Eve gets to the Tree of Knowledge, the more she finds herself in a vertiginous space, which metamorphoses into a simile in which a Night-wanderer, misled by a will o' the wisp, stands at its nucleus, "amaz'd" (book 9, line 640).

Milton's Archangel Michael's final prophetic history portends "A Paradise within thee happier far" (book 12, line 587). Tempted, Adam and Eve fall in order to achieve recompense, a spiritual horticulture that yields the inner fruit of the Christian life. In the eighteenth century, evangelical and political narratives intertwine with horticultural practice, but as the former became less necessary to the definition of national character, the rhetoric became deracinated and aestheticized, yet nevertheless still contains traces of its etiology. For the French, this includes the erasure of religion from horticultural practice, despite a dominant apparatus of state; in England, serpentine paths, ha-has, outlandish plants that brought botanicals from beyond the Hedge of Grace incorporated emblems of error while at the same time becoming enriched by a nationalistic political discourse: winding paths emblematized free feet; variety in plantings, mixed government; the boundless gaze, commonwealth; and the elimination of *allées* and *pattes d'oie*, emancipation from autocracy.

it illustrates a fruit garden enlivened with people of all sorts; the design is plain and has protective walls, but resembles a pleasure garden. Tropologically, the enclosed garden incorporates the Word: it exists under the aegis of Profit and Pleasure, which greet each other, and incorporates a text from the Song of Songs, which reminds us that Christ and the Church ("my sister") exist in terms of identity-in-difference, while Christ "knows" the Church as a husband knows his spouse. Anagogically, the combination of Word and figure produces an emblem of the Son, the Word of God and his express image; yet, at the anagogical level the image is noumnal and thus interrogates the reliability of images generally.

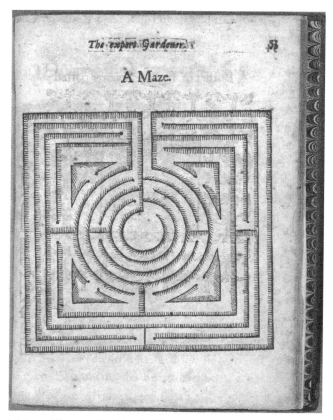

FIGURE 6.2: *A Maze*, Thomas Barker, fl. *The Expert Gardner* (1654), 53, RB 104446. This item is reproduced by permission of The Huntington Library, San Marino, California. Barker's pattern is identical to images of mazes in other manuals. This particular maze could well be called the English maze, since it is found in the first book on gardening published in English, by Thomas Hyll (Hill), and continued to be published well after 1654. Properly, the maze with its hedges is a type of broderie, but volitional and, in England, emblematic. Although the maze signifies wandering astray, the view from above associated with omniscience reveals its design. To reach the center of this most typical of mazes, the correct path first leads one away from the goal; only after the periphery of the maze has been traversed does the correct path begin to lead into the maze's heart. The maze thus measures a counterintuitive spiritual path, though the pattern is clear to those with redeemed vision.

THE EMBLEMATIC AND THE AESTHETIC

English and French treatises from the seventeenth century, whose authors matter of factly refer to an English style, provide a thread of continuity that suggests that despite changes in taste, a genuinely English formal style was recognized

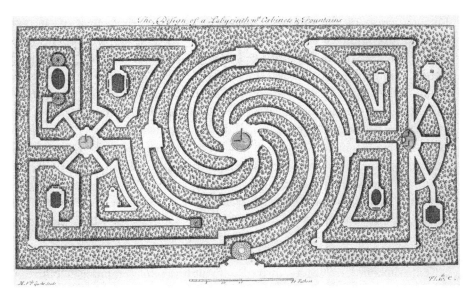

FIGURE 6.3: *Design of a Labyrinth with Cabinets and Fountains*, Antoine-Joseph
Dezallier, *The Theory and Practice of Gardening* (1712; 1728 ed.), Plate 10. C. RB
353474. Courtesy of The Huntington Library and Art Collections. In France, the maze
focuses on earthly delights. Errors, rather than terminating in dead ends, lead to private
cabinets, arbors, and fountains. Thus, the French maze discloses its more playful qualities: fundamentally a walk, the motion is not forward, and ornamented space provides
occasions for dalliance.

before 1700; the "natural" style between 1730 and 1790 did not constitute
a revolt against continental forms, because the formal style in England *was*
English. The Duc de Monconoys referred admiringly, for example, to "la mode
d'Angleterre" in 1630; Samuel Pepys spoke approvingly of the singular English penchant for plainness.[39] For Switzer, Queen Anne exemplified the plain
English style for "Rooting up the Box, and giving an English Model to the Old-
made Gardens at Kensington"; the Earl of Carlisle, writing of England's formal
style, contends that it brought horticulture to

> the highest Pitch that Natural and Polite Gard'ning can possibly ever
> arrive to: 'Tis there that Nature is truly imitated, if not excell'd; and from
> which the Ingenious may draw the best of their Schemes in Natural and
> Rural Gard'ning; 'Tis there that she is by a kind of fortuitous Conduct
> pursued thro' all her most intricate Mazes, and taught ev'n to exceed her
> own self in the Natura-Linear, and much more natural and promiscuous
> Disposition of all her Beauties.[40]

Like gardenists on the continent, who borrowed English elements such as the bowling green, gravel, and turf, the English borrowed, but the formal English style is based on three interwoven features: plain design; empirical thought, collection, and experiment; and grass and gravel, considered across Europe as the zenith of their kind. English gardenists, like the Dutch, discovered many of their garden elements among ordinary people in ordinary places: bowling greens were originally a feature of English pubs, and John Evelyn claimed they were "singular to the English nation"[41] though they were borrowed both for the king's garden at Het Loo and at Versailles. The *parterre à l'Anglaise*, fundamentally turf, was introduced during the reign of Charles I; gravel walks contributed uniquely to formal design, and at Oxford students were charged for their upkeep.[42] To be English also encompassed "Vegetative Philosophy,"[43] of which the Physick Gardens at Oxford and Chelsea provided examples: gardens renowned for their beauty, formal features, medicinal use, collections, and commitment to empirical experimentation. Beauty thrived with utility, while empiricism buttressed "the practical and plain Method" that characterized the writings of the greatest English gardeners of the seventeenth century,[44] and was sustained by the Protestant commitment to plain style and its recompense in profit and pleasure. The values of the plain and utilitarian were smuggled into English aesthetics as an aspect of beauty. For Immanuel Kant, beauty existed only when "purposiveness" is stripped of "purpose"[45] while "relative beauty," for British aesthetician Henry Home, Lord Kames, provided pleasure because of its utility.[46]

The long-standing characteristic of English singularity does not mean that the linguistic representation of the landscape in the first third of the eighteenth century remained static. Joseph Addison and Switzer's emphases on extent, the elimination of visible boundaries, and "nature" marked a desire for change.[47] A scrutiny of the work of writers such as Alexander Pope suggests that differences between the natural lines of *le jardin anglais* and the mode it replaced were not as stark as has been represented. The sinuous path is an indicator: it exchanges one geometrical form for another, but does not offer a new symbolic code; the sinuous line has no more claim to nature than the linear; the winding path restrains the feet as much as the straight. Emblems of Protestantism and English politics, such as the line, offer opposing meanings, but not structurally different models: in a Protestant emblematics, the serpentine path might insinuate the presence of controlled evil; in politics, the carefully controlled freedoms of English government—but both visualize control.

John Smith's imaginary estate elucidates this point when contrasted with Pope's 1731 critique of seventeenth-century garden design in his Epistle to Burlington;[48] Smith's description in *England's Improvement Reviv'd* (written

1653; published 1673) interrogates the extent to which Pope's critique represents a paradigmatic change rather than merely the obverse side of a structural opposition as it pursues a common political topic for its period, as may be inferred from *Paradise Lost*: the propagation of timber.[49] The fifth of Smith's six books provides a precise description of how timber may be incorporated into private property and offers a counterpoint, for us, to Pope's Epistle.

Smith uses conventional Protestant diction in his description of the estate, quoting directly from the English Bible, but excluding visual images from his text; his treatise thereby discloses the crisis the second commandment embodied for devout Protestants. For images, he substitutes an accumulation of mathematical information and iconic scriptural phrases, such as the common term *four-square* drawn from John's biblical dream vision of the New Jerusalem. In addition, he hybridizes the empirical with the emblematic, a strategy that underscores the treatise's eschatological geometry. In a first reading, empirical details heap up, producing a fascination in their own right; and, as in *Robinson Crusoe*, Smith's empirical diction creates a linguistic estate with extraordinary truth value subject to the same empirical deceits as Defoe's. For example, its 200 acres "four-square" provides a round rather than prime number and cannot therefore be truly accurate;[50] yet such error provokes the tropological plane of the image, compelling the imagination beyond the estate's literal dimensions. The explanatory language with which Peter Goodchild accompanies his meticulous conversion of the description into visual plans reveals how far from empirical precision Smith's measurements stray. Goodchild's accuracy also depends upon interpretive decisions signaled in his diction, from "inferred" and "if it was true" to "he does not indicate" and, most appealing, "This is a guess"; Goodchild points out that the location of the house, the central emblem, "has been interpreted."[51] As expressed by Smith, the Word requires interpretation the moment it leaves his hands, unless we could effect the impossible and intuit its indexical image.

More telling, the estate's profits take on a material rather than spiritual form when Smith converts labor, spirituality, and natural literacy into ready money. His reification of profit may seem mercenary, but in Protestantism's odd negotiation with wealth he rests on solid doctrinal ground: worldly success measures spiritual wealth. The peculiar convergence between frugality and riches became so important to garden representation the following century that Switzer, appealing to a wealthy audience, could assert, "this extensive Way of Design will be of Use: The Manner of doing which, will, I hope, appear delightful, besides the Cheapness in Performance, will (I doubt not) but be very agreeable to the frugal Planter."[52]

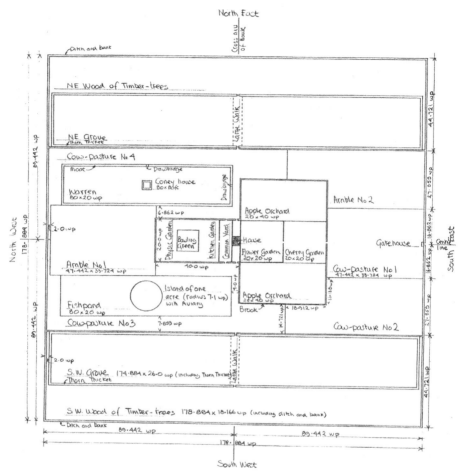

PLAN 1 : GENERAL LAYOUT OF THE ESTATE

FIGURE 6.4: *Schematic plan of the general layout of* [*John Smith's*] *estate.* Peter Goodchild, "John Smith's Paradise and Theatre of Nature: The Plans," *Garden History* 25, no. 1 (Summer 1997): Figure 1. Courtesy of the Garden History Society.

Though the departure from the seventeenth-century English formal man-ner would ultimately contribute to an aesthetic, Smith's ideal estate indicates how formality could have a native English character.[53] His rows of timber and groves, coney house and fishpond, kitchen and physic gardens, and other estate elements mirror each other. As his words lead us through the estate, they establish precedents for *le jardin anglais*, emulating elements from French formality without copying them. The walks, plats, and fountains of Smith's estate; its four streams, four mounts at the corners of the fruit garden, aviary, and apiary produce variety in the context of formal oppositions, while every feature is emblematic and useful. Smith's formality imparts a sense of imma- nence through the trope of a spiritual progress that adds a comic dimension to the visitor in Pope's Epistle to Burlington sweating up the terraces toward Timon's office. Similarly, structural opposition accrues the status of spiritual design: individual gardens emphasize places for contemplation, labor, and rec- reation, consistent with his insistence that contemplation should take prece- dence over disputation;[54] so the imaginary estate represents contemplation as a rational progress that attains increasing inwardness through interpretation. In the process of reading the description of the estate, we progress past timber trees and walled or hedged gardens that conceal the home. Smith designs the cherry orchard purposely to provide a "full view of the dwelling house,"[55] yet Goodchild's schematic reveals that one would have to stand in very particular spot to do so, as the view is compromised by the nine-foot walls that surround the cherry and flower gardens. Thus we move inward toward the architecture of companionate marriage. Rather than encountering the magisterial façade of a country house from a carriage approach, linguistic progress matches the progress of contemplation: the Christian moves further into the work of salva- tion to contemplate the goodly land of God's grace, while the estate gradually discloses marital unity as an excursion through profit and pleasure. The estate as a whole constitutes a tmesis that cuts through history, or fallen time, in order to mark the space between the garden of the human race's first innocence and the city four-square of the Protestant's eternal habitation.

A paradigmatic alteration away from an overt Protestant rhetoric does not genuinely occur in English garden writing until mid-century, when authors, fol- lowing the lead of philosophers, aestheticize descriptions. Indeed, kitchen gar- den manuals in the early eighteenth century produce identical formal designs for kitchen and pleasure gardens. I once thought these highly designed gardens with gravel paths and vegetable parterres were whimsical miniaturizations of pleasure gardens, but, aided by the example of Het Loo, I have come to see that authors and gardenists spin diminutive places into forms that do not privilege extent and instead rely on garden elements that favor increasing generations of miniaturization. Such spaces favor working gardens, in part, because they represent the aesthetic interests of an emerging middle class in countries such as England, France, and Germany.

Het Loo's emphasis on miniaturization and diminution exemplifies this point. More than many monarchical gardens, it represents the interests of the urban middle class; furthermore, it incorporates the symbolic landscape of the

Low Countries, maintained by the hydraulic dike and canal system. As Simon Schama has convincingly shown, the thriving seventeenth-century Dutch economy, like that of the English a century later, was driven by middle-class interests and working solutions, such as the salt trade—interests eschewed by mercantile-motivated economies such as Spain's in the sixteenth century before it collapsed under the weight of its bullion.[56] The English formal style was therefore pragmatic and imitated a structural principle that gardenists such as Ralph Austen believed immanent in nature but required human imagination, ingenuity, and labor to bring into visible form; the same structural principles were also proleptic of the eighteenth century, honored during that period without regard for critiques of littleness or rebukes of "fussy, Dutchified taste."[57] Urban and suburban taste drove these principles, which were adopted by a middle class that was growing, realizing its own power, and developing, adopting, or recuperating myths, legends (usually indigenous, such as Robin Hood and Dick Whittington), tales (sometimes imported like *The Thousand and One Nights*[58]), and metaphors that became symbols of their power by the end of the eighteenth century. The scorn that late eighteenth-century owners of small gardens who adopted the natural English manner endured reveals how much miniaturization exacerbated the differences between the classes: elfin winding paths, hummocks and rivulets produce a kitsch that threatened to make mockery of eighteenth-century class values.[59] A fundamental feature of *le jardin anglais* was, as Whately's treatise articulates, its attachment to an ideology of class; thus, "vast efforts in little objects are but ridiculous."[60]

The impact of alterations in eighteenth-century landscapes owes more to the kinds of gardens that accrued representational weight than to the number of gardens influenced by the natural style. After mid-century, the English landscape park became the fashion for garden design in the West. Meanwhile manuals devoted to useful or small gardens—those most likely to retain formal designs—lost visibility. How authors organize the contents of these publications illuminates the differences: the latter offer horticultural instructions such as planting, pruning, grafting, and manuring; they also classify plants and convey pharmaceutical information. Treatises on landscape parks organize their materials by the names of great estates, from Stowe to Studley Royal, Badminton to Blenheim, and emphasize design. Philip Miller's *Gardeners Dictionary* and less familiar calendars and almanacs, though also widely circulated, underwent such significant social erasure that historians have claimed that kitchen garden manuals were no longer written in the eighteenth century—yet the gardens they represented easily outnumbered landscape parks.

As Lancelot Brown's successor, Humphry Repton devoted his career to landscape parks until about 1803 when he begins to reveal his misgivings. He regrets the loss of "the precise line betwixt nature and art";[61] disparages devices designed to deceive the eye in the effort to possess the view; rejects the link between beauty and extent—all objections that derive from a principle central to his values from the inception of his career: the human dimension of his landscapes, intrinsic also to Het Loo's gardens before they were razed to follow the fashion for *le jardin anglais*. The outcome of this evolution reformulates the role of deceit in art as articulated by George Mason in 1752 with the phrase that introduces this chapter. "For deceit equals reality" sustained the rise in representational status of the landscape park, in part because the disguise of the disguise that facilitated boundless views and the highly designed "natural" contours of the *le jardin anglais* allowed massive earthworks to produce ascents for viewpoints, groves of young trees that would grow in time into the hanging woods for which England was famous, and artificially burbling streams stocked with trout, all de rigueur features of the landscape park. These represented a classed counterpart to England's well-defined internal boundaries of hedges and low stone walls memorialized in Wordsworth's "little lines of sporting woods run wild";[62] the slow, brown rivers meandering through the picturesque shires of England in Robert Louis Stevenson's beloved children's lyric, "Dark brown is the river/Golden is the sand/It flows along for ever/With trees on either hand."[63] In an alternative naturalization, the "natural" garden normalized the social demotion of useful gardens.

In *Mansfield Park* (1816), Jane Austen makes Repton's rejection of deceit in garden design both ambiguous and humorous, in part because she refers to him by name, thus motivating her narrative thaumaturgy: is he real person and fictional character? Beyond the comedy in which Repton straddles the categories of historical personage and pure invention, she portrays him as a disagreeable but complex figure. The fact that John Rushworth, the most obtuse character in the text, supports him only for fashion, reveals little. Without question she uses conversations about Repton to reveal personality facets of her characters. All but Repton's final treatise would have been available to Austen, demonstrating that over time many of his practices, like Austen's, changed. As an author, she would have been well aware of the flaws in treating the *Sketches and Hints* of 1795 like his later writings. He wrote his first treatise when he still considered himself Brown's disciple, but the French Revolution and Napoleonic wars, which straightened the finances of many of his clients, brought about a sea change in Repton's ideas and in English gardening generally. This included a shift in emphasis from the expansive lawns of the great estate to much smaller, even pocket-handkerchief gardens and city squares, from the serpentine lines of *le jardin anglais* to earlier rectilinear forms, from the appropriation of the view to the gemlike formalities of the gardenesque (often associated solely with J. C. and Jane Loudon), and from the dual deception necessary to sustain the deception of the boundless view to the reintroduction of the visible boundary. If not all of these ideas were articulated in *Designs for the Pavillon at Brighton*,[64] many were, and they would have been accessible. Austen's own work coincides directly with the period during which Repton's most salient ideas unfolded.

As his career matured, Repton placed the physical context of a commission ahead of design principles. His later decisions indicate a pleasure in recovering the "ancient" style, so long as it enhanced human comfort: "*the landscape ought to be adapted to the beings which are to inhabit it*—to men and not to beasts."[65] With the discovery over time of a reverence for "ancient" and, to his mind, indigenous British horticultural traditions, the later Repton would have approved of components of Sotherton Court, the Elizabethan estate owned by Austen's Rushworth—but not all: perhaps not the terrace, which was well out of fashion (though he would have approved of the visible line it created between house and garden, between nature and art), definitely not the wilderness with its sinuous paths: here Repton would have sympathized with Mary Crawford, who objected, "Oh! You do not consider how much we have wound about. We have taken such a very serpentine course;"[66] nor would he have approved of the ha-ha, which he had always thought misinterpreted by Brown's followers, and was doubtless relieved that it had now become outmoded; yet he would have approved of the iron fence that revealed the division between wilderness and park, as he believed that the line of separation should reveal itself; he would have approved of the straight path that ran along the ha-ha, since it mirrored the iron fence, and he would have approved of the building's southeast orientation, and of a less definable factor—its venerability. We may surmise that, unlike Rushworth, Repton would have approved of the approach to the house, which, by inference, was direct; and also surmise approval of the avenue of trees behind Rushworth's house, since it "leads from the West front to the top of the hill, you know"[67]—the crest of the hill, in Repton's view, permitting imaginative freedom, a value he treasured in landscape design. Though, in general, he did not like the artificiality of a line of trees, he would not have approved of cutting down any avenue in its entirety, but, like Brown, of cutting trees down here and there in order to open up vistas, often to other plantations; and he would likely have chosen trees that had been damaged over time. Unlike Rushworth, he did not lead with an axe. While this does not comprise a complete list of architectural details, landscape or built, on which Repton and Rushworth could have exchanged views (with the proviso that Austen's narrator would have to provide adequate information about Repton on Rushworth's behalf, and there is something unsporting about the fact that she does not, or perhaps she betrays a lack of effort on Repton's behalf—one hates to say laziness), it does reveal the curious and complex nature of the imaginary meeting of a character with an actual professional gardener, who is simultaneously two- and three-dimensional, simultaneously himself and his errant reputation.

Repton's mature principles, on the whole, betray an aestheticized Protestantism, exemplified by his objection to masking the points at which art and nature diverge, which has a precedent in the anxiety that images may lead to idolatry; his insistence on disclosing boundaries, to the treachery of the imagination; the reintroduction of the straight path, to an emblematic rectitude. Regarding the latter, history suggests that much of the discourse surrounding *le jardin anglais* concerns the geometry of the line, which inevitably raises the problem for gardenists of what to do when beauty and utility meet. Repton recognizes that any intervention in nature is a deceit that constitutes a form of art when he comments, "The most common attempts to improve may, indeed, be called deceptions;"[68] Although such deceits may characterize art, or perhaps because they do, he emphasizes utility: "By a strange perversion of terms," he says, "what is called modern, or English *gardening*, seldom includes the *useful garden*, and has changed the name of the *ornamental garden* into *pleasure ground*."[69] The useful parts of the estate, though hidden from the principal rooms of the house, should be kept conveniently nearby; paths should be straight, with manure easily wheeled to kitchen gardens and vegetables brought to the kitchen.[70] Repton's principles develop out of topographical contexts, pragmatism, and an interpretation of natural geometry as encompassing more than one form. In linking aesthetics and utility to nature, the straight path may indeed imitate nature more accurately than the serpentine, though both spring from geometry: one rectilinear, one curved (and perhaps in a covert bypath, Deutero-Isaiah's injunction that "the crooked shall be made straight."[71]

Paths, more than any other feature of the garden, formed a moving metaphorical line, an unstable boundary that was emblematically redrawn in the eighteenth century from a spiritual onto a political plane. Simultaneously, in a Protestant value system, utility contributed to the plain lifestyle, a by-product of self-disciplinary behaviors that governed social conventions as disparate as dress, the *sermo humilis*, storytelling, and garden design. Repton's recursive discussions of utility produce a passage on the advisability of winter walks that betrays none of this history. Protestant diction had become so much a part of ordinary vocabulary that garden culture had become post-Protestant in that its diction floats on the surface of representation unmoored to the concepts that originally grounded it. Repton begins by assuring his readers that he has no intention of "reviving the old [seventeenth-century] taste of gardening," yet, in this description, he, like Pope in the Epistle to Burlington, inverts the path we trod through Smith's estate. The home no longer radiates a center of immanence reached after the pilgrim's progress through goodly lands, but becomes an architectural feature with windows through which we gaze at that path's transposition:

> Our ancestors were so apt to be guided by utility, that they at length imagined it was in all cases a substitute for beauty; and thus we frequently see ancient houses surrounded not only by terraces, avenues, and fish-ponds, but even stables, and the meanest offices, formed a part of the view from the windows of their principal rooms. I am far from recommending a return to these absurdities; . . . and there is surely no object of greater comfort and utility belonging to a garden and a country mansion, than a dry, spacious walk for winter, sheltered by such trees as preserve their clothing, while all other plants are destitute of foliage.[72]

The beauty of the winter garden has no purpose without use; its deceptions, no function without utility. Perfect deceit may equal reality, but the pertinent reality in the late eighteenth century required the comfort of human beings in nature.

CHAPTER SEVEN

Visual Representations

ANNIE RICHARDSON

To portrait-painting . . . we subjoin, as the last branch of uninteresting subjects, that kind of landscape which is entirely occupied with the tame delineation of a given spot: an enumeration of hill and dale . . . what is commonly called views. These . . . may delight the owner of the acres they enclose, the inhabitants of the spot, perhaps the antiquary or the traveller, but to every other eye they are little more than topography.[1]

At that moment appeared Kent, painter enough to taste the charms of landscape, bold and opinionative enough to dare and to dictate . . . he realised the compositions of the greatest masters in painting. In general it is probably true that the possessor, must be the best designer of his own improvements.[2]

If the painter's landscape be indispensable to the perfection of gardening, it would surely be far better to paint it on canvas at the end of an avenue, as they do in Holland, than to sacrifice the health, cheerfulness, and comfort of a country residence, to the wild but pleasing scenery of a painter's imagination.[3]

History painter Henry Fuseli's disparagement of topographical art, Horace Walpole's praise of William Kent as painter followed by the note that the owner is the best designer, and, finally, Humphrey Repton's professional self-defense as a landscape designer introduce us to a key narrative in the rep-resentation of the garden in eighteenth-century Europe. This chapter will refer to the wider European period context, but will focus mainly on representations in England to decode and contextualize them. A growing market economy in early eighteenth-century Britain allowed specialization and professionalization in the production of images and designs.[4] This in turn produced a sense of competition around the social and professional location of tastes relevant to garden design, as we see in Walpole's and Repton's statements. The growth in market demand for the visual arts was dramatic enough to sustain specialist production, so that from the 1720s it became possible to produce a range of types of landscape so that the dominant estate view became only one of many possible types.[5] Toward the end of the eighteenth century, an adulatory patri-otic discourse arose that viewed some British landscape artists as mediators for the expression of a nationally rooted genius.[6] The "magical" transformations of natural phenomena wrought by the unique styles of J.M.W. Turner, Thomas Girtin, and others were felt to elevate them above the merely commercial cat-egories of landscape producer, the tame topographical delineator, or the sensa-tional showman of effects.

The concern here with perceptions of professional identities is designed to counterbalance the existing narratives in the relatively scarce literature on the representation of the garden in our period. The few treatments that have not been within the framework of garden history as such have tended to operate with the same narratives, singling out, as the most dramatic changes in the rep-resentations of the period, those that appear to be parasitic on stylistic changes in the design of the garden and the mode of its viewing, the bird's-eye view figuring the formal garden, and so on.[7] The effect of this focus on capturing a preexisting aesthetic has been a relatively narrow understanding of the range of meanings these representations might have held, in contrast to the breadth and multidisciplinary nature of histories of landscape painting in general. These have acknowledged the active agency of landscape representation[8] in the negotiation or disguise of class relations and ideological divisions,[9] the cultural enfranchisement of the polite tourist,[10] the construction of understandings of production and consumption, and, by the early nineteenth century, the marked avoidance of representations of specifically owned land in order to sustain a generic "rural" as locus of value and mythical form of identification.[11]

While garden historians have largely viewed garden imagery as document or design ideal, corrective calls for broader methodologies have emerged, sensi-tive to the role of schematic perceptual and conceptual models through which image makers would have perceived gardens,[12] and alert to the persuasive role of the very techniques apparently most designed for accuracy, often harnessed in the early modern period to relay social status in terms of cultural taste.[13] This chapter responds to these calls with a visual culture approach that considers the "equipment" of makers—their models, conventions, skills, and production methods—and the "equipment" of the viewer—the ways images might activate the cultural knowledge and values of an ideal historical viewer. A leading premise is that images create meanings about more than the objects they depict, since they organize the field of vision, operate with codes drawn from a range of cultural forms, and activate understandings of a social world.[14]

The first section analyzes a small number of case study images through visual culture approaches. The second section looks specifically at the visual culture of the landscape designer. The final section considers the garden in visual satire in recognition that images circulate not only to share but also to contest meanings within their wider culture.

THE GARDEN IMAGE IN VISUAL CULTURE

Llanerch Park, Denbighshire (ca. 1662), by an unidentified artist, is one of the earliest bird's-eye perspective views of a country house in Britain.[15] The garden was laid out by the owner, Mutton Davies, from a staunchly royalist family, after travels in Italy and elsewhere. It is generally assumed to be an Italianate-style garden, because of its terracing, grottoes, and statuary.[16] The primary conventions adopted by the artist are those of engraved architectural views of houses and gardens produced from the sixteenth century in Italy, France, and the Low Countries. The combination of viewpoints here—a plan-type viewpoint over the circular Neptune basin, and a viewpoint level with the top of the house for the rest—is attributed to a "naïve" or "journeyman" artist.[17] However, some seventeenth-century bird's-eye engraved views also combine perspectives from different viewpoints, for example where sloping ground would otherwise render the shape or identity of a garden feature unreadable or where the principal buildings are shown in elevation, in combination with a plan view of the grounds.[18] Estate maps combine plan views of fields and gardens with elevation views of the house. So what are the implications of using conventions from these two genres in a painted estate view?

Engraved architectural views of house and grounds were stimulated primarily by the growth of tourism to Italy and France, the desire for familiarity with prestigious gardens across Europe, sometimes to model a garden after them, and in order to glorify the monarchs and nobility of France and the Low Countries.[19] By the late seventeenth century, they were part of the nationalist

FIGURE 7.1: English school (seventeenth century), *The House and Garden of Llanerch Hall, Denbighshire*, ca. 1662–72, Yale Center for British Art, Paul Mellon Collection, USA/The Bridgeman Art Library.

or regional "propaganda machines" of France and the Netherlands in particular and served, through their detailed and exact notation of the features of formally planted gardens, to combine the record of a unique location with the signs of membership of a relatively homogeneous elite social group. The connotations of the conventions of the printed architectural estate view then included fashion, cultural prestige, and membership of an exclusive but collective identity.

The bird's-eye view became one of the most common formats for painted views of estates in Britain and the Netherlands, along with views of parts of a house and grounds from less elevated viewpoints. The bird's-eye view appears to have been common from the sixteenth century, not only to capture planting patterns and the axiality of layouts, but also to allow inclusion of land beyond the cultivated areas. This situated a property geographically, but also articulated a dialectic between inside and outside the property as, for example, between civilization and negatively viewed wilderness, or civilization and a positively viewed, divinely blessed natural order.[20] Engraved views used graphic techniques to heighten contrasts between cultivated and uncultivated areas and to create the overall effect of a minutely worked pristine concept.[21] The relative smoothness of areas of fields and walks in the Llanerch painting replicates these effects of contrast from engravings. Similarly, estate maps and improvement plans contrast the areas of park, garden, and fields.

From estate maps, the Llanerch painting employs the technique of representing a local settlement by depicting a church—here St Asaph's Cathedral on the horizon—and the technique of giving trees crisp, linear shadows. Estate maps were developed as administrative and legal tools when land became a commodity with the development of capitalism and professional land surveyors could service the need of landowners and tenants to "know their own" with a view to maximizing production.[22] The surveying profession could pride itself on providing extensive information about any aspect of a property in a way that appeared objective, permanent, and made sense "upon suddaine view."[23] Aesthetic sensibility grew not only alongside the development of estate maps in the seventeenth century, but was expressed through them, in combination with records of ownership. In elaborately decorated maps, illusionistic representations of birds, fruits, animals—especially deer—as well the owner's house, functioned to situate a "seigneurial emblem" within a sensory and aesthetic domain that fostered a poetic alongside a legal attachment to place.[24] By the end of the seventeenth century, an estate map was considered a necessity not only to secure a record of economic potential, but also because the map itself, as a little "commonwealth," could capture the symbolic status of an estate and the way this was "rooted" in land possession. It could also make the graphic visualization of this possession a delight, a neat ornament for the lord of the manor to hang in the study "so that at pleasure he may see his land before him" as *The Compleat Surveyor* of 1653 expressed it.[25] With devices such as title cartouches, compass roses, and brightly colored coats of arms, they offered a "symbol-fact" duality that focused political meanings.[26] The decorative devices would tend to be placed around the edges of the maps, and the placement of the basin and the church in the Llanerch view both suggest cartographic conventions, as does the heraldic brilliancy of the red coloring of the women's clothes. As Daniels suggests, "the basin looks like a medallion" and sets up a train of association making the water mill (with its circular wheel) and church (and presumably house) a series of emblems.[27]

Retaining the design ideal, prestige and display connotations of the architectural print, and the legal and management connotations of the map, the bird's-eye view is a relatively nonexperiential form, especially striking if we remember that the Llanerch landscape included tricks and devices as in Italian Renaissance gardens and offered far more than visual patterns. Lest we simply assume that the painting is a symptom of the lust for possessions that fueled the development of illusionism in Western art,[28] we should also recognize the associations of virtue in knowledge of the estate and its prudent management.

Commemoration of new build is likely to have been one motivation for this as for similar commissions.[29] However, generically and ideologically, this is an estate view: the house is prominent, if not central, and the framing, viewpoints, composition, and lighting of the whole create a significant series of emphases and relationships. The sunlight strikes the front of the house from the upper left. This not only lights the façade—a persistent generic convention— but the terrace walls, the smaller buildings, and the water mill. The eye is led from one "pool" of civilization to another. The framing and composition on the right-hand side vertically align the cathedral, the watermill, and the path from the Neptune basin. Semiotic methods alert us to the ways syntagmatic chains—associations produced by elements within the image—can combine with paradigmatic chains—examples of types or concepts. Perhaps what we have here are aligned forms of authority: the church and the divine (or the town), and the earthly power that harnesses the natural resources. The hallucinatory circle of the basin and its concentric hedging, containing as it does the statue of a classical deity associated with harnessing the power of the sea in decorative maps,[30] alludes to the authority of classical design, in association with national prosperity, and the perfection of geometric beauty echoing the heavenly spheres and thus divine order.[31] At Llanerch, the basin may well have contained fish, one of many creatures and products exemplifying the concept of nature's Edenic bounty as the reward for virtue and authority in the country house poem. Eels leap out onto the land, for example, in Ben Jonson's *To Penshurst* (1616). The basin echoes the sinuous protective frame of stream and bordering path. Perhaps the providential provision of resources and the virtues of harnessing these is alluded to here.

In the estate view, the garden proper is worked into a larger order, the estate as "microcosm," a universe of social influence imaged as a geographical one, as it also functioned in the estate map and the country house poem.[32] If by the end of the eighteenth century the painterly gaze replaced the cartographic in order to relinquish the "open relish of acquisitive power,"[33] the Llanerch view needs to be situated historically to embrace related but nonetheless different connotations of the prospect than simply power. In addition to the architectural print, the prospect view was associated with military surveys and fortification sightlines and with the "wonders" assembled in atlases, which included technological devices such as fountains.[34] In the seventeenth century, the term *prospect*, in its linguistic metaphorical usage, was linked to the technologies associated with vision: the technique of perspective and technological devices that enhanced vision, such as the telescope.[35] Thus the prospect referred to forms of interpretation that, as privileged forms of vision, linked inner and outer meanings. The garden itself, of course, as John Dixon Hunt has argued, is a representation, and it seems clear that someone like Mutton Davies, attempting to "English" an Italian garden, would have shared an awareness of some of the meanings Renaissance gardens held for foreign visitors.[36] They were perceived as microcosms: collections of rarities, and perfected versions of the imperfect world offering moral and political lessons.[37] Terrace gardens were recorded as providing magical visual effects since they offered views out of the garden and yet prevented viewers from seeing everything at once. They were considered as features belonging to classical gardens, along with statuary and the general idea of sacred spaces.[38] The prospect view itself symbolizes rather than reproduces the magical effects of the Italianate garden, since the viewer has been offered a privileged vision of everything at once. The multiple perspectives in the Llanerch painting should be considered not simply as "naïve," but as transcribing the tricks and deceits of the Renaissance garden, which Llanerch itself included,[39] and feeding the eye's imperious need for lordship, the rightly privilege of royalty, but available to the owners and visitors of buildings and gardens, according to seventeenth-century concepts of design.[40]

The Llanerch painting has four foreground figures, none of them in the garden itself. Topographical estate views do typically include figures, usually identifiable generically as wealthier folk, servants, and staff, as do some architectural prints, although the emphasis in the latter is generally on courtiers or visitors. All the figures in the Llanerch painting process centrifugally toward the house, the effect of gravitational pull reinforced by the deer that appear to stand to attention. The rider nearest the house appears better dressed and the rear women carry baskets on their heads. In order to consider the function of the figures, we can extend our "regime" of interrelated representations to include portraiture and Dutch genre. As Anne Lawrence has suggested, the estate view with its usually tiny figures reverses the situation of the outdoor human portrait where the house is relatively small.[41] Since the staff tend to be those who provide the immediate support for the household rather than agricultural laborers, Lawrence proposes that as in the Dutch genre and in the English and Dutch outdoor portrait, the generic theme is enjoyment of the "embarrassment of riches" rather than its production.[42] Interestingly, Lawrence asks how we might account for the perhaps unrealistic degree of social mix and integration shown in some of the estate views (though not Llanerch), given historical

evidence for an increasing spatial division of rank and gender in the English
country house in the post-Tudor period.[43]

The idealization of the estate as an organic community in the English country house poem provides an answer to this question. In our period, literary
sources, particularly poetry, have been essential aids to scholars for the ex-
cavation of perceptions about land and social relations and the metaphors
and fantasies supporting their visual representation.[44] Against the realities of
the commodification of land (the spur to the production of the estate map, as
discussed earlier) and display culture in the Stuart courts, the country house
poem hymned stable, virtuous, and "natural" social hierarchies through the
emblematic house "not built to envious show."[45] Natural elements such as
stone, wood, and water contrasted with gold and marble in Jonson's influential "To Penshurst," which insistently figured the ideology of the natural community and the magical pastoral transformation of the fruits of labor into the
fruits of nature. Visual prospects can convey the major themes of the poems:
religion "presides" over the education of the household, the coming and going
can suggest the contrast between city and country and the centrality and benevolence of the owner for all ranks, the ornaments of the garden and grounds
evoke notions of rural pastimes as sensory delights that are also studious and
innocent, flowers and fruit evince constant plenty or allegories of transience
(and thus still a reminder of the potential for virtue in a wealthy environment).
In several of the poems, animals and fish pay anthropomorphic "tribute," offering themselves willingly for slaughter, which seems to make sense of the
attentive postures of the Llanerch deer! Well managed, and a source of self-
conscious philosophical reflection, the estate and its gardens were "a prospect"
that could "restore man to his lost station: for God doubtless would never have
placed him in a paradise, had not a garden of pleasure been consistent with
innocence."[46] The painted prospect enables display and delight to be understood as allegory. The symmetry and beauty of one's own designs could also
be turned into an allegory of one's own creativity with something of the divine
stamped upon it.[47]

The watercolor views of Harewood House in Yorkshire undertaken by
Turner for Edward Lascelles in 1797 and '98 can help us to understand the
role of the estate view in a very different context at the end of the eighteenth
century. Lascelles's hospitality and patronage came toward the end of a tour
over several counties of northern England through which Turner's hundreds of
drawings could be the vehicle for future commissions or the setting for fiction-
alized landscapes, produced on his own initiative. Turner was working to his
own sense of purpose in an open market. Lascelles was a devoted patron of

contemporary British watercolor landscapes from artists endeavoring to make the medium a distinctive field of experiment and national expression.[48] Most of the views he commissioned of Harewood by Turner and others hung in the same room in his London house.[49] Included amongst Turner's four views of the house was *Harewood House from the South East* (1798), a viewpoint also selected in an earlier watercolor by Lascelles's father and later used by Girtin and Varley. The point presumably was comparison of the artists' respective styles and the representation of the estate with other types of scenery.

In this instance, the patron was an agent in the educational project enjoined on artists at the Royal Academy, and taken to heart by Turner, to assimilate the work of past masters and contemporaries and to measure oneself against them.[50] The estate view, given the longevity of the genre, was a useful vehicle, and Turner utilizes established traditions: varied viewpoints, light shining on and radiating from the house, extensive distances, subtle alignments, strongly differentiated light and dark areas, and small but legible details that indicate the management of the land (wagons, laborers, animals). His dense foreground detail responds to theories of picturesque beauty and its capacity to delight the eye, while darker expanses and vast distances respond to notions of the

FIGURE 7.2: J.M.W. Turner, *Harewood House from the South East*, 1798. Reproduced by the kind permission of the Earl and Countess of Harewood and trustees of the Harewood House.

visual sublime and its capacity to move. Such emphasis on subjective response would not have been available to the Llanerch Park artist, although of course that too is highly idealized in its way. Turner imposes himself wittily on convention, transforming the "politely" framed view of the house with trees and deer by his teacher Thomas Malton, an architectural draughtsman,[51] into an independent scene virtually animated by its picturesque roughness. Lascelles, and other landowning patrons who purchased a range of work from Turner as well as estate views, shared the artist's ambitious allegiance to an "elevated landscape" on the foundations of European traditions that could withstand Fuseli's "map-making aspersions."[52] At the end of the century, the estate view still enabled the display of virtuosity and creative reference to the past, but other landscape genres responded more effectively to demands for images of nation, expressive effects, and spiritual meanings. However, over the course of the seventeenth and eighteenth centuries, the representation of landed property remained a significant vehicle for the expression of social and moral ideas and the hybridization of genres adapting to market demand.

FIGURE. 7.3: Arthur Devis, *Sir George and Lady Strickland in the Grounds of Boynton Hall, near Bridlington, Yorkshire*, 1751, Ferens Art Gallery, Hull Museums, UK/The Bridgeman Art Library.

With Arthur Devis's *Lord and Lady Strickland* of Boynton Hall, Yorkshire (1751), we move from a landscape as portrait to landscape within a portrait. Devis's approach to portraiture came to seem "affected,"[53] as it perhaps does to us now, by the 1770s. However, the particular combination of theatrical postures, high-keyed figures, and a softly modulated parkland setting makes sense in context.

Devis was attempting to answer the formal demands on a marital portrait with an appropriate pictorial idiom. Gardens had featured in portraits since the fifteenth century as inset emblems, as "monument to dynastic pride," and as symbols of female virtue and fertility.[54] As in the estate view, they had harnessed the artist's skills in spatial representation to the portrayal of attributes extending beyond status and ownership. Devis has turned to the conversation piece, a genre of full-length group portraiture applied largely to families in which he specialized. Set back slightly from the foreground, attention was drawn to the figures' postures, possessions, and settings, as opposed to likeness, and the resulting staging of a social persona combined with perceptions of modish informality, sometimes enhanced by parkland settings, accounted for the explosive proliferation of the genre from the 1730s in Britain.[55] In her right hand, Lady Strickland holds a honeysuckle, emblem of "generous and deep affection."[56] It is held according to contemporary gestural codes in which grace signaled civility and gentility, and employs the specific code for "admiration."[57] Devis has brought together admiration and affection in a gesture that "affirms" husband and property.[58] The codified nature of the postures enabled the ideal spectator to understand the figures as enacting "complaisance": the dissemination of ease and refinement. The figures are set entirely to the left of the painting, leaving the sight of the serpentine water, distant hills, and sea for the viewer to enjoy, a form of "complaisance" for the viewer, normally signaled by the sitters' outward gazes. Although the amount of space devoted to the landscape here could be read as display or the artist's self-advertisement, it may also have served to translate the contemporary rationalization of codes of good breeding that recognized the importance not only of politically attuned niceties, but the tactful sensitivity required to negotiate the psychological needs and comforts of host and guest, with the viewer as a visitor who does not have the host's possessions forced upon him.[59]

A stimulus to the English outdoor conversation piece was the popularity of Jean-Antoine Watteau's fête galante,[60] a hybrid genre that mixed portraits with idealized generic types in conversations or musical and theatrical activities in parks and woodlands, as in *Fête in a Park* (1718–20). While these settings have been explained largely in terms of sources that also used landscape settings

such as French fashion plates, theater scenery, and prints with decorative
arabesque patterns incorporating figures in parklands, or the actual use of
gardens for theatrical and sociable activities, their relatively neglected-looking
appearance in Watteau's fête galante gave them a particular "charge" in their
French context. These were the *private* spaces of the garden, the bosquet or
wilderness, signifying *generalized* as opposed to *courtly* ideals of elite social-
ity and fulfillment—conversational reciprocity, gallantry, and bodies trained in
naturalized civility through social dance—whose viewing pleasures included
curvilinear movement along diagonal axes—echoed in the tracery patterns
for garden pathways and interior decorations.[61] The informality of Watteau's
overgrown settings was commensurate with the aspirational ideals of a French
bourgeoisie concerned with self-refinement through the adoption of aristocratic
manners.[62] In Devis's work, connotations of specifically Gallic refinement in an
English context may have played against connotations of old-fashioned formality created by the sitters' stiff postures.[63]

FIGURE 7.4: Jean-Antoine Watteau *Fête in a Park*, ca. 1718–20. By kind permission of
the trustees of the Wallace Collection, London. *Fête in a Park* is a larger, later reworking
of *Les Champs Elysées* (Watteau P389). The execution is perfunctory and the subject
appears curiously vapid on the large scale. With typical capriciousness, the fourth Mar-
quess of Hertford bought it at a sale in Paris in 1865 for thirty-one thousand francs
(about £1,240); ironically, the catalogue of this last sale used the fact that its pendant
had been sold seventeen years before to Lord Hertford for over a thousand pounds as
one of its main selling points.

Devis's setting is topographically inaccurate[64] and lacks any obvious iconography, but its suggestion of the contemporary challenge to geometry in
landscape design suggests the fashionable good taste the Stricklands may employ on future improvements. The extensiveness of the parkland setting, with
its connotations of exclusivity, reinforces the cultural status lent to the sitters
by their deportment and quietly advertises one of Devis's signature features—
landscape overmantels in his interior portraits—through which he could signify that his own good taste matched that of his sitters.

Whilst the pictorialist landscape itself lacks the means to connote order,
Devis's structural devices, such as diagonal "lines" created by the composi-
tional relationships, serves to figure notions of order and belonging. Blending of figures into landscapes became even more pronounced in marital and
society portraiture later in the century, according with the desire to combine
modishness with "high moral sensibility" expressed through response to
the landscaped garden,[65] and to signify the ways marriage expressed appropriate gender identities.[66] Devis's color blending of Lady Strickland's
dress with the landscape and the dog's adoring attention to her served to
align the generic identity of women and the private identity of men with
"nature," or perhaps more subtly stated, with natural sensibilities, more
fully the "property" of women. The pastoral setting endowed marriage with
the connotations of retirement, framing the woman in and with (rural) virtue, and allowing the man to absorb, temporarily, the softening qualities
of feminine sensibilities. These devices and connotations served to sustain
the ideology of the companionate marriage as the mutual polish of differently gendered natures.[67] Lord Strickland leans casually on a tree trunk (a
variant for a pedestal or balustrade in other outdoor portraits). The tree
of course is laden with latent symbolism in terms of landed power.[68] Lord
Strickland's physical distance and classically elegant masculine pose is nevertheless combined with absorption in his wife's gesture, and thus compatible with antiauthoritarian notions of the husband's role in contemporary
marriage discourses. These regularly argued that it was because of and not
in spite of the husband's greater legal authority and strength of mind that
he should have no need to exert authority but rather demonstrate affection
and esteem. Definitions of politeness in the earlier decades and the cult of
sensibility in the second half of the century, which overlap in their stress
on relative informality and their rhetorical rejection of ceremony, are both
prompted by concerns over artifice and their inappropriateness for Englishness and masculinity. This concern motivates developments in portrait
codes for (relative) informality.[69]

However, for all its theatricality to the later viewer, Devis's postures graft contemporary notions of portrait naturalism, social ease, breeding, taste, gender, and companionacy onto the portrait likenesses. They point to Lord Strickland's wisdom in his marriage choice and in the "ideal" template for the estate grounds, both indicating the likely fortunate "issue."[70] As in the Llanerch view, the landscape aids the representation of identity in terms of possessions, fashion, and rank to be transmuted into variously inflected signs of virtue in the social order and belonging in the natural order, and makes us aware that landscape design values, here serpentine waterways, are also social and behavioral.

VISUAL CULTURE AND THE PROFESSIONAL LANDSCAPE DESIGNER

A visual culture approach is particularly useful in investigating the visual design representations of designers in this period, since the second half of the century witnessed the emergence in Europe of the landscape designer as a distinctive professional with a named identity (landscape architect in France and landscape gardener in England) and a strategic use of visualization techniques. We can consider what techniques and codes were used to convey various types of information, what connotations they may have held, given their relationship with other types of contemporary imagery, and the ways they act as instruments of persuasion not only for the value of their improvements but professional intervention itself.

In France, the naturalistic garden style gave the signal for the emancipation of a profession distinct from architecture, the *"architecte-paysagiste."*[71] Elevated drawings expressed the pictorialist approach most appropriately, showing forms of ornaments, highlighting relationships between features, and allowing boundaries to remain hidden. However, the plan remained the key format, owing to the continued prestige and dominance of the architectural profession and the training of designers in surveying and engineering. Natural-style designers, such as Jean-Marie Morel, were able to incorporate into their plans drawing and wash techniques that relayed land contours and contrasted formal areas with darker-toned denser planting, producing a sense of the designer's deference to nature and the variegated textures and lighting that would result. Through the placement of structures, plans could also employ a rhetoric of suggested axiality, where none could be experienced on the ground, to suggest the degree of transformation in a makeover garden or the height of fashionability in a new one.[72] The light areas of hard-edged pathways served to emphasize the serpentine meanderings of the French *anglo-chinois* style as effectively as geometric shapes had expressed the patterns of the formal style. In Sweden, Fredrik Magnus Piper (1746–1824), supervisor of public works, court surveyor, and the foremost landscape gardener in the country, produced the most detailed and informative plans of his day, incorporating indications of land contours, atmosphere, and sightlines in addition to the more usual structural layouts and elevation drawings of buildings.[73] The coexistence of complementary visual formats and multiple forms of information within the plan were the expression of a profession seeking emancipation on the basis of its multiple forms of practical and theoretical knowledge.

In France, designers' publications of landscape theory and articulations of the role of the professional designer tended to be unillustrated since the idea was to follow the treatise formats already established by owners and intellectuals and to privilege the scientific understanding of and imaginative response to different types of landscape and the knowledge needed to make best use of them. In England, where large-scale elegant improvement plans were the norm in landscape design and only architects submitted reports as albums, Humphry Repton's Red Book albums make him a telling if not representative case study for professional self-presentation. Indeed the whole subject of the visual culture of designers and design publications in this period is under researched and merits further treatment.[74]

In England, the context for the emancipation of the landscape designer, or "landscape-gardener" as Repton termed it, was different to that in France. The rivals against which Repton competed either for commissions or for recognition included contract gardeners, estate managers, owner-improvers, theorists of landscape aesthetics, and—symbolically at least—landscape painters. When Repton justified the designation of landscape gardener in terms of the need to unite the "powers of the *landscape painter* and the *practical gardener*,"[75] he was not only presenting multiple skills, as was the claim in contemporary Europe, but arguing that his entry into the cultural world of genteel and aristocratic owners—with an understanding of the ways landscape design supported status, taste, and wealth creation—warranted his intervention.

The combative context for Repton's Red Book *Attingham in Shropshire— A Seat of the Right Honble. Lord Berwick* (1798) allows his strategic use of visual codes and text-image interaction to be seen at its most astringent. The red Morocco-bound quarto volume of thirty-four folios is typical of Repton's corporately styled improvement reports in combining rationales, theoretical statements, and didactic watercolor drawings, some of which demonstrate before and after versions of a scene with pull-up flaps. This report expressly addressed the politically enflamed wartime polemic around the use of "picturesque" notions of beauty in landscape improvement, which Herefordshire landowners and aesthetic theorists Richard Payne Knight and Uvedale Price had deployed against the Brownist parkland style, which they rightly saw Repton as continuing.[76] In question were the taste and integrity of any owner who saw fit to employ a professional. For Payne Knight and Price, Brown's belt-clump-and-shave aesthetic was the mechanical application of a fashion, insensitive to site and history, while for Repton's supporters and non-noble clients, a ready-made taste was a passport to integration alongside fashion-conscious neighbors. Repton used *Attingham* to present himself as a utilitarian conservative and to refute Payne Knight's mockery of the value placed on extensiveness as mark of status in his and Brown's designs, and Payne Knight and Price's insistence on the need for a painter's eye in landscape design: one attuned to connoisseurial conventions through familiarity with the old masters. Repton was continuing the strategy Price found understandably irksome, of insistently denying the importance of painting in visualizing landscape beauty in favor of notions of convenience and the enjoyment of places in real life, while illustrating changes with "the best pictures" he could make.[77]

In *Attingham*, as in all his Red Books, Repton referred self-denigratingly to his drawings as "sketches," partly to underplay their rhetorical role, and (paradoxically) partly to adopt the voice of the polite amateur artist disavowing professional engagement.[78] Although the books were attempts to integrate into the bibliophile material culture of the library as a polite social space,[79] their techniques—the overlays and the actualization of sequential circuit views—had been criticized as effeminate and commercial, akin to spectacular forms of entertainment such as the panorama.[80] With the term *sketch* then, Repton may have been seeking to distinguish the drawings from the turn to the temporary effects of the "atmospheric" in contemporary landscape painting, which stepped a fine line between the magic of genius and commercial theatricality,[81] and to allude to his own relative "accuracy" and consideration of permanent conditions.

However, Repton was not denying that landscape design was an art of responsibly planned deception. At Attingham, he argues, "apparent extent" is a "first principle."[82] As a recently enlarged, three-story pavilioned neoclassical pile, which dwarfed its front lawn, "apparent extent" was socially congruent (as polite tourists were pointing out), especially since the building faced the main road from London to north Wales. Designing only apparent extensiveness was also socially responsible in the light of current fears that too much land was unpatriotically unproductive, and Repton explicitly distanced himself from the "unnecessary extent" of Brown's "followers" in this.[83] Repton's development of this point, while appropriating the verbal discourse of aesthetics, the visual conventions of high art, the picturesque vignette-style amateur sketch as promulgated by William Gilpin, and the topographical seat-view print, is a tour de force that persuaded Lord Berwick to go ahead with his improvements and critics to concede his claims to pragmatism in the picturesque controversy.

Berwick had amassed a reputable collection of old masters on his grand tours. As his first illustration, *Elegance versus Decay*,[84] Repton draws a glimpsed colonnaded pavilion set behind the brick arches of a ruined mill by the side of the house, and busily brushed bushes and trees, parodying one of Berwick's Dutch landscapes in the style of Ruisdael, and a Gilpinesque sketch. The incongruent perception of the house as a ruined Greek temple, were such a view designed in reality, makes the point that, the formal appeal to the eye, so beloved of the picturesque theorists, would inevitably be cancelled out by offense to the understanding. Here and in his subsequent painted parody of Lord Berwick's Claude, Repton undermines the argument for painting as model without undermining the owner's taste or denying the value of high art conventions as signifying practices, while also engaging with aesthetic theory's support from the psychology of perception. The parody-Claude, perfectly composed with signature devices, such as shady foreground "wings" of tall trees, opens to an insipid panorama of regularly dotted planting accompanied by the cogent argument that the human angle of vision, particularly that of the inhabitants of the house standing at their breakfast room window, being five times wider than that presumed by the Claude, cannot be satisfied by a Claudeian gaze unless the viewer stands far back from the window.

Sketch 5, *View from the Bridge on to Attingham Hall*, likewise draws on and with picturesque conventions. The river Terne, passing in front of the house and seen by visitors from the highway, was liable to flooding. With the overlay flap in place, the unimproved muddy channels offer the "charms" of "irriguous appearances" to the painter who can select an appropriate level of water, whereas the "nobler" objective of the designer, as illustrated with the flap removed, is to create "an ample river majestically flowing" commensurate with the status implied by the building and "spreading cheerfulness on all around it."[85] Again picturesque conventions—the irregular shapes so accessibly captured by the amateur tourist and sketcher or the professional painter as magician—are associated here with professional dereliction of duty. The improved view courts comparison with Payne Knight's earlier satirical illustration of a fashionably trim Brownite/Reptonian river in front of a Palladian mansion.[86] With sketch 5 and the proposal for a new weir and embankment, Repton was also targeting Price's published criticisms of the artificial trimness of Brownite water improvements. "Cheerfulness" tactfully alludes to both the visual pleasures of the contemplation of (enlightened) light on emblematic water and the mental pleasure of an owner with significant investments in waterways distributing the coal from his coalfields. Price had claimed that his love of picturesque irregularity in landscapes, revealing effects of time and place, was intimately tied to his role as preserver of social "connection" in traditional paternalistic communities, and Repton's view of the Tern asserts the compatibility of aesthetic pleasures and pragmatism. Although Attingham was closed to the public,[87] the improved view is what the traveler on the road bridge would have seen. Appropriately then, Repton draws on the conventions of the printed seat view designed for the wider audience of tourist viewers in the latter half of the century, balancing the orderly modernity of improvement in seat and city views with the wildness of unimproved scenery.[88] Seat views generally showed the approach to the house. Angle and elevation might vary, but the house would be shown in enough detail to give a sense of style and placement, and legible signifiers of class and/or productivity from the Llanerch-style prospect view would be retained. Repton referred to these modes but drew even more from traditions more resonant for the owner: higher viewpoints, wider angles, and fewer figures. Unlike the view of Attingham from a similar but lower viewpoint in a printed set of seat views that offers elegant discoursing tourist staffage for identification and narrows the extent of visible lawn and river,[89] Repton has retained the emblematic tropes of the microcosm-estate.

If Repton's intense, discursive self-framing marks a new phase in the professionalization of landscape design, he also casts light on the huge importance of the status of art and artist in the creation of prestigious landscape designs. The triumphalist celebration of William Kent as "creator" of the pictorialist garden arose from his unassailable status within a patronage relationship with Lord Burlington and sketchy drawings, often based on fantasies. His imagination could easily be appropriated within the shared sensibility of a connoisseurial elite,[90] and in a similar way, in France, Hubert Robert's interchangeably styled Watteauesque parkland fantasies and animated projected designs indicate that a non-innocent eye projecting the signs of high visual culture was needed to mediate the concept of garden as a mise-en-scène for patrons projecting their cultivated personae as a poetic imagination.[91]

FIGURE 7.5: Humphrey Repton, *View from Tern Bridge*, plate V, from Repton's Red Book, *Attingham Park*, The Berwick Collection (The National Trust). ©NTPL/John Hammond.

FIGURE 7.6: Humphrey Repton, *View from Tern Bridge*, plate V, from Repton's Red Book, *Attingham Park*, The Berwick Collection (The National Trust). ©NTPL/John Hammond.

SATIRE

Elite landscaped gardens as such are not directly represented in visual satires. Here we consider why through an examination of some of the forms in which the garden *does* figure in them. These included the urban park and pleasure garden, the city merchant's country box, and garden statuary. A source of their humor was the "world turned upside down" where, for example, the "cit" (city of London trader) turned the country house into hell, but satires were constructed in a dialectical as well as antithetical relationship to high art, and they help us to reconstruct the field of meanings garden representations inhabited. Satires reminded viewers of the artifice and argument in normative visual conventions and remind us now of the vital dialectic between notions of country and city in the period in visualizing the good life in its widest sense.[92]

Visual satires in Britain became a significant commercial field of production fueled by opposition to Robert Walpole's ministry in the 1730s and extremes of fashionable display from the 1770s. Their primary orientation to metropolitan concerns is one reason for the lack of representations of the landscaped garden. As stylistic fusions of popular prints, Italian caricatures, and parodies of high art,[93] their audiences were similarly diverse, including the aristocracy as sponsors, collectors, and amateur designers. Since the aristocracy, as public figures, were prime individual targets in political caricature and generic targets in social caricature,[94] we might reasonably expect elite gardens to feature more than they do.

A long-standing source of instructive satirical humor was the paradox of claims for the virtues of country living coexisting with the acknowledgment of fulfilling self-importance in the urban hustle, a theme associated with the Roman satirist Horace (65–8 B.C.E.).[95] The dependence of a capacity for handling this paradox on the availability of morally refreshing rural living offers further insight into why estate landscapes fall largely outside the satirical spotlight. The major phase of growth in social caricature coincided with the nationalistic celebration of the natural garden style. As the examples considered here suggest, caricature's celebration of the failure of the British to assimilate politeness fully complemented claims to a national character based on constitutional freedoms, which contemporaries also saw as evidenced through landscape art and the naturalistic garden style.[96]

In visual satires, gardens are represented most frequently in the form of London's parks and commercial pleasure gardens, where they are settings for the motley crowd, the "cit" at leisure, or less edifying diversions. Comic dramas had already set amorous intrigues in urban pleasure gardens, and reveled in their urban-pastoral potential. Like the dramas, the visual satires depend for their bite on the existence of other "authentic" gardens and their patriarchal community, in which social identities could more easily be policed. (Or, as pleasure-seeking characters in comic dramas lament, in which the tedium of the country house life replaces urban adventure.) Urban parks were not marked with the singular identity of an owning family but were habitats for self-selecting promenaders in a display culture[97]: a visual culture distinct from but overlapping with landscape aesthetics and polite tourism.

Louis-Phillipe Boitard's *Taste à la Mode, 1745* (1745) figures a dense social "panorama." The conglomerate crowd, the relatively low, close viewpoint, and the recognizable setting (in front of Buckingham House in St James's Park, London) play with the conventions and viewing pleasures of the topographical prospect,[98] the conversation piece, and history painting. Buckingham House is drawn with the fine and precise lines of the topographical or architectural print. Its own restrained classicism and neat planting pose an understated question about sources of authority in taste and other matters. Unlike the generally empty foregrounds of town prospects, the scatterings of elegant staffage in garden views,[99] or the clearly distinguishable social types in earlier prospect views, the crowd in visual satires tends simply to mill about. The only activity offered to the gaze is the gazing of the promenaders enacting a cult of "visuality," of seeing and being seen.[100] Viewers are incited to "track" their sightlines.[101] Some individuals look at a particular person but others do not. The visual incoherence of a mutually spectating, emulatory "hodge-podge" seems to have been part of the point. As satirist Tom Brown expressed it, the London crowds in

FIGURE 7.7: Louis-Philllipe Boitard, *Taste à la Mode 1745*, 1745. Author's copy.

parks and walks were a spectacle for the satirical gaze, full of nations who did not know one another, the ladies taking on so many different characteristics (none virtuous) that they were "indefinable" and out quite simply to see and be seen.[102] The legibility and elegance of staffage and composition in the topographical estate view has been subverted to produce *anomie* and point up the indeterminacy of social relations in the microcosmic "town."

For their contemporary viewers, recognizing fashionable dress would have provided one source of pleasure.[103] Another would have been decoding the wildly different bodies through comic stereotypes from dramas and literary satires, which abounded with such types as the fop, the bumpkin, "oyster Betty," and so forth.[104] The horizontal layout of the crowd stimulates classification and prompts the question: what force has compelled them together? Fashion, social emulation, luxury, or the pervasiveness of prostitutes might have been the answers, since these were associated with the commonly lamented impossibility of detecting status from clothes. In the Boitard, a woman appears to be lifting up the skirt of her hoop petticoat suggestively to the man next to her, but the status of the most prominent woman in the foreground is unclear. She stares forward out of the picture plane, not catching anyone's attention. Dumpiness and fashionability in woman were often cit-signifiers, so she may be foregrounded as fashion victim rather than prostitute and designed to aid the projection of the abstract forces of fashion, luxury, and emulation onto women in general and the urban realm.

Visual satires reframed the polite spectatorial and sensory pleasures of the topographical view as narcissism and the grosser appetites, pleasures expunged from the realm of the aesthetic in contemporary philosophical theories. However, it is fair to assume that the "British," as constructed through such crowd in garden scenes, found their own unease with politeness, their relative impoliteness vis-à-vis the nobility and the French, a paradoxically reassuring source of amusement.[105]

Vauxhall Garden's decadent reputation, multiple entertainments, and heterogeneous styles of architectural ornament (classical, Gothic, and exotic), along with the arch hyperbolic puffs of its publicity machine, associating it with pastoral arcadias and Elysiums (where swains "discreetly were bold"), also provided rich pickings for political and social critique.[106] The Walpole opposition highlighted the parallel between its deceits—*trompe l'oeil* painted architecture in clashing styles, "vistas" and tin cascade—and its overblown marketing, and government screening of political corruption.[107] Vauxhall figured the state of the nation so aptly because the urban pleasure garden provided the archetypal trope for the ambivalence articulated in the luxury debates about consumption and social mobility. Its "deceits" must have been reassuringly illusory in contrast to the complexities associated with detecting identities in socially heterogeneous public arenas. Scholars of the luxury debates have given much attention to the role of philosophical and economic discourse in reconciling commercial consumption with optimistic concepts of morality and progress in eighteenth-century Britain.[108] However, satires too aided the rehabilitation of "luxury." They offered the pleasure of an apparent social incoherence to an anthropological eye and embraced the paradox of indulgent absorption in and critical distance from commercialized appetites. In satire, the eye could be ensnared in deceit and yet capable of detachment, as in a dream from which one could awaken.[109]

An anonymous etched and engraved caricature of 1771, *A common council man of Candlestick Ward, and his wife, on a visit to Mr. Deputy—at his modern built villa near Clapham* invokes the state of the nation through the theme of pretentious suburban luxury. The socially and geographically precise designations in the title allude to the idea that the tradesman is dignified in his sphere but ripe for rebuke when he moves out. The artist has used the devices of an overturned coach, a symbol of misgovernance, and a collage of

FIGURE 7.8: Anon, *A common council man of Candlestick Ward, and his wife, on a visit to Mr. Deputy—at his modern built villa near Clapham*, 1771, published by S. Hooper, London. Library of Congress. Prints and Photographs Division. [LC-USZ62–59607].

architectural styles to associate a physical disaster with a style disaster that might also suggest a national disaster: social miscegenation.[110] The viewing position is at anti-topographical eye level and illustrates a much-reproduced poem "The Cit's Country Box," in which the cit moves out of town, goaded by his wife's reminder of the need to keep up with other traders.[111] In the print, the cit's wig is on the horse's head, translating the idea of the loss of authority implied by following the dictates of wife and fashion.[112]

It would be easy to jump to the conclusion that patrician hostility to the increased spending power of the trading classes has been exercised here.[113] There is a degree of social realism to the image: city merchants tended to invest in properties in the suburbs rather than in country estates.[114] The cit, however, given the clichéd unwieldy plebeian body and the traits of the updated "boaster" from the ancient Greek writer Theophrastus, may have served as a "self-regulating instrument" for the middle classes who presumably engaged with elite tastes well enough to understand "emblem" in the era of "expression."[115] The poem was not understood as an attack on the middle classes per se.[116] Their "prudential virtues" must have continually clashed with actual consumption of the luxury goods they made or sold and urged them to juggle status expression with restraint.[117] By the beginning of the nineteenth century, middle-class people had evidently assimilated and reframed aristocratic ideals of rural retirement as self-improvement in the context of their suburban lifestyle.[118]

Visual satires saw consumption largely through conservative and masculine eyes. The landed classes were certainly represented as promoting excessive and immoral forms of consumption, and yet the landed estate itself appears to have been a *cordon sanitaire*, a gold standard, for the sorts of judgment, economic and aesthetic, polite viewers wished to see regulating the forces of consumption and symbolizing the nation. The 1780 etching *The Modern Paradise: or Adam and Eve Regenerated* shows a couple of aristocrats outside their country house, naked except for their elaborate wigs. The bills and references hanging from their "tree of life" are mainly for urban and fashionable pursuits. The house and grounds contain no obvious form of expenditure. It functions as an exception that proves the rule, its Brownite emptiness standing as reproach for their neglect of their true "estate" rather than as an emblem of conspicuous consumption. Visual satire's raiding of conventions from topography and high art suggests that it had the potential to turn to the elite landscaped garden, but chose not to use it. Its preferred stance was to ironize display culture by frequently setting it in urban or suburban gardens. Satire's comforting references to the age-old struggles between the lures of distinction and the forces of restraint, which made them inherent in human nature, contributed to the rehabilitation of the perception of consumption, displacing attention from rural vistas of fantasy, equally designed to "deceive the eye."

CONCLUSION

Ultimately, whatever was felt about the morals of consumption, the notion of property was sacred in eighteenth-century Europe, and in Britain it defined not only the aristocracy and gentry but "the middling rank," and ensured its "authority."[119] Satirists, as well as moralists, recognized or hoped that ideals and values, more than cultural practices, were shared by the upper and middling classes. The prescribed duties of the estate owner—improvement, wealth production, and the exertion of benevolent political and moral influence— were assumed to be translatable into middle-class circumstances.[120] Thus representations of the landscaped garden functioned to support cross-class elite self-imagining as metaphor for masculine rationality, governance, and influence.

The references to landscape garden structures in the French Revolutionary festival designs of the 1790s make an instructive final comparison with satirical and idealizing forms of representation of landscaped design, reinforcing the garden's value in representation as a means of imaging social authority. Although varied in overt theme, policy alignment, and symbols, the various festivals' need for syncretic, eclectic, and customized iconography (such as an altar with a Chinese canopy) to signify the coming of a new unified society, with accessible de-Christianized iconography, prompted recourse to neoclassical and militaristic mise-en-scène, with obvious debts to landscape garden design. Beyond the shared typology of structures and symbols (columns topped with statues, artificial mounds with grottoes, pyramids and obelisks with inscriptions, temples, etc.), the kinship between festival and garden design heightens our understanding of the cultural values associated with the latter. An iconography of nature is imposed on the city to support virtuous identities and attributes. Churches are made "pastoral" through imported lawns, mounds, and, in one case, a Temple of Philosophy, prompting reflection on the degree to which garden symbolism had previously been considered an explicit alternative or rival to religious iconography.[121] Long-standing topographical conventions in the painted and engraved representations of the festivals resonate ideologically: enormity of scale in the overall space depicted and the scale of the structures (assuming some exaggeration) presumably attempt to suggest the degree of political participation and change and their potential to expand, and small animated clusters of people observing and gesturing at orderly massed formations of the people's representatives visualize the often stated utopian purpose of the festivals in making the people themselves a work of art. The visual rhetoric, in contrast to the relatively depopulated or arbitrarily staffed spaces of the garden in topography, and as distinct from the unruly crowds in British satires, is of an orderly public's occupation of a space/state.

It is not surprising that garden design had some influence upon festival design, given its associations with theater, the influence of Jean-Jacque Rousseau on Revolutionary festival and garden design in France, the processional element in garden circuits, the immersive "pilgrimage" element in garden tourism, and the involvement of professional painters such as Jacques-Louis David and Hubert Robert (himself a noted designer of elite French gardens). Of wider significance, however, as we have seen, is the metaphorical capacity of garden imagery in this period to make the social order appear both legible and legitimate.

CHAPTER EIGHT

Gardens and the Larger Landscape

SARAH SPOONER AND TOM WILLIAMSON

The relationship between eighteenth-century gardens and the wider landscape might at first sight appear simple and straightforward. Many garden historians accept the story told by contemporary writers like Horace Walpole and argue that in the decades after about 1720, gardens steadily became both more "natural" in appearance and more integrated with the "natural" landscape of the surrounding countryside. As straight gravel paths, geometric parterres, and topiary were replaced by more sinuous and flowing features and planting, so external walls were removed and replaced by the sunken fence or "ha-ha." In the oft-quoted words of Horace Walpole, the crucial change came with William Kent, who "leapt the fence, and saw that all nature was a garden."

> The contiguous ground of the park without the sunk fence was to be harmonised with the lawn within; and the garden in its turn was to be set free from its prim regularity, that it might assort with the wilder country without.[1]

But as Walpole's account in part suggests, the ha-ha—widely adopted from the 1720s—was normally employed to open up views into the *park*, rather than across the wider working countryside. The countryside, that is, was only experienced through the intermediate space of the park, itself a form of landscape with a long and complex history. Moreover, the countryside was not "natural" in any meaningful sense, but shaped by long centuries of agricultural activity, and in the eighteenth century was in the process of being reshaped in radical new ways: by enclosure and "improvement" but also—in some areas—by what was, in effect, incipient suburbanization on the outskirts of expanding towns and cities. Only by understanding these wider spatial contexts of eighteenth-century gardens, and the iconographies attached to them, can we fully appreciate the social meanings of the "landscape" style.

THE ORIGINS OF THE PARK

In spite of what is often implied or stated, ornamental parks were not in themselves new in the eighteenth century, and their long pedigree carried particular connotations of status. In early medieval times, parks had been densely wooded venison farms and hunting grounds, usually located at a distance from manor houses.[2] Many contained a lodge, which provided accommodation for the owner not merely while hunting but also when wishing to withdraw from the daily ritualized social life of the mansion, to keep "secret house" with a restricted company of companions. By the thirteenth century, parks were among the only really "wild" landscapes left in England, areas in which the natural environment had been least modified by arable farming or by the kind of intensive grazing that had created and maintained open commons, heaths, and moors. And they had become—with the deer that lived in them—the exclusive province, and therefore the symbol par excellence, of the feudal elite.

During the late Middle Ages, the numbers of deer parks in England declined. The economic dislocations of the fourteenth century placed considerable strains on demesne incomes, while rising wages and the decline of customary services ensured that maintenance costs spiraled. Parks were increasingly restricted to the richest families. But more important, they were now more closely associated with residences, for as they dwindled in number the survivors were usually among the relatively few examples that had been located beside great houses; and as the number of parks began to increase once again during the fifteenth and sixteenth centuries, the new creations were, almost without exception, placed beside mansions.

There were changes, too, in the appearance of parks, with the emergence for the first time of true "parkland." Early medieval parks had been densely treed wood pastures, usually with relatively few open areas or "laundes." But as parks were brought into close association with mansions, they tended to become more open in appearance, and their layout and design were more carefully considered. The number of trees within them was reduced, for otherwise the house would have been hemmed in on one or more sides by woodland and, perhaps of greater importance, it would not have been possible to demonstrate the wealth of an owner able to put large areas of land out of cultivation in this manner. For while early medieval parks had been formed out of wood pasture "waste" on the fringes of cultivated land, most late medieval and early postmedieval parks were created at the expense of the latter, and their makers selectively retained existing hedgerow trees, woods, and copses. Already, designers of parkland were consulting, as their eighteenth-century successors did, the "genius of the place." In the seventeenth century, the park began to be wrapped around the mansion and its gardens and its boundary with the wider world began, in some places, to be hardened with the planting of a thick belt

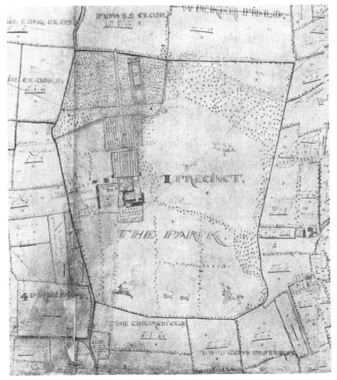

FIGURE 8.1: Somerleyon Hall, Suffolk, in 1652. The park is already wrapped completely around the house and its gardens. Note the belt of trees along the eastern perimeter and the prominent lines of trees where hedgerows have been removed but the timber retained. (Courtesy of University of East Anglia, Special Collections)

of trees. In the last decades of the century—for a few brief decades, lasting into the early eighteenth—the geometric design of the garden was extended out into the park in the form of avenues and geometric vistas, although these were essentially an intrusion into the park's natural informality, rather than a radical disruption or displacement of it. Long before the arrival of "Capability" Brown, the park was thus already a designed landscape with an immense pedigree loaded with significance and meaning.

TYPES OF EIGHTEENTH-CENTURY DESIGNED LANDSCAPE

In the course of the eighteenth century, parks became the accepted primary setting for the mansion, as not only formal gardens, but also a range of productive facilities and enclosures—kitchen gardens, orchards, fish ponds, and farm yards—were cleared away from fashionable façades. The ha-ha, by obscuring the division of the mown lawn of the pleasure ground from the grazed pasture of the park, gave the impression that the house stood alone in the midst of the latter. At the same time, the numbers of parks increased dramatically. At the beginning of the century, their ownership had been restricted to a relatively small landowning elite: by the end of the century, there were vast numbers of them, belonging to people much further down the social scale. While all displayed the open grassland, scattered trees, and blocks of woodland of the "traditional" park, most were no longer grazed by deer, but by sheep and cattle. Moreover, as they increased in number they developed a range of parallel forms, a variety only in part related to the styles of particular designers or the date of their creation. Indeed, a failure to appreciate the extent of this diversity has, perhaps more than anything else, hampered our understanding of eighteenth-century landscape design.

The very largest parks were owned by great landed families, and usually had their origins in earlier deer parks. Their perimeters were generally marked by belts of trees, selectively gapped to allow views of the wider countryside. They often contained garden buildings and large lakes, and their land surface was sometimes modified by subtle acts of earth movement, to open up views or close unappealing prospects. These were multipurpose landscapes: they served several different functions, not all aesthetic. Their sheer size meant that they could be subdivided into different areas, some more "designed" than others. The production of timber, for example, could thus be safely carried on within their confines without necessarily impinging on the view from the mansion. These were the kinds of park on which Brown most often worked: parks that were not only extensive, but which also normally had long and complex histories and a range of existing design elements of geometric character

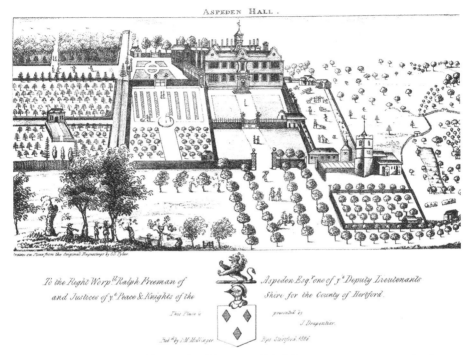

FIGURE 8.2: Aspenden Hall, Hertfordshire in 1700. Like most country seats in the period, Aspenden was surrounded by a complex of enclosures and facilities that included, besides the aesthetic gardens, orchards, nut grounds, farmyards, and a dovecote. Adopting the "landscape" style involved not only the removal of geometric gardens from the walls of the mansion, but also the destruction of a range of productive facilities, which had themselves traditionally functioned as important markers of status. (Courtesy of University of East Anglia, Special Collections)

that were usually removed or softened to make them acceptable to modern taste. Avenues, for example, might be felled, and complexes of geometric fish ponds thrown together to make fashionable, serpentine lakes, although at any places such archaic features were, in fact, retained right through the century. Most English counties contained at least ten or so landscape parks of this kind, and most of the more famous examples in England—Chatsworth, Holkham, Petworth—fall into this category.

On the next rung down the scale, and much more numerous, were the kinds of medium-sized parks owned by members of the local gentry, covering between 50 and 150 hectares. At the start of the century, members of this social group generally (although not invariably) lacked the luxury of a deer park, although they often possessed quite extensive geometric gardens. Parks like

FIGURE 8.3: Holkham, Norfolk, from the air. Typical of the largest parks in eighteenth-century England, this was internally subdivided, retained elements of its earlier, geometric phases of design, and included a home farm within its vast external belt. (Courtesy of University of East Anglia, Special Collections)

this were thus usually new creations made at the expense of working farmland, and today they often contain earthwork traces of field boundaries and roads, relics of this lost landscape. With their open grassland and belts of trees they resembled, in broad terms, the parks in our first category but they were less likely to contain lakes or elaborate buildings and had fewer economic functions—they did not, in particular, usually represent major forestry enterprises. Although their design was often carefully considered, and might be the work of professional designers like Nathaniel Richmond or Humphry Repton, they were on the whole less complex in their spatial organization.

Below these parks came a third tier, diminutive landscapes extending over less than fifty hectares. These were owned or leased by a broad group of people ranging from local squires, through wealthy bankers and merchants, army and naval officers, to members of the professional classes. Such "parks" were often little more than a group of pasture fields thrown together around a smart villa, and the smallest examples were often described by contemporaries as a "lawn" or "paddock" rather than as a "park." The residences with which these designs were associated often lacked an accompanying estate, and it was partly for this reason—a lack of available land—that parks in this category were seldom upgraded to medium-sized parks in the course of their history, in spite of the fact that their owners were often men whose fortunes rivaled or

FIGURE 8.4: Honing in Norfolk is typical of the smaller landscape parks created by the local gentry. It is simpler and less compartmentalized than Holkham, and the house is positioned close to its northern perimeter. (Courtesy of University of East Anglia, Special Collections)

exceeded those of established landowners. Humphry Repton, unlike Brown, often worked on parks in this third category, although many of his commissions involved sites in the second.

Some of these places were secondary residences for large landowners whose principal seat lay elsewhere. Marchmont House, near Hemel Hempstead in Hertfordshire, is a good example of this rather neglected type. A modest stuccoed box, the mansion appears at first sight to be the residence of a gentleman farmer or man of business, yet was built in the 1770s for the third Earl of Marchmont, Hugh Hume-Campbell. It was conveniently located close both to London and to the home of his son and daughter-in-law at Wrest Park in Bedfordshire. The house was carefully screened from the public road by a narrow "belt," little more than a thick hedge: the diminutive lawn contained trees retained from former boundaries of earlier houses and gardens cleared away when the house was erected. The windows of the house look out over a wide area of meadow land toward the River Gade, the latter an echo of the expanses

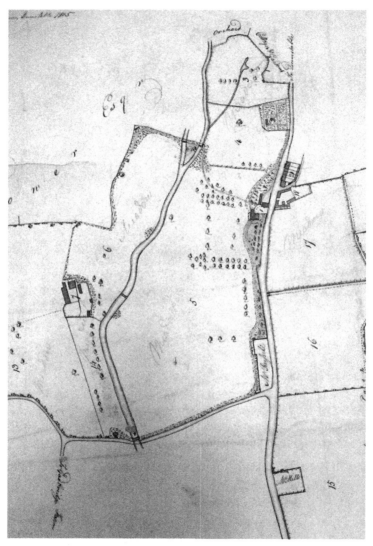

FIGURE 8.5: Marchmont House, Hemel Hempstead, Hertfordshire. A diminutive design in the "landscape" tradition created in the 1770s for the third Earl of Marchmont. (Reproduced with permission of Hertfordshire Archives and Local Studies)

of ornamental water found in larger parks (all shown on an 1805 estate map[3]). The house was placed toward the northern edge of the park in order to make it appear larger than it really was when viewed from the south-facing reception rooms: this was a common device in the design of these small parks, and even of some in our second category. Visitors would have been able to take in the whole of the grounds in a single glance, but they were divided from the much

larger Gadebridge Park, in separate ownership, by a narrow lane, and this
would have given the impression of uninterrupted, continuous grounds.

In addition to this broad threefold division of parks—and making all this
rather more complicated—another tradition of landscape design continued
to develop throughout the eighteenth and early nineteenth centuries, that of
the *ferme ornée*, or ornamented farmland, in which winding paths edged with
flowering shrubbery plants wound their way around little fields to various
garden seats and buildings. The ferme ornée in England is often associated
with places like Woburn Farm and The Leasowes—created in the 1740s by
Philip Southcote and William Shenstone respectively.[4] But it has a longer history. Even in the seventeenth century, the wider estate land might be ornamented with judicious planting, and in 1718 Stephen Switzer advocated a
form of "rural gardening" that explicitly linked the aesthetics of the formal
garden with the informality of the surrounding countryside. In his idealized
plans of imaginary designed landscapes, the gardens merge into ornamented
farmland and woodland.[5] Switzer has, in general, little to say about the park:
in effect, his designs dispensed with the buffer of the park and replaced it
with an aesthetically modified countryside. Arguably, this style was aimed at
smaller landowners who could not aspire to a park, which were expensive to
create and took up valuable arable land, but who nevertheless wanted to extend their gardening activities beyond the vicinity of their homes, although to
some extent there was an ideological aspect in these ideas—Switzer's style represented a form of "extensive gardening" that clearly, almost ostentatiously,
integrated the productive and the aesthetic, as well as the geometric and the
"natural."

The tradition of "ornamented farmland" continued strongly through the
later eighteenth century and into the nineteenth, although its later manifesta-
tions have received less attention from scholars than they deserve—in part,
perhaps, because they have left less obvious traces, on maps or in the modern
landscape, than the dominant "parkland" tradition. In fact, the largest parks
often had areas of ornamented farmland within their perimeter belts, especially (as at Woburn or Holkham) where their owners had a particular interest
in agricultural improvement. Even when home farm and park were spatially
distinct, they were usually contiguous, and the former might fulfill a particular
role in the lifestyle of the rural landowner, as Whateley explained:

A simple farm may undoubtedly be delightful; it will be particularly acceptable to the owner, if it be close to his park or his garden; the objects
which constantly remind him of his rank, impose a kind of constraint;
and he feels himself relieved, by retiring sometimes from the splendour

of a seat into the simplicity of a farm; it is more than a variety of scene; it is a temporary change of situation in life, which has all the charms of novelty, ease, and tranquillity to recommend it.[6]

Farmland lying well outside the park might be ornamented with plantations, and the view in this direction was revealed by making gaps in the perimeter belt. This was a device found at sites of all sizes but used with particular enthusiasm at those in our third, smallest category: Repton employed it regularly from the start of his career. Other ways of ornamenting the wider working countryside included the use of "ridings," another aspect of eighteenth-century landscape design that would benefit from more study. Whateley in 1770 described how gardening was "no longer confined to the spots from which it borrows its name, but regulates also the disposition and embellishments of a park, a farm, or a riding"; later explaining helpfully that the latter was a drive through the farmland of the estate, adorned with decorative planting to distinguish it from an ordinary road, that was supposed to lead "from one beauty to another, and be a scene of pleasure all the way."[7] Sometimes, as at Chatsworth in Derbyshire in the middle decades of the century, such ornamental rides terminated at detached areas of parkland positioned to command an agreeable prospect.[8] Throughout the eighteenth century, in other words, landowners found a variety of ways of ornamenting the wider estate land, and for smaller landowners such devices might make up for the meager extent of parks and pleasure ground, although those whose property was circumscribed might have limited aesthetic control over the surrounding farmland. In such circumstances, as we shall see, it made sense to choose as a place of residence an area already well supplied with parks and with a working landscape already possessing a vaguely "sylvan" appearance, with large amounts of pasture and trees.

THE RELATIONSHIP OF THE PARK TO WIDER LANDSCAPE

The character of the relationship of the gardens and park to the surrounding landscape, including the extent and character of any ornamented farmland, was in part related to our broad three-part division of designed landscapes. But it was also connected with the nature of the local landscape and topography. Wherever possible, landowners chose undulating terrain for their homes, in part because this provided pleasingly diversified views within and across the park itself, but also because of the prospects it provided outward, beyond it. Level interfluves, as much as wide flat marshlands, were avoided if at all possible. The Chiltern Hills of south Buckinghamshire and west Hertfordshire, for example, comprise a gently tilted plateau cut by widely spaced, relatively steep valleys. Most country houses of all sizes were located so that they overlooked a valley: the park usually stretched down the valley side, but did not normally extend very far behind the house, onto the level plateau above. The sides of the park were generally belted, but not the lower slopes, so that extensive, distant prospects could be viewed across the well-wooded Chiltern countryside. In addition, as many of the principal roads ran along the valley floors, such a disposition allowed the new landscape to be displayed to greatest advantage to passersby, albeit at a discreet distance.

Distant prospects like this might be enjoyed in all periods, but most parks only allowed in carefully selected views: anything undesirable was screened by planting. Smoke rising from a distant cottage was acceptable and picturesque: close views of villagers' pigs and washing were not. Moreover, certain *kinds* of land use were more appealing than others to the owners and creators of parks. Wooded slopes, other peoples' parks, or well-treed pasture land were more welcome than arable fields, while prospects of unenclosed open fields were generally shunned, as were views across areas of common land.

The extent of open fields and commons and the chronology of their disappearance are matters of some importance in the present context because many garden historians still assume that these forms of land use were extensive, if not ubiquitous, in England at the start of the eighteenth century; and that their disappearance, and the rise of "naturalistic" gardening, were thus contemporary, and perhaps in some way causally connected. As early as 1838, the great garden designer John Claudius Loudon argued:

> As the lands devoted to agriculture in England were, sooner than in any other country in Europe, generally enclosed with hedges and hedgerow trees, so the face of the country in England, sooner than in any other part of Europe, produced an appearance which bore a closer resemblance to country seats laid out in the geometrical style; and, for this reason, an attempt to imitate the irregularity of nature in laying out pleasure grounds was made in England . . . sooner than in any other part of the world.[9]

In the words of art historian Anne Bermingham, similarly:

> As the real landscape began to look increasingly artificial, like a garden, the garden began to look increasingly natural, like the pre-enclosed landscape. Thus a natural landscape became the prerogative of the estate . . . so that nature was a sign of property and property the sign of

nature. . . By conflating nature with the fashionable taste of a new social
order, it redefined the natural in terms of this order, and vice versa.[10]

In this way, according to Bermingham, vast yet arbitrary social inequalities
were made to appear natural and inevitable. Such arguments are seductive: but
they are difficult to support. Across most of the southeast of England, as in the
west of the country, open fields had either never existed or had been enclosed
in a gradual, piecemeal way in the three centuries before 1700. These regions
had irregular, organic landscapes of sinuous, well-timbered field boundaries
and lanes of the kind most contemporaries seem to have found visually attractive.[11] In all, more than three quarters of lowland England had been converted
to hedged fields in a variety of ways before large-scale, planned enclosures usually—although not invariably—by parliamentary act removed the remaining
commons and open fields in the course of the eighteenth and nineteenth centuries. This latter process formed the kind of countryside Loudon evidently saw
as a stimulus to the evolution of the "landscape" style: a landscape of straight
roads and large fields bounded by ruler-straight hawthorn hedges.

Enclosure by parliamentary act began in the early eighteenth century but
mostly occurred in two great waves of activity: the first peaking during the
1770s, and mainly concerned with the removal of arable open fields in the
Midlands; the second during the Napoleonic Wars, from about 1790 to 1815,
particularly associated with the enclosure of commons and other "wastes" to
increase the area of arable land at a time of rising prices and patriotic fervor.[12]
Parliamentary enclosure, because it was so concentrated spatially and chronologically, made a major impact on the landscape and on contemporary observ-
ers. But we should not exaggerate its importance. By the time the essential
form of the landscape park had become the common intellectual property of
the polite classes, enclosure had largely been completed.

The landscapes of recent enclosure were obviously modern and artificial
in character. But the fields produced by early enclosure, and even the unenclosed heaths, moors, and commons, generally so unattractive to contemporary eyes, were also entirely man-made. The latter areas had once been
covered in trees, and left to their own devices they would have returned to
woodland. Intensive and complicated forms of land use—grazing and the
cutting and removal of products like heather, gorse, and bracken—kept them
open, and no one even remotely connected with farming or land management
can have been in any doubt about their true status as environments shaped
by constant peasant use. The mania for "improving" such marginal land
was motivated in part by economics, in part by a hostility to old-fashioned

forms of land use that often allowed a measure of independence to small landowners and laborers. Their enclosure and reclamation, employing the innovative methods of the "agricultural revolution," can be read as part of a wider attempt to impose order and control over the rural landscape. But the idea of "improvement" was an all-embracing one that could be applied to the landscaping of the park as much as to the transformation of the working countryside. The landowners responsible for creating parks in the new, "natural" style also often sponsored schemes of enclosure, reclamation, and other "improvements" on their estates. Rather than seeing the development of the working countryside and of the landscape park in simple aesthetic opposition to each other, they should be read in terms of their strong relationship and in the context of gentlemanly attitudes toward improvement. Ornamented farmland of various kinds represented, in a sense, a mediation and convergence of the two aspects of improvement.

The landscape style was thus not simply a reaction against enclosure, nor did it involve any straightforward merging of the garden with the "natural" countryside outside it. The countryside was not "natural" in any meaningful sense and was usually viewed, very selectively, from the gardens beside the mansion as a distant backdrop to the landscape of the park, and often only after it had been suitably ornamented. Certain kinds of "natural" countryside, especially unenclosed commons, were rigorously excluded from the polite gaze and could never be included in a polite prospect.

SOME SOCIAL MEANINGS OF THE LANDSCAPE PARK

The relationship between the park and the wider landscape is important because it can tell us much about why the landscape style became so popular in the course of the eighteenth century, in particular why parks rather than gardens came to be the main setting for the homes of the wealthy. Even a cursory examination of surviving examples, or of contemporary maps and plans, indicates clearly that the park functioned primarily as a landscape of social exclusion: it was a symbol of the increasing segregation of landowners from local communities.[13] Eighteenth- and nineteenth-century parks were laid out in such a way that afforded their owners enhanced levels of privacy. Settlements were only occasionally removed when they were created, although individual farms and cottages were frequently demolished, and roads and footpaths within and around the park were almost invariably closed or diverted, legislative changes in 1778 making this process much easier than it had been before. Perimeter belts, as we have seen, obscured near views of the working landscape and of the homes of those who labored within it. Parks can be read almost as islands of gentility, of polite exclusion, within the wider working countryside.

Such an interpretation does not entirely explain the specific *style* of the landscape park. A park by itself would have achieved this aim without necessarily removing the formal planting of avenues and vistas within it or the geometric gardens from the immediate vicinity of the mansion. Moreover, late eighteenth-century society was highly complex, and did not consist simply of two opposed groups, the landed rich and the landless poor: the landscape style thus also needs to be understood in terms of the relationship between different levels within the propertied class, in particular in the context of a middle class expanding in numbers and affluence as the economy steadily grew. One useful way of examining changes in landscape design is in terms of the emergence of "polite society" in the middle decades of the eighteenth century.[14] As a number of social historians have emphasized, from the later seventeenth century the differences in status and lifestyle between the greatest landowners and the broader group of the propertied comprising the local gentry and wealthy professionals were consciously played down. Social encounters—at country houses or, increasingly, at urban assemblies and similar gatherings—became more relaxed and informal in character, as emphasis was placed on easy affability, wit, and conversation.[15] The upper ranks of society began to coalesce into a single cultural group and new social fault lines emerged between the gentry and professionals on one hand and the wider rural population on the other. Yet at the same time, with commercial and industrial expansion, there was increased upward social mobility; and with the proliferation of material goods many of the old markers of social distinction, in terms, for example, of dress, began to grow less distinct.

The landscape park can profitably be considered in terms of the emergence of the "polite." The park provided privacy at a time when landowners had less and less in common with their immediate neighbors and wished to socialize only with those of similar or greater social status. But in addition, the very style of the landscape park helped to mark off the "polite" clearly from the local farming community and the middle class. When the garden courts were removed from the vicinity of the house, so too were all the productive features and enclosures—many of which had been semi-ornamental in character—in which the gentry had once delighted, and which had symbolized their active involvement in the productive life of their estates—orchards, nut grounds, fish ponds, dovecotes, farm yards. This removal of productive clutter expressed a lack of involvement and empathy with the shared world of the agricultural community. At the same time, with the development of a more complex, commercial, consuming society—with members of the middle class busy making elaborate gardens of their own—the new style prioritized the ancient symbol of the park over elaborate gardens as the main setting for the homes of the wealthy. Not only was the park an ancient symbol of aristocratic privilege, it also demanded the commodity only the landed elite, or those wealthy enough to join them, possessed—an abundance of land.

The relationship between emergent social forms and landscapes was infinitely complex, however, and in part indirect, mediated in particular through new modes of architectural planning. The development of less structured forms of social interaction ensured that the old "formal" house plans of the late seventeenth and early eighteenth centuries, arranged round a series of *enfilades* and linear axes, were replaced by houses with more flowing circulation plans, which comprised suites of entertaining rooms forming a circuit in which a diverse range of activities—dancing, card games, conversation—could take place at the same time.[16] The serpentine, flowing lines of the landscape garden and the parkland beyond to some extent mirrored this development: with interior space no longer structured around linear vistas, people began to enjoy views toward and away from the mansion from a variety of angles, not only along axes that replicated and continued those inside it. And at the same time, the elegant, sweeping drives in the park and serpentine walks in the pleasure grounds provided additional contexts for "polite" social engagement.

PARKLAND AND SUBURBANIZATION

We must be careful, however, not to assume too simple a relationship—too direct an equivalence—between the traditional deer park of the sixteenth and seventeenth centuries and the new, more refined landscape park of the eighteenth. The one may have developed into the other, but not without significant changes. Deer parks had been characterized by indigenous trees, often fairly densely planted and scattered individually across the pasture. Landscape parks in contrast—whether new or created by adapting earlier parks—were generally more open in character, made more use of distinct clumps of trees, and often featured a higher proportion of new, fast-growing species, especially conifers. In part these stylistic features were directly derived from the Italianate pleasure grounds laid out—almost as three-dimensional versions of the paintings of Italian scenery by artists like Claude Lorraine—by William Kent in the 1730s, which were one of the important influences on the style of "Capability" Brown and his fellow landscapers. But to some extent they reflected the fact that planting trees like larch and pine provided more rapid results for those establishing a park from scratch. True, older trees, especially oaks, were incorporated from the previous landscape wherever possible to provide new parks with a veneer of established respectability. Most landscape parks in England contain old trees, often outgrown pollards, retained when hedges were grubbed out to provide the sweeping, uninterrupted prospects demanded by fashionable taste.[17] But for more structural planting, especially for clumps and belts, new trees with rapid growth were needed. All this was especially true of the smaller designs—those in our third and, to some extent, second categories—which were more likely to be laid out for the first time in the middle and later decades of the century. Humphry Repton tellingly lamented the clumps of fir trees in the long-established park at Henham in Suffolk, "only applicable to the recent Villa, and beneath the dignity of an Ancient inheritance."[18] While the larger parks often developed from earlier deer parks and retained the feel of ancient wood pastures, at least in their more secluded sections, the smaller designs newly created in the 1760s, '70s, and '80s were thus more elegant, more open, and more overtly designed spaces, partaking as much of the style of gardens and pleasure grounds as that of deer parks in the traditional sense.

The landscape park may have been a symbol and sign of the "polite" and of the emergence of a society that was horizontally stratified rather than vertically integrated, but we should not read it entirely in terms of *rural* social relations or rural lifestyles. Although the landscape style was self-consciously rural, the "polite" were not really a rural class. While many established landowners derived their income primarily from agricultural rents, equally numerous were those whose wealth stemmed principally from active investment in colonial enterprises, industry, and commerce: indeed, some of those who lived within parks of respectable size had made their fortunes in these sectors of the economy. Above all, in cultural terms the later eighteenth-century elite was unquestionably more urban than rural in character. Not only Bath and London, but most major towns, were the centers of their social universe, with shops, public spaces, assemblies, and other opportunities for fashionable consumption and display. Even in the 1720s, Daniel Defoe could describe a town like Bury St Edmunds—not a very large population center—as "the *Montpelier* of Suffolk . . . it being thronged with Gentry, People of Fashion, and the most polite conversation."[19]

From the later seventeenth century, many large, elegant urban houses were erected and the bigger towns and cities began to exhibit a measure of social zoning, with areas suitable for the homes of the "polite" contrasting with areas of poverty. Large town houses might resemble—more than we notice today, because of their settings—small country houses. Urban parks, pleasure grounds and other open spaces, both public and private, retained many features of the older geometric gardens, but increasingly adopted aspects (both in terms of planting, and layout) of the new landscape style. They provided arenas for a wide range of social engagements and for social display—for promenading, public picnics, concerts—paralleling to some extent the varied social use of private landscape parks.

The growth of towns and of urban culture is important because it means that we need to understand the geographical context of the eighteenth-century garden and park not simply in terms of the relationship between designed "core" and farmed "periphery" on the kinds of large estates usually studied, but also in terms of a countryside that had itself often been extensively "colonized" by designed landscapes. Improvements in communications with, in particular, the steady extension of the turnpike system in the second half of the eighteenth century ensured that major towns could be reached with relative ease from their rural hinterlands, which began to change accordingly: people who did not wish to reside within towns were usually keen to live close to them. While larger landowners, dwelling in large mansions at the center of extensive landed estates, generally remained on their ancestral acres, the newly rich, or those whose possessions included land close to a town, often chose to live within easy distance of urban attractions. As a consequence, most major towns and cities were, by the early nineteenth century, surrounded by a large number of country houses and parks, often of small or medium size. Such proximity not only provided easy access to the attractions and facilities urban centers had to offer. It also allowed those with interests in town—commercial or industrial—to keep a ready eye on business.

By the middle decades of the eighteenth century, many people thus lived in an increasingly suburbanized landscape in which parks, gardens, and ornamented farmland occupied large areas of ground. Perhaps most striking was the reshaping of the landscape around London along such lines, a process that began in earnest in the late seventeenth century, when the stretch of the Thames valley from Hampton Court to Kew became a fashionable and expensive retreat for the urban elite. London itself grew outward at an ever-increasing rate during the eighteenth century. Until the construction of Vauxhall Bridge (1811) and Waterloo Bridge (1811–17), the Thames was only spanned at three points—London Bridge, Westminster, and Blackfriars—and so the city's expansion was at first largely restricted to the north of the river. As villages like Islington and Marylebone came to be colonized by terraced streets and villas, those who wanted something grander were forced to move further away from the city in order to find a ready supply of potential farmhouses and old manor houses that could be upgraded to desirable residences. By the mid-eighteenth century, this outward migration of the "polite" had reached Hertfordshire and Essex, beyond the county of Middlesex. By the end of the century, the margins of these counties could be reached from the center of London in less than two hours by stagecoach; even their central districts were less than three hours journey time away. These were districts of anciently enclosed countryside, with abundant trees and woodlands, ideal for park making. The number of small and medium sized parks in these districts increased with particular rapidity between 1760 and 1820: many were the creation of individuals with fortunes derived from business and positions in the armed forces or the East India Company. No less than eleven members of the East India Company purchased estates in Hertfordshire, and at least twenty wealthy bankers made their home in the county, compared to just two in the more provincial Midland county of Northamptonshire.[20]

Small designed landscapes on the fringes of London all use the familiar grammar of Brown and his contemporaries—perimeter belts, clumps, trees scattered casually across turf, and curving entrance drives—but on a smaller, sometimes a much smaller, scale, as in the case of Marchmont House, discussed earlier. The aesthetic elements of informal parkland were, in the most diminutive examples, effectively shrunk and recast as pleasure gardens, but without the accompanying contrast of a "real" landscape park. In its place, these designs might rely on borrowed views into other, larger parks, or carefully framed prospects across the surrounding countryside. Indeed, small and medium-sized parks often formed clusters beside large, older ones, such as that which had, by the 1770s, developed around the southern boundary of the magnificent, ancient Hatfield Park in Hertfordshire. This included Bedwell Park, owned by the Whitbreads, the wealthy and successful brewing family; Birds Place, the residence of General Cornwallis; Popes, home of Sir Benjamin Truman; and Camfield Place, Woodside Place, Lower Woodside, and a number of other small but elegant residences owned by miscellaneous city gentlemen.

The histories of these places and the biographies of their owners reveal a world far removed from the archetypical "landed estate." The park at Woodside Place, which covered just 9 acres, lay at the heart of a small estate of about 200 acres built up by Robert Mackey, a banker and merchant from Cheapside, who speculated in Hertfordshire property throughout the 1770s and '80s. In 1778, Woodside was sold for eight thousand guineas, which Mackey reinvested in other, more ambitious projects like the acquisition of Marden Hill, near Panshanger, which he purchased in 1785.[21] He promptly pulled down the house and rebuilt it before selling the property and retiring to Kent with the profits.[22] Around the same time, the owner of Bedwell Park, Samuel Whitbread, acquired Woolmers near Hertford. He leased the house and grounds to a succession of tenants, but after his death the estate was sold to the Duke of Bridgewater who used it as a temporary residence during the extensive building work carried out at Ashridge in the west of the county. In 1803, the estate was sold again, to Sir John St Aubyn, a Cornish landowner who used the house as a base for his trips to London. In 1821, the estate was bought for thirty-five thousand pounds by Sir Gore Ousley, a former merchant and the ambassador to Persia. Ousley enlarged the house and spent another thirty-five thousand pounds on improvements to the property before selling it to Rear-Admiral George Hotham in 1836. In 1842, Hotham sold the estate to William Wodehouse, only six years after he had purchased it from Ousley.[23] Thus Woolmers had six different owners in just over four decades, not including the various tenants who leased it from Whitbread. Even the idea of the landed estate as the pinnacle of every gentleman's aspirations thus fails to ring true in areas like this, where such properties often changed hands at least once a generation. A country estate was not necessarily something to be acquired, maintained, improved, and extended and then passed on to heirs. It might be a short-term investment or a commodity to be enjoyed until something more prestigious could be acquired. The background to all this was a fevered land market in London's hinterland, which paralleled the increase in speculative building in the city itself.

Large numbers of landscape parks in the southeast of England thus developed within what were effectively suburbanizing landscapes, rather than simply within a working countryside. Repton himself, commenting upon the near-continuous parks along the Mimram valley between Hertford and Welwyn (Panshanger, Cole Green, Tewin Water, and Digswell), considered that their "united woods and lawns will by extending thro' the whole valley enrich the general face of the country."[24] And what was true of the hinterland of London was true of the countryside around most of the larger provincial towns and cities, albeit on a smaller scale. Norwich, for example, was by the 1780s surrounded by a dense cluster of small and medium-sized parks that included Catton, Repton's first paid commission, which was the home of Jeremiah Ives, a banker and businessman in the city.[25] The diminutive parkland (which Repton in fact embellished rather than created) was closely surrounded by neighboring residences, all set in small parks or pleasure grounds. Armstrong in 1781 described Catton as:

A very pleasant village, and the residence of many manufacturers, who have retired from Norwich, and built elegant houses. The air is reckonned very healthful, and many invalids resort thither for the benefit of it. It is distant from the city a mile and half north. . . The late Robert Roger, esq. and Robert Harvey, esq., both Aldermen of Norwich, have erected handsome seats in this village; as also Jeremiah Ives Harvey, esq. and Mr Suffield.[26]

Proximity to Norwich allowed such men to keep an eye on their business interests, but also to enjoy the society and leisure facilities the city afforded. But such facilities themselves migrated outward, into the city's suburbanized hinterland. Mulbarton Hall, set in its "beautiful fine Pleasure Garden," was put on the market when Philip Stannard, textile manufacturer, went bankrupt in 1770.[27] Lying some six kilometers outside Norwich, it was purchased by

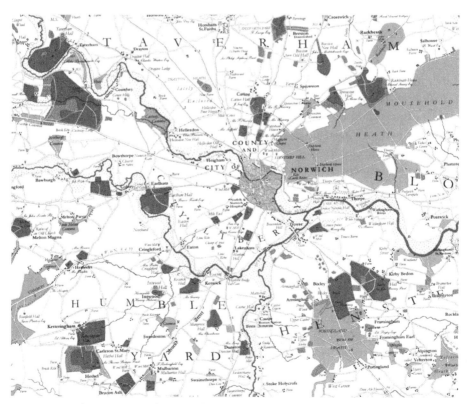

FIGURE 8.6: The area around Norwich shown on William Faden's county map of 1797. The landscape was full of small and medium-sized parks—it was already, in effect, becoming suburbanized. (Courtesy of University of East Anglia, Special Collections)

Robert Parkerson and reopened "for the reception of Gentlemen and Ladies, for Breakfasting, or Tea in the afternoon," the latter featuring "fine Strawberries, and other Fruit as they come into season." A coach operated several times a day, bringing customers from Norwich.[28]

CONCLUSION

We have emphasized the significance of the suburbanizing "fringe" as a type of landscape in eighteenth-century England in part because it is often neglected by historians of the landscape, but in part because a very high proportion of the "polite" actually lived there. The significance of the landscape style needs to be understood in this geographical context, as much as in that of the more traditional rural landed estate. Moreover, by emphasizing the essentially urban character of the "polite" in eighteenth-century England, we can perhaps better appreciate why this group found it so easy to interpret the manicured simplicity of the landscape park as, in any meaningful sense, "natural." For most of the people who lived in fashionable eighteenth- and early nineteenth-century mansions were far more divorced from the real world of the countryside—from nature and from the practical business of agriculture—than their predecessors had been half a century earlier. The removal of barns, yards, orchards, and the like from their immediate vicinity partly signaled a separation from farmers and laborers in the surrounding countryside. But it also reflected the fact that the "polite" had little interest in agricultural and horticultural production, and the features associated with such activities increasingly seemed to them to be primitive and uncouth. The change, it must be emphasized, was gradual, and even in the middle decades of the eighteenth century there remained substantial landowners in more remote regions who, like James Coldham of Anmer in Norfolk, happily noted in their diaries the number of young pigs born on their home farm each year.[29] But by the end of the century large landowners, while they often embraced a fashionable interest in estate management and agricultural improvement, usually did so in a hands-off way. Farming no longer took place in the immediate vicinity of, and in full sight of, their homes. While the "rural charms" of landscape parks were often vaunted by contemporaries, the popularity of the landscape style thus reflected, in reality, the effective divorce of the wealthy from real country life. A romanticization of the rural and of "nature" could only develop within a social group essentially urban in outlook and experience.

All this goes some of the way toward explaining why the English landscape park was, indeed, the *English* landscape park, ubiquitous in England but only

adopted rather sparingly in other countries in the course of the later eighteenth and nineteenth centuries—and then often in barely recognizable forms.
Broadly analogous styles of garden design did not emerge elsewhere in Europe
in the course of the eighteenth century simply because these different societies
engendered and maintained their own, particular styles of designed landscape.
We might, for example, have expected something similar to the landscape park
to have emerged in the Low Countries, a region as commercialized and as urbanized as England. Its failure to do so is partly due to the fact that Holland
was *too* urbanized, too bourgeois, in character. Few individuals were wealthy
enough to own land on a sufficient scale to lay out a park; indeed, there was
little tradition of the hunting park as a type of landscape in this crowded nation. In addition, the muted topography and the intensively farmed character
of the countryside further ensured the popularity of enclosed and highly artificial geometric gardens as the setting for the homes of wealthy merchants.[30] In
France, the situation was in many senses the reverse. Here there was land in
abundance and a landscape sufficiently undulating and wooded to provide all
the raw materials required for "naturalistic" design, while hunting parks had
long been a familiar feature. But France possessed a highly polarized society, in
which fashions were set by a small and wealthy group—the monarchy, court
aristocracy, and wealthy dignitaries. In the absence of a broader "polite society," a style of gardening emerged in the seventeenth century and continued
into the eighteenth in which the geometric elements of the enclosed gardens
were simply extended out though parks and forests in the form of avenues and
other linear alignments—a style that emphasized power, control, hierarchy,
and the centrality of the mansion in the landscape.[31]

A mixture of social and environmental factors likewise explains why the
landscape style "fell on relatively infertile soils across the Atlantic."[32] North
American landowners maintained and developed, throughout the eighteenth
century, the geometric and symmetrical styles handed down by European settlers: their gardens were enclosed, formal, and often terraced.[33] Here there was
too much nature. Even on the eastern seaboard, settlements were often surrounded by relatively untamed land that needed to be excluded from view
rather than used or emulated in the design of gardens. In addition, among the
European settlers there was, in most areas, less social polarization than in the
Old World, towns remained few and small, and most landowners remained
actively involved in agriculture and related activities. The wealthy often placed
their homes on high ground, displaying their status in the wider landscape: but
"few owned all the land they surveyed about them,"[34] and the old aesthetic of
domestic production ensured that farms, barns, and other useful facilities were
usually in full view, if not on proud display.

The landscape park was, in short, a product of the particular circumstances of eighteenth-century England: an obvious observation, perhaps, but one worth emphasizing. Yet the relationships between the landscape garden and its social and landscape contexts were (as we hope we have shown) many, complex, and subtle. Only by fully understanding these contexts can the real significance of the landscape style, including its meaning to contemporaries, be fully appreciated. It is effectively impossible to study the history of garden design, in this period and in this geographical area at least, as something isolated and separate from the history of the wider environment.

NOTES

Introduction

This volume has been some time in the making: my thanks go to all of the contributors for their support and patience along the way. Particular thanks must also go to Patrick Eyres, Matthew Johnson, and Annie Richardson, all of whom have helped me to shape this volume; thanks also to Gillian Dow and John Peacock for giving me such delightful European locations in which to work.

1. T. Williamson, *Polite Landscapes: Gardens and Society in Eighteenth-Century England* (Baltimore: Johns Hopkins University Press, 1995); J.D. Hunt, "Approaches (New and Old) to Garden History," in *Perspectives on Garden Histories: History of Landscape Architecture Symposium*, ed. M. Conan (Washington, D.C.: Dumbarton Oaks Research Library and Collection, 1999), 77–90; M. Conan, ed., *Perspectives on Garden Histories: History of Landscape Architecture Symposium* (Washington, D.C.: Dumbarton Oaks Research Library and Collection, 1999); M. Conan, ed. *Baroque Garden Cultures: Emulation, Sublimation, Subversion* (Washington, D.C.: Dumbarton Oaks Research Library and Collection, 2005).
2. See C. Goldstein, *Vaux and Versailles: The Appropriations, Erasures, and Accidents That Made Modern France* (Philadelphia: University of Pennsylvania Press, 2008).
3. Williamson, *Polite Landscapes*; C. Currie, *Garden Archaeology: A Handbook* (York: Council for British Archaeology, 2005).
4. R. Quaintance, "Walpole's Whig Interpretation of Landscaping History," *Studies in Eighteenth-Century Culture* 9 (1979): 285–300; S. Bending, "Horace Walpole and Eighteenth-Century Garden History," *Journal of the Warburg and Courtauld Institutes* 57 (1994): 209–26; M. Leslie, "History and Historiography in the English Landscape Garden," in *Perspectives on Garden Histories: History of*

Landscape Architecture Symposium, ed. M. Conan (Washington, D.C.: Dumbarton Oaks Research Library and Collection, 1999).

5. T. Longstaffe-Gowan, *The London Town Garden, 1700–1840* (New Haven, CT: Yale University Press, 2001).

6. But see C. A. Wilson, ed., *The Country House Kitchen Garden, 1600–1950* (Stroud: Sutton, 1998); S. Campbell, *A History of Kitchen Gardening* (London: Frances Lincoln, 2005).

7. For example, Conan, *Perspectives on Garden Histories*; B. Weltman-Aron, *On Other Grounds: Landscape Gardening and Nationalism in Eighteenth-Century England and France* (Albany: State University of New York Press, 2001); J. D. Hunt, *The Afterlife of Gardens* (London: Reaktion Books, 2004); M. Calder, ed., *Experiencing the Garden in the Eighteenth Century* (Bern: Peter Lang, 2006); Conan, *Baroque Garden Cultures*; S. M. Dixon, *Between the Real and the Ideal: The Accademia Degli Arcadi and Its Garden in Eighteenth-Century Rome* (Newark: University of Delaware Press, 2006); and the *New Arcadian Journal*, passim.

8. Examples are numerous but would include C. Mukerji, "Reading and Writing with Nature: Social Claims and the French Formal Garden," *Theory and Society* 19, no. 6 (1990): 651–79; S. Daniels, *Humphry Repton: Landscape Gardening and the Geography of Georgian England* (New Haven, CT: Yale University Press, 1999); T. Mariage, *The World of André Le Nôtre* (Philadelphia: University of Pennsylvania Press, 1999); Hunt, *The Afterlife of Gardens*; Conan, *Baroque Garden Cultures*; Dixon, *Between the Real and the Ideal*; S. Bending, "Miserable Reflections on the Sorrows of My Life: Letters, Loneliness and Gardening in the 1760s," *Tulsa Studies in Women's Literature* 25, no. 1 (2006): 31–47; S. Bending, "Mrs Montagu's Contemplative Bench: Bluestocking Gardens and Female Retirement," *Huntington Library Quarterly* 69, no. 4 (2006): 555–80.

9. T. Whately, *Observations on Modern Gardening* (London: T. Payne, 1770); R. Paulson, *Emblem and Expression: Meaning in English Art of the Eighteenth Century* (Cambridge, MA: Harvard University Press, 1975).

10. "The Political Temples of Stow," *New Arcadian Journal* 43/44 (1997).

11. C. Taylor, *The Archaeology of Gardens* (Aylesbury: Shire Archaeology, 1983); Williamson, *Polite Landscapes*; T. Williamson, *The Archaeology of the Landscape Park: Garden Design in Norfolk, England, c.1680–1840* (Oxford: British Archaeological Reports British Series, 1998); Currie, *Garden Archaeology: A Handbook*.

12. For example, Hunt, *The Afterlife of Gardens*; S. Bending, "One among the Many: Popular Aesthetics, Polite Culture and the Country House Landscape," in *The Country House in Georgian England*, ed. D. Arnold (Stroud: Alan Sutton Publishing, 1998).

13. D. Miller, *Material Culture and Mass Consumption* (Oxford: Blackwell, 1987).

14. M. Mosser and G. Teyssot, *The History of Garden Design: The Western Tradition from the Renaissance to the Present Day* (London: Thames and Hudson, 1991) would be another.

15. Most notably Williamson, *Polite Landscapes;* and Williamson, *The Archaeology of the Landscape Park.* Ostensibly outside of our period, the enormous amount of work currently being undertaken on medieval and Renaissance gardens will inevitably mean that accounts of innovation and change in our period will have to be revised.

16. H. Walpole, "The History of the Modern Taste in Gardening," in *Anecdotes of Painting in England: The Second Edition,* vol. 4 (London, Strawberry Hill, 1765–80).

17. Notably E. Gellner, *Nations and Nationalism: New Perspectives on the Past* (Ithaca, NY: Cornell University Press, 1983); E. J. Hobsbawm, *Nations and Nationalism since 1780: Programme, Myth, Reality* (Cambridge: Cambridge University Press, 1992).

18. See, for example, J. Hayman, "Notions of National Character in the Eighteenth Century," *Huntington Library Quarterly* 35 (1971): 1–17; J. D Hunt, " 'But Who Does Not Know What a Dutch Garden Is?' The Dutch Garden in the English Imagination," in *The Dutch Garden in the Seventeenth Century,* ed. J. D. Hunt (Washington, D.C.: Dumbarton Oaks Research Library and Collection, 1990); L. Colley, *Britons: Forging the Nation 1707–1837* (New Haven,CT: Yale University Press, 1992); D. Jacques, "Who Knows What a Dutch Garden Is?" *Garden History* 30, no. 2 (2002): 114–30.

19. R. Porter, *The Creation of the Modern World: The Untold Story of the British Enlightenment* (New York: W. W. Norton, 2000).

20. J. I. Israel, *Radical Enlightenment: Philosophy and the Making of Modernity 1650–1750* (Oxford: Oxford University Press, 2001).

21. See, for example, S. Schama, *The Embarrassment of Riches: An Interpretation of Dutch Culture in the Golden Age* (London: Collins, 1987); E. De Jong, "For Profit and Ornament: The Function and Meaning of Dutch Garden Art in the Period of William and Mary, 1650–1702," in *The Dutch Garden in the Seventeenth Century,* ed. J. D. Hunt (Washington, D.C.: Dumbarton Oaks Research Library and Collection, 1990), 13–48; and E. De Jong, *Nature and Art: Dutch Garden and Landscape Architecture 1650–1740* (Philadelphia: University of Pennsylvania Press. 2000); A. McRae, *God Speed the Plough: The Representation of Agrarian England, 1500–1660* (Cambridge: Cambridge University Press, 1996).

22. D. Lambin, "Pleasure with Profit: Some Aspects of Landscape Gardening," *Garden History* 3, no. 2 (1975): 29–36; Williamson, *Polite Landscapes*; P. Eyres, "Commercial Profit and Cultural Display in the Eighteenth-Century Landscape Gardens at Wentworth Woodhouse and Harewood," in *Bourgeois and Aristocratic Cultural Encounters in Garden Art, 1550–1850,* ed. M. Conan (Washington, D.C.: Dumbarton Oaks Research Library and Collection, 2002).

23. A. Young, *Travels, during the Years 1787, 1788, and 1789: Undertaken More Particularly with a View of Ascertaining the Cultivation, Wealth, Resources, and National Prosperity, of the Kingdom of France* (Bury St. Edmunds: J. Rackham, 1792), I, 54.

24. S. Bending, "The Improvement of Arthur Young: Agricultural Technology and the Production of Landscape in Eighteenth-Century England," in *Technologies*

of Landscape: From Reaping to Recycling, ed. D.E. Nye (Amherst: University of Massachusetts Press, 1999).

25. See K. Thomas, *Man and the Natural World: Changing Attitudes in England 1500–1800* (London: Allen Lane, 1983); M. Leslie and T. Raylor, *Culture and Cultivation in Early Modern England* (Leicester: Leicester University Press, 1992); McRae, *God Speed the Plough*.

26. E. Harwood, "Personal Identity and the Eighteenth-Century Garden," *Journal of Garden History* 13, nos. 1 and 2 (1993): 36–48; Williamson, *Polite Landscapes*.

27. J.D. Hunt, *Greater Perfections: The Practice of Garden Theory* (London: Thames and Hudson, 2000), 181.

28. Mariage, *The World of André Le Nôtre*. See also, for example, L.C. Halpern, "The Duke of Kent's Garden at Wrest Park," *Journal of Garden History* 15, no. 3 (1995): 149–78, which argues that because Wrest retained a formal layout it hasn't been deemed important by garden historians looking at the development of the English style; as she demonstrates, it featured in numerous tours and was not seen as old-fashioned by contemporaries.

29. D. Outram, *The Enlightenment* (Cambridge: Cambridge University Press, 1995); J.G.A. Pocock, *Barbarism and Religion* (Cambridge: Cambridge University Press, 1999); Porter, *The Creation of the Modern World*; D. Gordon, *Postmodernism and the Enlightenment: New Perspectives in Eighteenth-Century French Intellectual History* (New York: Routledge, 2001); J.I. Israel, *Radical Enlightenment*.

30. D. Spadafora, *The Idea of Progress in Eighteenth-Century Britain* (New Haven, CT: Yale University Press, 1990).

31. M. Baridon, "Understanding Nature and the Aesthetics of the Landscape Garden," in *Experiencing the Garden in the Eighteenth Century*, ed. M. Calder (Bern: Peter Lang, 2006).

32. As Roy Strong has convincingly argued, visual representations of gardens also reinforce the importance of religious symbolism. R. Strong, *The Artist and the Garden* (New Haven, CT: Published for the Paul Mellon Centre for Studies in British Art, Yale University Press, 2000).

33. J. Prest, *The Garden of Eden: The Botanic Garden and the Re-creation of Paradise* (New Haven, CT: Yale University Press, 1981).

34. Leslie and Raylor, *Culture and Cultivation in Early Modern England*; Hunt, *Greater Perfections*.

35. We might valuably compare this with modern Anglophone writing on Chinese gardens of the same period, which is insistent on the spiritual aspects of garden design. See, for example, O. Sirén, *Garden of China* (New York: Ronald Press, 1949); M. Keswick, *The Chinese Garden: History, Art and Architecture, with Contributions and Conclusion by Charles Jencks* (London: Academy Editions, 1978).

36. See, for example, M.F. Schulz, "The Circuit Walk of the Eighteenth-Century Landscape Garden and the Pilgrim's Circuitous Progress," *Eighteenth-Century Studies* 15, no. 1 (1981): 1–25; and M.F. Schulz, *Paradise Preserved: Recreations of Eden in 18th- and 19th-Century England* (Cambridge: Cambridge University Press, 1985).

37. R. Williams, *The Country and the City* (London: Chatto and Windus, 1973); G. M. MacLean, D. Landry, and J. P. Ward, *The Country and the City Revisited: England and the Politics of Culture, 1550–1850* (Cambridge: Cambridge University Press, 1999).

38. See, for example, J. Friday, *Art and Enlightenment: Scottish Aesthetics in the 18th Century* (Exeter: Imprint Academic, 2004).

39. Hunt, *Greater Perfections*, 81.

40. D. Cosgrove, *Social Formation and Symbolic Landscape* (London: Croom Helm, 1984), chapter 1; M. Andrews, *Landscape and Western Art* (Oxford History of Western Art, Oxford: Oxford University Press, 1999), chapter 3.

41. I. Ousby, *The Englishman's England: Taste, Travel, and the Rise of Tourism* (Cambridge: Cambridge University Press, 1990); Bending, "One among the Many."

42. Daniels, *Humphry Repton*.

43. M. Jourdain, *The Work of William Kent, Artist, Painter, Designer and Landscape Gardener* (London: Country Life, 1948); J. D. Hunt, *William Kent Landscape Garden Designer: An Assessment and Catalogue of His Designs* (London: A. Zwemmer, 1987).

44. M. Batey, "The Way to View Rousham by Kent's Gardener," *Garden History* 11, no. 2 (1983): 125–32.

45. J. Woodhouse, *Poems on Sundry Occasions* (London: R. and J. Dodsley et al., 1764).

46. For example, Ousby, *The Englishman's England*; Hunt, *The Afterlife of Gardens*: M. Calder, ed., *Experiencing the Garden in the Eighteenth Century* (Bern: Peter Lang, 2006).

47. W. Shenstone, "Unconnected Thoughts on Gardening," in *The Works, in Verse and Prose, of William Shenstone* (London: J. Dodsley, 1764).

48. Gilpin's notebooks are in the Bodleian Library; see MS. Eng. misc. 180(1), f.11; and MS. Eng. misc. f.179(2), "Particular Parts. Hagley & Leasowes."

49. T. Hull, ed., *Selected Letters between the Late Duchess of Somerset, Lady Luxborough, Mr. Whistler, Miss Dolman, Mr. R. Dodsley, William Shenstone, Esq. and Others; Including a Sketch of the Manners, Laws, &c. of the Republic of Venice, and Some Poetical Pieces; the Whole Now First Published from Original Copies, by Mr. Hull*, 2 vols. (London, 1778), 265–67.

50. Anon. *Journal of a Three Week Tour, in 1797, through Derbyshire to the Lakes: By a Gentleman of the University of Oxford* (1797). Vol. 5 of *The British Tourist; or, Traveller's Pocket Companion, through England, Wales, Scotland, and Ireland: Comprehending the Most Celebrated Tours in the British Islands*, ed. W. Mavor, 6 vols. (London, 1798–1800), 203.

51. J. Wesley, *The Journal of the Rev. John Wesley, A.M., Sometime Fellow of Lincoln College, Oxford, Enlarged from Original Mss., with Notes from Unpublished Diaries, Annotations, Maps, and Illustrations*, ed. N. Curnock, 8 vols. (London: R. Culley, 1909–16), Friday, August 25, 1769.

52. Outram, *The Enlightenment*, 80.

53. It is notable, for example, in the letters of the garden-obsessed Lennox sisters— especially Caroline Fox (later Holland)—that a Rousseauvian pleasure in the

garden is both delightful and unsettling; see E. Leinster, *Correspondence of Emily, Duchess of Leinster (1731–1814)*, ed. B. FitzGerald (Dublin: Stationery Office 1949–57).

54. On which, see C. Fabricant, "Binding and Dressing Nature's Loose Tresses: The Ideology of Augustan Landscape Design," in *Studies in Eighteenth-Century Culture*, vol. 8, ed. R. Runte (Madison: University of Wisconsin Press, 1979); W. Frith, "Castle Howard: Dynastic and Sexual Politics," *New Arcadian Journal* 29/30 (1990): 66–99; and W. Frith, "When Frankie Met Johnny: Sexuality and Politics in the Gardens at West Wycombe and Medmenham Abbey," *New Arcadian Journal* 49/50 (2000): 62–104.

55. But see S. G. Bell, "Women Create Gardens in Male Landscapes: A Revisionist Approach to Eighteenth-Century English Garden History," *Feminist Studies* 16, no. 3 (1990): 471–91; S. Bennet, *Five Centuries of Women and Gardens* (London: National Portrait Gallery Publications, 2000); Strong, *The Artist and the Garden*; T. Way, *Virgins Weeders and Queens* (Stroud: Sutton Publishing, 2006); M. Laird, *Mrs Delany and Her Circle* (New Haven, CT: Yale University Press, 2009).

56. S. Switzer, *Ichnographia Rustica; or, The Nobleman, Gentlemen, and Gardener's Recreation* (London: D. Browne, 1718), 1, 73–74.

57. On the genesis of the flower garden in England, see M. Laird, *The Flowering of the English Landscape Garden: English Pleasure Grounds 1720–1800* (Philadelphia: University of Pennsylvania Press, 1999).

58. No. 15, Saturday, March 17, 1711.

59. See also Laird, *Mrs Delany and Her Circle* for an excellent account of Mary Delany.

60. The majority of Montagu's letters are now at the Huntington Library, San Marino, though many are partially reprinted in E. Climenson, ed., *Elizabeth Montagu, The Queen of the Bluestockings: Her Correspondence from 1720 to 1761*, 2 vols. (New York: E. P. Dutton, 1906); and R. Blunt, ed., *Mrs Montagu, "Queen of the Blues": Her Letters and Friendships from 1762 to 1800*, 2 vols. (London: Constable, 1923).

61. Elizabeth Montagu to Lord Lyttelton, ca. 1760–62 (Huntington Library MS, MO 1407).

62. Bending, "Mrs Montagu's Contemplative Bench: Bluestocking Gardens and Female Retirement," 555–80; and S. Bending, *Women, Gardens and Eighteenth-Century Culture* (Cambridge: Cambridge University Press, 2013), chapter 3.

63. Lyttelton to Montagu, Ebrington, Glouc., May 21, 1764 (Huntington Library MS, MO 1321).

Chapter 1

1. For discussions of these gardens and illustrations, see P. Hayden, *Russian Parks and Gardens* (London: Frances Lincoln, 2005), 9–15.

2. Hayden, *Russian Parks and Gardens*, 9.

3. Hayden, *Russian Parks and Gardens*, 14.

4. Hayden, *Russian Parks and Gardens*, 14.

5. Hayden, *Russian Parks and Gardens*, 13.

6. Hayden, *Russian Parks and Gardens*, 13n12.

7. For a full account, see T. Mowl, *Gentlemen and Players: Gardeners of the English Landscape* (Stroud: Sutton, 2000), 11–34.

8. For an illustration, see Mowl, *Gentlemen and Players*, 13. For Dymock's rectangular plans for an ideal farm or estate, see J.D. Hunt, *Greater Perfections: The Practice of Garden Theory* (London: Thames and Hudson, 2000), figures 112a and 112b.

9. Illustrated in Mowl, *Gentlemen and Players*, 19.

10. Illustrated in Mowl, *Gentlemen and Players*, 21.

11. See Mowl, *Gentlemen and Players*, chapter 3, 23–34 for illustrations and a full description. For Beale and Backbury, see P. Goodchild, " 'No Phantastical Utopia but a Reall Place': John Evelyn, John Beale and Backbury Hill, Herefordshire," *Garden History* 19, no. 2 (1991): 105–27.

12. Illustrated in Mowl, *Gentlemen and Players*, 25. Also Hartlib MSS. 25/6/5. However, the idea of "wilderness" as part of a varied and thoughtful landscape was announced much earlier by sixteenth-century humanist discussions of different natures and then mirrored in most seventeenth-century and early eighteenth-century bird's-eye views of gardens.

13. Alexander Pope, "Epistle to Lord Burlington," l. 64.

14. 1709, translated into English in 1712 by John James.

15. Chambers made trips to Canton in 1743–45 and again to China in 1748–49 in connection with his duties in the Swedish East India Company.

16. L. de Rouvroy duc de Saint-Simon, *Saint-Simon at Versailles*, rev. ed., trans. L. Norton (New York: Harper, 1958), 262.

17. See L. Knyff and J. Kip, *Britannia Illustrata*, 1707, rev. ed., ed. J. Harris and G. Jackson-Stops (Bungay: Paradigm Press, 1984).

18. Alexander Pope, Epistle to Lord Burlington, lines 131–32.

19. A plan of Mollet's layout for St James's Park is illustrated in *Britannia Illustrata*, plate 3; see also Mowl, *Gentlemen and Players*, 48–50.

20. E. S. de Beer, ed., *The Diary of John Evelyn*, Oxford English Texts (Oxford: Oxford University Press, 1955), 573.

21. For a sound introduction, see M. Keswick, *The Chinese Garden: History, Art and Architecture, with Contributions and Conclusion by Charles Jencks* (London: Academy Editions, 1978).

22. For an impressive overview of eighteenth-century gardens in China and Europe, see O. Sirén, *China and Gardens of Europe in the Eighteenth Century*, with an introduction by H. Honour (Washington, D.C.: Dumbarton Oaks Research Library and Collection, 1950/1990); see also J. D. Hunt, *The Picturesque Garden in Europe* (London: Thames and Hudson, 2002). For a general history of Western landscape design, see M. Mosser and G. Teyssot, *The History of Garden Design: The Western Tradition from the Renaissance to the Present Day* (London: Thames and Hudson, 1991).

23. T. Mowl, *Historic Gardens of Worcestershire* (Stroud: Tempus, 2006), 64–106. For George I, see Mowl, *Historic Gardens of Worcestershire*, 64–106; see also R. Hatton, *George I: Elector and King* (London: Thames and Hudson, 1978).

24. Hunt, *The Picturesque Garden in Europe*; C. A. Brown, "Thomas Jefferson's Poplar Forest: The Mathematics of an Ideal Villa," *Journal of Garden History* 10 (1990): 117–39; E. T. Cooperman, *William Birch: Picturing the American Scene* (Philadelphia: University of Pennsylvania Press, 2010).
25. See plates 10, 11, and 12 of *Britannia Illustrata* for this obsessive garden park.
26. D. Jacques and A. J. van der Horst, *The Gardens of William and Mary* (London: Christopher Helm, 1988), 11.
27. Illustrations of all these centrally places gardens are in Jacques and van der Horst, *The Gardens of William and Mary*, chapter 3, "The Gardens of the Dutch Court of William III"; Heemstede, illustrated on pages 52 and 53, is the most impressive. See also J. D. Hunt and E. De Jong, eds., "The Anglo-Dutch Garden in the Age of William and Mary," *Journal of Garden History* nos. 2 and 3 (April–September 1988); and E. De Jong, *Nature and Art: Dutch Garden and Landscape Architecture 1650–1740* (Philadelphia: University of Pennsylvania Press, 2000). For a discussion of Dutch design, see D. Jacques, "Who Knows What a Dutch Garden Is?" *Garden History* 30 no. 2 (2002): 114–30.
28. Knyff and Kip, *Britannia Illustrata*, plate 71.
29. Knyff and Kip, *Britannia Illustrata*, plates 43 and 51.
30. Knyff and Kip, *Britannia Illustrata*, plates 41, 17, 39, and 40.
31. For a full account and illustrations, see T. Mowl and C. Hickman, *Historic Gardens of Northamptonshire* (Stroud: Tempus, 2008).
32. For two illustrations and a full account of Evelyn's lack of generosity, see Mowl, *Gentlemen and Players*, 38–40.
33. de Beer, *The Diary of John Evelyn*, 55.
34. Mowl, *Gentlemen and Players*, 41; J. D. Hunt, *Garden and Grove: The Italian Renaissance Garden in the English Imagination 1600–1750* (London: J. M. Dent, 1986).
35. T. Mowl, *Historic Gardens of Oxfordshire* (Stroud: Tempus, 2007).
36. Hunt makes a good case for the links between Hartlib and Switzer; see Hunt, *Greater Perfections*, 201–206.
37. Switzer, *Ichnographia Rustica*, 88.
38. Switzer, *Ichnographia Rustica*, 89.
39. Switzer, *Ichnographia Rustica*, 88.
40. Switzer, *Ichnographia Rustica*, 88.
41. Knyff and Kip, *Britannia Illustrata*, plate 59.
42. Knyff and Kip, *Britannia Illustrata*, plate 70.
43. See P. Willis, *Charles Bridgeman and the English Landscape Garden* (Newcastle: Elysium Press, 2002).
44. T. Mowl, *Historic Gardens of Wiltshire* (Stroud: Tempus, 2004), 68–70; Willis, *Charles Bridgeman and the English Landscape Garden*.
45. Which was exactly what Switzer had predicted in his *Ichnographia*.
46. Mowl, *Historic Gardens of Wiltshire*, 95. Quoted in Mowl, *Historic Gardens of Wiltshire*, 95. See also K. Woodbridge, *Landscape and Antiquity: Aspects of Culture at Stourhead 1718–1838* (Oxford: Oxford University Press, 1970); and K. Woodbridge, *The Stourhead Landscape: Wiltshire* (London: The National Trust, 1982).

47. Hunt, *Garden and Grove.*

48. For these continental examples, see Hunt, *The Picturesque Garden in Europe.* For Sweden particularly, see K. Lindegren, ed., *Frederick Magnus Piper and the Landscape Garden* (Sweden: Katrineholm, 1981); and M. Olausson, *Den engelska parken i Sverige under gustaviansk tid* [The English landscape garden in Sweden during the Gustavian era] (Stockholm: Piper Press, 1993).

49. Carmontelle's real name was Louis Carragis, quoted from his *Prospectus* to the Jardin de Monceau in D. Wiebenson, *The Picturesque Garden in France* (Princeton, NJ: Princeton University Press, 1978), 77.

50. The ponderous solemnity of French gardens meant that they took Thomas Whately's *Observations on Modern Gardening* seriously, with all its spurious categories. It was translated into French in 1771.

51. C.-H. Watelet, *Essay on Gardens: A Chapter in the French Picturesque*, rev. ed., trans. and ed. Samuel Danon, with introduction by Joseph Disponzio (Philadelphia: University of Pennsylvania Press, 1774, 2003); Wiebenson, *The Picturesque Garden in France.*

52. Hunt, *The Picturesque Garden in Europe*, 160.

53. Hunt, *The Picturesque Garden in Europe*, plate 89.

54. Hunt, *The Picturesque Garden in Europe*, plate 145.

55. M. Baridon in Hunt, *The Picturesque Garden in Europe.*

56. See Mowl, *Gentleman and Players*, chapter 12.

57. See J. Woudstra, ed., "Lancelot Brown (1716–83) and the Landscape Park," *Garden History* 29, no. 1 (2001). See also D. Stroud, *Capability Brown* (London: Country Life, 1950); and E. Hyams, *Capability Brown and Humphrey Repton* (New York: Charles Scribner's Sons, 1971).

58. J.-M. Morel, *Théorie des Jardins, ou l'Art des Jardins de la Nature*, 1802, second enlarged edition (Paris. Originally published in one volume, 1776); J. J. Disponzio, "A Catalogue of the Works of Jean-Marie Morel," *Studies in the History of Gardens and Designed Landscapes* (double issue) 21, nos. 3 and 4 (2001): 149–354; and J. J. Disponzio, "Jean-Marie Morel and the Invention of Landscape Architecture," in *Tradition and Innovation in French Garden Art*, ed. J.D. Hunt and M. Conan (Philadelphia: University of Pennsylvania Press, 2002).

59. See T. Mowl, *Historic Gardens of Worcestershire* (Stroud: Tempus, 2006), 45–56; also C. Gordon, *The Coventrys of Croome* (Chichester: Phillimore, 2000).

60. For Vanbrugh's work at Blenheim, see J. Bond and K. Tiller, *Blenheim: Landscape for a Palace* (Stroud: Sutton, 1997); also C. Ridgway and R. Williams, eds., *Sir John Vanbrugh and Landscape Architecture in Baroque England 1690–1730* (Stroud: Sutton, 2000).

61. For a discussion of the aesthetics of this period, see M. Andrews, *The Search for the Picturesque: Landscape Aesthetics and Tourism in Britain, 1760–1800* (Aldershot: Scolar, 1989).

62. See A. Rogger, *Landscapes of Taste: The Art of Humphrey Repton's Red Books* (London: Routledge, 2007). See also S. Daniels, *Humphry Repton: Landscape Gardening and the Geography of Georgian England* (New Haven, CT: Yale University Press, 1999); and D. Stroud, *Humphry Repton* (London: Country Life, 1962).

Chapter 2

1. For Versailles, see P.-A. Lablaude, *The Gardens of Versailles* (Paris: Éditions Scala, 1995); C. Constans, *Versailles: Château de la France et orgueil des rois* (Paris: Gallimard, 1996), a guidebook that usefully reprints one of Louis XIV's sets of instructions about how to show the gardens; and A. Friedman, "What John Locke Saw at Versailles," *Journal of Garden History* 9 (1989): 177–98.
2. Noticed by Mlle. de Scudèry in 1661.
3. In describing it in this way, I am trying to characterize the particular inflection given to the myth at Versailles. There is probably an allegory involved about Louis XIV's mother having had to deal with the rebellion of the Fronde during the Regency before he came of age.
4. See his contribution to J.D. Hunt and J. Wolschke-Bulman, eds., *The Vernacular Garden* (Washington, D.C.: Dumbarton Oaks Research Library and Collection, 1993).
5. S. Switzer, *Ichnographia Rustica; or, The Nobleman, Gentlemen, and Gardener's Recreation* (London: D. Browne, 1718), 197–98.
6. Switzer, *Ichnographia Rustica*, II, 186.
7. There is no evidence of Switzer having worked at Wentworth Castle, but the owner, the Earl of Strafford, bought a copy of Switzer's book in June 1728. See British Library, Add. Mss. 22258 f.137.
8. Switzer, *Ichnographia Rustica*, II, 187.
9. Switzer, *Ichnographia Rustica*, II, 199.
10. Switzer, *Ichnographia Rustica*, II, 200.
11. Switzer, *Ichnographia Rustica*, II, 188.
12. Switzer, *Ichnographia Rustica*, II, 221–22.
13. Hall Barn's "temple of Pan or Silvanus" was described by Lord Percevall in 1724, quoted in J.D. Hunt and P. Willis, eds., *The Genius of the Place: The English Landscape Garden 1620–1820* (London: Paul Elek, 1975), 165.
14. Florence Hopper claims this to be the first asymmetrical garden in the Netherlands, which is an ambitious claim: entry for Duin-en-Berg in *The Oxford Companion to Gardens* (Oxford University Press, 1986), 147. For Dutch gardens in general, see the special issue, "The Anglo-Dutch Garden in the Age of William and Mary," *Journal of Garden History* 8, nos. 2 and 3 (1988); C. Oldenburger-Ebbers, "Garden Design in the Netherlands in the Seventeenth Century," in *The Architecture of Western Gardens*, ed. M. Mosser and G. Teyssot (Cambridge, MA: MIT Press, 1991), 163–65; and Hopper's entry for the Netherlands in the *Oxford Companion*.
15. Sir Thomas Robinson, letter to the Earl of Carlisle, in *The Manuscripts of the Earl of Carlisle at Castle Howard* (Historical Manuscripts Commission, 1897), reprinted in M. Charlesworth, *The English Garden: Literary Sources and Documents* (Robertsbridge: Helm Information, 1993), vol. 2, 115.
16. Robinson in Charlesworth, *The English Garden*, 115.
17. Robinson in Charlesworth, *The English Garden*, 115.
18. See J. Colton, "Kent's Hermitage for Queen Caroline at Richmond," *Architectura* 2 (1974): 181–89 for the political importance of this feature.

19. M. Charlesworth, "Sacred Landscape: Signs of Religion in the Eighteenth-Century Garden," *Journal of Garden History* 13, nos. 1 and 2 (1993): 56–68.

20. Especially Bishop Butler, in his *Analogy of Natural and Revealed Religion* (London, 1736).

21. S. Clarke, *A Demonstration of the Being and Attributes of God Manifested in the Works of the Creation* (London, 1705).

22. *Encyclopaedia Britannica*, 1771, II, 6481.

23. First published in vol. 2 of W. Shenstone's *The Works, in Verse and Prose, of William Shenstone* (1764), reprinted in Charlesworth, *The English Garden*, vol. 2, 169–77, 169.

24. Stephen Bending and Andrew McRae's discussion of the word is more incisive than most. See S. Bending and A. McRae, *The Writing of Rural England 1500–1800* (London: Palgrave Macmillan, 2003), especially chapter 2, "The Discovery of Landscape."

25. W. Shenstone's "Unconnected Thoughts on Gardening," in Charlesworth, *The English Garden*, vol. 2, 174.

26. An excellent source for Girardin and his work is R.-L. de Girardin, *De la Composition des Paysages*, 1777, ed. Michel Conan (Paris: Editions du Champ Urbain, 1979), which also prints an anonymous guide to the gardens at Ermenonville and an extremely useful "Postface" by Conan.

27. Quoted and translated in B. Lassus, *The Landscape Approach* (Philadelphia: University of Pennsylvania Press, 1998), 47.

28. S. Daniels, *Humphry Repton: Landscape Gardening and the Geography of Georgian England* (New Haven, CT: Yale University Press, 1999).

29. M. Laird, *The Flowering of the English Landscape Garden: English Pleasure Grounds 1720–1800* (Philadelphia: University of Pennsylvania Press, 1999).

30. See Laird, *The Flowering of the English Landscape Garden*, 7, for an example of this at Brocklesby Park, Lincolnshire.

31. Laird, *The Flowering of the English Landscape Garden*, 83.

32. Laird, *The Flowering of the English Landscape Garden*, 303, quoting Woods. For Woods, F. Cowell, "Richard Woods (?1716–93): A Preliminary Account," *Garden History: The Journal of the Garden History Society* 14, no. 2 (1986), 85–119 is very useful.

33. For Nuneham, see Laird, *The Flowering of the English Landscape Garden*, 350–60.

34. M. Charlesworth, *Landscape and Vision in Nineteenth Century Britain and France* (Aldershot: Ashgate Publishing, 2008) contains extensive discussion of the significance of this on pages 81–84, 92–98, 112–15.

35. They are discussed throughout the literature. T. Williamson, *Polite Landscapes: Gardens and Society in Eighteenth-Century England* (Baltimore: Johns Hopkins University Press, 1995) emphasizes economic concerns throughout. He makes an error, however, on page 13, in the phrase "the Yarborough's Sledmere (Yorks.)." The Yarboroughs owned Brocklesby, Lincolnshire, while the Sykes family owned (and still owns) Sledmere, in east Yorkshire.

36. Beckford's journal for September 22, 1787, in B. Alexander, ed., *Journal of William Beckford in Portugal and Spain 1787–1788* (London: Hart-Davies, 1954), 205.

37. G. Carter, P. Goode, and K. Laurie, *Humphry Repton, Landscape Gardener 1752–1818* (London: Victoria and Albert Museum, 1982), 46–48.

38. An influential example was Salomon Gessner's *Rural Poems* (English translation 1762) and *New Idylls* (English translation 1776). See also J. Barrell, *The Dark Side of the Landscape: The Rural Poor in English Painting, 1730–1840* (Cambridge: Cambridge University Press, 1980).
39. Williamson, *Polite Landscapes*, on Holkham, the seat of the famous agricultural improver Coke of Norfolk, finds arable in the park, page 123.
40. Shenstone, *"Unconnected Thoughts,"* in Charlesworth, *The English Garden*, 177.
41. R. Williams, "Making Places: Garden-Mastery and English Brown," *Journal of Garden History* 3, no. 4 (1983): 382–85 emphasizes, however, just how many types of buildings were undertaken by the most prolific professional landscape designer.
42. For the Leasowes and Shenstone, see the primary sources collected in Charlesworth, *The English Garden*, vol. 2, 169–230.
43. The quotation is from Virgil's *First Georgic* l.168. (The Latin word *rus, ruris* could be equally well translated in this context as "countryside" or "fields." The translation "rural areas," while preserving the rustic connotation of the Latin, is too banal to allow here.)
44. R. Dodsley, "A Description of the Leasowes" (1764) quoted in Charlesworth, *The English Garden*, vol. 2, 210.
45. Exemplified by, but not confined to, D. Jacques, "On the Supposed Chineseness of the English Landscape Garden," *Garden History* 18, no. 1 (1990): 180–91.
46. Philip Yorke, journal for 1744, quoted in Charlesworth, *The English Garden*, vol. 2, 131. The building that emerged before Yorke's next visit in 1755 took a different Chinese form, however. See P. Conner, "China and the Landscape Garden: Reports, Engravings and Misconceptions," *Art History* 2 (1979): 429–40.
47. D. Ketcham, *Le Désert de Retz: A Late Eighteenth-Century French Folly Garden, the Artful Landscape of Monsieur de Monville* (San Francisco, CA: Arion Press, 1990; rev. ed., Cambridge, MA: MIT Press, 1994).
48. Discussion and quotation from Leibniz in A.O. Lovejoy, "The Chinese Origin of a Romanticism," in *Essays in the History of Ideas* (Baltimore: Johns Hopkins University Press, 1984), 99–135.
49. M. Tindal, *Christianity as Old as the Creation; or, The Gospel, a Republication of the Religion of Nature* (London, 1730), vol. 1, 405.
50. J.D. Hunt, "Approaches (New and Old) to Garden History," in *Perspectives on Garden Histories*, ed. M. Conan (Washington, D.C.: Dumbarton Oaks Research Library and Collection, 1999), 89–90.
51. M. Charlesworth, "Movement, Intersubjectivity, and Mercantile Morality at Stourhead," in *Landscape Design and the Experience of Motion*, ed. Michel Conan (Washington, D.C.: Dumbarton Oaks Research Library and Collection, 2003), 263–85.

Chapter 3

1. Collinson's Commonplace Book, Ms. 323a, 29, held by Linnean Society.
2. Linnean Society, Collinson MSS1, *Pococke's Tours 1754–1756*, 111.

3. J. C. Loudon, *Arboretum et Fruticetum Britannicum* (London: Longman et al., 1838), 73.
4. Loudon, *Arboretum et Fruticetum Britannicum*, 73.
5. Loudon, *Arboretum et Fruticetum Britannicum*, 62.
6. J.C. Loudon, *The Gardener's Magazine* 12 (1836): 502.
7. J.C. Loudon, *A Treatise on Farming, Improving and Managing Country Estates* (London, 1806), 343.
8. R. Desmond, *Kew: The History of the Royal Botanic Gardens* (London: Harvill Press, 1995), 39–40.
9. Loudon, *Arboretum et Fruticetum Britannicum*, 75.
10. D. Coombs, "The Garden at Carlton House of Frederick Prince of Wales and Augusta Princess Dowager of Wales," *Garden History* 25 (1997): 153–77.
11. E. Hyde, "The Cultivation of a King, or the Flower Gardens of Louis XIV," in *Tradition and Innovation in French Garden Art: Chapters of a New History*, ed. J.D. Hunt and M. Conan (Philadelphia: University of Pennsylvania Press, 2002), 1–21.
12. A. Tosi, "Fruit and Flower Gardens from the Neoclassical and Romantic Periods in Tuscany," in *The Italian Garden: Art, Design and Culture*, ed. J.D. Hunt (Cambridge: Cambridge University Press, 1996), 202–7.
13. H. Walpole, *The History of the Modern Taste in Gardening* (1771; New York: Ursus Press, 1995), 49.
14. Walpole, *The History of the Modern Taste in Gardening*, 46.
15. *For the Friends of Nature and Art: The Garden Kingdom of Prince Franz von Anhalt-Dessau in [the] Age of Enlightenment*, ed. Michael Sturmer et al. (Ostfildern-Ruit: Verlag Gerd Hatje, 1997), 53.
16. M. Symes, "Charles Hamilton at Bowood," *Garden History* 34 (2006): 206–7.
17. M. Laird, *The Flowering of the English Landscape Garden: English Pleasure Grounds 1720–1800* (Philadelphia: University of Pennsylvania Press, 1999), 46.
18. Laird, *The Flowering of the English Landscape Garden*, 59–60.
19. T. Whately, *Observations on Modern Gardening* (London: T. Payne, 1770), 188–89.

Chapter 4

1. S. Hall, *Representation: Cultural Representations and Signifying Practices* (Milton Keynes: Open University, 1997), 3.
2. "Lyme Park," The National Trust, http://www.nationaltrust.org.uk/main/w-vh/w-visits/w-findaplace/w-lymepark (accessed May 12, 2008).
3. W. Benjamin, "Theses on the Philosophy of History," in *Illuminations*, ed. H. Arendt (London: Fontana, 1982), 258.
4. P. Rabinow, ed., *The Foucault Reader* (London: Penguin, 1991), 82.
5. L. Smith, *Uses of Heritage* (London: Routledge, 2006), 3.
6. P. Mandler, *The Fall and Rise of the Stately Home* (New Haven, CT: Yale University Press), 1997.
7. Mandler, *The Fall and Rise of the Stately Home*, 266.
8. Smith, *Uses of Heritage*, 187.
9. Hall, *Representation*, 3–5.

10. Rabinow, *The Foucault Reader*, 82, 89.

11. D. Hicks, " 'Places for Thinking' from Anapolis to Bristol: Situations and Symmetries in 'World Historical Archaeologies,' " *World Archaeology* 37, no. 3 (September 2005): 387–88.

12. Scottish Natural Heritage, *Introducing Interpretation*, http://www.snh.org.uk/wwo/Interpretation (accessed May 12, 2008).

13. Smith, *Uses of Heritage*, 126.

14. Castle Howard, http://www.castlehoward.co.uk (accessed May 12, 2008).

15. There are some notable exceptions, such as the private Levens Hall guide which informs us of the modern labour of maintenance—the number of gardeners, the seasonal tasks, even the hardware involved: "four thirty-inch electric hedge trimmers powered by a generator" (Annette Bagot, *Levens Hall and Gardens*, nd, 30).

16. Smith, *Uses of Heritage*, 119.

17. Quotations from Chatsworth, http://www.chatsworth.org, accessed May 12, 2008.

18. Scottish Natural Heritage, *Introducing Interpretation*.

19. A. Greenspan, *Creating Colonial Williamsburg* (Washington, D.C.: Smithsonian Institute Press, 2002), 175.

20. M. Bywater, *Big Babies; or, Why Can't We Just Grow Up?* (London: Granta, 2006), 62.

21. F. Gibberd, "On Making Gardens and Landscapes" (lecture notes, 1982), Gibberd Archive, Gibberd Garden Trust. Quoted in A. de Verteuil, "The Gibberd Garden: Model of a Garden for Our Time?" unpublished MA diss., Bristol University, 2007.

22. See R. Hewison, *The Heritage Industry* (London: Methuen, 1987); and P. Wright, *On Living in an Old Country* (London: Verso, 1985), both summarized, with shortcomings pointed out, in Smith, *Uses of Heritage*, 38–42 passim.

23. Membership of the National Trust for England and Wales is over 3.5 million and rising.

24. Smith, *Uses of Heritage*, 5.

25. R. Samuel, *Theatres of Memory* (London: Verso, 1994), 271.

26. Stewart Harding, written response to English Heritage, draft *Conservation Principles Policies and Guidance for the Sustainable Management of the Historic Environment*, February 27, 2006, archives of the Parks Agency, Reading.

27. Smith, *Uses of Heritage*, 124.

28. J. D. Hunt, *The Afterlife of Gardens* (London: Reaktion Books, 2004), 205.

29. Acceptance speech at the Landscape Institute Annual Awards, November 2007.

30. National Trust, *Fountains Abbey and Studley Royal* (Swindon: National Trust, 2005), 38. It can be observed that such radical realignments of the approach to historic parks and gardens are quite commonplace, as a response to the needs and requirements of visitor processing. At Stowe the contemporary visitor approaches neither from the house nor the Triumphal Arch but via a path squeezed between the rear of the Temple of Concord and Victory and the new tea-room.

31. The steward's house had been converted to a tea-room as early as the 1890s, indicating how long a tradition public access has had at Studley. The garden and park including the Abbey were bought from descendants of the Aislabies by the County Council in 1966 before being acquired by the National Trust in 1983.

32. P. T. Harding and T. Wall, eds., *Moccas—An English Deer Park* (Peterborough: English Nature, 2000), 8.

33. S. Seymour et al., "Estate and Empire: Sir George Cornewall's Management of Moccas, Herefordshire and La Taste, Grenada, 1771–1819" (Dept. of Geography, University of Nottingham, Working Paper 28, August 1994).

34. Grade II* on the English Heritage Register in 1986.

35. W. Gilpin, *Three Essays: On Picturesque Beauty; on Picturesque Travel; and on Sketching Landscape* (London: Blamire, 1792), 3.

36. S. Lacey, *Gardens of the National Trust* (London: National Trust), 2005.

37. Lacey, *Gardens of the National Trust*, 322.

38. Lacey, *Gardens of the National Trust*, 322.

39. National Trust, *Stowe Landscape Gardens* (London: National Trust, 1997), 90.

40. G. Headley and W. Meulenkamp, *Follies: A National Trust Guide* (London: Jonathan Cape, 1986); and "Blast Folly: Bless Arcadia," special issue, *New Arcadian Journal* 24 (1986).

41. V. Joynt, "Utilior quam Dulce: A Utilitarian View of the Eighteenth-Century Model Farm," unpublished MA diss., Bristol University, 2007.

42. Hunt, *The Afterlife of Gardens*, 125.

43. See for example W. Frith, "Sexuality and Politics in the Gardens at West Wycombe and Medmenham Abbey," in *Bourgeois and Aristocratic Cultural Encounters in Garden Art, 1550–1850*, ed. M. Conan (Washington, D.C.: Dumbarton Oaks Research Library and Collection, 2002); J. G. Turner, "The Sexual Politics of Landscape: Images of Venus in Eighteenth-Century English Poetry and Landscape Gardening," *Studies in Eighteenth-Century Culture* 11 (1982): 346–66; P. Eyres, "Garden of Apollo & Venus," *New Arcadian Journal* 19 (1985); P. Eyres, "Studley Royal: Garden of Hercules and Venus," *New Arcadian Journal* 20 (1985): 4–29; R. Wheeler, " 'Pro Magna Charta' or 'Fay ce que Voudras': Political and Moral Precedents for the Gardens of Sir Francis Dashwood at West Wycombe," *New Arcadian Journal* 49/50 (2000): 26–60.

44. "These gardens were all about sex, but their history is being covered up by National Trust prudery. This makes it impossible to understand their true significance." Dan Cruikshank, quoted in M. Kennedy, "National Trust urged to abandon garden prudery," *The Guardian*, April 17, 2000, http://www.guardian.co.uk/uk/2000/apr/17/maevkennedy?INTCMP=SRCH (accessed November 26, 2012).

45. R. Higgs, "Stourhead Revisited," *The Follies Journal* 3 (2003): 40.

46. Quoted in R. Solnit, *Wanderlust: A History of Walking* (London: Verso, 2001), 92.

47. C. Tsu, *Inner Chapters*, rev. ed., trans. G.-F. Feng and J. English (London: Wildwood House, 1974), 30.

48. T. Mowl, *Historic Gardens of Oxfordshire* (Stroud: Tempus, 2007), 72.

49. "Lost Gardens of Heligan," Visit Cornwall, http://www.visitcornwall.com/things-to-do/south-cornwall/st-austell/pentewan/lost-gardens-heligan (accessed November 14, 2012).

50. "History and Restoration," The Lost Gardens of Heligan, http://heligan.com/the-story (accessed November 12, 2012).

51. See T. Petherick, and M. Eclaire, *The Kitchen Gardens at Heligan: Lost Gardening Principles Rediscovered* (London: Weidenfeld and Nicolson, 2006).

52. See "The Leasowes Project/Current Proposals," Dudley Metropolitan Borough Council, http://www.dudley.gov.uk/leisure-and-culture/parks-and-open-spaces/the-leasowes-project/current-proposals (accessed May 12, 2008).

53. For Shenstone's way of seeing what he termed "the fairy landscape," see D. Lambert, "William Shenstone and the Fairy Landscape," *Georgian Group Report and Journal* (1986): 67–73

54. H. Miller, *First Impressions of England and Its People* (Boston: Gould and Lincoln, 1860), 174–76.

55. Miller, *First Impressions of England and Its People*, 184.

56. H. Gilonis, "Emblematical and Expressive: The Gardenist Modes of William Shenstone and Ian Hamilton Finlay," *New Arcadian Journal* 53/54 (2002): 91–92.

57. P. Eyres, "Shenstone, The Leasowes and the Heritage Lottery Fund," *New Arcadian Journal* 53/54 (2002): 11.

58. S. Sontag, *On Photography* (Harmondsworth: Penguin), 1979.

59. The phrase is thought to be St. Augustine's; see "Solvitur ambulando," Everything2, http://everything2.com/title/solvitur+ambulando (accessed May 12, 2008).

60. Since this was written, the Gateway Gardens Trust has been dissolved as a result of lack of funding.

Chapter 5

1. T. Richardson, *The Arcadian Friends: Inventing the English Landscape Garden* (London: Bantam Press, 2007).

2. P. Eyres and F. Russell, "The Georgian Landscape Garden and the Victorian Urban Park," in *Sculpture and the Garden*, ed. P. Eyres and F. Russell (Aldershot: Ashgate Publishing, 2006).

3. P. Eyres, "Studley Royal: Garden of Hercules and Venus," *New Arcadian Journal* 20 (1985): 4–29.

4. J. Walker, "Studley Royal, 1716–1781," in *Mr Aislabie's Gardens*, ed. P. Eyres (Leeds: New Arcadian Press, 1981).

5. M. Charlesworth, "Thomas Wentworth's Monument: The Achievement of Peace," *New Arcadian Journal* 63/64 (2008): 37–63.

6. P. Eyres, "Wentworth Woodhouse: The Patriotism and Improvement of a Classic Whig Landscape," *New Arcadian Journal* 59/60 (2006): 51–146.

7. M. Symes, *Garden Sculpture* (Princes Risborough: Shire Publications, 1996).

8. P. Eyres, "The Rivalry between Wentworth Castle and Wentworth Woodhouse, 1695–1750," *New Arcadian Journal* 63/64 (2008): 11–35.

9. R. Wheeler, " 'Pro Magna Charta' or 'Fay ce que Voudras': Political and Moral Precedents for the Gardens of Sir Francis Dashwood at West Wycombe," *New Arcadian Journal* 49/50 (2000): 26–60.

10. R. Roscoe, "Peter Scheemakers and the Stowe Commission," *New Arcadian Journal* 43/44 (1997): 40–65.

11. P. Eyres, "British Naumachias: The Performance of Triumph and Memorial," in *Performance and Appropriation: Profane Rituals in Gardens and Landscapes*, ed. M. Conan (Washington, D.C.: Dumbarton Oaks Research Library and Collection, 2007).

12. G. B. Clarke, "Introduction," in *George Bickham: The Beauties of Stow*, ed. G. B. Clarke (The Augustan Reprint Society, 1977), i–xiv.

13. W. Frith, "Sexuality and Politics in the Gardens at West Wycombe and Medmenham Abbey," in *Bourgeois and Aristocratic Cultural Encounters in Garden Art, 1550–1850*, ed. M. Conan (Washington, D.C.: Dumbarton Oaks Research Library and Collection, 2002), 285–309.

14. W. Frith and P. Eyres, "In the Garden of Venus," *New Arcadian Journal* 33/34 (1992): 31–58.

15. Frith and Eyres, "In the Garden of Venus."

16. T. Mowl, *William Kent: Architect, Designer, Opportunist* (London: Jonathan Cape, 2006).

17. W. Frith, "Sex, Gender, Politics: The Venus de Medici in the Eighteenth-Century Landscape Garden," in *Sculpture and the Garden*, ed. P. Eyres and F. Russell (Aldershot: Ashgate Publishing, 2006).

18. W. Frith, "Castle Howard: Dynastic and Sexual Politics," *New Arcadian Journal* 29/30 (1990): 66–99.

19. M. Charlesworth, "Movement, Intersubjectivity, and Mercantile Morality at Stourhead," in *Landscape Design and the Experience of Motion*, ed. Michel Conan (Washington, D.C.: Dumbarton Oaks Research Library and Collection, 2003), 263–85.

20. P. Eyres, "Rambo in the Landscape Garden: The British Hercules as the Champion of the Protestant Succession," *New Arcadian Journal* 37/38 (1994): 11–43.

21. P. Eyres, "Kew and Stowe, 1757–1778: The Polarised Agendas of Royal and Whig Iconographies," *New Arcadian Journal* 51/52 (2001): 52–94.

22. R. Quaintance, "Kew Gardens 1731–1778: Can We Look at Both Sides Now?" *New Arcadian Journal* 51/52 (2001): 14–50.

23. J. Addison, *The Spectator*, 1712, ed. D. F. Bond, 5 vols. (Oxford: Clarendon Press, 1965).

24. P. Eyres, "The Invisible Pantheons of Thomas Hollis at Stowe and in Dorset," *New Arcadian Journal* 55/56 (2003): 45–120.

25. R. Williams, "The Leasowes, Hagley and Rural Inscriptions," *New Arcadian Journal* 53/54 (2002): 42–59.

26. W. Shenstone, "Unconnected Thoughts on Gardening," in *The Works, in Verse and Prose, of William Shenstone* (London: J. Dodsley, 1764).

27. M. Baker, *Figured in Marble: The Making and Viewing of Eighteenth-Century Sculpture* (London: Victoria and Albert Museum, 2000).

28. D. Lambert, "The Prospect of Trade: The Merchant Gardeners of Bristol in the Second Half of the Eighteenth Century," in *Bourgeois and Aristocratic Cultural Encounters in Garden Art, 1550–1850*, ed. M. Conan (Washington, D.C.: Dumbarton Oaks Research Library and Collection, 2002).

29. Eyres, "The Invisible Pantheons of Thomas Hollis at Stowe and in Dorset," 45–120.

30. M. Cousins, "William Shenstone: Jealous of Hagley?" *New Arcadian Journal* 53/54 (2002): 60–73.

31. P. Whiteley, "William Shenstone and 'The Judgement of Hercules': An Exercise in Politics," *New Arcadian Journal* 37/38 (1994): 81–99.

32. T. Whately, *Observations on Modern Gardening* (London: T. Payne, 1770).

33. F. Kielmansegge, *Diary of a Journey to England in the Years 1761–1762* (London: Longmans, Green and Co., 1902).

34. A. Young, *A Six Months' Tour through the North of England*, 2nd ed. (London, 1771).

35. P. Eyres, "Follies of Dissent and Omission: Monumental Reflections on the American War of Independence," *The Follies Journal* 7 (2007): 53–74.

36. Eyres, "Wentworth Woodhouse: The Patriotism and Improvement of a Classic Whig Landscape," 51–146.

37. Eyres, "Wentworth Woodhouse: The Patriotism and Improvement of a Classic Whig Landscape."

38. J. Lovie, Wentworth Woodhouse: Landscape Conservation and Management Plan (deposited in Sheffield Archives), 2008.

39. Kielmansegge, *Diary of a Journey to England in the Years 1761–1762.*

40. E. M. Burkdahl, *Johannes Wiedewelt: From Wincklemann's Vision of Antiquities to Sculptural Concepts of the 1980s*, rev. ed., trans. D. Hohnen (Copenhagen: Editions Bløndel, 1993).

41. Clarke, "Introduction," i–xiv.

42. B. W. Sarudy, *Gardens and Gardening in the Chesapeake, 1700–1805* (Baltimore: Johns Hopkins University Press), 1998.

Chapter 6

1. G. Mason, *An Essay on Design and Gardening* (1752, bound with T. Whatley, *Observations on Modern Gardening*; Dublin: John Exshaw, 1768).

2. J. W. Goethe, *Elective Affinities* (New York: Frederick Ungar, 1962), 20–24.

3. AV Isaiah 40:4. References from the Bible are from the Authorized Version (AV).

4. Goethe, *Elective Affinities*, 22.

5. AV Matthew 7:13–15.

6. F. Schlegel, *Dialogue on Poetry and Literary Aphorisms*, ed. E. Behler and R. Stuc (University Park: Pennsylvania State University Press, 1968), 138.

7. St. Augustine, *On Christian Doctrine*, rev. ed. (426; reprint, Indianapolis, IN: Bobbs-Merrill Educational Publishing, 1978).

8. J. Bunyan, *Pilgrims Progress from This World to That Which is to Come & Grace Abounding to the Chief of Sinners*, ed. J. F. Thornton and S. B. Varenne (1678; reprint, New York: Vintage, 2004), 29–36.

9. J. Addison, *The Spectator* (1712), ed. D. F. Bond, 5 vols. (Oxford: Clarendon Press, 1965), vol. 3, 560.

10. In later editions this became the subtitle of *Icnographia Rustica*.

11. A few of the many well-known and widely circulated treatises for useful gardens include those of John Abercrombie, Richard Bradley, Thomas Fairchild, Thomas

Knight, Thomas "Batty" Langley, George Mason, Stephen Switzer, and Richard Weston; in addition popular writers from the seventeenth century continued to circulate, including Ralph Austen and Jean de la Quintinye, among others.

12. I. Thompson, *The Sun King's Garden* (London: Bloomsbury, 2006).

13. J.D. Hunt, "Emblem and Expression in the Eighteenth Century Landscape Garden," *Eighteenth-Century Studies* 4, no. 3 (1971): 294–317. Hunt provides a Whig history of gardens quite different from my own that emphasizes the "mythology of prolepsis" (quoting Quentin Skinner), with which I agree, especially the mythology of prolepsis.

14. P. Hobhouse, *Gardening through the Ages* (New York: Barnes and Noble, 1997); C. Thacker, *The History of Gardens* (Berkeley: University of California Press, 1979); C. Quest-Ritson, *The English Garden: A Social History* (Boston: D. R. Godine, 2003).

15. I use the French term rather than the English because *le jardin anglais* has a specific connotation for the period from 1730 to 1790; as important, England's horticultural recognition on the continent simultaneously acknowledges its increasing political preeminence by associating its military preeminence with horticulture. Repton points out that groups of trees were given military names such as platoons and regiments; J. C. Loudon, *The Landscape Gardening and Landscape Architecture of the Late Humphry Repton, Esq.* (1840; West Mead: Gregg International Press, 1969), 233. Similarly, berms (low, grass-covered hillocks) were drawn from the military practice of throwing up earth behind which foot soldiers could lie down for cover.

16. S. Switzer, *The Nobleman, Gentleman, and Gardener's Recreation* (London: B. Barker and C. King, 1715), xiv.

17. W. Harris, *A Description of the King's Royal Palace and Gardens at Loo* (London: R. Roberts, 1699), 56.

18. Harris, *A Description of the King's Royal Palace and Gardens at Loo*, 71.

19. Harris, *A Description of the King's Royal Palace and Gardens at Loo*, 5.

20. Harris, *A Description of the King's Royal Palace and Gardens at Loo*, 45.

21. Harris, *A Description of the King's Royal Palace and Gardens at Loo*, 44–45.

22. J. Milton, *John Milton: Complete Poems and Major Prose*, rev. ed., ed. M. Y. Hughes (1667; Indianapolis, IN: Odyssey Press, 1957).

23. L. F. Baum, *The Wonderful Wizard of Oz* (Chicago: George M. Hill, 1900)

24. Harris, *A Description of the King's Royal Palace and Gardens at Loo*, 38; my emphasis.

25. Harris, *A Description of the King's Royal Palace and Gardens at Loo*, 40–42.

26. J. Evelyn, *Sylva; or, a Discourse of Forest-Trees, and the Propagation of Timber* (London: Royal Society Printers, 1665). On the connotations of the word *race* see R. Crawford, *Poetry, Enclosure, and the Vernacular Landscape 1700–1830* (Cambridge: Cambridge University Press, 2002), 125–26.

27. J.D. Hunt, *Garden and Grove: The Italian Renaissance Garden in the English Imagination 1600–1750* (London: J.M. Dent, 1986), 140–41.

28. Lines VIII, 66–75.

29. Lines IV, 236–37, 240–43. Milton likely borrowed Paradise's hydraulics from Homer's description of the garden of Alcinous. Homer, *The Odyssey*, rev.

ed., trans. Robert Fitzgerald (New York: Doubleday, 1963), lines 7.92–163. The description is even closer to Milton's in Laurence Eusden's translation as quoted by Switzer:

> Two plenteous Fountains the whole Prospect crown'd, This thro' the Garden leads its Streams the round, Visits each Plant, and waters all the Ground; While that in Pipes beneath the Palace flows, And thence in Current on the Town bestows. (Switzer, *The Nobleman, Gentleman, and Gardener's Recreation*, 7)

30. Denis Lambin associates the principle of the view with Pliny the Younger, but quotes the 1724 edition of Philip Miller's *Gardeners Dictionary*: without a view a garden "would be both disagreeable and unwholesome whereas a fine View, and the Prospect of a fine Country, are as agreeable Entertainment as a Garden can afford" (Miller, quoted by D. Lambin, "Pleasure with Profit: Some Aspects of Landscape Gardening," *Garden History* 3, no. 2 (1975): 29). As Lambin points out, "From a very early date, a sort of visual network extending beyond the actual limits of a garden was the necessary complement to a country estate, including, as it were, house, garden, park, and countryside" (Lambin, "Pleasure with Profit: Some Aspects of Landscape Gardening," 29).

31. Lines IV, 250–51.

32. E. Spenser, *Spenser's Complete Poetical Works*, 1590, rev. ed., ed. R. E. Neil Dodge (Cambridge: Riverside Press, 1936), lines II, xii, 58–59.

33. AV 1611, Matthew 5:45.

34. R. Austen, *A Dialogue between the Husbandman and His Fruit Trees* (Oxford: Thomas Rowman, 1635); R. Austen, *A Treatise of Fruit-Trees* (Oxford: Thomas Robinson, 1635).

35. For others, see almost every edition of William Lawson's manuals, including *A Country Housewife's Garden* (London: Roger Jackson, 1623); almost every edition of Thomas Hyll's (or Hill) kitchen garden manual, *The Gardener's Labyrinth* (1577; New York: Oxford, 1988); J. Rea, *Flora* (London: Richard Marriott, 1665); and his son-in-law Samuel Gilbert's *The Florists Vade-Mecum* (London: Thomas Simmons, 1682).

36. AV 1611, Exodus 20:4–6.

37. G. Flaubert, *The Works of Gustave Flaubert* (New York: Walter J. Black, 1904), 287–305.

38. E. Dickinson, *The Poems of Emily Dickinson*, ed. Thomas H. Johnson. (Cambridge, MA: The Belknap Press of Harvard University Press, 1955).

39. D. Jacques, "Garden Design in the Mid-Seventeenth Century," *Architectural History* 44 (2001): 371–72.

40. Switzer, *The Nobleman, Gentleman, and Gardener's Recreation*, 64.

41. Jacques, "Garden Design in the Mid-Seventeenth Century," 371.

42. Switzer, *The Nobleman, Gentleman, and Gardener's Recreation*, 44.

43. Quoted without attribution by Switzer, *The Nobleman, Gentleman, and Gardener's Recreation*, 43.

44. Switzer, *The Nobleman, Gentleman, and Gardener's Recreation*, 42.

45. I. Kant, *Critique of Judgment*, 1790, rev. ed., trans. J.H. Bernard (New York and London: Macmillan and Hafner Press, 1951), 45, 55.

46. H.H. Kames, *Elements of Criticism*, 3rd ed. (Edinburgh: A. Millar, A. Kincaid and J. Bell, 1765), 186–88.

47. See Joseph Addison's Pleasures of the Imagination Series, *The Spectator*, ed. D. F. Bond, 5 vols. (1712; Oxford: Clarendon Press, 1965), 411–20.

48. A. Pope, *The Complete Poetical Works of Alexander Pope*, rev. ed., ed. H.W. Boynton (Boston: Houghton Mifflin; Cambridge: Riverside Press, 1903), 170–73.

49. J. Smith, *England's Improvement Reviv'd* (London: Thomas Newcomb, 1673).

50. P. Goodchild, "John Smith's Paradise and Theater of Nature: The Plans," *Garden History* 25, no. 1 (1997): 28–44, 28. Smith uses Woodland Measure, for which see Goodchild, "John Smith's Paradise and Theater of Nature: The Plans."

51. Goodchild, "John Smith's Paradise and Theater of Nature: The Plans," 28, 30, 36.

52. Switzer, *The Nobleman, Gentleman, and Gardener's Recreation*, xxix.

53. I discuss formality in Milton's Paradise, the diction he uses to represent it, and the poetic tradition in which it is embedded in a forthcoming essay.

54. Smith, *England's Improvement Reviv'd*, 177.

55. Smith, *England's Improvement Reviv'd*, 177.

56. S. Schama, *The Embarrassment of Riches: An Interpretation of Dutch Culture in the Golden Age* (London: Collins, 1987).

57. Hunt, *Garden and Grove*, 187.

58. R. Burton, ed., *The Arabian Nights: Tales from a Thousand and One Nights* (1885; New York: Modern Library, 2001).

59. I do not judge kitsch negatively, as it comprises a complex aesthetic not genuinely esteemed until the later twentieth century; rather, I consider it within dominant aesthetic values of the eighteenth century.

60. T. Whately, *Observations on Modern Gardening* (London: T. Payne, 1770), 106.

61. Loudon, *The Landscape Gardening and Landscape Architecture of the Late Humphry Repton, Esq.*, 200. I use John Claudius Loudon's edition of Repton's works because Loudon intended this affordable edition for the middle classes, the target audience of Repton's later works; despite Repton's hostility for (or anxiety concerning) Loudon, Loudon's edition shows his admiration for Repton and builds a bridge to mid-nineteenth-century garden enthusiasts. Loudon compiles the following texts in this edition: *Sketches and Hints on Landscape Gardening* (1795), *Observations on the Theory and Practice of Landscape Gardening* (1803), *An Inquiry into the Changes of Taste in Landscape Gardening* (1806), *Designs for The Pavillon at Brighton* (1808), and *Fragments on the Theory and Practice of Landscape Gardening* (1816).

62. W. Wordsworth, *William Wordsworth Selected Poems*, ed. John O. Hayden (London: Penguin Books, 1994), 66.

63. R.L. Stevenson, *A Child's Garden of Verses* (1885; New York: Charles Scribner's Sons; London: John Lane, 1900), 24.

64. Repton, as reprinted in Loudon, *The Landscape Gardening and Landscape Architecture of the Late Humphry Repton, Esq.*

65. Loudon, *The Landscape Gardening and Landscape Architecture of the Late Humphry Repton, Esq.*, 111.

66. J. Austen, *Mansfield Park* (1816; Oxford: Oxford University Press, 1990), 85.

67. Austen, *Mansfield Park*, 49.

68. Loudon, *The Landscape Gardening and Landscape Architecture of the Late Humphry Repton, Esq.*, 76.

69. Loudon, *The Landscape Gardening and Landscape Architecture of the Late Humphry Repton, Esq.*, 330, 549.

70. Loudon, *The Landscape Gardening and Landscape Architecture of the Late Humphry Repton, Esq.*, 550.

71. Isaiah 40:4 (King James).

72. Loudon, *The Landscape Gardening and Landscape Architecture of the Late Humphry Repton, Esq.*, 236.

Chapter 7

1. H. Fuseli, "On Invention," Lecture IV, in *Lectures on Painting by the Royal Academicians Barry, Opie and Fuseli*, ed. R. N. Wornum (London: H. G. Bohn, 1848), 449.

2. H. Walpole, *The History of the Modern Taste in Gardening* (1771; New York: Ursus Press, 1995), 173–138, 149.

3. H. Repton, *A Letter to Uvedale Price, Esq.* (London, 1794), 6.

4. I. Pears, *The Discovery of Painting: The Growth of Interest in the Arts in England, 1680–1768* (New Haven, CT: Paul Mellon Centre for Studies in British Art, Yale University Press, 1988).

5. M. Rosenthal, *British Landscape Painting* (Oxford: Phaidon, 1982).

6. D. K. Kriz, *The Idea of the English Landscape Painter: Genius as Alibi in the Early Nineteenth Century* (New Haven, CT: Paul Mellon Centre for Studies in British Art, Yale University Press, 1997).

7. J. Harris, *The Artist and the Country House: A History of Country House and Garden View Painting in Britain 1540–1870* (London: For Sotheby Parke Bernet Publications by Philip Wilson Publishers, 1979); R. Strong, *The Artist and the Garden* (New Haven, CT: Paul Mellon Centre for Studies in British Art, Yale University Press, 2000).

8. M. Andrews, *Landscape and Western Art* (Oxford History of Western Art; Oxford: Oxford University Press, 1999).

9. J. Barrell, *The Dark Side of the Landscape: The Rural Poor in English Painting, 1730–1840* (Cambridge: Cambridge University Press, 1980); A. Bermingham, *Landscape and Ideology: The English Rustic Tradition* (Berkeley: University of California Press, 1986); S. Deuchar, *Sporting Art in Eighteenth-Century England: A Social and Political History* (New Haven, CT: Paul Mellon Centre for Studies in British Art, Yale University Press, 1988); N. Everett, *The Tory Idea of Landscape* (New Haven, CT: Paul Mellon Centre for British Art, Yale University Press, 1994).

10. M. Andrews, *The Search for the Picturesque: Landscape Aesthetics and Tourism in Britain, 1760–1800* (Aldershot: Scolar, 1989).

11. C. Payne, *Toil and Plenty: Images of the Agricultural Landscape in England, 1780–1890* (New Haven, CT: Yale Centre for British Art, Yale University Press, 1993).

12. L. C. Halpern, "The Uses of Paintings in Garden History," in *Garden History: Issues, Approaches, Methods*, ed. J. D. Hunt (Washington, D.C.: Dumbarton Oaks Research Library and Collection, 1992), 183–202.

13. D. Harris and D. L. Hays, "On the Use and Misuse of Historical Landscape Views," in *Representing Landscape Architecture*, ed. M Treib (London: Tayor and Francis, 2008), 22–41.

14. R. Howells, *Visual Culture* (Cambridge: Polity Press, 2003).

15. Harris, *The Artist and the Country House*, 54.

16. J. D. Hunt, *Garden and Grove: The Italian Renaissance Garden in the English Imagination 1600–1750* (London: J. M. Dent, 1986), 131; Strong, *The Artist and the Garden*, 127.

17. Harris, *The Artist and the Country House*, 49; Strong, *The Artist and the Garden*, 127.

18. V. T. Clayton, *Gardens on Paper: Prints and Drawings 1200–1900* (Washington, D.C.: National Gallery of Art, 1990), 5; Strong, *The Artist and the Garden*, 126.

19. J. D. Hunt and E. De Jong, "The Anglo-Dutch Garden in the Age of William and Mary," *Journal of Garden History* 8, nos. 2 and 3 (1988): 183; Strong, *The Artist and the Garden*, 130.

20. Andrews, *Landscape and Western Art*, 54.

21. Clayton, *Gardens on Paper: Prints and Drawings 1200–1900*.

22. C. Delano-Smith and R.J.P. Kain, *English Maps: A History* (British Library Studies in Map History, Book 2; London: The British Library, 1999), 116.

23. Delano-Smith and Kain, *English Maps: A History*, 118.

24. J. B. Harley, "Meaning and Ambiguity in Tudor Cartography," in *English Map Making 1500–1650*, ed. S. Tyacke (London: The British Library, 1983), 37.

25. Delano-Smith and Kain, *English Maps: A History*, 122–23.

26. J. B. Harley, "Maps, Knowledge and Power," in *The Iconography of Landscape*, ed. D. Cosgrove and S. Daniels (Cambridge: Cambridge University Press, 1988).

27. S. Daniels, "Goodly Prospects: English Estate Portraiture 1670–1730," in *Mapping the Landscape: Essays on Art and Cartography* (Nottingham: University Art Gallery and Castle Museum Nottingham, 1990), 10.

28. J. Berger, *Ways of Seeing* (London: British Broadcasting Corporation and Penguin Books, 1972), 83–190.

29. Harris, *The Artist and the Country House*; Strong, *The Artist and the Garden*.

30. Harley, "Meaning and Ambiguity in Tudor Cartography," 36.

31. F. Hutcheson, *An Inquiry into the Original of Our Ideas of Beauty and Virtue; in Two Treatises*, 2nd ed. (London, 1726), 20.

32. Rosenthal, *British Landscape Painting*, 22; Daniels, "Goodly Prospects: English Estate Portraiture 1670–1730," 9.

33. Daniels, "Goodly Prospects: English Estate Portraiture 1670–1730," 12.

34. R. Dubbini, *The Geography of the Gaze: Urban and Rural Vision in Early Modern Europe* (Chicago: University of Chicago Press, 2000), 28.

35. J. G. Turner, "Landscape and the 'Art Prospective' in England 1584–1660," *Journal of the Warburg and Courtauld Institutes* 42 (1979): 290–93.

36. Hunt, *Garden and Grove*; J. D. Hunt, *Greater Perfections: The Practice of Garden Theory* (London: Thames and Hudson, 2000), 76–115.

37. Hunt, *Garden and Grove*.

38. Hunt, *Garden and Grove*, 10.

39. Daniels, "Goodly Prospects: English Estate Portraiture 1670–1730," 10.

40. Hunt, *Garden and Grove*, 119.

41. A. Lawrence, "Space, Status and Gender in English Topographical Paintings c.1660–c.1740," *Architectural History* 46 (2003): 81–94.

42. S. Schama, *The Embarrassment of Riches: An Interpretation of Dutch Culture in the Golden Age* (New York: Knopf, 1988).

43. Lawrence, "Space, Status and Gender in English Topographical Paintings c.1660–c.1740," 91.

44. Barrell, *The Dark Side of the Landscape*; Rosenthal, *British Landscape Painting*; D. H. Solkin, *Richard Wilson: The Landscape of Reaction* (London: The Tate Gallery, 1982).

45. From the opening lines of Ben Jonson's "To Penshurst" (1616), one of the linguistically richest and most influential country house poems. On the country house poem as political discourse, see R. Williams, *The Country and the City* (London: Chatto and Windus, 1973); M. Kelsall, *The Great Good Place: The Country House in English Literature* (New York: Harvester Wheatsheaf, 1993); and A. Fowler, *A Cabinet of Seventeenth-Century Estate Poems and Related Items* (Edinburgh: Edinburgh University Press, 1994).

46. T. Nourse, "Of a Country House," in *Campania Foelix; or, A Discourse of the Benefits and Improvements of Husbandry* (London, 1700; 2nd ed., 1706), 339–40.

47. Nourse, "Of a Country House," 341.

48. D. Hill, *Harewood Masterpieces: English Watercolours and Drawings* (Harewood: Harewood House Trust, 1995); S. Smiles, *The Turner Book* (London: Tate Publishing, 2006).

49. Hill, *Harewood Masterpieces*, 57–58.

50. Smiles, *The Turner Book*, 200, 24.

51. Hill, *Harewood Masterpieces*, 9.

52. Smiles, *The Turner Book*, 32.

53. E. G. D'Oench, *The Conversation Piece: Arthur Devis and His Contemporaries* (New Haven, CT: Yale Center for British Art, 1980), 31–32; K. Retford, *The Art of Domestic Life: The Family Portrait in Eighteenth-Century England* (New Haven, CT: Paul Mellon Centre for Studies in British Art, Yale University Press, 2006), 56.

54. Strong, *The Artist and the Garden*, 54–56.

55. In 1729, George Vertue recorded conversation pieces as being "a portrait of small figures from the life in their habits & dress of the Times. Well disposd gracefull and naturall easy actions suteable to the characters of the persons and their portraitures—well toucht to the likeness and air." Vertue Notebooks in *Walpole Society* 22 (1933–34), cited in D'Oench, *The Conversation Piece*, 3.

56. J. H. Ingram, *Flora Symbolica; or, the Language and Sentiment of Flowers* (London: Frederick Warne, 1887), 350.

57. T. Page, *The Art of Painting in Its Rudiments, Progress and Perfection* (London, 1720), cited by D'Oench, *The Conversation Piece*, 15.

58. D'Oench, *The Conversation Piece*, 15–16.

59. H. Fielding, "Essay on Conversation" (1743; reprint, H. K. Miller, ed., *Miscellanies*, Oxford: Clarendon Press, 1972).

60. D. H. Solkin, *Painting for Money: The Visual Arts and the Public Sphere in Eighteenth-Century England* (New Haven, CT: Paul Mellon Centre for Studies in British Art, Yale University Press, 1993), 74.

61. D. Posner, *Antoine Watteau* (London: Weidenfeld and Nicolson, 1984); M. Vidal, *Watteaux's Painted Conversations: Art, Literature and Talk in Seventeenth and Eighteenth-Century France* (New Haven: Yale University Press, 1992); S. J. Cohen, *Art, Dance and the Body in French Culture of the Ancien Régime* (Cambridge: Cambridge University Press, 2000).

62. Posner, *Antoine Watteau.*

63. D'Oench, *The Conversation Piece*, 5–6, 10–11.

64. J. Hayes and S. Sartin, *Polite Society by Arthur Devis 1712–1787: Portraits of the English Country Gentleman and His Family* (Preston: The Harris Museum and Art Gallery, 1983), 53.

65. M. Rosenthal and M. Myrone, *Gainsborough* (London: Tate Britain, 2003), 172.

66. Retford, *The Art of Domestic Life*, 42–82.

67. Retford, *The Art of Domestic Life*, 59–72.

68. S. Daniels, "The Political Iconography of Woodland in Later Georgian England," in *The Iconography of Landscape: Essays on the Symbolic Representation, Design and Use of Past Environments*, ed. D. Cosgrove and S. Daniels (Cambridge: Cambridge University Press, 1998).

69. On tensions between masculinity and polite manners and the quest for "authenticity" in sensibility, see P. Carter, *Men and the Emergence of Polite Society in Britain 1660–1800* (Harlow: Pearson Education, 2001).

70. Contemporary social caricatures, which played with the tasteful postures and settings of the conversation piece to mock the extremes of arranged marriages, as in Hogarth's *Marriage a la Mode*, or those repented at leisure, indicated the significance of signs of taste and good breeding as markers of sound judgment in the marriage market (Retford, *The Art of Domestic Life*, 59–65).

71. J. J. Disponzio, "Jean-Marie Morel and the Invention of Landscape Architecture," in *Tradition and Innovation in French Garden Art*, ed. J. D. Hunt and M. Conan (Philadelphia: University of Pennsylvania Press, 2002), 134, 142; D. L. Hays, "Francesco Bettini and the Pedagogy of Garden Design in Late Eighteenth-Century France," in *Tradition and Innovation in French Garden Art*, ed. J. D. Hunt, M. Conan, and C. Goldstein (Philadelphia: University of Pennsylvania Press, 2002), 109.

72. Hays, "Francesco Bettini and the Pedagogy of Garden Design in Late Eighteenth-Century France"; D. L. Hays, "Figuring the Commonplace at Ermenonville," in *Experiencing the Garden in the Eighteenth Century*, ed. M. Calder (Bern: Peter Lang, 2006).

73. T. Andersson, "From Paper to Park," in *Representing Landscape Architecture*, ed. M. Treib (London: Taylor and Francis, 2008), 74–95.

74. Estate plans have received attention, for example, S. Bendall, *Maps, Land and Society: A Carto-Bibliogaphy of Cambridgeshire Estate Maps c. 1600–1836* (Cambridge: Cambridge University Press, 1992), but we need to know more about the flow of conventions from estate maps to improvement plans and the ways eyes attuned to contemporary conventions would have read them.

75. S. Daniels, *Humphry Repton: Landscape Gardening and the Geography of Georgian England* (New Haven, CT: Yale University Press, 1999), 13.

76. S. Daniels, S. Seymour, and C. Watkins, "Border Country: The Politics of the Picturesque in the Middle Wye Valley," in *Prospects for the Nation: Recent Essays in British Landscape 1750–1880*, ed. M. Rosenthal, C. Payne, and S. Wilcox (New Haven, CT: Paul Mellon Centre for Studies in British Art and the Yale Center for British Art, Yale University Press, 1997), 157–81; Daniels, *Humphry Repton*, 103–47.

77. Daniels, *Humphry Repton*, 125.

78. K. Sloan, *"A Noble Art": Amateur Artists and Drawing Masters c.1600–1800* (London: British Museum Press, 2000).

79. M. Girouard, *Life in the English Country House* (1978; Harmondsworth: Penguin Books, 1980).

80. Daniels, *Humphry Repton*, 25.

81. Kriz, *The Idea of the English Landscape Painter*, 53–54, 141.

82. *Attingham* fol. 3; A. Rogger, *Landscapes of Taste: The Art of Humphrey Repton's Red Books* (London: Routledge, 2007), 226.

83. *Attingham* fol. 6; Rogger, *Landscapes of Taste*, 227.

84. Rogger, *Landscapes of Taste*, 155.

85. *Attingham* fol. 15; Rogger, *Landscapes of Taste*, 229–30.

86. Daniels, *Humphry Repton*, 112.

87. Rogger, *Landscapes of Taste*, 173.

88. A. Kennedy, "British Topographical Print Series in Their Social and Economic Context c1720—c1840," unpublished PhD diss., Courtauld Institute of Art, London, 1998.

89. Rogger, *Landscapes of Taste*, 150.

90. J.D. Hunt, *William Kent Landscape Garden Designer: An Assessment and Catalogue of His Designs* (London: A. Zwemmer, 1987).

91. J. de Cayeux, *Hubert Robert et les jardins* (Paris: Herscher, 1987).

92. For example, a print entitled *Emblem of a Modern Marriage* attributed to James Gillray, British Museum, appropriates the late eighteenth-century promenade marital portrait. It has as its "emblem" Cupid in the sky with his torch turned upside down, but the scene below, which fuses an estate prospect with the marital promenade, is also shown as a highly contrived artifice. A male skeleton in finery, in the Apollo Belvedere senatorial pose used by artists to elevate society portraiture, points with his clothed female companion, as in the gendered conventions of the promenade portrait, to a distant overblown Palladian palace, to signify the death of love in (aristocratic) arranged marriages. Reproduced in Retford, *The Art of Domestic Life*, 67.

93. M. Bills, *The Art of Satire: London in Caricature* (London: Museum of London and Philip Wilson Publishers, 2006), 17–26.

94. D. Donald, "'Characters and Caricatures': The Satirical View," in *Reynolds*, ed. N. Penny (London: Royal Academy of Arts, Weidenfeld and Nicolson, 1986), 15, 98–108.

95. On the popularity of Horace in the seventeenth and eighteenth centuries, see C. Martindale and D. Hopkins, eds., *Horace Made New* (Cambridge: Cambridge University Press, 1993).

96. The third Earl of Shaftesbury, calling for a national cultural identity to be expressed in humane classically oriented history painting and a less formal garden style, viewed ridicule as another rational weapon in the same cultural war against the reappearance of religious or courtly tyrannies and their delusions; D. Donald, *The Age of Caricature: Satirical Prints in the Reign of George III* (New Haven, CT: Yale University Press, 1996), 31–32, 208fn59.

97. P. Borsay, *The English Urban Renaissance: Culture and Society in the Provincial Town 1660–1770* (Oxford: Clarendon Press, 1989).

98. M. Hallett, *The Spectacle of Difference: Graphic Satire in the Age of Hogarth* (New Haven, CT: Paul Mellon Centre for the Study of British Art, Yale University Press, 1999), 178–82.

99. Elegant staffage was a central component of French topographical garden views, as in the drawings and engravings of Israel Silvestre and Adam Perelle, from where it entered British garden series views. In Jacques Rigaud's drawings of Stowe, for example, the recognizable figures amongst the generically elegant crossed over from Hogarthian satires and may have been designed to further the practice of garden tourism; see R. Quaintance, "Who's Making the Scene: Real People in Eighteenth-Century Topographical Prints," in *The Country and the City Revisited: England and the Politics of Culture 1550–1850*, ed. G. Macclean, D. Landy, and J. P. Wood (Cambridge: Cambridge University Press, 1999), 134–59.

100. M. Ogborn, *Spaces of Modernity: London's Geographies 1680–1780* (New York London: The Guilford Press, 1998), 116–57.

101. Hallett, *The Spectacle of Difference*, 194.

102. T. Brown, *Amusements Serious and Comical: Calculated for the Meridian of London* (London, 1702), 68–72.

103. Hallett, *The Spectacle of Difference*, 180–82.

104. See, for example, the types enumerated in the satires on Vauxhall Gardens such as *A Trip to Vaux-hall; or, a General Satyr on the Times* (1737) reproduced in Solkin, *Painting for Money*, 121–23.

105. Donald, *Age of Caricature*, 136.

106. The typical ambiguity of the phrase "The swains thus discreetly were bold" is from the text of the song "The Adieu to Spring Gardens" (1737), written by John Lockman and engraved by George Bickham and reproduced with Hubert Francois Gravelot's title vignette in a series entitled *The Musical Entertainer* (1738), reproduced in Solkin, *Painting for Money*, 126. The ambiguous tone around the imagery of sensory overload in Arcadian innocence is found in both the publicity and the satires.

107. The engraving and etching by a pseudonymous "M. Ramano," assumed to be George Bickham junior, *Spring Gardens, Vauxhall* (1741), is reproduced in Solkin, *Painting for Money*, 128.

108. On the luxury debates, see J. Sekora, *Luxury: The Concept in Western Thought, Eden to Smollett* (Baltimore: Johns Hopkins University Press, 1977); and C. Berry, *The Idea of Luxury: A Conceptual and Historical Investigation* (Cambridge: Cambridge University Press, 1994). The focus on theory is extended to material culture and themes in representation in M. Berg and E. Eger, eds., *Luxury in the Eighteenth Century: Debates, Desires and Delectable Goods* (Basingstoke: Palgrave Macmillan, 2003).

109. See, for example, Henry Fielding's essay "Of the Luxury of the English and a Description of Ranelagh Gardens and Vaux-hall in a Letter from a Foreigner to his Friend at Paris," from *The Champion* no. 424 (August 5), reprinted in *The Gentleman's Magazine* 12 (1742): 418–20, and the analyses by Solkin (*Painting for Money*, 115–17) and Ogborn (*Spaces of Modernity*, 125–28).

110. See, for example, John Gay's *Trivia* (1716) where a coach containing a beau is overturned by a dustman, signifying the idea of the city streets as a place of class antagonism (Hallett, *The Spectacle of Difference*, 184). The overturned coach was a symbol of misgovernance in political caricatures and of punishment of fashionable excess in social caricatures.

111. A poem by Robert Lloyd, "The Cit's Country Box," 1757, in *The Connoisseur*, 3rd ed., 1757–60, vol. 4 of 4, and R. Lloyd, *Poems: By Robert Lloyd* (London, 1762), 43–49.

112. On the visual motif of the wig and masculine authority in portraits and satires, see chapter 4, "Dangerous Excrescences: Wigs, Hair and Masculinity," in M. Pointon, *Hanging the Head: Portraiture and the Social Formation in Eighteenth-Century England* (New Haven, CT: Paul Mellon Centre for the Study of British Art, Yale University Press, 1993), 107–39.

113. During the Seven Years' War (1756–63) and its accompanying unstable ministries and tensions around city support for the war, anti-luxury writing focused on fashionable tastes such as "Chinese Madness" as the sign of the power and corruption of "New Gentry of the City." J. G. Cooper, *Letters on Taste*, 3rd ed. (London), 58, cited by Solkin, *Richard Wilson*, 58.

114. D. Donald, "'Mr Deputy Dumpling and Family': Satirical Images of the City Merchant in Eighteenth-Century England," *The Burlington Magazine* 1040 (1989): 755–63, 75.

115. Diana Donald has shown how the eighteenth-century *parvenu* or *arriviste* built on classical "character" tropes, for example through imitations and updates of the fourth-century B.C.E. writer Theophrastus. *Imitations of the Characters of Theophrastus* (1774) updated a boaster—a type of social pretender—into a cit who furnishes his rented house in the Eastern taste to prove he is intimate with the great nabobs (Donald, "'Mr Deputy Dumpling and Family': Satirical Images of the City Merchant in Eighteenth-Century England," 761).

116. "The Cit's Country Box" was reproduced, among many other publications, in *The Farmer's Magazine and Useful Family Companion* (1776–80; 3, 239–40).

117. Prudential virtues rather than gentry emulation were key to the middle-class ethos in the high-risk era before limited liability, easy credit, and insurance (J. D. Hunt, ed., *The Italian Garden: Art, Design and Culture* (Cambridge: Cambridge University Press, 1996).

118. Davidoff and Hall's representative early nineteenth-century middle-class man, a jewelry manufacturer from Birmingham, retires to a suburb whose garden appears to reincarnate Shenstone's and enacts the country house poem ideal of making the home a representation of self; see L. Davidoff and C. Hall, *Family Fortunes: Men and Women of the English Middle Class 1780–1850* (Chicago: University of Chicago Press, 1987), 14–17.

119. D. Hume, "Of Luxury," in *Essays and Treatises on Several Subjects* (London, 1758), 162; P. Langford, *A Polite and Commercial People: England 1727–1783* (Oxford: Clarendon Press, 1989), 592.

120. The Reverend Thomas Gisborne, in *An Enquiry into the Duties of Men in the Higher and Middle Classes of Society in Great Britain*, explains that the duties of those who live on their estate income are incumbent upon "almost every individual, belonging to any one of the classes and professions" (1794; 573). Although the duties he lists are specific to the estate owner—such as well-researched agricultural improvement and moral influence in the locality—the middling male is expected to translate these into his own sphere of business. If the estate owner is enjoined to think of the country estate, rather than the city, as the proper sphere for his governance and influence, then the non-landed gentleman will have to understand the country estate as a metaphor for masculine governance and influence.

121. M. Ozouf, *Festivals and the French Revolution*, rev. ed., trans. A. Sheridan (Cambridge, MA: Harvard University Press, 1988), 102.

Chapter 8

1. H. Walpole, *The History of the Modern Taste in Gardening* (1771; New York: Ursus Press, 1995), 53.

2. O. Rackham, *The History of the Countryside* (London: Dent, 1986); R. Hoppitt, "Hunting Suffolk's Parks: Towards a Reliable Chronology of Emparkment," in *The Medieval Park: New Perspectives*, ed. R. Liddiard (Macclesfield: Windgather, 2007), 146–64, 162.

3. Hertfordshire Archives and Local Studies (HALS), Hertford, England, DE/X/134/P2.

4. R. Bisgrove, *The National Trust Book of the English Garden* (London: Viking Books, 1990), 89–91.

5. S. Switzer, *Ichnographia Rustica; or, The Nobleman, Gentlemen, and Gardener's Recreation* (London: D. Browne, 1718).

6. T. Whately, *Observations on Modern Gardening* (London: T. Payne, 1770), 94.

7. T. Whately, *Observations on Modern Gardening*, 164–65.

8. J. Barnatt and T. Williamson, *Chatsworth: A Landscape History* (Macclesfield: Windgather, 2005), 120.

9. Loudon, 1838, 162.

10. A. Bermingham, *Landscape and Ideology: The English Rustic Tradition* (Berkeley: University of California Press, 1986), 14.

11. Rackham, *The History of the Countryside*, 2–5.

12. M. Turner, *English Parliamentary Enclosure* (Folkstone: Dawson-Archon Books, 1980).

13. T. Williamson, *Polite Landscapes: Gardens and Society in Eighteenth-Century England* (Baltimore: Johns Hopkins University Press, 1995), 100–109.

14. Williamson, *Polite Landscapes*, 109–18.

15. M. Girouard, *Life in the English Country House* (1978; Harmondsworth: Penguin Books, 1980), 188–93.

16. Girouard, *Life in the English Country House*, 125–26.

17. T. Williamson, *The Archaeology of the Landscape Park: Garden Design in Norfolk, England, c.1680–1840* (Oxford: British Archaeological Reports British Series, 1998), 135–36; O. Rackham, *The History of the Countryside* (London: Dent, 1986).

18. H. Repton, Red Book for Hengrave Hall, Suffolk (Private Collection), 1791.

19. D. Defoe, *Tour through the Whole Island of Great Britain* (Harmondsworth: Penguin, 1971), 73–74.

20. L. Stone and J. Fawtier-Stone, *An Open Elite? England 1540–1880* (Oxford: Clarendon, 1986), 204.

21. HALS D/EX55/E1.

22. W. Branch-Johnson, *The Carrington Diary 1797–1810* (London: C. Johnson, 1956), 100.

23. Stone and Fawtier-Stone, *An Open Elite?* 168–69.

24. H. Repton, Red Book for Tewin Water, Hertfordshire (HALS D/Z42 Z1 P 21 A), 1799.

25. S. Daniels, *Humphry Repton: Landscape Gardening and the Geography of Georgian England* (New Haven, CT: Yale University Press, 1999), 79–80.

26. W. Armstrong, *History and Antiquities of the County of Norfolk*, vol. 9, *Taverham Hundred* (Norwich, 1781), 15.

27. *Norwich Mercury*, May 12, 1770.

28. *Norwich Mercury*, July 28, 1770.

29. Norfolk Records Office (NRO), Norwich, MC 40/1104.

30. J.D. Hunt and E. De Jong, "The Anglo-Dutch Garden in the Age of William and Mary," *Journal of Garden History* 8, nos. 2 and 3 (1988); F. Hopper, "The Dutch Classical Garden and André Mollet," *Journal of Garden History* 2, no. 1 (1982): 25–40.

31. E. B. MacDougall and F. H. Hazlehurst, *The French Formal Garden* (Washington, D.C.: Dumbarton Oaks Research Library and Collection, 1974); T. Mariage, *The World of André Le Nôtre* (Philadelphia: University of Pennsylvania Press, 1999).

32. A. Leighton, *American Gardens in the Eighteenth Century: "For Use or for Delight"* (Amherst: University of Massachusetts Press, 1986), 362.

33. B. W. Sarudy, *Gardens and Gardening in the Chesapeake, 1700–1805* (Baltimore: Johns Hopkins University Press, 1998), 20–49.

34. Sarudy, *Gardens and Gardening in the Chesapeake, 1700–1805*, 32.

BIBLIOGRAPHY

Aall, S.S., and N. Barlow. *Follies and Fantasies: Germany and Austria*. New York: Harry N. Abrams, 1994.

Adams, W.H. *The French Garden 1500–1800*. New York: George Braziller, 1979.

Addison, J. *The Spectator* (1712), ed. D.F. Bond, 5 vols. Oxford: Clarendon Press, 1965.

Album du Comte du Nord [Recueil des Plans des Chateaux Parcs et Jardins de Chantilly, 1784], reduced facsimile, with introduction by Jean-Pierre Babelon, Saint-Rémy-en-l'Eau, 2000.

Alexander, B., ed. *Journal of William Beckford in Portugal and Spain 1787–1788*. London: Hart-Davies, 1954.

Allen, B.S. *Tides in English Taste (1619–1800): A Background for the Study of Literature*. New York: Rowman and Littlefield, 1969.

Andersson, T. "From Paper to Park." In *Representing Landscape Architecture*, ed. M. Treib. London: Taylor and Francis, 2008.

Andrews, M. *Landscape and Western Art*. Oxford History of Western Art. Oxford: Oxford University Press, 1999.

Andrews, M. *The Search for the Picturesque: Landscape Aesthetics and Tourism in Britain, 1760–1800*. Aldershot: Scolar, 1989.

Anon. *A Description of the Gardens and Buildings at Kew*. London, 1762, n.d. after 1762.

Anon. *Journal of a Three Week Tour, in 1797, through Derbyshire to the Lakes: By a Gentleman of the University of Oxford* (1797). Vol. 5 of *The British Tourist; or, Traveller's Pocket Companion, through England, Wales, Scotland, and Ireland: Comprehending the Most Celebrated Tours in the British Islands*, ed. W. Mavor, 6 vols. London, 1798–1800.

Anon. *Letters to Honoria and Marianne*. London: J. Dodsley, 1784.

Armstrong, W. *History and Antiquities of the County of Norfolk*. Vol. 9, *Taverham Hundred*. Norwich, 1781.

Arnold, D. *The Georgian Country House: Architecture, Landscape and Society*. Stroud: Sutton, 1998.

Attiret, J.D. *A Particular Account of the Emperor of China's Gardens near Pekin*. Translated by "Sir Harry Beaumont" (i.e., Joseph Spence). 1752. Reprint, New York: Garland, 1982.

Augustine, St. *On Christian Doctrine*, 426. Reprint, Indianapolis, IN: Bobbs-Merrill Educational Publishing, 1978.

Austen, J. *Mansfield Park*, 1818. Reprint, Oxford: Oxford University Press, 1990.

Austen, R. *A Dialogue between the Husbandman and His Fruit Trees*. Oxford: Thomas Rowman, 1635.

Austen, R. *A Treatise of Fruit-Trees*. Oxford: Thomas Robinson, 1635.

Bagatti Valsecchi, P. F., and A. Kipar. *Il giardino paesaggistico tra Settecento e Ottocento in Italia e in Germania: Villa Vigoni e l'opera di Giuseppe Balzaretto*. Kepos, 8. Milano: Guerini e associate, 1996.

Bagot, A. *Levens Hall and Gardens*. Norwich: Jarrold Colour Publications, 1971.

Baker, M. *Figured in Marble: The Making and Viewing of Eighteenth-Century Sculpture*. London: Victoria and Albert Museum, 2000.

Bald, R.C. "Sir William Chambers and the Chinese Garden." In *Discovering China: European Interpretations in the Enlightenment*, ed. J. Ching and W.G. Oxtoby, 142–75. Rochester, NY: University of Rochester Press, 1992.

Baltrusaitis, J. "Gardens and Lands of Illusions." In *Aberrations: An Essay on the Legend of Forms*. Cambridge, MA: MIT Press, 1989.

Baridon, M. "The Garden of the Perfectibilists Mereville and the Désert de Retz." In *Tradition and Innovation in French Garden Art*, ed. J.D. Hunt and M. Conan. Philadelphia: University of Pennsylvania Press, 2002.

Baridon, M. *A History of the Gardens of Versailles*. Arles, 2003. Reprint, Philadelphia: University of Pennsylvania Press, 2008.

Baridon, M. *Les Jardins*. Paris, 1998.

Baridon, M. "Ruins as a Mental Construct." *Journal of Garden History* 5, no. 1 (1985): 84–96.

Baridon, M. "Understanding Nature and the Aesthetics of the Landscape Garden." In *Experiencing the Garden in the Eighteenth Century*, ed. M. Calder. Bern: Peter Lang, 2006.

Barker, T. *The Expert Gardener*, 1651. Bound with *The Country-mans Recreation*. London: William Shears, 1654.

Barnatt, J., and T. Williamson. *Chatsworth: A Landscape History*. Macclesfield: Windgather, 2005.

Barrell, J. *The Dark Side of the Landscape: The Rural Poor in English Painting, 1730–1840*. Cambridge: Cambridge University Press, 1980.

Barrell, J. "The Public Prospect and the Private View: The Politics of Taste in Eighteenth-century Britain." In *Reading Landscape: Country–City–Capital*, ed S. Pugh, 19–40. Manchester: Manchester University Press, 1990.

Batey, M., ed. *A Celebration of John Evelyn: Proceedings of a Conference to Mark the Tercentenary of His Death*. Surrey: Surrey Gardens Trust, 2007.

Batey, M. "The Way to View Rousham by Kent's Gardener." *Garden History* 11, no. 2 (1983): 125–32.

Baum, L. F. *The Wonderful Wizard of Oz*. Chicago: George M. Hill, 1900.

Bell, S.G. "Women Create Gardens in Male Landscapes: A Revisionist Approach to Eighteenth-Century English Garden History." *Feminist Studies* 16, no. 3 (1990): 471–91.

Bending, S. *Green Retreats: Women, Gardens and Eighteenth-Century Culture*. Cambridge: Cambridge University Press, 2013.

Bending, S. "Horace Walpole and Eighteenth-Century Garden History." *Journal of the Warburg and Courtauld Institutes* 57 (1994): 209–26.

Bending, S. "The Improvement of Arthur Young: Agricultural Technology and the Production of Landscape in Eighteenth-Century England." In *Technologies of Landscape: From Reaping to Recycling*, ed. D.E. Nye. Amherst: University of Massachusetts Press, 1999.

Bendall, S. *Maps, Land and Society: A Carto-Bibliogaphy of Cambridgeshire Estate Maps c. 1600–1836*. Cambridge: Cambridge University Press, 1992.

Bending, S. "Miserable Reflections on the Sorrows of My Life: Letters, Loneliness and Gardening in the 1760s." *Tulsa Studies in Women's Literature* 25, no. 1 (2006): 31–47.

Bending, S. "Mrs Montagu's Contemplative Bench: Bluestocking Gardens and Female Retirement." *Huntington Library Quarterly* 69, no. 4 (2006): 555–80.

Bending, S. "A Natural Revolution? Garden Politics in Eighteenth-Century England." In *Refiguring Revolutions: British Politics and Aesthetics, 1642–1789*, ed. K. Sharpe and S. Zwicker, 241–66. Berkeley: University of California Press, 1998.

Bending, S. "One among the Many: Popular Aesthetics, Polite Culture and the Country House Landscape." In *The Country House in Georgian England*, ed. D. Arnold, 61–78. Stroud: Alan Sutton Publishing, 1998.

Bending, S. "Uneasy Sensations: Shenstone, Retirement and Fame." *New Arcadian Journal* 53/54 (2002): 42–59.

Bending, S., and A. McRae. *The Writing of Rural England 1500–1800*. London: Palgrave Macmillan, 2003.

Benjamin, W. "Theses on the Philosophy of History." In *Illuminations*, ed. H. Arendt. London: Fontana, 1982.

Bennet, S. *Five Centuries of Women and Gardens*. London: National Portrait Gallery Publications, 2000.

Berg, M., and E. Eger, eds. *Luxury in the Eighteenth Century: Debates, Desires and Delectable Goods*. Basingstoke: Palgrave Macmillan, 2003.

Berger, J. *Ways of Seeing*. London: British Broadcasting Corporation and Penguin Books, 1972.

Berger, R.W. *Diplomatic Tours in the Gardens of Versailles under Louis XIV*. Philadelphia: University of Pennsylvania Press, 2008.

Berger, R.W. *In the Garden of the Sun King: Studies on the Park of Versailles under Louis XIV*. Washington, D.C.: Dumbarton Oaks Research Library and Collection, 1985.

Bermingham, A. *Landscape and Ideology: The English Rustic Tradition*. Berkeley: University of California Press, 1986.

Berry, C. *The Idea of Luxury: A Conceptual and Historical Investigation*. Cambridge: Cambridge University Press, 1994.

Bettey, J. H. *Estates and the English Countryside*. London: B. T. Batsford, 1993.

Bevington, M. "Stowe: The Bibliography." *New Arcadian Journal* 55/56 (Supplement, 2004).

Bickham, G. *The Beauties of Stow* (1750). Reprint, The Augustan Reprint Society, 1977.

Bills, M. *The Art of Satire: London in Caricature*. London: Museum of London and Philip Wilson Publishers, 2006.

Birch, W. R., ed. *The Country Seats of the United States*. Introduction by E. T. Cooperman. Philadelphia: University of Pennsylvania Press, 2009.

Bisgrove, R. *The National Trust Book of the English Garden*. London: Viking Books, 1990.

Blake, S. *The Compleat Gardeners Practice*. London: Thomas Pierrepoint, 1664.

"Blast Folly: Bless Arcadia." Special issue, *New Arcadian Journal* 24 (1986).

Blondel, J.-F. *De la Distribution des maisons de plaissance*. Paris, 1737.

Blunt, R., ed. *Mrs Montagu, "Queen of the Blues": Her Letters and Friendships from 1762 to 1800*, 2 vols. London: Constable, 1923.

Bond, D. F., ed. *The Spectator*, 5 vols. Oxford: Clarendon Press, 1965.

Bond, J., and K. Tiller. *Blenheim: Landscape for a Palace*. Stroud: Sutton, 1997.

Bonnefoy, Y. "Le Désert de Retz et l'experience dulieu." In *Le Nuage Rouge: Dessin, couleur et lumière*. Paris: Mercure de France, 1977.

Borsay, P. *The English Urban Renaissance: Culture and Society in the Provincial Town 1660–1770*. Oxford: Clarendon Press, 1989.

Branch-Johnson, W. *The Carrington Diary 1797–1810*. London: C. Johnson, 1956.

Brewer, J. *The Pleasures of the Imagination: English Culture in the Eighteenth Century*. London: Harper Collins, 1997.

Brix, M., and S. Lindberg. *The Baroque Landscape: André Le Nôtre & Vaux le Vicomte*. New York: Rizzoli, 2004.

Brown, C. A. "Thomas Jefferson's Poplar Forest: The Mathematics of an Ideal Villa." *Journal of Garden History* 10 (1990): 117–39.

Brown, T. *Amusements Serious and Comical: Calculated for the Meridian of London*. London, 1702.

Brownell, M. R. *Alexander Pope and the Arts of Georgian England*. Oxford: Clarendon Press, 1978.

Brownell, M. R. "The Garden and the Topographical View." *Journal of Garden History* 1, no. 3 (1981): 271–78.

Bunyan, J. *Pilgrims Progress from This World to That Which Is to Come & Grace Abounding to the Chief of Sinners*, 1678. Reprint, J. F. Thornton and S. B. Varenne, eds. New York: Vintage, 2004.

Burkdahl, E. M. *Johannes Wiedewelt: From Wincklemann's Vision of Antiquities to Sculptural Concepts of the 1980s*. Rev. ed. Translated by D. Hohnen. Copenhagen: Editions Bløndel, 1993.

Burton, R., ed. *The Arabian Nights: Tales from a Thousand and One Nights*, 1885. Reprint, New York: Modern Library, 2001.

Butler, J. *Analogy of Natural and Revealed Religion*. London, 1736.

Bywater, M. *Big Babies; or, Why Can't We Just Grow Up?* London: Granta, 2006.

Calder M., ed. *Experiencing the Garden in the Eighteenth Century*. Bern: Peter Lang, 2006.

Campbell, S. *A History of Kitchen Gardening*. London: Frances Lincoln, 2005.

Carita, H., and H. Cardoso. *Portuguese Gardens*. Woodbridge: Antique Collectors' Club, 1989.

Carter, G., P. Goode, and K. Laurie. *Humphry Repton, Landscape Gardener 1752–1818*. London: Victoria and Albert Museum, 1982.

Carter, P. *Men and the Emergence of Polite Society in Britain 1660–1800*. Harlow: Pearson Education, 2001.

Cayeux, J., de. *Hubert Robert et les jardins*. Paris: Herscher, 1987.

Chambers, D. *The Planters of the English Landscape Garden: Botany, Trees, and the Georgics*. New Haven, CT: Yale University Press, 1993.

Chambers, W., J. Barrier, M. Mosser, and C. B. Chiu. *Aux jardins de Cathay: l'imaginaire anglo-chinois en Occident*. Collection Jardins et paysages. Besançon: Editions de l'imprimeur, 2004.

Charlesworth, M. *The English Garden: Literary Sources and Documents*. Robertsbridge: Helm, 1993.

Charlesworth, M., ed. *The Gothic Revival, 1720–1870: Literary Sources and Documents*, 3 vols. Robertsbridge: Helm, 2002.

Charlesworth, M. "Hercules, Apollo and the Hermit: Exploring Stourhead." *New Arcadian Journal* 37/38 (1994): 65–76.

Charlesworth, M. *Landscape and Vision in Nineteenth Century Britain and France*. Aldershot: Ashgate Publishing, 2008.

Charlesworth, M. "Sacred Landscape: Signs of Religion in the Eighteenth-Century Garden." *Journal of Garden History* 13, nos. 1 and 2 (1993): 56–68.

Charlesworth, M. "Thomas Wentworth's Monument: The Achievement of Peace." *New Arcadian Journal* 63/64 (2008): 37–63.

Charlesworth, M. "The Wentworths: A Georgian Landscape with Towers." *New Arcadian Journal* 59/60 (2006): 12–27.

Chase, I.W.U. *Horace Walpole: Gardenist*. Princeton, NJ: Princeton University Press, 1943.

Chastel-Rousseau, C. "The King in the Garden: Royal Statues and the Naturalisation of the Hanoverian Dynasty in Early Georgian Britain, 1714–1760." In *Sculpture and the Garden*, ed. P. Eyres and F. Russell. Aldershot: Ashgate Publishing, 2006.

Chatel de Brancion, L. *Carmontelle au jardin des illusions*. Saint-Rémy-en-l'Eau: Monelle Hayot, 2003.

Clark, H. F. *The English Landscape Garden*. London: Pleiades Books, 1948.

Clarke, G. B. *Descriptions of Lord Cobham's Gardens at Stowe 1700–1750*. Buckingham Record Society, 26. 1990.

Clarke, G. B. "Introduction." In *George Bickham: 'The Beauties of Stow,'* ed. G. B. Clarke, i–xiv. Los Angeles: The Augustan Reprint Society, 1977.

Clarke, S. *A Demonstration of the Being and Attributes of God Manifested in the Works of the Creation*. London, 1705.

Clayton, V. T. *Gardens on Paper: Prints and Drawings 1200–1900*. Washington, D.C.: National Gallery of Art, 1990.

Climenson, E., ed. *Elizabeth Montagu, The Queen of the Bluestockings: Her Correspondence from 1720 to 1761*, 2 vols. New York: E. P. Dutton, 1906.

Coffin, D. *The English Garden: Meditation and Memorial*. Princeton, NJ: Princeton University Press, 1994.

Coffin, D., ed. *The Italian Garden*. Washington, D.C.: Dumbarton Oaks Research Library and Collection, 1972.

Cohen, S. J. *Art, Dance and the Body in French Culture of the Ancien Régime*. Cambridge: Cambridge University Press, 2000.

Colley, L. *Britons: Forging the Nation 1707–1837*. New Haven, CT: Yale University Press, 1992.

Colton, J. "Kent's Hermitage for Queen Caroline at Richmond." *Architectura* 2 (1974): 181–189.

Conan, M., ed. *Baroque Garden Cultures: Emulation, Sublimation, Subversion*. Washington, D.C.: Dumbarton Oaks Research Library and Collection, 2005.

Conan, M., ed. *Bourgeois and Aristocratic Cultural Encounters in Garden Art, 1550–1850*. Washington, D.C.: Dumbarton Oaks Research Library and Collection, 2002.

Conan, M., ed. *Landscape Design and the Experience of Motion*. Washington, D.C.: Dumbarton Oaks Research Library and Collection, 2003.

Conan, M. "The New Horizons of Baroque Garden Cultures." In *Baroque Garden Cultures: Emulation, Sublimation, Subversion*, ed. M. Conan. Washington, D.C.: Dumbarton Oaks Research Library and Collection, 2005.

Conan, M. *Perspectives on Garden Histories: History of Landscape Architecture Symposium*. Washington, D.C.: Dumbarton Oaks Research Library and Collection, 1999.

Conner, P. "China and the Landscape Garden: Reports, Engravings and Misconceptions." *Art History* 2 (1979): 429–40.

Conner, P. *Oriental Architecture in the West*. London: Thames and Hudson, 1979.

Constans, C. *Versailles: Château de la France et orgueil des rois*. Paris: Gallimard, 1996.

Coombs, D. "The Garden at Carlton House of Frederick Prince of Wales and Augusta Princess Dowager of Wales." *Garden History* 25 (1997): 153–77.

Cooperman, E. T. *William Birch: Picturing the American Scene*. Philadelphia: University of Pennsylvania Press, 2010.

Cosgrove, D. *Social Formation and Symbolic Landscape*. London: Croom Helm, 1984.

Cosgrove, D., and S. Daniels, S., eds. *The Iconography of Landscape: Essays on the Symbolic Representation, Design and Use of Past Environments*. Cambridge: Cambridge University Press, 1988.

Cousins, M. "William Shenstone: Jealous of Hagley?" *New Arcadian Journal* 53/54 (2002): 60–73.

Coutu, J. *Persuasion and Propaganda: Monuments of the Eighteenth-Century British Empire*. Montreal: McGill-Queen's University Press, 2006.

Coutu, J. "Stowe: A Whig Training Ground." *New Arcadian Journal* 43/44 (1997): 66–78.

Cowell, F. "Richard Woods (?1716–93): A Preliminary Account." *Garden History: The Journal of the Garden History Society* 14, no. 2 (1986): 85–119.

Cowper, W. *The Poems of William Cowper*, 2 vols., ed. J. D. Baird and C. Ryskamp. Oxford: Clarendon Press, 1995.

Cracraft, J., and D. B. Rowland. *Architectures of Russian Identity: 1500 to the Present.* Ithaca, NY: Cornell University Press, 2003.

Crawford, R. *Poetry, Enclosure, and the Vernacular Landscape 1700–1830.* Cambridge: Cambridge University Press, 2002.

Cross, A. "The English Garden in Catherine the Great's Russia." *Journal of Garden History* 13 (1993): 172–81.

Curl, J. S. "Symbolism in Eighteenth Century Gardens: Some Observations." In *Symbolism in 18th Century Gardens: The Influence of Intellectual and Esoteric Currents, Such as Freemasonry,* ed. J.A.M. Snoek, M. Scholl, and A. A. Kroon. Den Haag: OVN, 2006.

Currie, C. *Garden Archaeology: A Handbook.* York: Council for British Archaeology, 2005.

Daniels, S. "Goodly Prospects: English Estate Portraiture 1670–1730." In *Mapping the Landscape: Essays on Art and Cartography.* Nottingham: University Art Gallery and Castle Museum Nottingham, 1990.

Daniels, S. "Gothic Gallantry: Humphry Repton, Lord Byron, and the Sexual Politics of Landscape Gardening." In *Bourgeois and Aristocratic Cultural Encounters in Garden Art, 1550–1850,* ed. M. Conan, 311–36. Washington, D.C.: Dumbarton Oaks Research Library and Collection, 2002.

Daniels, S. *Humphry Repton: Landscape Gardening and the Geography of Georgian England.* New Haven, CT: Yale University Press, 1999.

Daniels, S. "The Political Iconography of Woodland in Later Georgian England." In *The Iconography of Landscape: Essays on the Symbolic Representation, Design and Use of Past Environments,* ed. D. Cosgrove and S. Daniels. Cambridge: Cambridge University Press, 1998.

Daniels, S., S. Seymour, and C. Watkins. "Border Country: The Politics of the Picturesque in the Middle Wye Valley." In *Prospects for the Nation: Recent Essays in British Landscape 1750–1880,* ed. M. Rosenthal, C. Payne, and S. Wilcox. New Haven, CT: Paul Mellon Centre for Studies in British Art and the Yale Center for British Art, Yale University Press, 1997.

Dantec, D., and J.-P. le Dantec. *Le roman des jardins de France, leur histoire.* Paris: Paris Plon, 1987. Republished as *Reading the French Garden, Story and History.* Cambridge, MA: MIT Press, 1990.

Davidoff, L., and C. Hall. *Family Fortunes: Men and Women of the English Middle Class 1780–1850.* Chicago: University of Chicago Press, 1987.

de Beer, E. S., ed. *The Diary of John Evelyn* (Oxford English Texts). Oxford: Oxford University Press, 1955.

Defoe, D. *Robinson Crusoe,* 1719. Rev. ed. Edited by M. Shinagel. 2nd ed. New York: Norton, 1994.

Defoe, D. *Tour through the Whole Island of Great Britain.* Harmondsworth: Penguin, [1724–27] 1971.

De Jong, E. "For Profit and Ornament: The Function and Meaning of Dutch Garden Art in the Period of William and Mary, 1650–1702." In *The Dutch Garden in the Seventeenth Century,* ed. J.D. Hunt, 13–48. Washington, D.C.: Dumbarton Oaks Research Library and Collection, 1990.

De Jong, E. *Nature and Art: Dutch Garden and Landscape Architecture 1650–1740.* Philadelphia: University of Pennsylvania Press, 2000.

Delano-Smith, C., and R.J.P. Kain. *English Maps: A History. British Library Studies in Map History, Book 2*. London: The British Library, 1999.

Delile, Abbe J. *Les Jardins. Poeme*. Paris, 1782, with many subsequent editions and translations.

Dennerlein, I. *Die Gartenkunst der Régence und des Rokoko in Frankreich*. Worms: Werner'sche Verlagsgesellschaft, 1981.

Desmond, R. *Kew: The History of the Royal Botanic Gardens*. London: Harvill Press, 1995.

Deuchar, S. *Sporting Art in Eighteenth-Century England: A Social and Political History*. New Haven, CT: Paul Mellon Centre for Studies in British Art, Yale University Press, 1988.

Dezallier, A.-J. *The Theory and Practice of Gardening*, 1712. Reprint, London: Bernard Lintot, 1728.

Diary of a Scotch Gardener (on Thomas Blaikie), ed. Francis Birrell. London, 1931.

Dickinson, E. *The Poems of Emily Dickinson*, ed. Thomas H. Johnson. Cambridge, MA: The Belknap Press of Harvard University Press, 1955.

Dingwall, C. "The Hercules Garden at Blair Castle, Perthshire." *Garden History* 20, no. 2 (1992): 153–72.

Disponzio, J.J. "A Catalogue of the Works of Jean-Marie Morel." *Studies in the History of Gardens and Designed Landscapes* (double issue) 21, nos. 3 and 4 (2001): 149–354.

Disponzio, J.J. "Jean-Marie Morel and the Invention of Landscape Architecture." In *Tradition and Innovation in French Garden Art*, ed. J.D. Hunt and M. Conan. Philadelphia: University of Pennsylvania Press, 2002.

Dixon, S.M. *Between the Real and the Ideal: The Accademia Degli Arcadi and Its Garden in Eighteenth-Century Rome*. Newark: University of Delaware Press, 2006.

Dodsley, R., ed. *The Works in Verse and Prose of William Shenstone*. London, 1764.

D'Oench, E.G. *The Conversation Piece: Arthur Devis and His Contemporaries*. New Haven, CT: Yale Center for British Art, 1980.

Dohna, U. *Die Gärten Friedrichs des Grossen und seiner Geschwister*. Berlin: Stapp Verlag, 2000.

Donald, D. *The Age of Caricature: Satirical Prints in the Reign of George III*. New Haven, CT: Yale University Press, 1996.

Donald, D. "'Characters and Caricatures': The Satirical View." In *Reynolds*, ed. N. Penny. London: Royal Academy of Arts, Weidenfeld and Nicolson, 1986.

Donald, D. "'Mr Deputy Dumpling and Family': Satirical Images of the City Merchant in Eighteenth-Century England." *The Burlington Magazine* 1040 (1989): 755–63.

Drayton, M. *The Poly-Olbion: A Chorographicall Description of Great Britain*, 1622. Reprint. Publications of the Spenser Society, n.s., no. 1. Manchester: Charles E. Simms, 1889.

Dubbini, R. *The Geography of the Gaze: Urban and Rural Vision in Early Modern Europe*. Chicago: University of Chicago Press, 2000.

Ehrlich, T.L. "Pastoral Landscape and Social Politics in Baroque Rome." In *Baroque Garden Cultures: Emulation, Sublimation, Subversion*, ed. M. Conan. Washington, D.C.: Dumbarton Oaks Research Library and Collection, 2005.

Encyclopaedia Britannica; or, a Dictionary of the Arts and Sciences Compiled upon a New Plan: By a Society of Gentlemen in Scotland. Edinburgh, 1771.

Erdberg, E. von. *Chinese Influence on European Garden Structures.* Cambridge, MA: Harvard University Press, 1936.

Evelyn, J. *The Diaries of John Evelyn,* 6 vols. 3. rev. ed. Edited by E. S. de Beer. London: Oxford University Press, 1959.

Evelyn, J. *Sylva; or, a Discourse of Forest-Trees, and the Propagation of Timber.* London: Royal Society Printers, 1665.

Everett, N. *The Tory Idea of Landscape.* New Haven, CT: Paul Mellon Centre for Studies in British Art, Yale University Press, 1994.

Eyres, P. "British Naumachias: The Performance of Triumph and Memorial." In *Performance and Appropriation: Profane Rituals in Gardens and Landscapes,* ed. M. Conan. Washington, D.C.: Dumbarton Oaks Research Library and Collection, 2007.

Eyres, P. "Celebration and Dissent: Thomas Hollis, the Society of Arts and Stowe Gardens." *The Medal* 38 (2001): 31–50.

Eyres, P. "Commercial Profit and Cultural Display in the Eighteenth-Century Landscape Gardens at Wentworth Woodhouse and Harewood." In *Bourgeois and Aristocratic Cultural Encounters in Garden Art, 1550–1850,* ed. M. Conan. Washington, D.C.: Dumbarton Oaks Research Library and Collection, 2002.

Eyres, P. "Follies of Dissent and Omission: Monumental Reflections on the American War of Independence." *The Follies Journal* 7 (2007): 53–74.

Eyres, P. "Garden of Apollo & Venus." *Rousham, New Arcadian Journal* 19 (1985): 26–35.

Eyres, P. "Hackfall: A Sublime Landscape." *Studley Royal and Hackfall, New Arcadian Journal* 20 (1985): 37–44.

Eyres, P. "The Invisible Pantheons of Thomas Hollis at Stowe and in Dorset." *New Arcadian Journal* 55/56 (2003): 45–120.

Eyres, P. "Kew and Stowe, 1757–1778: The Polarised Agendas of Royal and Whig Iconographies." *New Arcadian Journal* 51/52 (2001): 52–94.

Eyres, P. " 'Patriotizing Strenuously, the Whole Flower of His Life': The Political Agenda of Thomas Hollis's Medallic Programme." *The Medal* 36 (2000): 8–23.

Eyres, P., ed. "The Political Temples of Stowe." *New Arcadian Journal* 43/44 (1997).

Eyres, P. "Rambo in the Landscape Garden: The British Hercules as the Champion of the Protestant Succession." *New Arcadian Journal* 37/38 (1994): 11–43.

Eyres, P. "The Rivalry between Wentworth Castle and Wentworth Woodhouse, 1695–1750." *New Arcadian Journal* 63/64 (2008): 11–35.

Eyres, P. "Shenstone, The Leasowes and the Heritage Lottery Fund." *New Arcadian Journal* 53/54 (2002): 6–19.

Eyres, P. "Studley Royal: Garden of Hercules and Venus." *New Arcadian Journal* 20 (1985): 4–29.

Eyres, P. "Wentworth Woodhouse: The Patriotism and Improvement of a Classic Whig Landscape." *New Arcadian Journal* 59/60 (2006): 51–146.

Eyres, P., and Russell, F. "The Georgian Landscape Garden and the Victorian Urban Park." In *Sculpture and the Garden,* ed. P. Eyres and F. Russell. Aldershot: Ashgate Publishing, 2006.

Fabricant, C. "Binding and Dressing Nature's Loose Tresses: The Ideology of Augustan Landscape Design." In *Studies in Eighteenth-Century Culture*, vol. 8, ed. R. Runte. Madison: University of Wisconsin Press, 1979.

Fabricant, C. "The Literature of Domestic Tourism and the Public Consumption of Private Property." In *The New Eighteenth Century: Theory and Politics and English Literature*. London: Methuen, 1987.

Ferriolo, M. V. *Giardino e paessaggio dei Romantici*. Milan, 1998.

Fielding, H. "Essay on Conversation." 1743. Reprint, H. K. Miller, ed. *Miscellanies*. Oxford: Clarendon Press, 1972.

Fielding, H. "Of the Luxury of the English and a Description of Ranelagh Gardens and Vaux-hall in a Letter from a Foreigner to His Friend at Paris." *The Gentleman's Magazine* 12 (1742): 418–20.

Flaubert, G. *The Works of Gustave Flaubert*. New York: Walter J. Black, 1904.

Floryan, M. *Gardens of the Tsars: A Study of the Aesthetics, Semantics, and Uses of the Late 18th Century Russian Gardens*. Aarhus, Denmark: Aarhus University Press, 1996.

For the Friends of Nature and Art: The Garden Kingdom of Prince Franz von Anhalt-Dessau in [the] Age of Enlightenment, ed. Michael Sturmer et al. Ostfildern-Ruit: Verlag Gerd Hatje, 1997.

Fowler, A. *A Cabinet of Seventeenth-Century Estate Poems and Related Items*. Edinburgh: Edinburgh University Press, 1994.

Frederik Magnus Piper and the Landscape Garden, exhibition catalogue. Stockholm: Kunlg. Akademien For De Fria Konstema, 1981.

Frederik Magnus Piper and the Landscape Garden: Description of the Idea and General-Plans for an English Park, Written during the Years 1811 and 1812 (title also in Swedish), facsimile text and commentary, in Swedish and English, 2 vols. Stockholm: Byggforlaget, 2004.

Friday, J. *Art and Enlightenment: Scottish Aesthetics in the 18th Century*. Exeter: Imprint Academic, 2004.

Friedman, A. "What John Locke Saw at Versailles." *Journal of Garden History* 9 (1989): 177–98.

Frith, W. "Castle Howard: Dynastic and Sexual Politics." *New Arcadian Journal* 29/30 (1990): 66–99.

Frith, W. "Sex, Gender, Politics: The Venus de Medici in the Eighteenth-Century Landscape Garden." In *Sculpture and the Garden*, ed. P. Eyres and F. Russell. Aldershot: Ashgate Publishing, 2006.

Frith, W. "Sexuality and Politics in the Gardens at West Wycombe and Medmenham Abbey." In *Bourgeois and Aristocratic Cultural Encounters in Garden Art, 1550–1850*, ed. M. Conan, 285–309. Washington, D.C.: Dumbarton Oaks Research Library and Collection, 2002.

Frith, W. "When Frankie Met Johnny: Sexuality and Politics in the Gardens at West Wycombe and Medmenham Abbey." *New Arcadian Journal* 49/50 (2000): 62–104.

Frith, W., and P. Eyres. "In the Garden of Venus." *New Arcadian Journal* 33/34 (1992): 31–58.

Fuseli, H. "On Invention." Lecture IV. In *Lectures on Painting by the Royal Academicians Barry, Opie and Fuseli*, ed. R. N. Wornum. London: H.G. Bohn, 1848.

Ganay, E., de. "Les Jardins à l'anglaise en France au dix-huitième siècle (de 1750 a 1789)." Unpublished manuscript held in the library of the Musée des Arts Décoratifs, Paris, n.d.

Garten der Goethe Zeit, ed. Harri Gunther. Leipzig, 1993.

[Il] Giardino paesaggistico tra settecento e ottocento in Italia e Germania, ed. Pier Fausto Bagatti Valsecchi and Andreas Kipar. Milan: Guerini e Associati, 2000.

[Il] Giardino romantico, exhibition catalogue. Florence: Alinea, 1986.

Gellner, E. *Nations and Nationalism: New Perspectives on the Past*. Ithaca, NY: Cornell University Press, 1983.

Gerndt, S. *Idealisierte Natur: die literarische Kontroverse um den Landschaftsgarten des 18. und frühen 19. Jahrhunderts in Deutschland*. Stuttgart: Metzler, 1981.

Gilbert, S. *The Florists Vade-Mecum*. London: Thomas Simmons, 1682.

Gilonis, H. "Emblematical and Expressive: The Gardenist Modes of William Shenstone and Ian Hamilton Finlay." *New Arcadian Journal* 53/54 (2002): 86–109.

Gilpin, W. *Three Essays: On Picturesque Beauty; on Picturesque Travel; and on Sketching Landscape*. London: Blamire, 1792.

Girardin, R.-L., de. *An Essay on Landscape; or, the Means of Improving and Embellishing the Country round our Habitations*, 1783. Rev. ed. Translated by Daniel Malthus. Reprint, New York: Garland, 1982.

Girardin, R.-L., de. *De la Composition des Paysages*, 1777. Reprint, Michel Conan, ed. Paris: Editions du Champ Urbain, 1979.

Girouard, M. *Life in the English Country House*, 1978. Reprint, Harmondsworth: Penguin Books, 1980.

Gisborne, T. *An Enquiry into the Duties of Men in the Higher and Middle Classes of Society in Great Britain*. London, 1794.

Goethe, J. W. *Elective Affinities*. New York: Frederick Ungar, 1962.

Goldstein, C. *Vaux and Versailles: The Appropriations, Erasures, and Accidents that Made Modern France*. Philadelphia: University of Pennsylvania Press, 2008.

Goodchild, P. "John Smith's Paradise and Theater of Nature: The Plans." *Garden History* 25, no. 1 (1997): 28–44.

Goodchild, P. " 'No Phantastical Utopia but a Reall Place': John Evelyn, John Beale and Backbury Hill, Herefordshire." *Garden History* 19, no. 2 (1991): 105–27.

Gordon, C. *The Coventrys of Croome*. Chichester: Phillimore, 2000.

Gordon, D. *Postmodernism and the Enlightenment: New Perspectives in Eighteenth-Century French Intellectual History*. New York: Routledge, 2001.

Green, D. *Gardener to Queen Anne: Henry Wise (1653–1738) and the Formal Garden*. Oxford: Oxford University Press, 1956.

Greenspan, A. *Creating Colonial Williamsburg*. Washington, D.C.: Smithsonian Institute Press, 2002.

Habermann, S. *Bayreuther-Culmbach im 17. und 18. Jahrhundert*. Worms: Werner'sche Verlagsgesellschaft mbH, 1982.

Hadfield M. *A History of British Gardening*. London: Spring Books, 1960.

Hajós, G. *Romantische Garten der Aufklarung. Englische Landschaftskultur des 18. Jahrhunderts in und um Wien*. Vienna and Cologne: Bohlau, 1989.

Hall, S. *Representation: Cultural Representations and Signifying Practices*. Milton Keynes: Open University, 1997.

Hallett, M. *The Spectacle of Difference: Graphic Satire in the Age of Hogarth*. New Haven, CT: Paul Mellon Centre for Studies in British Art, Yale University Press, 1999.

Halpern, L. C. "The Duke of Kent's Garden at Wrest Park." *Journal of Garden History* 15, no. 3 (1995): 149–78.

Halpern, L. C. "The Uses of Paintings in Garden History." In *Garden History: Issues, Approaches, Methods*, ed. J. D. Hunt. Washington, D.C.: Dumbarton Oaks Research Library and Collection, 1992.

Harding, P. T., and T. Wall, T., eds. *Moccas—An English Deer Park*. Peterborough: English Nature, 2000.

Harley, J. B. "Maps, Knowledge and Power." In *The Iconography of Landscape*, ed. D. Cosgrove and S. Daniels. Cambridge: Cambridge University Press, 1988.

Harley, J. B. "Meaning and Ambiguity in Tudor Cartography." In *English Map Making 1500–1650*, ed. S. Tyacke. London: The British Library, 1983.

Harris, D. "Landscape and Representation: The Printed View and Marc'Antonio dal Re's *Ville di Delizi*." In *Villas and Gardens in Early Modern France and Italy*, ed. M. Benes and D. Harris. Cambridge: Cambridge University Press, 2001.

Harris, D. "The Postmodernization of Landscape: A Critical Historiography." *Architectural History* 58, no. 3 (1999/2000): 434–43.

Harris, D., and D. L. Hays. "On the Use and Misuse of Historical Landscape Views." In *Representing Landscape Architecture*, ed. M Treib. London: Taylor and Francis, 2008.

Harris, J. *The Artist and the Country House: A History of Country House and Garden View Painting in Britain 1540–1870*. London: For Sotheby Parke Bernet Publications by Philip Wilson Publishers, 1979.

Harris, W. *A Description of the King's Royal Palace and Gardens at Loo*. London: R. Roberts, 1699.

Harvey, J. H. *The Availability of Hardy Plants of the Late Eighteenth Century*. London: Garden History Society, 1988.

Harwood, E. "Personal Identity and the Eighteenth-Century Garden." *Journal of Garden History* 13, nos. 1 and 2 (1993): 36–48.

Hatton, R. *George I: Elector and King*. London: Thames and Hudson, 1978.

Hayden, P. *Russian Parks and Gardens*. London: Frances Lincoln, 2005.

Hayes, J. *Thomas Gainsborough*. London: The Tate Gallery, 1980.

Hayes, J., and S. Sartin. *Polite Society by Arthur Devis 1712–1787: Portraits of the English Country Gentleman and his Family*. Preston: The Harris Museum and Art Gallery, 1983.

Hayman, J. "Notions of National Characters in the Eighteenth Century." *Huntington Library Quarterly* 35 (1971): 1–17.

Hays, D. L. "Figuring the Commonplace at Ermenonville." In *Experiencing the Garden in the Eighteenth Century*, ed. M. Calder. Bern: Peter Lang, 2006.

Hays, D. L. "Francesco Bettini and the Pedagogy of Garden Design in Late Eighteenth-century France." In *Tradition and Innovation in French Garden Art*, ed. J. D. Hunt, M. Conan, and C. Goldstein. Philadelphia: University of Pennsylvania Press, 2002.

Hays, D.L. "'This is not a *Jardin Anglais*': Carmontell, the Jardin de Monceau, and Irregular Garden Design in Late-Eighteenth-Century France." In *Villas and Gardens in Early Modern France and Italy*, ed. M. Benes and D. Harris. Cambridge: Cambridge University Press, 2001.

Headley, G., and W. Meulenkamp. *Follies: A National Trust Guide*. London: Jonathan Cape, 1986.

Heimburger-Ravelli, M. *Disegni di giardini e opera minori di un artista del '700, Francesco Bettini*. Florence: L. S. Olschki, 1981.

Henrey, B. *British Botanical and Horticultural Literature Before 1800*. Oxford: Oxford University Press, 1975.

Herzog, G. *Hubert Robert und das Bild im Garten*. Worms: Werner, 1989.

Hewison, R. *The Heritage Industry*. London: Methuen, 1987.

Hicks, D. "'Places for Thinking' from Anapolis to Bristol: Situations and Symmetries in 'World Historical Archaeologies.'" *World Archaeology* 37, no. 3 (2005): 387–88.

Higgs, R. "Stourhead Revisited." *The Follies Journal* 3 (2003): 7–10.

Hill, D. *Harewood Masterpieces: English Watercolours and Drawings*. Harewood: Harewood House Trust, 1995.

Hirschfeld, C.C.L. *Theorie der Gartenkunst*, 5 vols. Leipzig, 1779–85. Reprint, 2 vols., Zurich: George Olms, 1973 and 1985.

Hobhouse, P. *Gardening through the Ages*. New York: Barnes and Noble, 1997.

Hobhouse, P. *Plants in Garden History*. London: Pavilion Books, 1992.

Hobsbawm, E.J. *Nations and Nationalism since 1780: Programme, Myth, Reality*. Cambridge: Cambridge University Press, 1992.

Hobson, D. "'Leasure and Decorum': Thomas Hollis in West Dorset." *New Arcadian Journal* 55/56 (2003): 17–43.

Homer. *The Odyssey*. Rev. ed. Translated by R. Fitzgerald. New York: Doubleday, 1963.

Hopper, F. "The Dutch Classical Garden and André Mollet." *Journal of Garden History* 2, no. 1 (1982): 25–40.

Hoppitt, R. "Hunting Suffolk's Parks: Towards a Reliable Chronology of Emparkment." In *The Medieval Park: New Perspectives*, ed. R. Liddiard, 146–64. Macclesfield: Windgather, 2007.

Howells, R. *Visual Culture*. Cambridge: Polity Press, 2003.

Hull, T., ed. *Selected Letters between the Late Duchess of Somerset, Lady Luxborough, Mr. Whistler, Miss Dolman, Mr. R. Dodsley, William Shenstone, Esq. and Others; Including a Sketch of the Manners, Laws, &c. of the Republic of Venice, and Some Poetical Pieces; the Whole Now First Published from Original Copies, by Mr. Hull.* 2 vols. London, 1778.

Hume, D. "Of Luxury." In *Essays and Treatises on Several Subjects*. London, 1758.

Hunt, J.D. *The Afterlife of Gardens*. London: Reaktion Books, 2004.

Hunt, J.D. "Approaches (New and Old) to Garden History." In *Perspectives on Garden Histories*, ed. M. Conan, 77–90. Washington, D.C.: Dumbarton Oaks Research Library and Collection, 1999.

Hunt, J.D. "Bridges, Friendship, and the Picturesque Garden." *Wege zum Garten. Gewidmet Michael Seiler zum 65, Geburtstag*. Leipzig: Koehler & Amelang, 2004.

Hunt, J.D. "'But Who Does Not Know What a Dutch Garden Is?' The Dutch Garden in the English Imagination." In *The Dutch Garden in the Seventeenth Century*, ed. J.D. Hunt. Washington, D.C.: Dumbarton Oaks Research Library and Collection, 1990.

Hunt, J.D., ed. *The Dutch Garden in the Seventeenth Century*. Washington, D.C.: Dumbarton Oaks Research Library and Collection, 1990.

Hunt, J.D. "Emblem and Expression in the Eighteenth Century Landscape Garden." *Eighteenth-Century Studies* 4, no. 3 (1971): 294–317.

Hunt, J.D. *The Figure in the Landscape: Poetry, Painting, and Gardening in the Eighteenth Century*. Baltimore: Johns Hopkins University Press, 1976.

Hunt, J.D. *Garden and Grove: The Italian Renaissance Garden in the English Imagination 1600–1750*. London: J. M. Dent, 1986.

Hunt, J.D., ed. *Garden History: Issues, Approaches, Methods*. Washington, D.C.: Dumbarton Oaks Research Library and Collection, 1992.

Hunt, J.D. *Greater Perfections: The Practice of Garden Theory*. London: Thames and Hudson, 2000.

Hunt, J.D., ed. *The Italian Garden: Art, Design and Culture*. Cambridge: Cambridge University Press, 1996.

Hunt, J.D. *The Picturesque Garden in Europe*. London: Thames and Hudson, 2002.

Hunt, J.D. *William Kent Landscape Garden Designer: An Assessment and Catalogue of His Designs*. London: A. Zwemmer, 1987.

Hunt, J.D., and E. De Jong. "The Anglo-Dutch Garden in the Age of William and Mary." Special issue, *Journal of Garden History* 8, nos. 2 and 3 (1988).

Hunt, J.D., and P. Willis, eds. *The Genius of the Place: The English Landscape Garden 1620–1820*. London: Paul Elek, 1975.

Hunt, J.D., and J. Wolschke-Bulman, eds. *The Vernacular Garden*. Washington, D.C.: Dumbarton Oaks Research Library and Collection, 1993.

Hunt, M.R. *The Middling Sort: Commerce, Gender and the Family in England 1680–1780*. Berkeley: University of California Press, 1996.

Hussey, C. *English Gardens and Landscapes, 1700–1750*. London: Country Life, 1967.

Hutcheson, F. *An Inquiry into the Original of Our Ideas of Beauty and Virtue: in Two Treatises*. 2nd ed. London, 1726.

Hyams, E. *Capability Brown and Humphrey Repton*. New York: Charles Scribner's Sons, 1971.

Hyde, E. "The Cultivation of a King, or the Flower Gardens of Louis XIV." In *Tradition and Innovation in French Garden Art: Chapters of a New History*, ed. J.D. Hunt and M. Conan. Philadelphia: University of Pennsylvania Press, 2002.

Hyll, T. *The Gardener's Labyrinth*, 1577. Reprint, New York: Oxford, 1988.

Ingram, J.H. *Flora Symbolica; or, the Language and Sentiment of Flowers*. London: Frederick Warne, 1887.

Israel, J.I. *Radical Enlightenment: Philosophy and the Making of Modernity 1650–1750*. Oxford: Oxford University Press, 2001.

Jackson-Stops, G. *The Fashioning and Functioning of the British Country House*. Washington, D.C.: National Gallery of Art, 1989.

Jacques, D. "Garden Design in the Mid-Seventeenth Century." *Architectural History* 44 (2001): 365–76.

Jacques, D. "On the Supposed Chineseness of the English Landscape Garden." *Garden History* 18, no. 1 (1990): 180–91.

Jacques, D. "Who Knows What a Dutch Garden Is?" *Garden History* 30, no. 2 (2002): 114–30.

Jacques, D., and A. J. van der Horst. *The Gardens of William and Mary*. London: Christopher Helm, 1988.

[Les] Jardins d'Ermonville racontés par René Louis marquis de Girardin, ed. Jean-Claude Curtil. Saint-Rémy-en-l'Eau: M. Hayot, 2003.

[Les] Jardins des Lumièresen Ile-de-France (2005), ed. Dominique Césari. Paris: Parigramme, 2005.

Jardins en France, 1760–1820: Pays d'illusions, Terre d'expérience, exhibition catalogue. Paris: Caisse Nationale des Monuments Historiques et des Sites, 1978.

Jefferson, T., and E. M. Betts. *Thomas Jefferson's Garden Book, 1766–1824, with Relevant Extracts from His Other Writings*. Charlottesville: Thomas Jefferson Memorial Foundation, 1999.

Jekyll, G. *Homes and Gardens*. London: Longman's, 1900.

Jellicoe, G., S. Jellicoe, P. Goode, and M. Lancaster. *The Oxford Companion to Gardens*. Oxford: Oxford University Press, 1986.

Joudiou, G. *La Folie de M. de Sainte-James. Une demeure, un jardin pittoresque.* Neuilly-sur-Seine: Spiralinthe Editions, 2001.

Jourdain, M. *The Work of William Kent, Artist, Painter, Designer and Landscape Gardener*. London: Country Life, 1948.

Joynt, V. "Utilior quam Dulce: A Utilitarian View of the Eighteenth-Century Model Farm." Unpublished MA diss., Bristol University, 2007.

Junker-Mielke, S. *Barocke Gartenlust: auf Spurensuche entlang der BarockStraße SaarPfalz*. Regensburg: Schnell & Steiner, 2008.

Kames, H. H. *Elements of Criticism*, 3rd ed. Edinburgh: A. Millar, A. Kincaid and J. Bell, 1765.

Kant, I. *Critique of Judgment*, 1790. Rev. ed. Translated by J. H. Bernard. New York: Macmillan and Hafner Press, 1951.

Kelsall, M. *The Great Good Place: The Country House in English Literature*. New York: Harvester Wheatsheaf, 1993.

Kelso, W. M. "Landscape Archaeology and Garden History Research: Success and Promise at Bacon's Castle, Monticello, and Poplar Forest Virginia." In *Garden History: Issues, Approaches, Methods*, ed. J. D. Hunt. Washington, D.C.: Dumbarton Oaks Research Library and Collection, 1992.

Kennedy, A. "British Topographical Print Series in their Social and Economic Context c1720–c1840." Unpublished PhD diss., London: Courtauld Institute of Art, London, 1998.

Kennedy, M. "National Trust Urged to Abandon Garden Prudery." *Guardian*, April 17, 2000.

Keswick, M. *The Chinese Garden: History, Art and Architecture, with Contributions and Conclusion by Charles Jencks*. London: Academy Editions, 1978.

Ketcham, D. *Le Désert de Retz: A Late Eighteenth-Century French Folly Garden, the Artful Landscape of Monsieur de Monville*. Arion, 1990. Reprint, Cambridge, MA: MIT Press, 1994.

Kielmansegge, F. *Diary of a Journey to England in the Years 1761–1762*. London: Longmans, Green and Co. 1902.

Kip, J., and L. Knyff. *Britannia Illustrata*. London: Henry Overton, 1714.

Knyff, L., and J. Kip. *Britannia Illustrata*, 1707. Rev. ed. Edited by J. Harris and G. Jackson-Stops. Bungay: Paradigm Press, 1984.

Krafft, J.-C. *Plans des plus beaux jardins pittoresques de France, d'Angleterre et d'Allemagne*. Paris, 1809.

Kriz, D. K. *The Idea of the English Landscape Painter: Genius as Alibi in the Early Nineteenth Century*. New Haven, CT: Paul Mellon Centre for Studies in British Art, Yale University Press, 1997.

Kuyper, W. *Dutch Classicist Architecture: A Survey of Dutch Architecture, Gardens and Anglo-Dutch Architectural Relations from 1625 to 1700*. Delft: Delft University Press, 1980.

Lablaude, P.-A. *The Gardens of Versailles*. Paris: Éditions Scala, 1995.

Laborde, A., de. *Description des nouveaux jardins de la France et de ses anciens chateaux*, Paris, 1809. Reprint, Paris: Connaissance et Mémoires, 2004.

Laborde, A., de. *Discours sur la vie de Campagne et la Composition des Jardins*. Paris, a reprinting of the essay originally included in the previous volume, 1808.

Lacey, S. *Gardens of the National Trust*. London: National Trust, 2005.

Laird, M. "The Culture of Horticulture: Class, Consumerism and Gender in the English Landscape Garden." In *Bourgeois and Aristocratic Cultural Encounters in Garden Art, 1550–1850*, ed. M. Conan. Washington, D.C.: Dumbarton Oaks Research Library and Collection, 2002.

Laird, M. *The Flowering of the English Landscape Garden: English Pleasure Grounds 1720–1800*. Philadelphia: University of Pennsylvania Press, 1999.

Laird, M. *Mrs Delany and Her Circle*. New Haven, CT: Yale University Press, 2009.

Lambert, D. "The Meaning and Re-Meaning of Sculpture in Victorian Public Parks." In *Sculpture and the Garden*, ed. P. Eyres and F. Russell. Aldershot: Ashgate Publishing, 2006.

Lambert, D. "The Prospect of Trade: The Merchant Gardeners of Bristol in the Second Half of the Eighteenth Century." In *Bourgeois and Aristocratic Cultural Encounters in Garden Art, 1550–1850*, ed. M. Conan. Washington, D.C.: Dumbarton Oaks Research Library and Collection, 2002.

Lambert, D. "William Shenstone and the Fairy Landscape." *Georgian Group Report and Journal* (1986): 67–73.

Lambin, D. "Ermenonville Today," *Journal of Garden History* 8, no. 1 (1988): 42–59.

Lambin, D. "The Landscape Gardens at Goldney and Warmley: Hercules and Neptune and the Merchant Gardeners of Bristol." *New Arcadian Journal* 37/38 (1994): 45–63.

Lambin, D. "Pleasure with Profit: Some Aspects of Landscape Gardening." *Garden History* 3, no. 2 (1975): 29–36.

Langford, P. *A Polite and Commercial People: England 1727–1783*. Oxford: Clarendon Press, 1989.

Langford, P. *Walpole and the Robinocracy*. Cambridge: Chadwyck-Healey, 1989.

Langley, B. *New Principles of Gardening*. London: A. Bettesworth and J. Batley; J. Pemberton; T. Bowles, J. Clarke; and J. Bowles, 1728.

Laplana Gil, J. E. *La cultura del barroco. Los jardines–arquitectura, simbolismo y literatura: actas del I y II curso en torno a Lastanosa.* Huesca: Instituto de Estudios Altoaragoneses, Diputación de Huesca, 2000.

Lassus, B. *The Landscape Approach.* Philadelphia: University of Pennsylvania Press, 1998.

Lauterbach, I. *Der französische Garten am Ende des Ancien Régime: "schöne Ordnung" und "geschmackvolles Ebenmass."* Worms: Werner, 1987.

Lawrence, A. "Space, Status and Gender in English Topographical Paintings c.1660–c.1740." *Architectural History* 46 (2003): 81–94.

Lawson, W. *A Country Housewife's Garden.* London: Roger Jackson, 1623.

Lawson, W. *A New Orchard and Garden.* London: Roger Jackson, 1618.

Leatherbarrow, D. "Character, Geometry and Perspective: The Third Earl of Shaftesbury's Principles of Garden Design." *Journal of Garden History* 4, no. 4 (1984): 332–58. Republished in D. Leatherbarrow, *Topographical Stories: Studies in Landscape and Architecture.* Philadelphia: University of Pennsylvania Press, 2004.

Leighton, A. *American Gardens in the Eighteenth Century: "for Use or for Delight."* Amherst: University of Massachusetts Press, 1986.

Leinster, E., *Correspondence of Emily, Duchess of Leinster (1731–1814)*, ed. Brian FitzGerald. Dublin: Stationery Office, 1949–57.

Le Ménahèze, S., and M. Baridon. *L'invention du jardin romantique en France 1761–1808.* Neuilly-sur-Seine: Editions spiralinthe, 2001.

Le Rouge, G. L. *Détails des nouveaux jardins à la mode, otherwise referred to as Les jardins anglo-chinois.* Paris, ca.1776–88. Reprinted as loose leaf plates, Paris: Connaissance et Mémoires, 2004.

Leslie, M. "History and Historiography in the English Landscape Garden." In *Perspectives on Garden Histories: History of Landscape Architecture Symposium*, ed. M. Conan. Washington, D.C.: Dumbarton Oaks Research Library and Collection, 1999.

Leslie, M., and T. Raylor. *Culture and Cultivation in Early Modern England.* Leicester: Leicester University Press, 1992.

Lewis, C. S. *The Last Battle*, 1958. Reprint, Toronto: Bodley Head, 1972.

Ligne, C.-J., de. *Coup d'Oeil at Beloil and a Great Number of European Gardens.* Translated and introduced by Basil Guy. Berkeley: University of California Press, 1991.

Lindegren, K., ed. *Frederick Magnus Piper and the Landscape Garden.* Sweden: Katrineholm, 1981.

Linnean Society. Collinson MSS, Large Book.

Linnean Society. Collinson MSS, *Pococke's Tours 1754–1756.*

Lloyd, R. "The Cit's Country Box," 1757–60. *The Connoisseur*, 3rd ed., no. 135, vol. 4 of 4.

London, G., and H. Wise. *The Retir'd Gardener*, vol. 2. London, 1706.

Longstaffe-Gowan, T. *The London Town Garden, 1700–1840.* New Haven, CT: Yale University Press, 2001.

Loudon, J. C. *Arboretum et Fruticetum Britannicum.* London: Longman et al., 1838.

Loudon, J. C. *The Gardener's Magazine* 12 (1836).

Loudon, J.C. *The Landscape Gardening and Landscape Architecture of the Late Humphry Repton, Esq*, 1840. Reprint, West Mead: Gregg International Press, 1969.

Loudon, J.C. *The Suburban Gardener and Villa Companion*. London, 1838.

Loudon, J.C. *A Treatise on Farming, Improving and Managing Country Estates*. London, 1806.

Lovejoy, A.O. "The Chinese Origin of a Romanticism." In *Essays in the History of Ideas*, 99–135. Baltimore: Johns Hopkins University Press, 1984.

Lovie, J. Wentworth Woodhouse: Landscape Conservation and Management Plan (deposited in Sheffield Archives), 2008.

Maccubin, R.P., and P. Martin, eds. *"British and American Gardens."* Special edition, *Eighteenth Century Life* 8, no. 2 (1983).

MacDougall, E.B., and F.H. Hazlehurst. *The French Formal Garden*. Washington, D.C.: Dumbarton Oaks Research Library and Collection, 1974.

MacLean, G.M., D. Landry, and J.P. Ward. *The Country and the City Revisited: England and the Politics of Culture, 1550–1850*. Cambridge: Cambridge University Press, 1999.

Magannari, G. *Trattato della composizione e dell'ornamento de' giardini*, ed. Lina Danielli. Bologna: Edagricole, 1837/1994.

Magnani, L. "The Rise and Fall of Gardens in the Republic of Genoa, 1528–1797." In *Bourgeois and Aristocratic Cultural Encounters in Garden Art, 1550–1850*, ed. M. Conan. Washington, DC: Dumbarton Oaks Research Library and Collection, 2002.

Maier-Solgk, F., and A. Greuter. *Landschaftsgarten in Deutschland*. Stuttgart: Deutsche Verlags-Anstalt, 2000.

Mandler, P. *The Fall and Rise of the Stately Home*. New Haven, CT: Yale University Press, 1997.

Mariage, T. *The World of André Le Nôtre*. Philadelphia: University of Pennsylvania Press, 1999.

Martin, P. *The Gardening World of Alexander Pope*. Hamden: Archon Press, 1984.

Martindale C., and D. Hopkins, eds. *Horace Made New*. Cambridge: Cambridge University Press, 1993.

Mason, G. *An Essay on Design and Gardening*, 1752. Bound with T. Whatley, *Observations on Modern Gardening*. Dublin: John Exshaw, 1768.

Mason, W. *The English Garden*. London, 1772–81.

Mayer, M. *Nicolas Michot ou l'introduction du jardin anglais en France*. Paris: Editions d'Art et d'Histoire, 1942.

McDayter, M. "Poetic Gardens and Political Myths: The Renewal of St James's Park in the Restoration." *Journal of Garden History* 15, no. 3 (1995): 135–48.

McKendrick, N., J. Brewer, and J.H. Plumb. *The Birth of Consumer Society: The Commercialization of Eighteenth-Century England*. London: Hutchinson, 1982.

McRae, A. *God Speed the Plough: The Representation of Agrarian England, 1500–1660*. Cambridge: Cambridge University Press, 1996.

Michalska, A.K. "The Influence of Freemasonry and Esoteric Ideas on Polish Landscape Gardens during the Age of Enlightenment." In *Symbolism in 18th Century Gardens: The Influence of Intellectual and Esoteric Currents, such as Freemasonry*, eds. J.A.M. Snoek, M. Scholl, and A.A. Kroon. Den Haag: OVN, 2006.

Middleton, R. "The Chateau and Gardens of Mauperthuis: The Formal and the Informal." In *Garden History: Issues, Approaches, Methods*, ed. J.D. Hunt. Washington, D.C.: Dumbarton Oaks Research Library and Collection, 1992.

Miller, D., ed. *Acknowledging Consumption*. London: Routledge, 1995.

Miller, D. *Material Culture and Mass Consumption*. Oxford: Blackwell, 1987.

Miller, H. *First Impressions of England and Its People*. Boston: Gould and Lincoln, 1860.

Miller, P. *The Gardeners and Florists Dictionary; or, a Complete System of Horticulture &c.*, 8 vols. London: Charles Rivington, 1724–68.

Milton, J. *John Milton: Complete Poems and Major Prose*, 1667. Rev. ed. Edited by M. Y. Hughes. Indianapolis, IN: Odyssey Press, 1957.

Morel, J.-M. *Théorie des Jardins, ou l'Art des Jardins de la Nature*, 1802, second enlarged edition, Paris. Originally published in one volume, 1776.

Mosser, M., and G. Teyssot. *The History of Garden Design: The Western Tradition from the Renaissance to the Present Day*. London: Thames and Hudson, 1991.

Mowl, T. *Gentlemen and Players: Gardeners of the English Landscape*. Stroud: Sutton, 2000.

Mowl, T. *Historic Gardens of Gloucestershire*. Stroud: Tempus, 2002.

Mowl, T. *Historic Gardens of Oxfordshire*. Stroud: Tempus, 2007.

Mowl, T. *Historic Gardens of Wiltshire*. Stroud: Tempus, 2004.

Mowl, T. *Historic Gardens of Worcestershire*. Stroud: Tempus, 2006.

Mowl, T. *William Kent: Architect, Designer, Opportunist*. London: Jonathan Cape, 2006

Mowl, T., and C. Hickman. *Historic Gardens of Northamptonshire*. Stroud: Tempus, 2008.

Mukerji, C. "Reading and Writing with Nature: Social Claims and the French Formal Garden." *Theory and Society* 19, no. 6 (1990): 651–79.

Müllenbrock, H.-J. "The 'Englishness' of the English Landscape Garden and the Genetic Role of Literature: A Reassessment." *Journal of Garden History* 8, no. 4 (1988): 97–103.

Murray, C. *Sharawadgi: The Romantic Return to Nature*. London: International Scholars Publications, 1999.

Myers, S.H. *The Bluestocking Circle: Women, Friendship, and the Life of the Mind in Eighteenth-Century England*. Oxford: Clarendon Press, 1990.

National Trust. *Fountains Abbey and Studley Royal*. Swindon: National Trust, 2005.

National Trust. *Stowe Landscape Gardens*. London: National Trust, 1997.

Neave, D., and D. Turnbull. *Landscaped Parks and Gardens of East Yorkshire*. Hull: Georgian Society for East Yorkshire, 1992.

Nourse, T. "Of a Country House." In *Campania Foelix; or, A Discourse of the Benefits and Improvements of Husbandry*. London, 1700. 2nd ed. 1706.

Ogborn, M. *Spaces of Modernity: London's Geographies 1680–1780*. New York: The Guilford Press, 1998.

Olausson, M. "The Aesthetic and Social Reception and Development of the Baroque Garden in Sweden." In *Baroque Garden Cultures: Emulation, Sublimation, Subversion*, ed. M. Conan. Washington, D.C.: Dumbarton Oaks Research Library and Collection, 2005.

Olausson, M. *Den engelska parken i Sverige under gustaviansk tid* [The English landscape garden in Sweden during the Gustavian era]. Stockholm: Piper Press, 1993.

Olausson, M. "Freemasonry, Occultism and the Picturesque Garden towards the End of the 18th Century." *Art History* 8 (1985): 413–35.

Oldenburger-Ebbers, C. "Garden Design in the Netherlands in the Seventeenth Century." In *The Architecture of Western Gardens*, ed. M. Mosser and G. Teyssot, 163–65. Cambridge: MIT Press, 1991.

O'Malley, T. "Art and Science in the Design of Botanic Gardens, 1730–1830." In *Garden History: Issues, Approaches, Methods*, ed. J.D. Hunt. Washington, D.C.: Dumbarton Oaks Research Library and Collection, 1992.

O'Malley, T. *Keywords in American Landscape Design*. Washington, D.C.: Center for Advanced Study in the Visual Arts, 2010.

Ousby, I. *The Englishman's England: Taste, Travel, and the Rise of Tourism*. Cambridge: Cambridge University Press, 1990.

Outram, D. *The Enlightenment*. Cambridge: Cambridge University Press, 1995.

Ozouf, M. *Festivals and the French Revolution*. Rev. ed. Translated by A. Sheridan. Cambridge, MA: Harvard University Press, 1988.

Parshall, L. "C.C.L. Hirschfeld's Concept of the Garden in the German Enlightenment." *Journal of Garden History* 13, no. 3 (1993): 125–71.

Paulson, R. *Emblem and Expression: Meaning in English Art of the Eighteenth Century*. Cambridge, MA: Harvard University Press, 1975.

Payne, C. *Toil and Plenty: Images of the Agricultural Landscape in England, 1780–1890*. New Haven, CT: Yale Center for British Art, Yale University Press, 1993.

Pears, I. *The Discovery of Painting: The Growth of Interest in the Arts in England, 1680–1768*. New Haven, CT: Paul Mellon Centre for Studies in British Art, Yale University Press, 1988.

Petherick, T., and M. Eclaire. *The Kitchen Gardens at Heligan: Lost Gardening Principles Rediscovered*. London: Weidenfeld and Nicolson, 2006.

Pevsner, N. *The Picturesque Garden and Its Influence outside the British Isles*. Washington, D.C.: Dumbarton Oaks Research Library and Collection, 1974.

Pocock, J.G.A. *Barbarism and Religion*. Cambridge: Cambridge University Press, 1999.

Pointon, M. *Hanging the Head: Portraiture and the Social Formation in Eighteenth-century England*. New Haven, CT: Paul Mellon Centre for Studies in British Art, Yale University Press, 1993.

"The Political Temples of Stow." Special issue, *New Arcadian Journal* 43/44 (1997).

Pope, A. *The Complete Poetical Works of Alexander Pope*. Rev. ed. Edited by Henry W. Boynton. Boston: Houghton Mifflin; Cambridge: Riverside Press, 1903.

Porter, R. *The Creation of the Modern World: The Untold Story of the British Enlightenment*. New York: W. W. Norton, 2000.

Posner, D. *Antoine Watteau*. London: Weidenfeld and Nicolson, 1984.

Prest, J. *The Garden of Eden: The Botanic Garden and the Re-creation of Paradise*. New Haven, CT: Yale University Press, 1981.

Pugh, S. *Garden, Nature, Language*. Cultural Politics. Manchester: Manchester University Press, 1988.

Pugh, S. *Reading Landscape: Country, City, Capital*. Cultural Politics. Manchester: Manchester University Press, 1990.

Puppe, R. "Saxon Baroque Gardens (1694–1733): Nature's Entertainment Palaces." In *Baroque Garden Cultures: Emulation, Sublimation, Subversion*, ed. M. Conan. Washington, D.C.: Dumbarton Oaks Research Library and Collection, 2005.

Quaintance, R. "Kew Gardens 1731–1778: Can We Look at Both Sides Now?" *New Arcadian Journal* 51/52 (2001): 14–50.

Quaintance, R. "Towards Distinguishing Theme Park Publics: William Chambers' Landscape Theory vs. His Kew Practice." In *Theme Park Landscapes: Antecedents and Variations*, ed. T. Young and R. Riley. Washington, D.C.: Dumbarton Oaks Research Library and Collection, 2001.

Quaintance, R. "Walpole's Whig Interpretation of Landscaping History." *Studies in Eighteenth-Century Culture* 9 (1979): 285–300.

Quaintance, R. "Who's Making the Scene: Real People in Eighteenth-Century Topographical Prints." In *The Country and the City Revisited: England and the Politics of Culture 1550–1850*, ed. G. Macclean, D. Landy, and J.P. Wood. Cambridge: Cambridge University Press, 1999.

Quest-Ritson, C. *The English Garden: A Social History*. Boston: D. R. Godine, 2003.

Quintinye, J. *The Complete Gardner*. London: Matthew Gillyflower, 1693.

Rabinow, P., ed. *The Foucault Reader*. London: Penguin, 1991.

Rackham, O. *The History of the Countryside*. London: Dent, 1986.

Radisich, P. R. *Hubert Robert; Spaces of the Enlightenment*. Cambridge: Cambridge University Press, 1998.

Rea, J. *Flora*. London: Richard Marriott, 1665.

Repton, H. *A Letter to Uvedale Price, Esq*. London, 1794.

Repton, H. Red Book for Attingham in Shropshire—A Seat of the Right Honble. Lord Berwick. The Berwick Collection (The National Trust), 1798.

Repton, H. Red Book for Hengrave Hall, Suffolk (Private Collection), 1791.

Repton, H. Red Book for Tewin Water, Hertfordshire (HALS D/Z42 Z1 P 21 A), 1799.

Retford, K. *The Art of Domestic Life: The Family Portrait in Eighteenth-Century England*. New Haven, CT: Paul Mellon Centre for Studies in British Art, Yale University Press, 2006.

Richards, S. "A Magazine for the Friends of Good Taste: Sensibility and Rationality in Garden Design in Late 18th-Century Germany." *Studies in the History of Gardens* 20 (2000): 229–48.

Richardson, T. *The Arcadian Friends: Inventing the English Landscape Garden*. London: Bantam Press, 2007.

Ridgway, C., and R. Williams, eds. *Sir John Vanbrugh and Landscape Architecture in Baroque England 1690–1730*. Stroud: Sutton, 2000.

Ridley, G. "Studley Royal: Landscape as Sculpture." In *Sculpture and the Garden*, eds. P. Eyres and F. Russell. Aldershot: Ashgate Publishing, 2006.

Robins, T., J. Harris, and M. Rix. *Gardens of Delight: The Rococo English Landscape of Thomas Robins the Elder*. London: Basilisk Press, 1978.

Roche, D. *A History of Everyday Things: The Birth of Consumption in France 1600–1800*. Rev. ed. Translated by B. Peace. Cambridge: Cambridge University Press, 2000.

Rogger, A. *Landscapes of Taste: The Art of Humphrey Repton's Red Books*. London: Routledge, 2007.

Roosevelt, P. R. *Life on the Russian Country Estate: A Social and Cultural History*. New Haven, CT: Yale University Press, 1995.

Roscoe, R. "Peter Scheemakers and the Stowe Commission." *New Arcadian Journal* 43/44 (1997): 40–65.

Rosenthal, M. *British Landscape Painting*. Oxford: Phaidon, 1982.

Rosenthal, M. "Landscape as High Art." In *Glorious Nature: British Landscape Painting 1750–1850*, ed. K. Baetjer. London: Zwemmer, 1993.

Rosenthal, M., and M. Myrone. *Gainsborough*. London: Tate Britain, 2003.

Ross, S. *What Gardens Mean*. Chicago: University of Chicago Press, 1998.

Rousseau, J. J. *Eloisa; or, a Series of Original Letters Collected and Published by J. J. Rousseau*. Rev. ed. Translated by W. Kenrick. London: R. Griffiths et al., 1761.

Royet, V. *Georges Le Rouge. Les jardins anglo-chinois. An Annotated Catalogue of Le Rouge's Cahiers*. Paris: Bibliothèque nationale de France and Editions Connaissance et Mémoires, 2004.

Russell, T. M., and A.-M. Thornton. *Gardens and Landscapes in the* Encyclopédie *of Diderot and D'Alenbert: The Letterpress Articles and Selected Engravings*, 2 vols. Aldershot: Ashgate, 1999.

Saisselin, R. G. "The French Garden in the 18th Century: From *Belle Nature* to the Landscape of Time." *Journal of Garden History* 5 (1985): 284–97.

Samuel, R. *Theatres of Memory*. London: Verso, 1994.

Sands, M. *The Eighteenth-Century Pleasure Gardens of Marylebone, 1737–1777*. London: The Society for Theatre Research, 1987.

Sarudy, B. W. *Gardens and Gardening in the Chesapeake, 1700–1805*. Baltimore: Johns Hopkins University Press, 1998.

Schama, S. *The Embarrassment of Riches: An Interpretation of Dutch Culture in the Golden Age*. London: Collins, 1987.

Schlegel, F. *Dialogue on Poetry and Literary Aphorisms*, ed. E. Behler and R. Stuc. University Park: Pennsylvania State University Press, 1968.

Schulz, M. F. "The Circuit Walk of the Eighteenth-Century Landscape Garden and the Pilgrim's Circuitous Progress." *Eighteenth-Century Studies* 15, no. 1 (1981): 1–25.

Schulz, M. F. *Paradise Preserved: Recreations of Eden in 18th- and 19th-Century England*. Cambridge: Cambridge University Press, 1985.

Scottish Natural Heritage. *Introducing Interpretation*. http://www.snh.org.uk/wwo/Interpretation. Accessed November 14, 2012.

Scott, S. *A Description of Millenium Hall, and the Country Adjacent: Together with the Character of the Inhabitants*. London: J. Newberry, 1762.

Searson, J. *Mount Vernon: A Poem, Rural, Romantic and Descriptive*. Philadelphia, 1799.

Sekora, J. *Luxury: The Concept in Western Thought, Eden to Smollett*. Baltimore: Johns Hopkins University Press, 1977.

Seymour, S., et al. "Estate and Empire: Sir George Cornewall's Management of Moccas, Herefordshire and La Taste, Grenada, 1771–1819." Dept. of Geography, University of Nottingham, Working Paper 28, August 1994.

Shenstone, W. "Unconnected Thoughts on Gardening." In *The Works, in Verse and Prose, of William Shenstone*. London: J. Dodsley, 1764.

Shteir, A. B. *Cultivating Women, Cultivating Science: Flora's Daughters and Botany in England 1760–1860*. Baltimore: Johns Hopkins University Press, 1996.

Shvidkovskii, D. O. *The Empress & the Architect: British Architecture and Gardens at the Court of Catherine the Great*. New Haven, CT: Yale University Press, 1996.

Silva, E. *Dell' Arte de' Giardini Inglesi*, ed. Gianni Venturi. Milano, 1801/1976.

Sirén, O. *China and Gardens of Europe in the Eighteenth Century*. Washington, D.C.: Dumbarton Oaks Research Library and Collection, 1950/1990.

Sirén, O. *Garden of China*. New York: Ronald Press, 1949.

Sloan, K. *"A Noble Art": Amateur Artists and Drawing Masters c.1600–1800*. London: British Museum Press, 2000.

Smiles, S. *The Turner Book*. London: Tate Publishing, 2006.

Smith, J. *England's Improvement Reviv'd*. London: Thomas Newcomb, 1673.

Smith, L. *Uses of Heritage*. London: Routledge, 2006.

Solkin, D. H. *Painting for Money: The Visual Arts and the Public Sphere in Eighteenth-century England*. New Haven, CT: Paul Mellon Centre for Studies in British Art, Yale University Press, 1993.

Solkin, D. H. *Richard Wilson: The Landscape of Reaction*. London: The Tate Gallery, 1982.

Solnit, R. *Wanderlust: A History of Walking*. London: Verso, 2001.

Sontag, S. *On Photography*. Harmondsworth: Penguin, 1979.

Spadafora, D. *The Idea of Progress in Eighteenth-Century Britain*. New Haven, CT: Yale University Press, 1990.

Spence, J. *Observations, Anecdotes and Characters of Books and Men*, ed. J. M. Osborn. Oxford: Clarendon Press, 1966.

Spenser, E. *Spenser's Complete Poetical Works*, 1590. Rev. ed. Edited by R. E. Neil Dodge. Cambridge, MA: Riverside Press, 1936.

Stevenson, R. L. *A Child's Garden of Verses*, 1885. Reprint, New York: Charles Scribner's Sons; London: John Lane, 1900.

Stone, L., and J. Fawtier-Stone. *An Open Elite? England 1540–1880*. Oxford: Clarendon, 1986.

Strong, R. *The Artist and the Garden*. New Haven, CT: Paul Mellon Centre for Studies in British Art, Yale University Press, 2000.

Stroud, D. *Capability Brown*. London: Country Life, 1950.

Stroud, D. *Humphry Repton*. London: Country Life, 1962.

Swift, J., *Gulliver's Travels*. London: Benjamin Motte, 1726.

Switzer, S. *Ichnographia Rustica; or, the Nobleman, Gentlemen, and Gardener's Recreation*. London: D. Browne, 1718.

Switzer, S. *Ichnographia Rustica; or, the Nobleman, Gentleman, and Gardener's Recreation: Being Directions for the general Distribution of a Country Seat, into Rural and Extensive Gardens, Parks, Paddocks etc.*, 1718. Facsimile reprint, New York: Garland Publishing, 1982.

Switzer, S. *The Nobleman, Gentleman, and Gardener's Recreation*. London: B. Barker and C. King, 1715.

Symes, M. "Charles Hamilton at Bowood." *Garden History* 34 (2006): 206–20.

Symes, M. *Garden Sculpture*. Princes Risborough: Shire Publications, 1996.

Taigel, A., and T. Williamson. *Parks and Gardens*. London: B. T. Batsford, 1993.

Tait, A. A. *The Landscape Garden in Scotland, 1735–1835*. Edinburgh: Edinburgh University Press, 1980.

Taylor, C. *The Archaeology of Gardens*. Aylesbury: Shire Archaeology, 1983.

Taylor, P. *Thomas Blaikie, The "Capability" Brown of France, 1751–1838*. East Linton: Tuckwell Press, 2001.

Taylor-Leduc, S. "Luxury in the Garden: La Nouvelle Héloise Reconsidered." *Journal of Garden History* 19 (1999): 74–85.

Thacker, C. *The History of Gardens*. Berkeley: University of California Press, 1979.

Thomas, K. *Man and the Natural World: Changing Attitudes in England 1500–1800*. London: Allen Lane, 1983.

Thompson, I. *The Sun King's Garden*. London: Bloomsbury, 2006.

Tindal, M. *Christianity as Old as the Creation; or, The Gospel, a Republication of the Religion of Nature*, vol. 1. London, 1730.

Tosi, A. "Fruit and Flower Gardens from the Neoclassical and Romantic Periods in Tuscany." In *The Italian Garden: Art, Design and Culture*, ed. J. D. Hunt. Cambridge: Cambridge University Press, 1996.

Tsu, C. *Inner Chapters*. Rev. ed. Translated by G.-F. Feng and J. English. London: Wildwood House, 1974.

Turner, J. G. "Landscape and the 'Art Prospective' in England 1584–1660." *Journal of the Warburg and Courtauld Institutes* 42 (1979): 290–293.

Turner, J. G. "The Sexual Politics of Landscape: Images of Venus in Eighteenth-Century English Poetry and Landscape Gardening." *Studies in Eighteenth-Century Culture* 11 (1982): 346–66.

Turner, M. *English Parliamentary Enclosure*. Folkstone: Dawson-Archon Books, 1980.

Turner, R. *Capability Brown and the Eighteenth-Century Landscape*. London: Weidenfeld and Nicholson, 1985.

Versailles à Stockholm, exhibition catalogue for the Nationalmuseum. Stockholm: Nationalmuseum (Sweden), 1985.

Verteuil, A., de. "The Gibberd Garden: Model of a Garden for Our Time?" Unpublished MA diss., Bristol University, 2007.

Vidal, M. *Watteaux's Painted Conversations: Art, Literature and Talk in Seventeenth and Eighteenth-Century France*. New Haven, CT: Yale University Press, 1992.

Visentini, M. A. "Islands of Delight: Shifting Perceptions of the Borromean Islands." In *Baroque Garden Cultures: Emulation, Sublimation, Subversion*, ed. M. Conan. Washington, D.C.: Dumbarton Oaks Research Library and Collection, 2005.

Voltaire. *Candide & Zadig*, 1759. Rev. ed. Edited by L. G. Crocker. Translated by T. G. Smollet. New York: Washington Square Press, 1962.

Walker, J. "Studley Royal, 1716–1781." In *Mr Aislabie's Gardens*, ed. P. Eyres. Leeds: New Arcadian Press, 1981.

Walpole, H. "The History of the Modern Taste in Gardening." In *Anecdotes of Painting in England: The Second Edition*, vol. 4. London, Strawberry Hill, 1765–1780.

Walpole, H. *The History of the Modern Taste in Gardening*, 1771. Reprint, New York: Ursus Press, 1995.

Watelet, C.-H. *Essay on Gardens; A Chapter in the French Picturesque.* Rev. ed. Translated and edited by Samuel Danon. Philadelphia: University of Pennsylvania Press, 1774, 2003.

Way, T. *Virgins Weeders and Queens.* Stroud: Sutton Publishing, 2006.

Weltman-Aron, B. *On Other Grounds: Landscape Gardening and Nationalism in Eighteenth-Century England and France.* Albany: State University of New York Press, 2001.

Wesley, J., *The Journal of the Rev. John Wesley, A.M., Sometime Fellow of Lincoln College, Oxford, Enlarged from Original Mss., with Notes from Unpublished Diaries, Annotations, Maps, and Illustrations,* ed. N. Curnock, 8 vols. London: R. Culley, 1909–16.

Whately, T. *Observations on Modern Gardening.* London: T. Payne, 1770.

Wheeler, R. " 'Pro Magna Charta' or 'Fay ce que Voudras': Political and Moral Precedents for the Gardens of Sir Francis Dashwood at West Wycombe." *New Arcadian Journal* 49/50 (2000): 26–60.

Whelan, A. "On the Statuary in the Garden of Pulawy." *Studies in the History of Gardens and Designed Landscapes* 29, nos. 1/2 (2009): 57–71.

Whiteley, P. "William Shenstone and 'The Judgement of Hercules': An Exercise in Politics." *New Arcadian Journal* 37/38 (1994): 81–99.

Wiebenson, D. *The Picturesque Garden in France.* Princeton, NJ: Princeton University Press, 1978.

Williams, R. *The Country and the City.* London: Chatto and Windus, 1973.

Williams, R. "The Leasowes, Hagley and Rural Inscriptions." *New Arcadian Journal* 53/54 (2002): 42–59.

Williams, R. "Making Places: Garden-Mastery and English Brown." *Journal of Garden History* 3, no. 4 (1983): 382–85.

Williamson, T. *The Archaeology of the Landscape Park: Garden Design in Norfolk, England, c.1680–1840.* Oxford: British Archaeological Reports British Series, 1998.

Williamson, T. *Polite Landscapes: Gardens and Society in Eighteenth-Century England.* Baltimore: Johns Hopkins University Press, 1995.

Williamson, T. *The Transformation of Rural England: Farming and the Landscape 1700–1870.* Exeter: Exeter University Press, 2002.

Williamson, T., and L. Bellamy. *Property and Landscape: A Social History of Land Ownership and the English Countryside.* London: George Philip, 1987.

Willis, P. *Charles Bridgeman and the English Landscape Garden.* Newcastle: Elysium Press, 2002.

Willis, P. "Rousseau, Stowe and le jardin anglais." *Studies on Voltaire and the Eighteenth Century* 90 (1972): 1791–98.

Wilson, C. A., ed. *The Country House Kitchen Garden, 1600–1950.* Stroud: Sutton, 1998.

Wittkower, R. "English Neo-Palladianism, the Landscape Garden, China, and the Enlightenment." *L'Arte* 2, no. 6 (1969): 18–35.

Wittkower, R. *Palladio and English Palladianism.* London: Thames and Hudson, 1974.

Woodbridge, K. *Landscape and Antiquity: Aspects of Culture at Stourhead 1718–1838.* Oxford: Oxford University Press, 1970.

Woodbridge, K. *The Stourhead Landscape: Wiltshire*. London: The National Trust, 1982.

Woodhouse, J. *Poems on Sundry Occasions*. London: R. and J. Dodsley et al., 1764.

Wordsworth, W. *William Wordsworth Selected Poems*, ed. John O. Hayden. London: Penguin Books, 1994.

Woudstra, J., ed. "Lancelot Brown (1716–83) and the Landscape Park." Special issue, *Garden History* 29, no. 1 (2001).

Wright, P. *On Living in an Old Country*. London: Verso, 1985.

Young, A. *A Six Months' Tour through the North of England*, 2nd ed. London, 1771.

Young, A. *Travels, during the Years 1787, 1788, and 1789: Undertaken More Particularly with a View of Ascertaining the Cultivation, Wealth, Resources, and National Prosperity, of the Kingdom of France*. Bury St. Edmunds: J. Rackham, 1792.

CONTRIBUTORS

Stephen Bending is a senior lecturer in English at the University of Southampton. He has written numerous articles on eighteenth-century landscape (most recently on women, loneliness, and depression); he is co-editor of *The Writing of Rural England 1500–1800* (Palgrave, 2003) and of a number of eighteenth-century texts including Henry Mackenzie's sentimental novel *The Man of Feeling* (Oxford University Press, 2001) and Thomas Day's novel for children *Sandford and Merton* (Broadview Press, 2009); he is also a series editor of the *Pickering and Chatto Chawton House Library Series* of women's novels, travels, and memoirs. His book *Women and Gardens in the Eighteenth Century* will be published by Cambridge University Press in 2013.

Rachel Crawford is a professor at the University of San Francisco. She is the author of *Poetry, Enclosure and the Vernacular Landscape, 1700–1800* (Cambridge University Press, 2002), and her articles have been placed in journals including *ELH*, *Studies in Romanticism* and its British counterpart, *Romanticism*, and *Literary Compass*, among others. She has also published in several edited collections. Her teaching life includes courses in both the gender and sexualities minor and English literature. Her courses span the long eighteenth century and aspects of critical theory. She is currently writing a book on the relationship between poetry and space as interpreted through the language of cartography.

Timothy Mowl is emeritus professor of history of architecture and designed landscapes, University of Bristol, and professorial research fellow in the

Humanities Research Institute, University of Buckingham. After two decades of architectural history and biography, he turned in 2000 to garden history with *Gentlemen & Players: Gardeners of the English Landscape* (Sutton, 2000), which charted the influence of aristocrats and professionals on the creation of landscape parks and gardens. He is now embarked on a Leverhulme Trust-funded nationwide series of the historic landscapes and gardens of England, which has produced twelve county volumes to date.

Dr. Patrick Eyres is editor-publisher of the *New Arcadian Journal*, which engages with the cultural politics of landscape gardens and specializes in Georgian Britain. The year 2011 saw the fiftieth issue of *NAJ* in thirty years. He is also editor of *Wentworth Castle and Georgian Political Gardening* (Wentworth Castle Heritage Trust, 2012), co-editor of *Sculpture and the Garden* (Ashgate, 2006), and has published in numerous books and other journals. Patrick is on the boards of the Wentworth Castle Heritage Trust (restoring the 500-acre Grade 1 landscape) and the Little Sparta Trust (conserving the garden of Ian Hamilton Finlay) as well as the Garden History Society and the Leeds Arts Fund.

Michael Symes is an author, lecturer, and garden historian. He specializes in the eighteenth century in Britain and in Europe, and has written numerous scholarly articles and several books, including most recently *Mr Hamilton's Elysium: The Gardens of Painshill* (Frances Lincoln, 2010) and *The Picturesque and The Later Georgian Garden* (Redcliffe Press, 2012). He established the master's degree in garden history at Birkbeck, University of London in 2000, and has organized many conferences and study days, with particularly close involvement with the Garden History Society and the London Parks and Gardens Trust. He is the president of the Birkbeck Garden History Group, a lively organization that promotes lectures and visits. His contribution to the new "Chelsea Fringe," run in connection with the Chelsea Flower Show in 2012, was to run a period barn dance in the Garden Museum.

Michael Charlesworth is a professor of art history at the University of Texas at Austin. His critical biography of filmmaker Derek Jarman was published by Reaktion Books in 2011. His books include *Landscape and Vision in Nineteenth-Century Britain and France* (Ashgate, 2008), *The English Garden 1550–1910* (Helm, 3 vols., 1993), and *The Gothic Revival* (Helm, 3 vols., 2002). He has written about Stourhead in *Landscape Design and the Experience of Motion* (Dumbarton Oaks, 2003) and in *Word & Image* (1995). Since a first article in 1986 in *Garden History*, he has also published a series of articles on Wentworth Castle in *Art History* and the *New Arcadian Journal*.

Annie Richardson is a senior lecturer in design history at the University of Lincoln. She is the author of several articles on William Hogarth's book *Analysis of Beauty* and eighteenth-century concepts of dance. She has co-edited *Women's Travel Writings in Italy*, Volumes 1–4 (Pickering & Chatto 2009), and is completing research on Lady Anna Riggs Miller's *Letters from Italy* (1777) and female connoisseurship.

David Lambert is a director of the Parks Agency, a consultancy specializing in historic landscape research and public parks. He was previously conservation officer for the Garden History Society and has been closely involved with the Heritage Lottery Fund in its programs for public parks. He has held research fellowships at the University of York and De Montfort University and has written and campaigned on a wide range of conservation issues. He has been a special adviser to three parliamentary select committee inquiries, and currently serves on a number of advisory panels including the National Trust, English Heritage, the World Monuments Fund, and Historic Royal Palaces.

Tom Williamson is a professor of landscape history at the University of East Anglia, Norwich, UK, and has written widely on agricultural history, landscape archaeology, and the history of landscape design. His books include *Polite Landscapes: Gardens and Society in Eighteenth-Century England* (Sutton, 1995); *The Archaeology of the Landscape Park* (Archaeopress, 1998); *The Transformation of Rural England: Farming and the Landscape 1700–1870* (Exeter University Press, 2002); *Chatsworth: a Landscape History* (Windgather, 2005); and *Rabbits, Warrens and Archaeology* (Tempus, 2007).

Dr Sarah Spooner is a Lecturer in Landscape History at the University of East Anglia, with a particular interest in eighteenth-century landscape design

INDEX

Made in United States
North Haven, CT
10 October 2023

42577677R00167